# ANNUAL EDITIONS

# Drugs, Society, and Behavior

*Twenty-Second Edition*

## 07/08

W9-AZH-291

**EDITOR**

**Hugh T. Wilson**

*California State University—Sacramento*

Professor Hugh Wilson received his Bachelor of Arts degree from California State University, Sacramento, and a Master of Arts degree in Justice Administration and a Doctorate in Public Administration from Golden Gate University in San Francisco. Dr. Wilson is currently a Professor within the Criminal Justice Division at California State University, Sacramento, one of the largest such programs in the United States. He has taught drug abuse recognition, enforcement, and policy to students, educators, and police officers for 30 years. Dr. Wilson interacts regularly with primary and secondary educators in the interests of drug-related youth at risk. His primary professional and academic interest lies in the study and reduction of Fetal Alcohol Syndrome within Native American populations.

 **Contemporary Learning Series**

2460 Kerper Blvd., Dubuque, IA 52001

Visit us on the Internet
*http://www.mhcls.com*

# Credits

1. **Living with Drugs**
   Unit photo—Jim Arbogast/Getty Images
2. **Understanding How Drugs Work—Use, Dependency, and Addiction**
   Unit photo—Stockbyte/PictureQuest
3. **The Major Drugs of Use and Abuse**
   Unit photo—Dynamic Graphics/Jupiterimages
4. **Other Trends in Drug Use**
   Unit photo—The McGraw-Hill Companies, Inc./Gary He, photographer
5. **Measuring the Social Costs of Drugs**
   Unit photo—Royalty-Free/CORBIS
6. **Creating and Sustaining Effective Drug Control Policy**
   Unit photo—The McGraw-Hill Companies, Inc./John Flournoy, photographer
7. **Prevention, Treatment, and Education**
   Unit photo—Getty Images/PhotoLink/Kent Knudson

# Copyright

Cataloging in Publication Data
Main entry under title: Annual Editions: Drugs, Society, and Behavior 2007/2008.
1. Drugs, Society, and Behavior—Periodicals. I. Wilson, Hugh, comp. II. Title: Drugs, Society, and Behavior.
ISBN-13: 978–0–07–339742–9      MHID: 0–07–339742–3      658'.05      ISSN: 1091–9945

Twenty-Second Edition

Cover image Lisa Zador/Getty Images and Photo.com
Compositor: Laserwords Private Limited

# Editors/Advisory Board

Members of the Advisory Board are instrumental in the final selection of articles for each edition of ANNUAL EDITIONS. Their review of articles for content, level, currentness, and appropriateness provides critical direction to the editor and staff. We think that you will find their careful consideration well reflected in this volume.

# Preface

In publishing ANNUAL EDITIONS we recognize the enormous role played by the magazines, newspapers, and journals of the public press in providing current, first-rate educational information in a broad spectrum of interest areas. Many of these articles are appropriate for students, researchers, and professionals seeking accurate, current material to help bridge the gap between principles and theories and the real world. These articles, however, become more useful for study when those of lasting value are carefully collected, organized, indexed, and reproduced in a low-cost format, which provides easy and permanent access when the material is needed. That is the role played by ANNUAL EDITIONS.

It is difficult to define the framework by which Americans make decisions and develop perspectives on the use of drugs. There is no predictable expression of ideology. A wide range of individual and collective experience defines our national will toward drugs.

Despite drug prevention efforts, millions of Americans use illegal drugs on a monthly basis and over 22 million are estimated to need drug treatment. Social costs from drugs are measured in the billions. Drugs impact almost every aspect of public and private life. Drugs are the subjects of presidential elections, congressional appointments, and military interventions. Financial transactions from smuggling help sustain terrorist organizations. Drugs impact families, schools, health care systems, and governments in more places and in more ways than many believe imaginable.

Although it takes little effort to expose social costs manifested by the abuse of drugs, there are tiny victories through which harm from drug abuse can be reduced. Scientific discovery relative to creating a new understanding of the processes of addiction is one. New treatment modalities, the successful use of drug courts and the political support to expand these concepts has reduced drug-related impacts. In 2007 the federal government refunded a $98 million grant to states and local communities for the Access to Recovery program which assists individuals and provides them options in obtaining treatment and recovery services. Although good evidence suggests that many of the most egregious forms of drug abuse have leveled off or been reduced, other disturbing trends, such as the non-medical use of prescription drugs and the manufacture, abuse, and trafficking of methamphetamine are worsening. Drug abuse is a multifaceted problem requiring a multifaceted response. Complacency, encouraged by positive trends, has finally been recognized as a fatal mistake.

The articles contained in *Annual Editions: Drugs, Society, and Behavior 07/08* are a collection of facts, issues, and perspectives designed to provide the reader with a framework for examining current drug-related issues. The book is designed to offer students something to think about and something with which to think. It is a unique collection of materials of interest to the casual as well as the serious student of drug-related social phenomena. Unit 1 addresses the significance that drugs have in affecting diverse aspects of American life. It emphasizes the often-overlooked reality that drugs—legal and illegal—have remained a pervasive dimension of past as well as present American history. The unit begins with an emphasis on the continuing ways that so

many lives are affected by illegal drugs, crime, and violence and continues through diverse discussions about drugs and ordinary life. Unit 2 examines the ways that drugs affect the mind and body that result in dependence and addiction. Unit 3 examines the major drugs of use and abuse, along with issues relative to understanding the individual impacts of these drugs on society. It addresses the impacts produced by the use of legal and illegal drugs and emphasizes the alarming nature of widespread methamphetamine abuse and prescription drug abuse. Unit 4 reviews the dynamic nature of drugs as it relates to changing patterns and trends of use. It gives special attention this year to drug trends among youth, including discussions of 'pharming' and inhalant use. Unit 5 focuses on the social costs of drug abuse and why the costs overwhelm many American institutions. It examines through personal accounts the problems of drug abuse, victimization, and chaos that disproportionately exist in the lives and families of Native American women. Unit 6 illustrates the complexity in creating and implementing drug policy, such as the Synthetic Drug Control Policy, and the recent large-scale initiative to counter the widening efforts by Mexican criminal syndicates to cultivate enormous marijuana growth on federal park lands. Unit 7 concludes the book with discussions of current strategies for preventing and treating drug abuse. Can we deter people from harming themselves with drugs, and can we cure people addicted to drugs? What does work and what does not? Special attention is given to programs that address at-risk youth and programs that reduce criminal offender rehabilitation and recidivism.

*Annual Editions: Drugs, Society, and Behavior 07/08* contains a number of features that are designed to make the volume "user friendly." These include a *table of contents* with abstracts that summarize each article and key concepts in boldface, a *topic guide* to help locate articles on specific individuals or subjects, *Internet References* that can be used to further explore the topics, and a comprehensive *Index*.

We encourage your comments and criticisms on the articles provided and kindly ask for your review on the postage-paid rating form at the end of the book.

*Hugh T. Wilson*

Hugh T. Wilson
*Editor*

# Contents

## UNIT 1
## Living with Drugs

The concepts in bold italics are developed in the article. For further expansion, please refer to the Topic Guide and the Index.

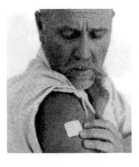

# UNIT 2
## Understanding How Drugs Work—Use, Dependency, and Addiction

The concepts in bold italics are developed in the article. For further expansion, please refer to the Topic Guide and the Index.

# UNIT 3
## The Major Drugs of Use and Abuse

# UNIT 4
## Other Trends in Drug Use

The concepts in bold italics are developed in the article. For further expansion, please refer to the Topic Guide and the Index.

# UNIT 5
## Measuring the Social Costs of Drugs

The concepts in bold italics are developed in the article. For further expansion, please refer to the Topic Guide and the Index.

# UNIT 6
## Creating and Sustaining Effective Drug Control Policy

The concepts in bold italics are developed in the article. For further expansion, please refer to the Topic Guide and the Index.

# UNIT 7
## Prevention, Treatment, and Education

The concepts in bold italics are developed in the article. For further expansion, please refer to the Topic Guide and the Index.

The concepts in bold italics are developed in the article. For further expansion, please refer to the Topic Guide and the Index.

# Topic Guide

This topic guide suggests how the selections in this book relate to the subjects covered in your course. You may want to use the topics listed on these pages to search the Web more easily.

On the following pages a number of Web sites have been gathered specifically for this book. They are arranged to reflect the units of this *Annual Edition*. You can link to these sites by going to the student online support site at *http://www.mhcls.com/online/*.

**ALL THE ARTICLES THAT RELATE TO EACH TOPIC ARE LISTED BELOW THE BOLD-FACED TERM.**

## Youth and Drugs

# Internet References

The following Internet sites have been carefully researched and selected to support the articles found in this reader. The easiest way to access these selected sites is to go to our student online support site at *http://www.mhcls.com/online/*.

# AE: Drugs, Society, and Behavior 07/08

The following sites were available at the time of publication. Visit our Web site—we update our student online support site regularly to reflect any changes.

## General Sources

### Higher Education Center for Alcohol and Other Drug Prevention
*http://www.edc.org/hec*

The U.S. Department of Education established the Higher Education Center for Alcohol and Other Drug Prevention to provide nationwide support for campus alcohol and other drug prevention efforts. The Center is working with colleges, universities, and preparatory schools throughout the country to develop strategies for changing campus culture, to foster environments that promote healthy lifestyles, and to prevent illegal alcohol and other drug use among students.

### Narconon
*http://www.youthaddiction.com*

This site contains drug information, information on addiction, rehab information, online consultations, and other related resources.

### National Clearinghouse for Alcohol and Drug Information
*http://ncadi.samhsa.gov*

This site provides information to teens about the problems and ramifications of drug use and abuse. There are numerous links to drug-related informational sites.

### NSW Office of Drug Policy Home Page
*http://www.druginfo.nsw.gov.au*

This is an Australia government based website with a great deal of drug related information. The site includes information about: illicit drugs (Amphetamines, Pseudoephedrine, GHB, Heroin, Ketamine, Rohypnol, Marijuana, Paramethoxyamphetamines [PMA], Steroids, Cocaine, Hallucinogens, Inhalants, Ecstasy, Ritalin, and Psychostimulants), Information and resources, Treatment services, Law and Justice, Illicit Drug Diversion, and Medical Cannabis. It also includes statistics on drug use in Australia.

### ONDCP (National of Drug control policy)
*http://www.whitehousedrugpolicy.gov*

This Site contains a vast amount of drug related information, resources and links. Included is information about drug policy, drug facts, publications, related links, prevention, treatment, science and technology, enforcement, state and local along with international facts, and policies, and programs. The site is easy to use and understand.

### US Department of Health and Human Services
*http://ncadi.samhsa.gov/research*

This site contains links, and resources on various topics that include, but are not limited to: Substance Abuse and Mental Health Data Archive, OAS Short Reports (on such drugs as marijuana, crack cocaine, inhalants, club drugs, heroin, alcohol, and tobacco). Also included are government studies and an online library and databases.

## Unit 1: Living With Drugs

### Freevibe Drug Facts
*http://www.freevibe.com/Drug_Facts/why_drugs.asp#1*

This website contains information on Drug Facts with links on: drug information, why people take drugs, the physical effects and drug related behavior, drug recognition, and discussions of addiction. The site also includes personal accounts by addicts.

### National Council on Alcoholism and Drug Dependence, Inc.
*http://www.ncadd.org*

According to its Web site, The National Council on Alcoholism and Drug Dependence provides education, information, help, and hope in the fight against the chronic, and sometimes fatal, disease of alcoholism and other drug addictions.

### Parents. The Anti-Drug
*http://www.theantidrug.com*

Tips and links for helping children avoid drugs can be found at this site. Also provided is help in parenting with drug related issues such as how to advise young persons about the drug related influences of peer pressure.

## Unit 2: Understanding How Drugs Work–Use, Dependency, and Addiction

### AddictionSearch.com
*www.addictionsearch.com*

Check this site out for information on addiction and rehabilitation. Some of the other features of this site are the use of statistics, identifies social issues, provides resources for treatment, facility listings for the United States, and analyzes types of addictions by race, sex and age of human populations.

### Addiction Treatment Forum
*www.atforum.com*

News on addiction research and reports on substance abuse are available here.

### APA Help Center from the American Psychological Association
*http://www.apahelpcenter.org/articles/article.php?id=45*

This site is a good resource with several articles and information mostly on alcohol.

### British Broadcasting Company Understanding Drugs
*http://www.bbc.co.uk/health/conditions/mental_health/drugs_use.shtml*

This is a good reference for information about drug use, addiction, and dependence. Includes links.

### Centre for Addiction and Mental Health (CAMH)
*http://www.camh.net*

One of the largest addictions facilities in Canada, CAMH advances an understanding of addiction and translates this knowledge into resources that can be used to prevent problems and to provide effective treatments.

### Dealing with Addictions
*http://kidshealth.org/teen/your_mind/problems/addictions.html*

This site contains information on addictions, and includes a quiz on substance abuse. There are categories for: Your Mind, Your Body, Sexual Health, Food and Fitness, Drugs and Alcohol, Diseases and Conditions, Infections, School and Jobs, Staying Safe, and questions and answers. Much of this site is available in Spanish.

### Drugs and the Body: How Drugs Work
*http://www.doitnow.org/pdfs/223.pdf*

This site pinpoints some basic but critical points in a straight-forward manner. It explains how drugs can be administered, the processes through the body, effects, changes over time. Included are drug related information resources and links.

### The National Center on Addiction and Substance Abuse at Columbia University
*http://www.casacolumbia.org*

The National Center on Addiction and Substance Abuse at Columbia University is a unique think/action tank that brings together all of the professional disciplines (health policy, medicine and nursing, communications, economics, sociology and anthropology, law and law enforcement, business, religion, and education) needed to study and combat all forms of substance abuse—illegal drugs, pills, alcohol, and tobacco—as they affect all aspects of society.

### National Institute on Drug Abuse (NIDA)
*http://www.nida.nih.gov*

NIDA's mission is to lead the nation in bringing the power of science to bear on drug abuse and addiction.

### Public Agenda
*http://www.publicagenda.org/issues/frontdoor.cfm?issue_type5illegal_drugs*

A guide on illegal drugs has links that include: understanding the issues, public opinions, and additional resources. Includes several links for each of these groups.

### Understanding Addiction-Regret, Addiction and Death
*http://teenadvice.about.com/library/weekly/aa011501a.htm*

This site has several resources and articles related to drug use by young persons.

## Unit 3: The Major Drugs of Use and Abuse

### National Institute on Drug Abuse
*www.drugabuse.gov*

This is the National Institute on Drug Abuse web site that identifies the major drugs of use and abuse. It provides resources and information for students, parents, and teachers, as well as reports on drug trends.

### Office of Applied Studies
*www.oas.samhsa.gov*

Data and statistics on the major drugs of use and abuse along with reports on the effects of these drugs focusing on the emotional, social, psychological and physical aspects are contained at this site. Also available are extensive survey findings on drug use related to evolving patterns of drug abuse.

### QuitNet
*http://www.quitnet.org*

The QuitNet helps smokers control their nicotine addiction. This site operates in association with the Boston University School of Public Health.

### The American Journal of Psychiatry
*http://ajp.psychiatryonline.org/cgi/content/abstract/155/8/1016*

This site contains a study on female twins and cannabis.

## Unit 4: Other Trends in Drug Use

### Drug Story.org
*http://www.drugstory.org/drug_stats/druguse_stats.asp*

This site contains lots of information—"Hard Facts, Real Stories, Informed Experts"; information on drugs and their effects. Also covered are prevention and treatment, drugs and crime, drug trafficking, drug use statistics, costs of drugs, and subtopics including: healthcare costs, loss of productivity in the workplace, and crime statistics.

### Marijuana as a Medicine
*http://mojo.calyx.net/~olsen*

This site promotes the concept of marijuana as medicine. This is a controversial issue that has been in the news quite a bit over the past few years. At this site, you will find numerous links to other sites that support this idea, as well as information developed specifically for this site.

### Monitoring the Future
*www.monitoringthefuture.org*

Located at this site is a collaboration of drug trend data tables from 2005 focusing on students in the eighth, tenth, and twelfth grades; also described are trends in the availability of drugs, the attitudes of users, and the use of major drugs.

### Prescriptions Drug Use and Abuse
*http://www.fda.gov/fdac/features/2001/501_drug.htm*

This site contains lots of resources and links related to prescription drug use and abuse.

### SAMHSA
*http://www.drugabusestatistics.samhsa.gov/trends.html*

This link is to the office of applied studies, where you can link to numerous drug related resources. It includes the latest and most comprehensive drug survey information in the U.S.

### United States Drug Trends
*www.usdrugtrends.com*

Provided at this site are drug trends for each state in the United States, such as information where each drug is most likely to be used in each state, cost of the drug, and where the drug supply is coming from.

## Unit 5: Measuring the Social Costs of Drugs

### BMJ.com a publishing group
*http://bmj.bmjjournals.com/cgi/content/abridged/326/7383/242/a*

This is an intriguing report related to the social costs of smoking. It includes numerous links.

### Drug Enforcement Administration
*http://www.usdoj.gov/dea*

The mission of the Drug Enforcement Administration is to enforce the controlled substances laws and regulations of the United States.

### Drug Use Cost to the Economy
*www.ccm-drugtest.com/ntl_effcts1.htm*

This site identifies the economic and social costs associated with drug use and abuse in the United States.

### Drug Policy Alliance
*www.drugpolicy.org/database/index.html*

News about drug policies and articles critiquing the real social and economic costs associated with drug abuse versus the cost of the drug war policies can be found here.

### National Drug Control Policy
*http://www.ncjrs.org/ondcppubs/publications/policy/ndcs00/chap2_10.html*

This site contains information about the consequences of illegal drug use including: economic loss, drug related death, drug related medical emergencies, spreading of infectious diseases, homelessness, and drug use in the workplace.

## The November Coalition
*http://www.november.org*

The November Coalition is a growing body of citizens whose lives have been gravely affected by the present drug policy. This group represents convicted prisoners, their loved ones, and others who believe that U.S. drug policies are unfair and unjust.

## TRAC DEA Site
*http://trac.syr.edu/tracdea/index.html*

The Transactional Records Access Clearinghouse (TRAC) is a data gathering, data research, and data distribution organization associated with Syracuse University. According to its Web site, the purpose of TRAC is to provide the American people—and institutions of oversight such as Congress, news organizations, public interest groups, businesses, scholars, and lawyers—with comprehensive information about the activities of federal enforcement and regulatory agencies and the communities in which they take place.

## United Nations Chronicle—online edition
*http://www.un.org/Pubs/chronicle/1998/issue2/0298p7.html*

This site contains information about the global nature of drugs.

# Unit 6: Creating and Sustaining Effective Drug Control Policy

## Drug Policy Alliance
*www.drugpolicy.org*

This site explores and evaluates drug policy in the United States and around the world.

## DrugText
*http://www.drugtext.org*

The DrugText library consists of individual drug-related libraries with independent search capabilities.

## Effective Drug Policy: Why journey's end is legalisations
*http://www.drugscope.org.uk/wip/23/pdfs/journey.pdf*

This site contain the Drug scope policy and public affairs in the United Kingdom.

## The Higher Education Center for Alcohol and Other Drug Prevention
*http://www.edc.org/hec/pubs/policy.htm*

"Setting and Improving Policies for Reducing Alcohol and Other Drug Problems on Campus: A Guide for School Administrators."

## The National Organization on Fetal Alcohol Syndrome (NOFAS)
*http://www.nofas.org*

NOFAS is a nonprofit organization founded in 1990 dedicated to eliminating birth defects caused by alcohol consumption during pregnancy and improving the quality of life for those individuals and families affected. NOFAS is the only national organization focusing solely on fetal alcohol syndrome (FAS), the leading known cause of mental retardation.

## National NORML Homepage
*http://www.norml.org*

This is the home page for the National Organization for the Reform of Marijuana Laws.

# Unit 7: Prevention, Education and Treatment

## American Council for Drug Education
*www.acde.org*

This site educates employers, parents, teachers, and health professionals about drugs and includes information on recognizing the signs and symptoms of drug use.

## D.A.R.E.
*http://www.dare-america.com*

This year 33 million schoolchildren around the world—25 million in the United States—will benefit from D.A.R.E. (Drug Abuse Resistance Education), the highly acclaimed program that gives kids the skills they need to avoid involvement in drugs, gangs, or violence. D.A.R.E. was founded in 1983 in Los Angeles.

## Drug Watch International
*http://www.drugwatch.org*

Drug Watch International is a volunteer nonprofit information network and advocacy organization that promotes the creation of healthy drug-free cultures in the world and opposes the legalization of drugs. The organization upholds a comprehensive approach to drug issues involving prevention, education, intervention/treatment, and law enforcement/interdiction.

## Join Together
*www.jointogether.org*

Contained here are multiple types of resources and web links regarding youth drug prevention for parents, teachers, community members, public officials and faith leaders.

## Marijuana Policy Project
*http://www.mpp.org*

The purpose of the Marijuana Policy Project is to develop and promote policies to minimize the harm associated with marijuana.

## National Institute on Drug Abuse
*http://www.nida.nih.gov/Infofacts/TreatMeth.html*

Information on effective drug treatment approaches, costs for treating drug addiction, and the different treatment options (inpatient, outpatient, group, etc) can all be found at this site.

## Office of National Drug Control Policy (ONDCP)
*http://www.whitehousedrugpolicy.gov*

The principal purpose of ONDCP is to establish policies, priorities, and objectives for the nation's drug control program, the goals of which are to reduce illicit drug use, manufacturing, and trafficking; drug-related crime and violence; and drug-related health consequences.

## Hazelden
*http://www.hazelden.org*

Hazelden is a nonprofit organization providing high quality, affordable rehabilitation, education, prevention, and professional services and publications in chemical dependency and related disorders.

## KCI (Koch Crime Institute) The Anit-Meth Site
*http://www.kci.org/meth_info/faq_meth.htm*

This site contains Frequently Asked Questions on Methamphetamine. Very interesting.

## The Drug Reform Coordination Network (DRC)
*http://www.drcnet.org*

According to its home page, the DRC Network is committed to reforming current drug laws in the United States.

## United Nations International Drug Control Program (UNDCP)
*http://www.undcp.org*

The mission of UNDCP is to work with the nations and the people of the world to tackle the global drug problem and its consequences.

**We highly recommend that you review our Web site for expanded information and our other product lines. We are continually updating and adding links to our Web site in order to offer you the most usable and useful information that will support and expand the value of your Annual Editions. You can reach us at: *http://www.mhcls.com/annualeditions/*.**

# Unit 1

# Living with Drugs

## Unit Selection

## Key Points to Consider

- Why is history important when attempting to understand contemporary drug-related events?

- How does the American response to drug-related issues compare to that which occurs in other countries?

- What role do the media play in American society's perception of drug-related events?

- How have national crises such as the war in Iraq and shootings in high schools influenced thinking about drugs?

- What important drug-related issues do you believe the American public is uninformed about?

## Student Website
www.mhcls.com/online

## Internet References
Further information regarding these websites may be found in this book's preface or online.

**Freevibe Drug Facts**
*http://www.freevibe.com/Drug_Facts/why_drugs.asp#1*
**National Council on Alcoholism and Drug Dependence, Inc.**
*http://www.ncadd.org*
**Parents. The Anti-Drug**
*http://www.theantidrug.com/*

**W**hen attempting to define the American drug experience, one must examine the past as well as the present. Too often drug use and its associated phenomena are viewed through a contemporary looking glass relative to our personal views, biases, and perspectives. Although today's drug scene is definitely a product of the counterculture of the 1960s and 1970s, the crack trade of the 1980s, and the worsening methamphetamine problem of the 1990s, it is also a product of the more distant past. This past and the lessons it has generated, although largely unknown, forgotten, or ignored, provide one important perspective from which to assess our current status and to guide our future in terms of optimizing our efforts to manage the benefits and control the harm from legal and illegal drugs.

The American drug experience is often defined in terms of a million individual realities, all meaningful and all different. In fact, these realities often originated as pieces of our national, cultural, racial, religious, and personal past that combine to influence present-day drug-related phenomena significantly. The contemporary American drug experience is the product of centuries of human attempts to alter or sustain consciousness

through the use of mind-altering drugs. Early American history is replete with accounts of the exorbitant use of alcohol, opium, morphine, and cocaine.

Further review of this history clearly suggests the precedents for Americans' continuing pursuit of a vast variety of stimulant, depressant, and hallucinogenic drugs. Drug wars, drug epidemics, drug prohibitions, and escalating trends of alarming drug use patterns were present throughout the early history of the United States. During this period the addictive properties of most drugs were largely unknown. Today, the addictive properties of almost all drugs are known. So why is it that so many drug-related lessons of the past repeat themselves in the face of such powerful new knowledge? Why does Fetal Alcohol Syndrome remain as the leading cause of mental retardation in infants? How is it that the abuse of drugs continues to defy the lessons of history? How big is the American drug problem and how is it measured?

One important way of answering questions about drug abuse is by conducting research and analyzing data recovered through numerous reporting instruments. These data are in turn used to assess historical trends and make policy decisions in response to what has been learned. For example: the leading source of information about drug use in America is the annual federal Substance Abuse and Mental Health Services Administration's National Survey on Drug Use and Health. Released again in September of 2006, it reports that there continues to be about 19.1 million Americans over 12 years of age who are current users of illicit drugs. The most widely used illicit drug is marijuana with 14.6 million users—a figure that has remained constant for the past 4 years. Approximately 51.8 percent of Americans over 12 are drinkers of alcohol; over 40 percent of full-time enrolled college students are binge drinkers (defined as consuming 5 or more drinks during a single drinking occasion). Approximately 30 percent of Americans over 12 use tobacco. Almost 23 million people are believed to be drug-dependent on alcohol or illicit drugs—a slight increase from the figures reported in last year's survey. This year's survey identified a steadily increasing 4.7 million persons using prescription painkillers for non-medical reasons, an alarming trend. The size of the economy associated with drug use is staggering; Americans continued to spend more than $70 billion last year on illegal drugs alone.

Drugs impact our most powerful public institutions on many fronts. Drugs are *the* business of our criminal justice system, and drugs compete with terrorism, war, and other major national security concerns as demanding military issues. Over $720 million dollars to fight drugs were pledged to South American countries again this past year to continue the Andean Counter Drug Initiative. Only terrorism and war distract the continuing military emphasis on drug fighting. And as the war in Iraq, Afghanistan, and Pakistan continues, American drug agents in those countries struggle to contain the heroin trade, a major source of funding for the Taliban. As you read through the pages of this book, the pervasive nature of drug-related influences will become more apparent.

The lessons of our drug legacy are harsh, whether they are the subjects of public health or public policy. Methamphetamine is now recognized as having surpassed crack as the drug associated with the most serious consequences. The entire dynamic of illicit drug use is changing. Once quiet rural cities, counties, and states are now reporting epidemics of methamphetamine abuse that suggest comparisons to the inner-urban crack epidemics of the 1980s—only worse. The non-medical use of prescription drugs, particularly pain relievers such as oxycodone, has surged the past three years. This issue is competing for the most widely cited emerging drug problem. Families, schools, and workplaces continue to be impacted by the many facets of drug abuse. One in three Americans has a close relationship to someone who abuses drugs. It is only because of war and terrorism that more public attention toward drug problems has been diverted.

The articles and graphics contained in this unit illustrate the evolving nature of issues influenced by the historical evolution of legal and illegal drug use in America. The changing historical evolution of drug-related phenomena is reflected within the character of all issues and controversies addressed by this book. Unit 1 presents examples of the contemporary and diverse nature of current problems, issues, and concerns about drugs and how they continue to impact all aspects of public and private life. The drug related events of today continue to forecast the drug related events of tomorrow. The areas of public health, public policy, controlling crime, and education exist as good examples for discussion. As you read this and other literature on drug-related events, the dynamics of past and present drug-related linkages will become apparent.

# Hey, You Don't Look So Good

## As diagnoses of once-rare illnesses soar, doctors say drugmakers are "disease-mongering" to boost sales

CATHERINE ARNST

If you have high blood pressure, you may be at risk for heart disease. And given that an estimated 65 million Americans have hypertension, it's not surprising that drugs to treat it are among the most prescribed medicines in the world. But why stop at prescribing drugs to people whose readings are 140/90 or higher, the standard definition of high blood pressure? In the Apr. 20 issue of *The New England Journal of Medicine*, a research team reported on "prehypertension," the condition of being in danger of developing hypertension.

Prehypertension was first identified in 2003, and some studies claim as many as 50 million U.S. adults have the condition, defined as blood pressure readings from 120/80 to 139/89. This risk of being at risk can be modified with diet and exercise, but the *NEJM* study reports that it can also be treated with Atacand, a drug from AstraZeneca Pharmaceuticals PLC.

To a growing chorus of physicians and health-care specialists, the very idea of treating the risk of a risk is wrong. They have labeled the phenomenon "disease-mongering," defined as the corporate-sponsored creation or exaggeration of maladies for the purpose of selling more drugs. Prehypertension "is a classic case of a risk factor being turned into the disease," says Dr. Steven Woloshin of the Veterans Affairs Outcomes Group in White River Junction, Vt. "If you make a cut-off for blood pressure that's close to the normal range, then just about everyone can be diagnosed." An AstraZeneca spokesman responds that the trial was considered important enough to be published in the prestigious *NEJM*. "I think that speaks for itself."

## Demand for a Quick Fix

According to critics, disease-mongering is on the rise. It starts when a drug is developed for some once-rare condition. Then heavily promoted disease-awareness campaigns kick into gear, leading to increasing numbers of diagnoses and prescriptions. The list of suspects includes restless legs syndrome, social anxiety disorder, premenstrual dystrophic disorder, irritable bowel syndrome, female sexual dysfunction, and more. "Of course, some people have these diseases very seriously," says Dr. Robert L. Klitzman, a psychiatrist and bioethicist at Columbia

University. "The problem is that mild cases are being made to seem more serious than they are."

The other problem, say the anti-disease-mongerers, is that the vagaries of everyday life, such as sadness, shyness, forgetfulness, and the occasional upset stomach, are being turned into medical conditions. Before Pfizer Inc.'s Viagra was introduced, erectile dysfunction was a medical problem only when associated with an underlying biological cause, such as diabetes or prostate cancer. Now, Pfizer's Web site claims that half of all men over 40 have problems getting or maintaining an erection. Social anxiety disorder, defined as severe shyness, was rarely seen until GlaxoSmithKline PLC's Paxil was approved to treat it. A disease-awareness campaign by Glaxo in the late 1990s, with the tag line "imagine being allergic to people," was quickly followed by rising prevalence estimates.

Disease promotion is not just the purview of drug companies. "Doctors should set more boundaries," asserts Dr. David Henry, a pharmacology professor at the University of Newcastle in Australia and a leading critic of disease-mongering. Then there are patients seeking a quick fix for conditions that might better be treated through lifestyle changes. "Drug companies are playing off the desire we all have to get rid of things that bother us," says Klitzman. But ridding oneself of bothersome symptoms without changing the behaviors that contribute to them can mean taking a pill every day for years, a proposition that is both risky and costly.

## Younger and Younger

Also of concern are efforts to expand the definition of serious diseases to cover more and more people. Loosened criteria for bipolar disorder, a dire psychological disease once thought to affect only 0.1% of the population, have led some experts to claim prevalence rates of anywhere from 5% to 10%. Dr. David Healy of Cardiff University in Wales says the higher estimates are based on ill-defined surveys that followed the introduction in the mid-1990s of mood stabilizer drugs, promising relief even for people with mild emotional swings. In the U.S., children as young as age 2 are being diagnosed as bipolar even though, in the classic definition of the illness, symptoms don't usually show up until the teens. "These young kids are started on two or three medicines when there isn't even any evidence that any of them work in children," says Dr. Jon McClellan at the University of Washington in Seattle.

Disease-mongering isn't new. The term was coined by Lynn Payer in her 1994 book *Disease-Mongers: How Doctors, Drug Companies, and Insurers are Making You Feel Sick.* But the advent of direct-to-consumer advertising in the U.S. in 1999 fanned the trend, say drug industry critics. Their complaints reached a critical mass this spring. The April issue of the journal *PLoS Medicine* ran 11 articles on disease-mongering to coincide with the first conference devoted to the topic, held Apr. 11-13 in Newcastle.

Drugmakers say they're only trying to educate patients who are struggling with serious illnesses. "We realize that not every medicine is for every person," says a spokeswoman for Glaxo, which makes drugs for restless legs syndrome, social anxiety disorder, and other diagnoses that are under fire. "The labels contain important information about whether it's appropriate, and we're confident that doctors consulting with patients will assess their health-care issues and the risks and rewards and make an appropriate decision."

## Skeptics note that MDs get much of their continuing education from the drug industry

The skeptics aren't convinced that doctors will be so discriminating, in part because many get their information about disease treatment from the drug industry. Pharmaceutical companies routinely subsidize continuing medical education courses for doctors. They fund research for diseases that then gets published in medical journals, and they underwrite patient advocate groups, which in turn promote the underwriter's drugs on their Web sites. Witness the Child & Adolescent Bipolar Foundation: It lists four pharmaceutical companies as major donors, including Eli Lilly & Co. and Janssen LP, makers of leading mood stabilizers.

All these factors come into play with restless legs syndrome, a case history detailed in *PLoS Medicine.* Defined as the urge to constantly move one's legs, the condition can be truly disruptive for people with severe symptoms, but such severity is considered rare. That didn't stop GlaxoSmithKline from launching a disease awareness campaign in 2003. The company kicked off the blitz with a press release stating that a "new survey reveals a common yet under recognized disorder—restless legs syndrome—is keeping Americans awake at night." News articles proliferated, most stating that the condition affects up to 10% of adults in the U.S., based on the study Glaxo promoted.

In 2005, Glaxo's Requip, a treatment for Parkinson's disease, was approved for restless legs. At the same time the Restless Legs Syndrome Foundation, which receives funding from Glaxo, issued a press release about "a new national survey that shows [the] syndrome is largely under recognized and poorly understood." A Glaxo spokeswoman says that most Requip prescriptions are written for Parkinson's.

The VA's Dr. Woloshin grants that some people are helped by Requip, Paxil, and Viagra. But he worries that over treatment drains money from research into more serious illnesses. "None of these companies is coming up with a cure for TB," he notes. That's a disease no one is trying to monger.

# Living the High Life. The Role of Drug Taking in Young People's Lives

**The vast majority of young drug users see substance use as a positive experience. Why else would they continue to take them? Most research on the other hand pathologises drug use by looking solely at the negative consequences, contributing to the misunderstanding that young people are increasingly self-indulgent and, in a meaningless world, hell-bent on self-destruction. In this refreshing new article Karenza Moore and Steven Miles try to understand the social roles of drug use in the everchanging lives of young people and come up with an alternative view. Rather than seeing drugs as a destructive force, Moore and Miles portray drug-taking as a stabilising factor in the volatile world of growing up.**

KARENZA MOORE

STEVEN MILLER

C lubbing is a leisure pursuit enjoyed by millions of young people. So-called 'dance drugs', predominately ecstasy, amphetamines, cocaine and 'new' substances such as GHB and ketamine, are an integral part of localised and globalised club cultures.

There is a considerable danger that in the midst of media and academic conjecture the impact of drugs upon young people's lives and the role that drugs partake in the active construction of young people's lifestyles is neglected in favour of a melodramatic vision of young people as risk-takers, and of young clubbers as being at the forefront of such 'risk behaviour'.

We argue that much like other forms of consumption, young people's use of drugs in clubbing settings (pre-club bars, in-club spaces, dance music festivals, after-parties) is less about exploring the unpredictability of risk or about the corruption of innocence, and more about young people actively maintaining a sense of stability in their everyday lives.

## Exploring the Nature of Drug Use

To explore this alternative view of young people's drug consumption we draw on our small-scale survey of young clubbers in Manchester and Sheffield and two years of observation in various clubbing settings within these two cities.

Many commentators have noted that young people's lives are perhaps increasingly precarious, not least in light of the apparently vast number of choices and hurdles that lie between them and their futures. In order to understand the role of drugs in young people's lives it is important to have some comprehension of the broader nature of their social experience.

Young people do not consume drugs in isolation. The consumption of drugs represents an active expression of how young people cope with the demands of the social structures within which they operate. Drug consumption, and most particularly that found in club settings, is one such way that young people can actually impart some control over their everyday lives.

# Drug Use Has Meaning for Young People

The apparently mundane contexts in which young people consume drugs are particularly useful in understanding what drug consumption actually *means*. The fact that young people's cultural lives are not always deemed to be of significant policy interest has a dangerous side-effect insofar as it serves to magnify the problematisation of young people—a phenomenon already encountered among services that deal with drug use among young people.

Clubbing can offer young people a sense of identity that goes beyond the antics of the weekend. It can have an impact upon a person's sense of self, their identifications with others and their sense of 'belonging' in sometimes confusing and menacing urban spaces.

Clubbing may provide some young people with a sense of stability in their lives, opening up a space in which they can depend on something, in a world in which arguably at least they can depend on very little.

Such aspects of young people's drug use, notably within club settings, are often overlooked in moralistic prescriptions of zero tolerance and the dominant 'war on drugs' discourse.

# Dedication to Clubbing and Drugs

To 'be a clubber' is hard work. Young people who regularly go clubbing invest considerable time and effort ensuring that their nights out, and dancing till the early hours of the morning, will be fun, and to a certain extent trouble-free. Clubbers demonstrate considerable local (and wider) knowledge about clubs, DJs, music and musical genres.

Preparation for some nights out clubbing starts weeks or even months in advance, while at other times a more spontaneous decision to go clubbing is made. In terms of preparation, procuring desired substances sometimes takes place days in advance and can be a source of considerable anxiety.

# The Routine

Due to the very familiarity of the practices that have to be undertaken in order for the night out to run smoothly, these preparations act as basis for the expectations that clubbers build up around a night. When clubbers have 'sorted' themselves out in terms of deciding where to go and obtaining substances, this adds to the excitement and anticipation.

Events, such as being caught in-club with drugs, undermine the 'flow' of a night out, and the possibility that such events may occur contributes to the anxiety that some clubbers experience. Of course mundane clubbing practices such as obtaining, hiding and consuming 'dance drugs' form the basis for the more spectacular aspects of clubbing, such as when a crowd is 'brought up' by the DJs with a popular record.

# Broadening Social Encounters

There are other mundane and possibly routine practices on which the spectacular aspects of clubbing rest. Many young dance drug users for example see interacting with strangers in-club as a 'natural' part of clubbing.

> 'Normally I'm quite shy but when I'm out clubbing I just chat to anyone and hug and dance with everyone. That's the best thing about it. If I like someone's hair or what they're wearing, or they just look friendly, I'll go right up and tell them' (Male, age 26)[1].

> 'It makes you feel special, like you're out clubbing with the whole club' (Male, age 20).

# Sociability, Indicators and Rules

Mundane practices undertaken pre-club and in-club play a part in the more spectacular feeling of 'clubbing with the whole club'. Young clubbers share water, chewing gum and 'poppers' with friends and strangers, and use physical contact as a 'marker' for the friendliness and togetherness of a crowd, and an indication of a good night out.

> 'You can tell it's a good one if the crowd are there with their hands in the air, jumping up and down with each other and hugging random people!' (Female, age 19, Sat 12 July 2003: Manchester).

Many of the young people we spoke to said they would help a fellow clubber who appeared to be in trouble, by calling security or a paramedic for example. Such practices relate to the social etiquette that surrounds the consumption of substances in the clubbing space.

Extravagant displays of 'self-expression' in settings where it may be presumed that 'anything goes' rest on the nuances of behaviours that are deemed socially, culturally and contextually acceptable or unacceptable.

Some young people for example thought that ketamine users in clubs can somehow break the 'rules', describing users as *'like zombies roaming around the club'* (Male, age 20).

# Drugs of Choice

The northwest of England is similar to many areas of the UK in providing a huge range of club nights, all playing a wide variety of dance music genres, often under the same roof. On a single night out clubbers may consume alcohol, ecstasy, GHB, amyl nitrate (poppers), ketamine and cannabis (Saturday 13 September 2003: Sheffield).

Many young clubbers take a range of drugs, although ecstasy remains the drug of choice for many. This seems to be related to the perception that ecstasy makes people friendlier than any other 'clubbing drug', especially alcohol.

'People are all very nice on pills' (Female, age 21)

Musical genre affects what drugs people take and how: Our respondents said they are more likely to take ecstasy (and for some ketamine) at hard house, trance, and hard trance nights. Those that attend funky/soulful house nights say they are more likely to take alcohol at such events than at other nights (such as hard trance).

'You will rarely find clubbers taking Ket in a trance club. It's not that type of scene. You would also rarely find people taking cocaine in a hard house/trance environment, because it makes you more arrogant and unsociable' (Male, age 20).

'Funky house: people are more likely to take cocaine due to the pretensions associated with it. Hard house and trance: Ecstasy is more commonly used' (Male, age 20).

Here we see a process occurring in which clubbers distinguish between the friendliness of a crowd depending on the genre of music being played and the related substance use. There may not actually be any substantive differences in the types of substances being consumed according to musical genre in the club setting but clubbers perceive there to be a difference.

Young clubbers also report experiencing what are ostensibly the 'same' substances differently according to musical genre and (club) setting. Some clubbers indicated that they consume less, if any, alcohol at hard house nights than they do at funky/soulful house nights.

'I drink alcohol at funky house nights, don't know why just seems like the thing to do. Also I always end up feeling more f\*\*ked at hard house nights and the comedowns are worse' (Female, age 27).

## Knowing the Score and Feeling in Control

Many young clubbers perceive that they are well informed about drug harm and risk-reduction techniques.

'Have a nice bath when I get in, sleep! Drink plenty of water, orange juice, take 5-HTP (to aid replenishment of Serotonin) and Echinacea (to boost immune system). Eat healthily, ie, lots of vegetables, fruit etc. Be around people/friends for comedown company!' (Male, age 20).

In addition to clubbers' perceptions that they know 'what pills do to you', young people deployed the notion of

'balance' between clubbing and 'real-life' as itself a harm-reduction technique.

'I make sure I still do other things I love like playing football, and I take a break every couple of weekends. I know one really smart guy that went to Imperial in London and basically fucked up his life from too many pills and too much clubbing' (Male, age 21, Saturday 25 October 2003: Manchester).

## Clubbing Folklore and Setting Boundaries

Clubbers tell anecdotes about people who had 'overdone' clubbing, or become too 'hardcore', letting their weekend activities interfere with 'normal' life. While the use of ecstasy in club culture may be becoming 'normalised', this does not necessarily entail the existence of a 'reckless' chemical generation.

Clubbers engage with discourses surrounding drug 'abuse' and distance themselves from the notion of abuse by referring to the ways in which they 'manage' their 'recreational' drug use so that it does not interfere with their everyday lives.

The general feeling among many young clubbers is that 'recreational' drug consumption in club settings is a temporary pursuit and that at some point in the future they will stop.

'When I get older, I suppose I'll grow out of it. If I carried on, I'd look out of place. I believe it's a phase people go through. Eventually I'll stop taking them. I've cut down a lot of the stuff I used to do already. I never have to take drugs when I'm out' (Male, age 20).

However, from our participant observation in dubs in the northwest of England, it is dear that there are substantial numbers of older people who continue to enjoy dance–drug dubbing.

## The Social Benefits of Clubbing

However this view appears not to detract from the symbolic importance that many young clubbers attribute to dubbing, particularly in terms of the friendship groups they had built up around dubbing activities.

'The music, dancing, the feeling/energy doing pills gives you, enjoying myself and seeing other people I know and care about enjoying themselves, sense of community and feeling "special"!' (Male, age 20).

This again suggests that young clubbers' drug consumption is strategic in nature. Strategic in the sense that it provides young people with something very tangible in the short-term: the feeling that they belong to something that has its own structure and language that takes them away from their broader life-concerns while simultaneously being formed by, and forming, those concerns.

# Importance of a Non-pathological View

If we resist the temptation to pigeonhole and demonise young people, we may begin to comprehend the pragmatic and at times rational ways with which they cope with social change. Involvement in club culture may be one way in which young people are negotiating such changes.

## Note

1. These responses are taken from the aforementioned questionnaire on young 'clubbers' in Manchester and Sheffield.

**Acknowledgement**—An extended version of this paper is available in *Addiction, Research and Theory*. The full reference for this is:

KARENZA MOORE and STEVEN MILES (2004) Young people, dance and the sub-cultural consumption of drugs. *Addiction, Research and Theory 12* (6) 507–523
**k.moore@salford.ac.uk**

# Methamphetamine Across America: Misconceptions, Realities and Solutions

**The abuse of methamphetamine (meth) continues to spread across the country, straining the already limited resources for law enforcement, environmental clean up, and addiction treatment. This article examines the perceived and actual nature of the meth problem and presents possible solutions.**

CAROL L. FALKOWSKI, HAZELDEN FOUNDATION

Methamphetamine (meth) abuse is changing the American landscape unlike any other illegal drug before it, sweeping across our small towns, rural areas, suburbs and cities. Meth casts a dark shadow and leaves behind a wake of shattered lives and communities.

Some trends in drug abuse come and go, such as the explosion of crack cocaine in the 1980s, and later GHB, the "date rape" drug, and "ecstasy." Other drug abuse trends hold constant such as nicotine addiction with 400,000 lives lost annually to tobacco-related disease, and alcohol abuse claiming 100,000 lives annually. Underage drinking persists even 20 years after states adopted 21 as the legal drinking age, and marijuana is still used by almost half of students before graduation from high school.

So what makes the rising tide of methamphetamine abuse so different? Plenty.

## Meth – The Drug

First, consider the drug itself, a synthetic, man-made stimulant that can be consumed in multiple ways: smoked, injected or snorted. "Glass" or "ice" is the most potent, smokable form of the drug. Yet unlike most other drugs of abuse, its duration of action is longer, and for some, the effects can persist long after discontinuation of regular use.

A person under the influence of meth may be in an altered state for eight to 12 hours. After the initial euphoric "rush," the behavioral effects include heightened concentration, increased alertness, high energy, wakefulness and loss of appetite. With meth the progression from occasional use to addiction can occur over a period of months. As with other drugs of abuse, addiction to meth can also trigger psychosis in people who are predisposed.

Unlike many other drugs of abuse, methamphetamine is a neurotoxin. This means that it not only affects the release and reuptake of certain brain chemicals (mostly dopamine), but also damages the neural tissue within the brain, the effects of which can be long-lasting. Meth exposure can damage the areas of the brain related to both cognition and memory. In some cases, even years after discontinuation of use, some brain functioning may not be fully restored to pre-meth levels. For this reason, meth addiction places an individual at heightened risk of long-term, possibly irreversible behavioral, cognitive, and psychological problems over the course of a lifetime.

## Meth – The Addiction

Addiction is not simply "a lot of drug abuse," but a diagnosable medical disorder wherein a person's compulsive drug use dominates every aspect of life. For an addict, the acquisition and use of the drug is the primary focus of life, in spite of negative consequences that are directly attributable to drug use (loss of employment, family, personal relationships, and physical and psychological health). Because of the insatiable, compulsive craving for the drug, addicts will do almost anything to obtain it. This can include behaviors they may have never considered possible prior to their addiction—behaviors that violate their value system or that are criminal.

Drug testing data from urinalysis obtained from males who were arrested (for all types of crime, not just drug offenses), reflect the degree to which meth abuse underlies a significant amount of criminal activity. Nationwide in 2003, the cities with the highest rate of methamphetamine-positive male arrestees were Honolulu with 40.3 percent, followed by Phoenix (38.3 percent) and Sacramento (37.6 percent). Rates in the central states include Des Moines (27.9 percent), Omaha (21.4 percent), Tulsa (17.4 percent), Albuquerque (10.1 percent), Dallas (5.8 percent) and Minneapolis (3.3 percent). Meth abuse has not reached comparable levels in some eastern parts of the country. Less than 1 percent of arrestees tested positive for methamphetamine in Albany, Anchorage, Boston, Charlotte, Cleveland, Miami, New York City, Philadelphia and Washington D.C. The median across all cities was 4.7 percent.

Addicts use increasing amounts of meth (due to the resultant physical tolerance) over extended periods of time—sometimes days at a time—during which they do not eat or sleep. This pattern of meth use results in extreme sleep and food deprivation, so that the physical deterioration is often more rapid and pronounced than with other drugs.

Eventually most meth addicts develop strong paranoid delusions, sometimes known as "methamphetamine psychosis." They see things that aren't really there, including illusive "shadow people." They hear things that aren't really there—auditory hallucinations. A defining feature of this delusional state is when meth addicts believe that everyone is "out to get them," even innocent strangers or inanimate objects.

For example, a meth addict can spend hours on end peering out of a window into the front yard, nearly paralyzed with fear and convinced that someone is watching him and coming to "get him," when in fact there is nothing threatening in the front yard, just an unoccupied parked car or a few shrubs and bushes. It is this phenomenon, in particular, that makes meth addicts such a hazard to people they may encounter, and hence the public safety.

# Meth Labs

Many meth abusers eventually attempt to make the drug themselves, in the privacy of their own apartment, office, barn, workshop, home or car. Recipes are readily accessible online or by word of mouth from one "cook" to another. Using ingredients that can be readily stolen or purchased at farm supply stores (anhydrous ammonia), hardware stores (muriatic acid, camping fuel, automotive de-icer, gun scrubber, to name a few), and grocery or drug stores (ephedrine, pseudoephedrine, matches, batteries, iodine), they "cook" it up themselves.

Mixing these volatile, poisonous, and flammable substances has toxic and sometimes explosive results. Because they are not trained chemists working in controlled laboratory conditions, meth cooks typically are also unable to safely correct minor mistakes that happen along the way, a problem that contributes to sudden explosions and unexpected flash fires.

Every unit of "finished product" of meth produces six units of dangerous waste. The fumes, ingredients, and waste byproducts contaminate surrounding buildings, groundwater, wells, and bodies of water, land and air. For these reasons trained, hazardous response teams conduct meth lab clean up.

Those who live in proximity to operational or abandoned meth production areas are harmed as well. People can unknowingly live in an apartment unit that is adjacent to an operational meth lab, stay in a motel where meth was produced just hours before, or purchase property that was once used as a meth dumpsite or lab.

Innocent children who live in homes where meth is made are particularly damaged, suffering chemical burns, lung irritation, blood disorders, and the increased risk of permanent neuro-logical and developmental damage. Multiple law enforcement sources have reported meth labs located in close proximity to children's eating, sleeping and bathing areas.

Whenever the primary caretakers of children are addicted, the potential for child abuse and neglect is heightened. More often than not, children's physical, safety and emotional needs are unmet. When caregivers are both addicted to meth and making it themselves, add to the picture the ill effects on children of prolonged exposure to dangerous environmental toxins, and the elevated risk of spills, accidental ingestion, sudden explosions or fires.

# Meth Treatment

Addiction is a chronic, relapsing disease, such as asthma, diabetes and hypertension. Treatment for addiction is as effective as treatment for these other chronic diseases. In addiction treatment, patients look at the consequences related to their addiction, and with the respectful help of professionals, slowly develop tools and skills necessary to negotiate the challenges of life without the drug. Once diagnosed and treated, behavior change and periodic professional services are necessary to effectively manage addiction over the course of a lifetime.

Can methamphetamine addiction be successfully treated? Absolutely. Yet often we hear an elected official, environmental health officer, or law enforcement agent definitively state, "Treatment for meth addicts doesn't work." For those of us in the addiction field this statement is sadly reminiscent of what people said about alcoholics 60 years ago, and about crack addicts in the 1980s. Perhaps you've even said it yourself. Yet it is simply not the case. Methamphetamine addiction can be successfully treated.

Consider the primary research-based principles of addiction treatment according to the National Institute on Drug Abuse. First, treatment needs to be readily available. In reality, though, addiction treatment is not readily accessible for many who need it in this country. By some estimates, up to two-thirds of those who need addiction treatment do not receive it. One reason for this is that treatment is often not fully covered by health insurance.

Second, research finds that remaining in treatment for an adequate period of time is critical for treatment effectiveness and that longer treatment exposure enhances the likelihood of sustained sobriety. In reality, however, there are often caps or restrictions on both on the length and type addiction treatment benefits, even for those with health insurance. For public pay clients, especially in non-urban areas, options may be even more limited.

Further, research finds that short periods of abstinence, like detox or time spent in jail, in the absence of treatment, do little to change behavior and support recovery in the long haul. Jail is not the same as treatment. Therefore no one should be surprised, for example, when an addict who has not received treatment continues to use while out on pre-trial release.

A more accurate assessment is that treatment is not as accessible as it should be, especially for meth addicts—most of whom have lost their jobs, their assets, their homes, their

## Principles of Effective Treatment

- Treatment needs to be readily available.
- Treatment does not need to be voluntary to be effective.
- Medical detoxification is only the first stage of addiction treatment and by itself does little to change long-term drug use.
- Remaining in treatment for an adequate period of time is critical for treatment effectiveness. Research indicates that for most patients the threshold of significant improvement is reached at three months, and that additional treatment can produce further progress toward recovery.
- Effective treatment addresses the multiple needs of the individual: drug use and the associated medical psychological, legal, social and vocational problems. Addiction and co-existing mental disorders should be treated in an integrated way.
- Recovery from addiction can be a long-term process and frequently requires multiple episodes of treatment.

*Source: Principles of Addiction Treatment: A Research-Based Guide, National Institute on Drug Abuse, NIH Publication No. 99-4180, 1999.*

families, their freedom and their health. With meth addicts, in particular, an adequate length of treatment is necessary in order to determine which psychiatric disorders are pre-existing and which are associated with meth use itself.

Following primary treatment, halfway houses or supported, transitional living situations are often indicated for recovering meth addicts because they have no safe, drug-free residence to which to return. Yet in reality, these too, are not always accessible to all who need them.

## Solutions to the Meth Problem

Retailers, distributors and wholesalers of precursor substances need continuing education in how to identify possible meth lab purchases, and encouragement in reporting suspicious purchases to authorities without fear of repercussions. Beyond that, every individual needs to be vigilant in reporting suspicious activity to law enforcement officials. People making meth use enormous amounts of legal products. So when we notice these piled up in our neighbor's trash, or smell a strong chemical odor, or see people coming and going from a business or dwelling at all hours of the day or night, we need to report these suspicions.

Curtailing the supply of foreign, imported precursors and meth must also be part of a comprehensive solution. While meth labs are a growing public nuisance, the majority of methamphetamine consumed in this country is imported from Mexico.

States should examine their criminal codes to see if they adequately address the range of activities related to methamphetamine abuse. At least 28 states have addressed meth production

by limiting the sale of precursor substances used in meth production at the retail or wholesale level. Some states have stiffened penalties for the theft of anhydrous ammonia and other precursors, or for the production of meth. Varying approaches have been met with varying degrees of success.

If meth addicts who are serving long prison terms receive no formal addiction treatment, nothing has been done to address their addiction. Once released, their long-term prognosis is poor. Hence, some states have made advances in offering treatment in correctional settings, followed by up to a year of highly structured, supervised community living.

Our children need to appreciate the dangers of meth use, especially young teenage girls who may be initially attracted by the weight loss effects. We need to have realistic, factual and heartfelt conversations with our children. And we need to engage not just our families, but our schools, and entire communities. Research finds that drug abuse prevention is effective only when it consists of the same message delivered by multiple messengers. The message here is clear—"speed kills."

## Conclusions

Meth-related problems continue to spread across the country. It seems by the time meth addicts finally get the help they need, it is under the worst of circumstances. Many of our public systems that respond to the associated problems are short-staffed and operate severely curtailed budgets, which renders them marginally effective even under the best of circumstances.

Meth addicts interface with multiple public agencies at enormous public expense: criminal justice, human services, environmental health, child protection and emergency medicine. Therefore, both sufficient financial resources and the multidisciplinary coordination of effort are essential to any strategic solution.

Without adequate resources, communities cannot absorb the astronomical costs of meth lab clean up, nor can a state provide effective treatment and supported aftercare to all who need it. Without coordination of services, law enforcement cannot deliver a timely response to suspected meth lab activity, school social workers cannot adequately investigate and intervene with the growing number of children living in meth lab homes, nor can overstretched service providers or drug court professionals keep up with the burgeoning challenges presented by meth addicts and their families.

Policymakers must acknowledge the significant magnitude and far-reaching dimensions of the escalating meth problem, and address it with an appropriate high level of response. "Business as usual," which these days means "doing more with less," will not curtail the rising tide of methamphetamine abuse.

## References

*Arrestee Drug Abuse Monitoring (ADAM) Program,* (2003) National Institute of Justice, U.S. Department of Justice.

Falkowski, Carol L., *Dangerous Drugs: An Easy-to-Use Reference for Parents and Professionals,* (2003) 2nd edition, Hazelden Publishing.

McLellan, Thomas A., Lewis, David C., O'Brien, Charles P., Kleber, Herbert D., "Drug Dependence, a Chronic Medical Illness: Implications for Treatment, Insurance, and Outcomes Evaluation," (2000) *Journal of the American Medical Association*, Vol. 284: No. 13, p. 1689–95.

*Principles of Addiction Treatment: A Research-Based Guide*, (1999) US Department of Health and Human Services, National Institutes of Health, National Institute on Drug Abuse, NIH Publication No. 99-4180.

Thompson, Paul M., Hayashi, Kiralee M., Simon, Dara L., Geaga, Jennifer A., et al, "Abnormalities in the Brains of Human Subjects Who Use Methamphetamine," (2004) *Journal of Neuroscience*, Vol. 24: p. 6028–36.

CAROL L. FALKOWSKI is the director of research communications at the Hazelden Foundation, and author of Dangerous Drugs: An Easy-to-Use Reference of Parents and Professionals. She has monitored drug abuse trends for nearly 20 years as part of an ongoing epidemiological drug abuse surveillance network of the National Institute on Drug Abuse. The nonprofit Hazelden Foundation, is an international provider of programs, services, and publications for individuals, families, and communities affected by addiction. Online at: www.hazelden.org. P.O. Box 11, Center City, MN 55012. (800) 257–7800. CFalkowski@Hazelden.org.

# Balding, Wrinkled and Stoned

## The '60s are gone, but for some baby boomers, the drugs aren't. A guide to the cost of a 40-year high

JEFFREY KLUGER WITH JEFFREY RESSNER

Few people know the perils of drug abuse better than a 55-year-old former schoolteacher whose job it used to be to teach that very topic—which is why it's particularly ironic that she's a cocaine addict today. More than 30 years ago, Gwen—who prefers to keep it to one name when discussing her addiction—spent her days teaching in the Virginia school system and drafting the schools' drug-and-alcohol-abuse curriculum. She spent her nights researching the subject firsthand.

"I started using alcohol and pot in college," she says. "Then I turned to sniffing cocaine and freebasing. By the time I began teaching, I was spending big-time money. My body knew that I got out of school at 3:30 every day, and then I'd have to go out and get my drugs."

Today Gwen spends most of her time far from Virginia, living in New York City and attending regular sobriety meetings in the Odyssey House ElderCare treatment program in East Harlem. It's not how she envisioned her retirement. "I never thought the drug-abuse classes I taught applied to me," she says. "But here I am."

She's hardly alone. Of the more than 75 million baby boomers who came of age in the 1960s and '70s, millions experimented with drugs during their impressionable teenage years, and millions went on to enter middle age—and are now headed into their senior years—with decades-long addictions. Hard numbers are not easy to come by, but older addicts are clearly a growth sector in the drug-recovery industry. There are an estimated 1.7 million Americans over age 50 addicted to drugs, according to the Substance Abuse and Mental Health Services Administration (SAMHSA), a division of the Department of Health and Human Services. By 2020 SAMHSA expects the number to reach 4.4 million. Already an ongoing federal study has found that the number of older Americans seeking help for heroin or cocaine abuse roughly quadrupled from 1992 to 2002. Odyssey House, which was founded to treat younger addicts, now has a separate division, with both inpatient and outpatient facilities, to deal specifically with older users.

What makes the problem especially hard for seniors is that the wages of drug abuse are cumulative. A lifetime of recreational chemistry also means a lifetime of neglect of overall health—as a recent morning meeting at Odyssey House illustrated. There were too many canes in evidence for a group so comparatively young—the legacy of joints wrecked by years of undertreated diabetes—and too many bad hearts and bum livers and vascular systems fighting hypertension. "This is the first generation to have a high incidence of using recreational drugs," says SAMHSA epidemiologist Joseph Gfroerer. "All this puts them at risk for problems."

But why did those baby boomers stay aboard the drug carousel when so many millions more climbed off? And what exactly have 40 years of experimental pharmacology done to them? It would not have been possible—much less ethical—to recruit subjects when the 1960s drug circus got started, send them off for four decades of substance abuse and bring them back for study. But now that the ad hoc longitudinal experiment those aging boomers have been conducting on themselves is reaching its endgame, addiction experts are pouncing on what the doctors and psychiatrists treating the abusers are learning. What they uncover may help not only the surviving victims of the early drug years but younger users as well.

Of all the drugs the boomers have used, perhaps the four most notorious have been marijuana, hallucinogens, cocaine and heroin. Researchers have devoted enormous effort to studying those drugs' long-term effects. The results have been decidedly mixed.

## There are too many canes in use for people in their 50s and 60s, too many bad hearts and bum livers

**Marijuana** The so-called demon weed turned out to be a lot less devilish than advertised. The popular image of the goofy, smoky slacker notwithstanding, a 2003 study in the *Journal of the International Neuropsychological Society* found that even among regular users, there is no proof that pot causes irreversible cognitive damage. Memory does get cloudy, and learning new information does get harder, but those effects fade if the user does kick the habit. The drug may also diminish libido and fertility. (So much for its promised free-love properties.) And as with any intoxicating chemical, pot use can become chronic and compulsive, crowding out room for much else. "If you came to our adolescent program and saw the 16-year-old kids whose lives have become unmanageable as a result of pot use, you'd understand it's addictive," says psychologist Peter Provet, president of Odyssey House. "But a lot of people who use pot don't become addicts."

Scientists haven't settled on whether repeated chestfuls of unfiltered marijuana smoke increase the risk of pulmonary disease and cancers of the mouth, throat and lungs. Although a recent study out of UCLA says no, practitioners in the field disagree. "There's certainly strong if not definitive evidence that long-term smokers take in a lot of particulates and carcinogens," says Dr. Robert Raicht, medical director of Odyssey House.

**Hallucinogens** Things are trickier when it comes to LSD and its hallucinogenic kin, but reports suggest that most '60s trips ended relatively benignly. The most rigorous studies of hallucinogens have been conducted not on boomers, who used the drugs intermittently and furtively, but on Native American populations for whom consumption of the hallucinogen peyote is part of their cultural and religious fabric. In November researchers from the McLean psychiatric hospital outside Boston released a five-year study that found no cognitive or psychological problems among Native American regular users, some of whom even performed better on psychological tests than those with minimal substance use. It's certainly too much to say that every peyote user emerges undamaged by the drug, and the lead researcher on the study, Dr. John Halpern, takes care to stress that his findings apply only to the Native American groups he studied.

LSD and mescaline, which are often whipped up in unpoliced labs in uncontrolled ways, present different problems. The condition that the experts call HPPD (hallucinogen persisting perception disorder) and that users call flashbacks is a very real problem. But Halpern says it is relatively rare, striking mostly people who use LSD specifically. But there are other risks too. Some trips have ended catastrophically, with suicides or fatal accidents. In other cases, the disaster was not physical but emotional. "There were a lot of people who decompensated into major mental illness," says Dr. Charles Grob, a professor of psychiatry at UCLA's school of medicine. "But you could make the case that these were people who were vulnerable to begin with."

## 1.7 million

Estimated number of Americans over 50 who were abusing drugs in 2001

## 4.4 million

Number of over-50 abusers by 2020, when baby boomers will be 56 to 74

**Cocaine** The coke party started late for most boomers—not until the 1980s—but when it hit, it hit hard. Even cocaine apologists admit that the drug is dangerously addictive and sometimes lethal. Coke-triggered strokes and heart attacks—both of which can occur in people with no known cardiovascular disease—are the real deal, caused by the sudden elevation of blood pressure and spasms of vessels. "The damage can be done suddenly and acutely," says Raicht, "or slowly and chronically."

Whether periodic cocaine use develops into disabling addiction can be something of a crapshoot. "There's a tendency for most people who have any kind of stake in conventional life to modulate their use and not let it get out of hand," says Craig Reinarman, a sociologist at the University of California at Santa Cruz and a co-author of two books on cocaine. For most people, he says, the breaking point for cocaine use is about an eighth of an ounce a week. But that's just a very general rule, and for many people, the threshold can be lower. And when it comes to crack—crystallized and smoked instead of snorted—addiction, often from the first use, is much harder to avoid.

**Heroin** Easily the most lethal of the gang of four, heroin frequently hooks users for the rest of their lives, unless it simply kills them first. One long-term study, published in May 2001 in the *Archives of General Psychiatry*, followed 581 male heroin users from 1962 to 1997. Nearly half the subjects were dead by the time the study ended. Of those still alive, many were self-medicating with multiple other illicit drugs or alcohol and 67% smoked cigarettes. Not surprisingly, heroin users suffer from a wide range of medical ills, including hypertension, liver and pulmonary diseases and HIV. But the most common cause of death from heroin is overdose, with 22% of the subjects in the long-term study dying that way. Some of the health problems associated with heroin come from the impurities it is cut with. Overdoses often spring from an uncut batch that is unexpectedly pure.

## Aging metabolisms cause drugs to hit harder and linger longer, doing more damage with the same dose

The ultimate impact of any of those drugs, of course, depends on the users. No one has yet been able to tease out the precise mix of genetics, temperament and environment that makes one person a recreational user and another a lifelong addict, but clearly there is no single cause. "There are inherited components, hormonal components, psychosocial variables such as poverty," says Provet. And then, of course, there is mere opportunity—something the '60s provided in abundance.

"That was the era," says Evelyn, 56, an Odyssey House graduate and an addiction counselor there. "If the drugs hadn't been so available, I wouldn't have been apt to go looking for them."

As drug users mature, geriatric biology and life circumstances tend to tighten the drugs' hold. Reduced body mass, slower metabolism and less efficient kidneys and liver mean that the same quantity of drug hits harder and stays in the body longer. Older users who think they're keeping their doses fixed are thus, in effect, steadily increasing them. What's more, the loss of a spouse or job or merely the boredom of retirement could tip the nonuser into experimentation and the borderline user into full-blown addiction. Moses, 57, never touched heroin until 2001, when his wife died. But when he picked it up, he got hooked fast. "I missed my wife. I was lonely," he says. "I didn't want to live, but I didn't have the nerve to put a gun to my head."

For the seniors who do get clean—and the millions more who will need to in the years to come—there are a few factors that drive recovery. Seeing peers die of addiction certainly scares some straight. So too do late-life worries about the legacy one is going to leave. "You get to a point when you think about having a dignified end," says Jon Roberts, another Odyssey House veteran who is now a counselor. "You think about family reunification, about giving back through community service, about having spent your life as more than an addict."

It's rare for teenagers of any generation to think that far ahead, never mind the cohort that reached adolescence at the height of the drug boom. It may be impossible to slow the demographic conveyor belt that's going to dump so many of them into the senior population with a habit they picked up during their summers of love. But it's not too late for them to shake it off, achieving the peace in the last chapters of their lives that the drugs promised them in the first.

# America's Most Dangerous Drug

**It creates a potent, long-lasting high—until the user crashes and, too often, literally burns. How meth quietly marched across the country and up the socioeconomic ladder—and the wreckage it leaves in its wake. As law enforcement fights a losing battle on the ground, officials ask: are the Feds doing all they can to contain this epidemic?**

DAVID J. JEFFERSON

The leafy Chicago suburb of Burr Ridge is the kind of place where people come to live the American dream in million-dollar homes on one-acre lots. Eight years ago Kimberly Fields and her husband, Todd, bought a ranch house here on a wooded lot beside a small lake, and before long they were parents, with two sons, a black Labrador and a Volvo in the drive. But somewhere along the way this blond mother with a college degree and a $100,000-a-year job as a sales rep for Apria Healthcare found something that mattered more: methamphetamine. The crystalline white drug quickly seduces those who snort, smoke or inject it with a euphoric rush of confidence, hyperalertness and sexiness that lasts for hours on end. And then it starts destroying lives.

Kimberly tried drug rehab but failed, and she couldn't care for her children, according to divorce papers filed by her husband, who moved out last year. She was arrested three times for shoplifting—most recently, police say, for allegedly stealing over-the-counter cold pills containing pseudoephedrine, the key ingredient used in making meth. By the time cops came banging on her door with a search warrant on June 1, Kimberly, now 37, had turned her slice of suburbia into a meth lab, prosecutors allege, with the help of a man she'd met eight months earlier in an Indiana bar, Shawn Myers, 32. (Both Fields and Myers pleaded not guilty to possessing meth with an intent to distribute, though Kimberly told police that she is addicted to the drug.) Dressed in a pink T shirt printed with the words ALL STRESSED OUT, Kimberly looked about 45 pounds thinner than when police first booked her for shoplifting two years ago. Her leg bore a knee-to-ankle scar from a chemical burn, and police found anhydrous ammonia, also used in cooking meth, buried in a converted propane tank in her backyard. As officers led Kimberly away in handcuffs, her 6-year-old son Nicholas was "only concerned that his brother had his toys and diapers," recalls Detective Mike Barnes. Meanwhile, police evacuated 96 nearby homes, fearing the alleged meth lab might explode.

Once derided as "poor man's cocaine," popular mainly in rural areas and on the West Coast, meth has seeped into the mainstream in its steady march across the United States. Relatively cheap compared with other hard drugs, the highly addictive stimulant is hooking more and more people across the socioeconomic spectrum: soccer moms in Illinois, computer geeks in Silicon Valley, factory workers in Georgia, gay professionals in New York. The drug is making its way into suburbs from San Francisco to Chicago to Philadelphia. In upscale Bucks County, Pa., the Drug Enforcement Administration last month busted four men for allegedly running a meth ring, smuggling the drug from California inside stereo equipment and flat-screen TVs. Even Mormon Utah has a meth problem, with nearly half the women in Salt Lake City's jail testing positive for the drug in one study.

More than 12 million Americans have tried methamphetamine, and 1.5 million are regular users, according to federal estimates. Meth-making operations have been uncovered in all 50 states; Missouri tops the list, with more than 8,000 labs, equipment caches and toxic dumps seized between 2002 and 2004. Cops nationwide rank methamphetamine the No. 1 drug they battle today: in a survey of 500 law-enforcement agencies in 45 states released last month by the National Association of Counties, 58 percent said meth is their biggest drug problem, compared with only 19 percent for cocaine, 17 percent for pot and 3 percent for heroin. Meth addicts are pouring into prisons and recovery centers at an ever-increasing rate, and a new generation of "meth babies" is choking the foster-care system in many states. One measure of the drug's reach: Target, Wal-Mart, Rite-Aid and other retailers have moved nonprescription cold pills behind the pharmacy counter, where meth cooks have a harder time getting at them.

The active ingredient in those pills is pseudoephedrine, a chemical derivative of amphetamine. The "pseudo" is extracted from the cold pills, and cooked with other chemicals like iodine and anhydrous ammonia—using recipes readily available on the Internet—over high heat. The resulting compound, when ingested, releases bursts of dopamine in the brain, producing a strong euphoric effect.

And, amid the wreckage, a pressing political debate: are we fighting the wrong drug war? The Bush administration has made marijuana the major focus of its anti-drug efforts, both because there are so many users (an estimated 15 million Americans) and because it considers pot a "gateway" to the use of harder substances. "If we can get a child to 20 without using marijuana, there is a 98 percent chance that the child will never become addicted to any drug," says White House Deputy Drug Czar Scott Burns, of the Office of National Drug Control Policy. "While it may come across as an overemphasis on marijuana, you don't wake up when you're 25 and say, 'I want to slam meth!'" But those fighting on the front lines say the White House is out of touch. "It hurts the federal government's credibility when they say marijuana is the No. 1 priority," says Deputy District Attorney Mark McDonnell, head of narcotics in Portland, Ore., which has been especially hard hit. Meth, he says, "is an epidemic and a crisis unprecedented."

## Terry Silvers quit his job rather than get help. When his wife confronted him, he hit her. 'I think meth is one of the plagues the bible talks about,' she says.

Indeed, few municipalities, especially in rural areas, have the resources to deal with the drug's ravages: lab explosions that maim and kill cooks and their families; the toxic mess (for each pound of meth, five pounds of toxic waste are left behind); the strain on social services; the increase in violent crime. "All the social and environmental issues surrounding this drug affect society more than any of the other drugs," says Bill Hansell, president-elect of the National Association of Counties. In its survey of local law enforcement, 70 percent said robberies or burglaries have increased because of meth, as have domestic violence, assaults and identity theft; 40 percent of child-welfare officials reported an increase in out-of-home placements last year due to meth.

State and local officials generally give high marks to the Drug Enforcement Administration, which has increased its meth budget from $127.5 million in fiscal 2001 to $151.4 million in fiscal 2004 (though these figures exclude major expenses like training costs and overtime pay for local task forces) and sends Mobile Enforcement Teams to areas of the country with limited resources or experience in dealing with meth. The Justice Department is turning up the heat; in a July 18 speech to district attorneys, Attorney General Alberto Gonzales said that "in terms of damage to children and to our society, meth is now the most dangerous drug in America." And the drug czar's office has started to wake up to the problem: last year, for the first time, it took a serious look at meth and outlined what needs to be done to fight it. Its Web site for parents, www.theantidrug. com, now prominently features information like how to "Talk to Your Teen About Meth."

But a growing number of officials around the country want to see more concrete action from the White House. The drug czar's office hasn't made any legislative proposals, or weighed in on any of those coming from Capitol Hill; officials there say they want to get a better sense of what works before throwing their weight around. Members of Congress whose districts have been ravaged by the drug are forcing the issue: the ranks of the House's bipartisan "meth caucus" have swelled from just four founding members in 2000 to 118 today, and the group has been fighting the administration's efforts to cut federal spending on local law enforcement. (The House has voted to restore much of the funding; the issue awaits action in the Senate.) "To the extent that we have to choose between fighting meth and marijuana, we need to be fighting meth," says Sen. Jim Talent, Republican of Missouri, who along with Sen. Dianne Feinstein, Democrat of California, has introduced the first big federal bill to address the problem, which would put strict restrictions on the sale of pseudoephedrine-based products.

On the Hill last week, the deputy drug czar walked into a buzz saw, as members vented their frustration over his office's level of attention to the problem. "This isn't the way you tackle narcotics," said GOP Rep. Mark Souder of Indiana. "How many years do we have to see the same pattern at an increasing rate in the United States until there's something where we have concrete recommendations, not another cotton-pickin' meeting? . . . This committee is trying desperately to say, 'Lead!'" Despite the congressional clamor, the White House has been loath to just throw money at the problem. "Meth is a serious priority for us, as evidenced by programs like drug-endangered children, access to recovery, drug courts and community coalitions, among others," says Tom Riley, spokesman for ONDCP. "I'm afraid there's also an element of people 'crying meth' because it's a hot new drug."

The policy debate doesn't mean much to Terry Silvers, who is one of the victims in this war. Silvers, 34, worked for 19 years at Shaw carpet mill in Dalton, Ga., dreaming of the day he could open his own body shop. He had a wife, three kids and a 401(k), and he'd never missed more than a few days of work his entire life. The only illegal drug he'd tried was pot, which he used twice. One day when he was drinking with his buddies they talked him into doing some meth to wake him up for the drive home. "I snorted a line and within five seconds it was like I'd had 12 hours of sleep and wasn't drunk anymore." Soon, Silvers was snorting once or twice a week. Then someone taught him how to smoke it. When the thrill wore off, he started injecting: "firing" or "slamming," addicts call it. "Golly, it's the best feeling you ever had. It's like your mind is running 100 miles an hour, but your feet aren't moving." His weight dropped so drastically—from 180 pounds to 140—that his wife, Lisa, thought he had cancer. He grew increasingly hyperactive and began having seizures and hallucinations. When his wife figured out what the real problem was, she called the carpet mill and tried to get him into its drug-treatment program. He decided to quit his job rather than get help. Fed up, his wife confronted him one Sunday in May and told him she was leaving. "He hit me and knocked a hole in my eardrum," his wife says. His daughter Heather called 911 as her father was dragging Lisa down the steps of a neighbor's house. When Newsweek met with Terry Silvers earlier this summer, he was in Whitfield County Jail, wearing leg shackles and handcuffs. "I'm not as hardened as all this looks," said a gaunt and embarrassed Silvers, who is charged with manufacturing the drug. "I think meth is one of the plagues the Bible talks about," his wife says.

In urban gay communities from New York to Los Angeles, the meth plague has been linked to an even deadlier one: AIDS. Meth makes many users feel hypersexual and uninhibited, and in the gay community that has meant a sharp increase in unsafe sex. The link between meth and HIV is undeniable: in L.A., nearly one in three homosexual men who tested positive for HIV last year reported using crystal, and that percentage has tripled since 2001, according to a new study of 19,000 men by the Los Angeles Gay & Lesbian Center. As in the early days of AIDS, the gay community is fighting to get men to change their behavior: in L.A., activists hand out buttons that declare dump tina (one of meth's many nicknames). But the entreaties fall on ears deafened by meth's siren call. At this spring's annual Black Party in Manhattan, one of the big bacchanals on the gay party circuit, volunteers from Gay Men's Health Crisis handed out condoms to a crowd shaken by recent reports that a meth user had contracted what might be a new, supervirulent strain of HIV. Not 10 feet away, two revelers high on crystal were having unprotected anal sex.

Meth-fueled sex is hardly the exclusive province of gay men. Dr. Alex Stalcup, medical director of New Leaf Treatment Center in Lafayette, Calif., sees plenty of straight high school and college men who use meth to have "speed sex." "They'll get a bunch of speed and go up to a cabin with some girls on Friday night and just have sex all weekend," Stalcup says. The irony is that meth can cause impotence. For many women, weight loss is an even bigger draw. Stalcup tells of one 5-foot-8 patient who weighed less than 90 pounds when she came to him. "People call it the Jenny Crank diet," says Patrick Fleming, head of the Salt Lake County Division of Substance Abuse Services, which now sees more women with addictions to meth than to alcohol.

A lot of people never saw the meth epidemic coming. Unlike crack cocaine, which erupted in the nation's urban centers in the 1980s and quickly gained the attention of media and government, meth took hold in rural areas far from America's power brokers. "It does not have the same hold on policymakers that crack did 20 years ago. I think that's one of the things that has helped the epidemic build in severity, kind of under the radar," says Jack Riley of RAND Corp., the Santa Monica, Calif., think tank. Methamphetamine isn't a new drug, though it has become more powerful as the ingredients and the cooking techniques have evolved. It was first synthesized by a Japanese chemist in 1919, and was used by both Axis and Allied troops in World War II to keep them alert and motivated; kamikaze pilots were said to have taken high doses of the stuff before their missions. In the 1950s, it was commonly prescribed as a diet aid, to fight depression and give housewives a boost. The federal government criminalized the drug in 1970 for most uses (it's still legally available in low doses for the treatment of attention-deficit disorder and narcolepsy). But by then it was illegally being manufactured and distributed by motorcycle gangs in the West. In the early '90s, Mexican trafficking organizations began taking over production, setting up "superlabs" in the California countryside that were able to crank out 50 pounds of meth or more in a weekend. To put that in perspective: an "eight ball" of meth, one eighth of an ounce, is enough to get 15 people high.

Back when bikers controlled the trade, legislators tried to restrict supplies of the core ingredient they were using to make crank, so nicknamed because they would hide meth in their motorcycles' crankcases. So the cooks simply changed the recipe to use ephedrine, a chemical then found in cold medications. Lawmakers got wise, and clamped down on ephedrine; the cooks switched to a related compound, pseudoephedrine. When the United States began restricting bulk sales of "pseudo" in the mid-1990s, meth manufacturers turned to Canada. They also began buying hundreds of thousands of boxes of Sudafed and other pseudoephedrine-based drugs ("smurfing," cooks call it, when they go from store to store buying or stealing pills). When Canada strengthened regulation of large sales of pseudoephedrine in 2003, production jumped south to Mexico, where pseudo has been arriving in ever-larger doses from Asia. Today about half the meth in the United States is made in Mexico, smuggled across the border and ferried around the country in cars with secret compartments that would make James Bond proud. "It'll be the kind where you turn on the windshield wiper, hit the brakes, hit the door lock and then the compartment will open up," says the DEA's Rodney Benson, special agent in charge of the four-state Seattle Field Division. The DEA is working with its foreign counterparts from Mexico to Hong Kong to intercept pseudoephedrine shipments from overseas and prevent cross-border trafficking into the United States. "I think, increasingly, meth will be seen from our point of view as a smuggled drug," says the agency's Mike Heald.

But meth is a two-front war, and Mexican drug dealers are only part of the problem. Because the drug is relatively easy to make, thousands of labs manned by addicts or local dealers have sprung up around the country. Legislators are now trying to make it harder for these mom-and-pop labs to get their hands on pseudo. Last year Oklahoma became the first state to put pseudoephedrine pills behind the counter; as a result, "meth labs have all but disappeared in Oklahoma," says Mark Woodward, press aide for the Oklahoma Bureau of Narcotics, which reports a 90 percent drop in lab seizures since the legislation was enacted. Seventeen other states have followed Oklahoma's example, and a total of 40 states put some sort of restriction on the sale of pseudo. Drug manufacturers, having fought hard against such laws, have started reformulating their cold medicines using a different chemical—one that cannot be used to make meth.

Still, there will be no easy victory. As law enforcement is all too aware, Anytown, U.S.A., can be turned into a meth den almost overnight. Take Bradford County in northeast Pennsylvania, a place law-enforcement officials nationwide now refer to as Meth Valley. Five years ago a cooker from Iowa named Les Molyneaux set up shop in Towanda, a town of 3,000 along the Susquehanna River. Hardly anyone in Towanda had heard of the drug, but by the time Molyneaux was arrested and pleaded guilty in 2001 to conspiracy to manufacture meth, he'd shared his recipe with at least two apprentices. From there, "it just spread like wildfire," says Assistant U.S. Attorney Christopher Casey. Today police have identified at least 500 people who are using or cooking the drug in Bradford County, and the actual tally is probably "significantly worse" than that, Casey says. The drug has seduced whole families and turned them into "zombies," says Randy Epler, a police officer in Towanda. "I see walking death."

The sobering fact is that, like addiction itself, this epidemic can only be arrested, not cured. "There are a lot more regular people doing it than society has a clue," says Dominic Ippolito, who for a decade dealt meth to doctors, lawyers, designers, accountants and working moms across California. He also smoked the stuff—every day for 10 years—even as he held down a job as a claims manager for a big supermarket chain. But then he lost his job and started dealing drugs full time. He finally got caught on his 42nd birthday, after a customer fingered him in a plea bargain. He pleaded guilty to two counts of possession with intent to sell. He wound up serving 9½ months behind bars, where he got to see firsthand the impact of the drug he dealt. "The whole meth-mouth thing is true: I saw hundreds and hundreds of guys with no teeth. A lot of them couldn't even chew the prison food." Some inmates would grind up antidepressants and snort them, attempting to replicate the high of speed. "They were total meth heads. That's what everybody is in prison."

Now off meth ("that's part of the parole"), the 46-year-old Ippolito says that whatever the government is doing to fight this epidemic, it's failing. He paraphrases a bit of dialogue from the movie "Traffic," in which a defiant drug dealer mocks a DEA agent about the futility of the drug war: "You think you guys are making a difference?!," Ippolito says. They had better. Hundreds of thousands of lives depend on it.

# With Scenes of Blood and Pain, Ads Battle Methamphetamine in Montana

KATE ZERNIKE

Kalispell, Mont., Feb. 18—The camera follows the teenager as she showers for her night out and looks down to discover the drain swirling with blood. She turns and sees her methamphetamine-addicted self cowering below, oozing from scabs she has picked all over her body because the drug made her think there were bugs crawling beneath her skin, and she lets out a scream worthy of "Psycho."

Turn on prime time television here, and chances are this or another commercial like it will interrupt.

The spots are part of the Montana Meth Project, a saturation campaign paid for by Thomas M. Siebel, a software billionaire and part-time resident who fell in love with Montana's vast skies and soaring mountains as a ranch hand in college and now wants to shock the state away from a drug that has ravaged it.

Since it began in September, the project has become the biggest advertiser in the state, blanketing radio, television, newspapers and billboards with advertisements so raw that officials quickly asked that they be removed from television before 7 p.m. Now, with other states expressing interest in the campaign, Mr. Siebel and state officials say they want to make it a national template for halting a problem that has cursed many largely poor, rural states.

The advertisements have inspired poems and raps. High school groups have replayed them in place of morning announcements and devoted newspaper issues to them. Students readily quote dialogue and characters from them and cringe recalling, for instance, how a methamphetamine-addicted teenager in one calmly plucks out her entire eyebrow, oblivious, in her drug-induced compulsion, to the blood and pain.

In a state of fewer than a million people—as one school principal said, "a small town with very long highways"—it can seem that every parent meeting turns to talk of "those ads."

"People are talking about this like I've never seen anything in our state," said Attorney General Mike McGrath, whose office was flooded with hundreds of calls, pro and con, demanding to know who was behind the ads. "When they first came out, I couldn't walk anywhere without someone asking about it."

At Flathead High School on the edge of Glacier National Park here in northwest Montana, students complained that the television spots were too gross to watch first thing in the morning—but they did watch.

"It's like a car wreck, you can't take your eyes off it," said Dillon Foley, 18. "It's totally gross, totally graphic, you know it's going to be bad, but all you can do is watch it go down."

The project reflects frustration with fighting the methamphetamine problem, which began here about a decade ago and is now enough of a public concern that a meeting about it on a recent Friday night in Kalispell drew 600 people.

Like most states, Montana has restricted pseudoephedrine, the cold medicine that is the key ingredient in homemade methamphetamine, only to discover that demand for the drug remains just as high and has been met by imported methamphetamine.

State officials say the drug is responsible for 80 percent of the prison population—and 90 percent of female inmates—and about half the foster care population.

"It's destroying families; it's destroying our schools; it's destroying our budgets for corrections, social services, health care," Gov. Brian Schweitzer said. "We're losing a generation of productive people. My God, at the rate we're going, we're going to have more people in jail than out of jail in 20 years.

"This isn't just a few ads," he said. "If this thing works, it can be a template all over rural America."

The commercials ranked in the Top 20 on AdCritic.com, a Web site covering the advertising industry, and Mr. Siebel has been asked to speak to the National Governors Association and before a Congressional town hall meeting. People mob him at speeches around the state, offering ideas, testimonials, checks.

"You may not like the ads, but they're effective," said Robert A. Nystuen, the president of Glacier Bank in Kalispell, who approached Mr. Siebel after a presentation and offered to sponsor radio spots.

Peg Shea, a former drug treatment specialist who signed on as the project's executive director in late September, said she started out a skeptic, considering most antidrug commercials "dorky." "Then I saw these ads, and heard them," she said. "I saw the quality and the impact."

Mr. Siebel, who recently sold the software company he founded to Oracle, his former employer, began hearing of methamphetamine's damage while fishing with a sheriff friend. "There's a human tragedy of magnificent proportion taking place here," Mr. Siebel said. "I don't think putting everyone in jail is contributing to a solution."

Few people think the commercials will stop addicts; the aim is to deter new ones. While users tend to be older than 25, the project focuses on teenagers, who are at an age when decisions about drug use start.

Surveying 12- to 24-year-olds, the campaign found that most said methamphetamine was readily available; 26 percent said they had been offered the drug in the last year. A quarter did not see great risk in trying it, and more than a third saw benefits: losing weight and feeling happier or more energetic.

Mr. Siebel, 52, set out to "unsell" methamphetamine. He hired Tony Kaye, the director of the stark 1998 movie "American History X," to make commercials graphic enough to, as he said, "break through the clutter."

## Gruesome warnings have captured teenagers' attention.

The radio spots are particularly powerful, some say, because they use real addicts, not actors, recovering from methamphetamine addiction. One girl introduces herself: "Hi, my name is Cindy. I'm 15 years old. I'm from Browning, Montana, and I started doing meth when I was 12." She then tells how she prostituted herself for the drug. Tim, who started using meth at age 19, talks about how using the drug cost him his home and his job and left him no memory of a period of several months, but plenty of regrets: "I did things that, you know, only God can forgive you for."

Teenagers say the spots succeed because they are showing the effects of the drug rather than preaching.

"You see a fast-food commercial, and you want to go buy some because it looks so good," said Marcus Hafferman, 18, a senior at Flathead High. "Or you see a car doing tricks on an ad, and you want to buy it because it looks so good. These commercials are exactly like fast food or cars, except they show how bad it is."

Donna Feist, 18, a student at C. M. Russell High in Great Falls, agreed. "Kids are too desensitized to gore and violence," she said. "They see gory television, gory movies, so the only thing that's going to get their attention is blood and gore."

Others, though, doubt that any ad can break through to jaded teenagers. "The ads are dead on, that's exactly the way it is," said Wendy Kongstvedt, 17, a student at Helena High School. "But it's just another thing adults are telling us not to do."

In the project's survey and in interviews, parents said they had rarely before discussed the drug with their children. "The meth ads have given us a focal point," said Matt Dale, a Helena parent whose son is 15. "Without the ads, if you say to kids, 'Don't do meth,' there's an allure; you've intrigued them."

So far, the Montana Meth Project has run 30,000 minutes of advertisements on radio, 30,000 minutes on television and 150 pages in newspapers, with a budget of $5.5 million for 2006.

It tests new advertisements in focus groups to make sure they are shocking, but not so much so that teenagers dismiss them as unlikely. It is now testing spots by a documentary filmmaker who visited hotels to film desperate and strung-out addicts, including a pregnant teenager who says she fears for her baby but soothes that fear with more methamphetamine.

Mr. Siebel, though, worries that these may simply be too real.

# My Mother the Narc

## Do home drug-testing kits help or hurt teens?

SARAH CHILDRESS

It took Mike Peterson three years to find out that his 15-year-old son had a drug problem. He'd noticed that the once-charming A and B student with a love of Superman paraphernalia had become angry and withdrawn, and was in danger of flunking out of school. But his son repeatedly denied using drugs. Finally, at home in St. Clair, Mo., Peterson turned to the Internet, where he found a site that sold home drug-testing kits for parents. He told his son he wasn't leaving the house until he turned over a urine sample. Peterson was stunned and hurt when his son tested positive for cocaine, marijuana and amphetamines. "He had a problem—a genuine problem," Peterson says. "Thank God we caught it before he hit rock bottom."

Parents used to rifle through their kid's coat pockets to figure out if he was using drugs. Now they can just hand him a little cup and point to the bathroom door. Home drug-testing has boomed as a cheap, private and, advocates say, foolproof way to monitor teenage behavior. Online sales of the kits, which range from $15 to $25, have exploded in the last decade, with some 200 Web sites aimed at parents. Particularly popular are simple urine tests that show results in minutes. Now the industry's getting even more of a boost. Over the past two years, the Office of National Drug Control Policy has championed the controversial practice of random drug testing in middle and high schools. But for some school officials, the high cost of tests and the threat of legal challenges

and protests from outraged parents have led them to pass the cup. In states like Missouri, Wisconsin and Texas, schools are hanging banners, passing out pamphlets and holding information sessions to encourage parents to visit a Web site, buy a kit and drug-test their own teenagers at home.

St. James R-1 School District in meth-ravaged Missouri was the first to try it out this fall. It called on Mason Duchatschek, owner of testmyteen.com to help promote the program to parents. It held an information session at the high school, hoping to attract 100 parents. About 700 showed up. Parents responded so well, officials say, that the district is applying for a $100,000 federal grant to expand the program to eighth graders.

There's already a heated debate over testing in schools, which hasn't been proved conclusively to deter drug use. Not everybody thinks home testing is a good idea, either. Online stores don't always educate parents about how to perform the tests or interpret results accurately, according to a 2004 study from the Center for Adolescent Substance Abuse Research at Children's Hospital in Boston. Other critics say it erodes the trust between parents and children and may create a mind-set of secrecy that discourages parents from seeking professional help.

But kit sellers argue that home tests are just the first step in dealing with drug use. They're most effective in deterring teens who haven't tried drugs, which is why they say no home with a teenager should be without them. "Parents tell me, 'My kid's in the choir!' Well, you know what? Whitney Houston was in the choir," says Duchatschek. So was Peterson's son. Now 16, he's been clean for nine months, but Peterson still doesn't hesitate to wake him at 3 a.m. for a urine test. "It kinda makes me feel like he doesn't trust me sometimes, but I can kinda see where he's coming from," says the younger Peterson. It was, he says, the only way he could come clean.

# Pass the Weed, Dad

**Parents are smoking dope with their kids. What are they thinking? Marni Jackson investigates.**

MARNI JACKSON

"**It was a little weird,** seeing my parents stoned," Tom confesses. The Toronto high school student was describing the first time he'd smoked marijuana—at home last spring, just after turning 17, when he shared a joint with his hard-working, middle-class parents. "But I had an amazing, fantastic connection with my dad, and it was a good experience for all of us. They showed me how to take the seeds and stems out of the pot. Then, basically, we ate. My mom ordered sushi, and we made a mountain of nachos. It kind of felt like a rite of passage."

After his family initiation, Tom bought six or seven joints of his own for a camping trip, "and that was cool too." But his new girlfriend didn't approve of pot, or him on it. "She said there was this separation thing that happened whenever I smoked." So Tom gave it up, even though his older sister had just given him a nice handmade pipe for his birthday. "But my other sister could care less about pot. Lots of kids try it and don't like it. I think it's totally individual."

Nicole, who maintained a scholarship throughout university and has now graduated, grew up in a household where pot smoking was as casually present as wine with dinner. "Marijuana was so integrated into our social life that it didn't seem to make sense to hide it," says her father, a lawyer. "So we didn't. She began smoking pot when she was around 16. This was in the nineties, when the police were pretty aggressive about it, so we thought that it was safer for her to smoke at home than in the streets. And then when she was in college, there were definitely times when she and I would smoke a joint together. Or I might buy some dope and give her some."

"But lately, we've made some new rules. No smoking dope together. No tobacco in the house. We are rethinking things in general."

He pauses. "Yes, we were open about smoking pot around her. But was it a good idea? I don't know."

Nicole, now 24, says she's "always believed it was a good thing that it wasn't hidden or taboo. I've seen a lot of sheltered kids who got into it at 12 or 13, as rebellion. I wasn't interested till later. I tried it and thought, 'Hey, this is good!' It was relaxing, and fun, and it numbs you out, which can be a good thing."

**Most parents,** of course, aren't sitting around the family bong with their kids. They go along with the authorities who view marijuana as a drug with addictive potential that turns kids into over-snacking, under-motivated, learning-impaired couch potatoes. But the 1.5 million Canadian adults who, according to the Canadian Medical Association, smoke marijuana recreationally might not agree. In fact, a recent Canadian Addiction Survey found that 630,000 of us aged 15 and older smoke cannabis every day. And among middle-aged Canadians, dope use in the past year has increased from 1.4 per cent in 1994 to 8.4 per cent in 2004.

Perhaps as a consequence of this ongoing boomer buzz, some parents feel a zero-tolerance policy with teenagers simply doesn't work and may only increase the allure of pot. They would rather keep the lines of communication open, talk to their children about the genuine risks of individual drugs, and help them develop their own good judgment about drug use—whether it's tobacco, alcohol or marijuana.

## 'When she was in college, there were definitely times when she and I would smoke a joint together'

Sharing a joint with your 16- or 17-year-old may be pushing it. Nevertheless, parents who talk about "drugs" as if they're all the same, equating pot with more lethal substances like cocaine or crystal meth—a popular form of amphetamine that is wildly addictive and blatantly destructive—run the risk of not being listened to at all. When we demonize drugs, ironically we tend to empower the drugs, rather than our kids.

Families have changed since the days of *Father Knows Best* (the equivalent show today would be "Father Tokes Best"). Many parents are veterans of the counterculture who did a lot more than inhale in the sixties. For some, marijuana was just an ambient phase, like black-light posters. Others have grown up into successful, civilized, recreational pot smokers who don't want to lie to their kids. They consider the moderate use of pot to be a relatively benign activity—and certainly better than drinking eight beers and getting behind the wheel of a car. Binge drinking, which has become epidemic among college students, can also be fatal, but no one has ever died from a marijuana overdose (although it carries its own health risks, affects driving ability, and has certainly caused repeated screenings of bad movies).

One thing is clear, though: regardless of whether their parents are strict or permissive, most kids will try cannabis sooner or later. By the time they exit their teen years, the Canadian Addiction Survey reports, 70 per cent of them will have smoked a joint at some point—if not in the past hour. Among everyone who's tried it, 18 per cent smoke daily.

Tom and Nicole waited longer than most teenagers to experiment with marijuana. The average age of first use has gone down, from 14.5 years in 1995 to 13.7 in 2003. In fact, Toronto's Centre for Addiction and Mental Health (CAMH) reports that five per cent of school kids have tried pot before the end of Grade 6. (Can the preschool doobie be far behind? Hemp soothers?) Twenty-eight per cent of students who've finished Grade 9 will have smoked pot in the past year. Roughly the same percentage, it's worth noting, have never tried any drugs, including alcohol or tobacco, and—before we get too hysterical—47 per cent of Canadian high school students "strongly disapprove of regular marijuana smoking."

Nevertheless, cannabis remains the No. 1 illicit drug in North America. And its reputation may be shifting, as science uncovers new medical potential for the cannabinoids that are the active ingredients in marijuana. Last month, a Saskatchewan study reported that a cannabis-like substance injected into rats caused new nerve-cell growth in the hippocampus, suggesting the possibility that marijuana might actually improve certain brain functions—contrary to its reputation as a memory-shredder. (It should be added that the rats were getting a drug 100 times more powerful than THC, the compound that gives marijuana its high.) A study published in a recent issue of the journal *Nature* also suggested that marijuana may "more closely resemble an antidepressant than a drug of abuse." And, of course, the much-debated medical benefits of cannabis for people suffering with chronic pain, AIDS or multiple sclerosis are already well known.

Marijuana is also firmly embedded in popular culture, from the slim green leaves featured on the cover of Willie Nelson's recent CD (reggae, of course), to the phenomenon of "bud porn" (coffee-table books featuring photos of dewy, resin-oozing exotic strains of cannabis), to *Weeds*, the new series currently airing on Showcase. It stars Mary-Louise Parker as a freshly widowed mother who supports her family by dealing pot in her upscale Californian suburb. ("But not to kids," she explains, setting the moral high bar of the show.)

## 'We call them Jell-O-heads. Boys who can't really think. My son and his friends just seem sedated.'

The series traffics in lame stereotypes (her suppliers are a trash-talkin' black family whose mother cleans and bags her product at the kitchen table). But it flies in the face of George W. Bush's $35-billion War on Drugs, which focuses many of its public awareness programs on the evils of smoking pot while largely ignoring the scourge of crystal meth use in North America. And it's one more sign that marijuana is not about to be weeded out of the culture any time soon.

If this is the case, what sort of limits should parents offer, when their 13-year-old comes home from a party to announce—because they encourage the kid to be open—that he has just smoked his first joint? Of course, they turn off David Letterman, pour a glass of wine, sit down and say, "We don't want you smoking marijuana, sweetheart. You're too young." Then he says, with a red-eyed glare, "Why not? You do."

How does a parent respond to that? With a lecture on how dope impairs concentration and learning, and may not be the best thing for the lungs? Or with a mini-joint and some Neil Young on the CD player?

# The Pot (Smoker) Calling the Kettle Black.

"When it comes to my own son, I'm totally protective—I veer right into *Reefer Madness* territory," says Ray, a Toronto father and regular grass smoker who was introduced to hash at the age of 15 by his own, scientist father. (Note: not even the most nonchalant pot smoker would agree to be named here. Apparently no one, 15 or 55, wants to be known as a pothead—or arrested. So the names and some identifying details in these stories have been changed.)

"When my son asked if I smoked dope, I simply lied and said no," Ray continues. "But his older sister was with us. She knew that I smoked, and said, 'What are you talking about, dad? Of course you do!'" But Ray's double standard is just fine with his son; kids don't necessarily want their parents to be cool. The writer and film director Nora Ephron once observed that if children are given the choice between a happy, gratified parent off boogie-boarding in Hawaii, or a suicidal parent in the next room, they'll pick the miserable, available one every time. The baby boomer pursuit of pleasure and openness may have produced parents who resemble party-hearty older siblings rather than helpful, boring authority figures. "Even though in the real world, marijuana may occupy an unclear, grey zone," says Bob Glossop, a spokesman for the Vanier Institute for the Family, "one of the roles of the parent is to simplify their kids' world, and offer limits."

Some parents are open about their dope smoking while drawing firm lines about drug use for their kids. Patrick is a Toronto writer, poet, parent and cannabis fan. He finds a joint in the late afternoon helps him write. "When my son confronted me and said, 'But you do it,' I said, 'Yes, I smoke pot, but I also earn a living. You are 12 and in Grade 8 and you shouldn't smoke marijuana." Patrick mostly confines his habit to his workspace, but he has always smoked in the house. "My line with my two sons was clear. I told them, 'If you want to finish your education, don't smoke weed.' It tends to de-motivate kids regarding school. I know it brought out my own rebellion, and made me want to quit school and fight the system."

Patrick's relationship to marijuana goes back 27 years, when his stepson, then six, entered his life. "The vibe around pot smoking was different then; it was a more legitimate activity. I smoked in the house, but I explained to my stepson that it was an herb—coltsfoot—that I had to smoke, for my lungs." He sounds a bit sheepish here. "So, yeah, it was a lie, but not entirely; it was an herbal supplement."

His stepson grew up to become a very conservative adult, and a non-smoker, but "surprisingly tolerant" of marijuana. "Coltsfoot has become a kind of joke between us," says Patrick.

When he had his own sons, they both ignored his advice and took up dope smoking around 13. His eldest, Richard, then started dealing; he encountered some violence, got robbed, and finally decided that the dope life was not a good one. "Although I do think he honed his business skills when he was selling," Patrick muses. "He was making good money." Gradually, Richard gave up dope. "He saw that all his friends were dropping out of school, and he didn't want to. He's now in university, studying philosophy, doing well, and he rarely smokes pot. He'd rather argue about philosophy now, which drives me crazy, because . . ."—and here the truly committed pot smoker can be detected—"it's so damn rational."

But Patrick remembers his sons' drug years as a "worrying time. I was really concerned." And he's not alone. Parents worry about the dangers associated with the criminal aspect of marijuana—which is, after all, still an illegal substance, carrying a maximum fine of $1,000 and/or six months in jail for simple possession. The government may be pondering the wisdom of spending millions on imprisoning cannabis offenders when gunshot deaths seem to be everywhere, and white collar crime flies under the radar.

With 69 per cent of Canadians favouring decriminalization of pot possession, according to a February 2003 poll, the feds have taken a step to acknowledging the country's dope use. Last year, they introduced a bill that would decriminalize possession of small amounts of cannabis. But it's currently sitting with a Commons committee and is unlikely to become law before the next federal election.

As they step out onto their back decks to have a quick after-dinner toke, noticing that thick feeling in their lungs again, parents also worry about the long-term effects of marijuana on a 13-year-old's developing mind and body. (Many experts believe regular pot smoking damages the lungs, though there's debate over whether it's more or less harmful than tobacco.) And then there's the school issue: chronic use is linked to declining school work and dropping out.

## One Toke Too Many Over the Line.

Young people who have already smoked marijuana for a decade are discovering what some of their parents know—it is more habit-forming than its reputation suggests. Eric, who works as a fly-fishing guide near Vancouver, is 19 and has been smoking pot daily—except for the brief periods when he's tried to stop—for about seven years. He lives in a province where more than half the population has tried pot and many are regular users.

Eric's parents were both involved in the political upheaval of the sixties. His mother once spent a night in jail for possession of pot, and, Eric says, "my father told me that he tried everything once, which I tend to believe." Eric's dad, Dmitri, is now a criminal psychologist who is in favour of the legalization of marijuana—although he no longer smokes it himself, and dearly wishes his son would stop too. Despite his liberal perspective, Dmitri views the heavy pot smoking among his son's circle as "insidiously costly." Eric—whom his father proudly describes as a "beautiful, athletic, creative, sensitive young man"—couldn't agree more.

"I would like to quit, a lot," Eric says. "And every single friend I know who smokes heavily wants to stop too. Dope is okay in moderation, but when your life starts to revolve around it every day, it becomes like any other addiction. You lose your motivation. Your senses get numbed. And you don't get out of life what you could if you weren't stoned all the time. It was fun to party at 14. But the older you get, the more you kind of want to pull up your socks and get your life going. I've quit a few times, but it's hard. I don't even have to go out and buy it—it's all around me."

**'Yes we were open about smoking pot around her. But was it a good idea? I don't know.'**

Bestselling American health and wellness author Dr. Andrew Weil could not be called anti-pot by any stretch. And the 2004 edition of his book, *From Chocolate to Morphine*, is an unhysterical guide to a wide spectrum of mind-altering drugs. But Weil is very clear about the risks of habitual use. "Marijuana dependence can be sneaky in its development," he writes. "It doesn't appear overnight like cigarette addiction . . . but rather builds up over a long time. The main danger of smoking marijuana is simply that it will get away from you, becoming more and more of a repetitive habit and less and less of a useful way of changing consciousness."

Elizabeth Ridgely is a Toronto therapist and executive director of the George Hull Centre for Children and Families, which has a substance-abuse program open to heavy pot smokers. "The most important thing for parents to know is that marijuana is stronger than it used to be in the Woodstock days," she says. "People who use it habitually use it to soothe themselves, and when they stop, they can feel agitated and anxious. It can really mess up a kid. But kids are surprised to hear this—families aren't having those kinds of conversations about drugs."

# Dreams Gone Up in Smoke.

"We call them Jell-O-heads," says Tanya, a 52-year-old photo-archivist who lives in Toronto. "Boys who can't really think." She is referring to her 19-year-old son and his friends, who regularly smoke dope on the third floor of her house. "When they come in the door and go up the stairs, it's like having large cedar trees in the house. Everything shakes and rattles. Then they go up to my son's room, and the music starts, and the laughing."

Tanya is a former pot smoker who now considers dope a "real time-waster. I wasted so many years as a hippie, smoking. But it was part of the language back then. It was social, it was anti-authority, it was very sensual. I don't see that with my son's crowd. They just seem sedated. They use a bong, and the drug is really clean and refined and incredibly potent—it's not the ditch weed we used to smoke. It doesn't give you the big fuzzy body stone we used to get from dope. They just get high. I think it dumbs my kid down. The thing that bothers me is that he doesn't seem present when he's stoned.

"My son gave me some of his dope once," says Tanya. "I thought it would be a good way to, you know, talk about it. I didn't want to smoke, so I ate it, and suddenly my eyelids had no function—I mean, I would close my eyes and it would just go on forever. When will this be over, I thought."

After some ineffective drug counseling, her son eventually cut down on his own. "Now he says he only smokes it to get to sleep, as a sedative." She laughs. "Remember when we thought smoking marijuana made us more aware?"

A friend of Tanya's, a Gestalt therapist, has a theory about the downside of heavy pot smoking for teenagers. She considers it a "dream-stealer. At the age when they should be generating their own fantasies and dreams, a drug can usurp that. The visions belong to the drug, not to them."

# Smokescreen for Other Problems.

Mario, a handsome, athletic 23-year-old, went the whole nine yards with drugs and teen rebellion. He started smoking dope, taking acid and staying out till 4 a.m. when he was 12 and 13. He and his friends would get stoned and go chase skunks through the park in the middle of the night, until somebody called the cops. "If there was a rule, he would break it," remembers his father. He had separated from the boy's mother and was living with his new partner. The separation was civil, and Mario and his younger brother, Paul, were welcome in both households.

"My mother didn't hide the fact that she would smoke around the house occasionally," Mario says. "But she didn't glamorize it. If you're going to have a parent who smokes pot, she went about it the right way. Kids are supersensitive to anything that's hypocritical, especially in their parents. It breaks trust." But his parents worried about the effect Mario's behaviour was having on Paul. They asked him to honour one final rule—no smoking pot in the house, or around his younger brother. When Mario broke that one, his father asked him to move out.

So at the age of 15, for almost two years, Mario was out on the street, couch-surfing at friends' houses and living for a time in a hostel for street kids. He quit school after three weeks of Grade 9. "We gave him money to buy toiletries, which he probably spent on dope," his father says. They stayed in touch, though, and finally his mother said, "That's enough," and let him move in with her. He went back to high school and graduated. He reconnected with the rest of his family, was accepted at Queen's and got a degree in anthropology, and by his late teens had lost interest in pot.

Mario now looks back on those years with hard-earned intelligence and insight. "As far as our family problems go, I think dope was more of a flashpoint than the real issue. My pot smoking was an abrasive thing, and my parents concentrated on that. And it did have tangible fallout—in terms of punctuality and procrastination and school. You know, if a kid isn't getting his work done, and he's smoking dope, it's an easy equation to make. But there's usually more than dope going on."

Poor parents—they always seem to miss the point. And what has become the ultimate parental sin now that pot is out of the closet? Smoking cigarettes. Mario also has a sister, Lucy. At the age of 11, she came home one night to find a dinner party in progress, and her non-smoking mother sitting back with a lit cigarette in hand. "She went ballistic," recalls the mother, "and after everyone left, Lucy came down and sprayed the room with perfume. It was a big deal—kids hate it when their parents do anything self-destructive."

So, a memo to all you law-breaking, pot smoking parents: if you want your kids not to worry, just say no—to tobacco.

# Did Prohibition Really Work?

## Alcohol Prohibition as a Public Health Innovation

The conventional view that National Prohibition failed rests upon an historically flimsy base. The successful campaign to enact National Prohibition was the fruit of a century-long temperance campaign, experience of which led prohibitionists to conclude that a nationwide ban on alcohol was the most promising of the many strategies tried thus far. A sharp rise in consumption during the early 20th century seemed to confirm the bankruptcy of alternative alcohol control programs.

The stringent prohibition imposed by the Volstead Act however, represented a more drastic action than many Americans expected. Nevertheless, National Prohibition succeeded both in lowering consumption and in retaining political support until the onset of the Great Depression altered voters' priorities. Repeal resulted more from this contextual shift than from characteristics of the innovation itself.

JACK S. BLOCKER JR, PHD

Probably few gaps between scholarly knowledge and popular conventional wisdom are as wide as the one regarding National Prohibition. "Everyone knows" that Prohibition failed because Americans did not stop drinking following ratification of the Eighteenth Amendment and passage of its enforcement legislation, the Volstead Act. If the question arises why Americans adopted such a futile measure in the first place, the unnatural atmosphere of wartime is cited. Liquor's illegal status furnished the soil in which organized crime flourished. The conclusive proof of Prohibition's failure is, of course, the fact that the Eighteenth Amendment became the only constitutional amendment to be repealed.

Historians have shown, however, that National Prohibition was no fluke, but rather the fruit of a century-long series of temperance movements springing from deep roots in the American reform tradition. Furthermore, Americans were not alone during the first quarter of the 20th century in adopting prohibition on a large scale: other jurisdictions enacting similar measures included Iceland, Finland, Norway, both czarist Russia and the Soviet Union, Canadian provinces, and Canada's federal government.[1] A majority of New Zealand voters twice approved national prohibition but never got it. As a result of 100 years of temperance agitation, the American cultural climate at the time Prohibition went into effect was deeply hostile to alcohol, and this antagonism manifested itself clearly through a wave of successful referenda on statewide prohibition.

Although organized crime flourished under its sway, Prohibition was not responsible for its appearance, as organized crime's post-Repeal persistence has demonstrated. Drinking habits underwent a drastic change during the Prohibition Era,

and Prohibition's flattening effect on per capita consumption continued long after Repeal, as did a substantial hard core of popular support for Prohibition's return. Repeal itself became possible in 1933 primarily because of a radically altered economic context—the Great Depression. Nevertheless, the failure of National Prohibition continues to be cited without contradiction in debates over matters ranging from the proper scope of government action to specific issues such as control of other consciousness-altering drugs, smoking, and guns.

We historians collectively are partly to blame for this gap. We simply have not synthesized from disparate studies a compelling alternative to popular perception.[2] Nevertheless, historians are not entirely culpable for prevalent misunderstanding; also responsible are changed cultural attitudes toward drinking, which, ironically, Prohibition itself helped to shape. Thinking of Prohibition as a public health innovation offers a potentially fruitful path toward comprehending both the story of the dry era and the reasons why it continues to be misunderstood.

## Temperance Thought Before National Prohibition

Although many prohibitionists were motivated by religious faith, American temperance reformers learned from an early point in their movement's history to present their message in ways that would appeal widely to citizens of a society characterized by divergent and clashing scriptural interpretations. Temperance, its advocates promised, would energize political reform, promote community welfare, and improve public health. Prohibitionism, which was inherently political, required even more urgent pressing of such claims for societal improvement.[3] Through local contests in communities across the nation, liquor control in general and Prohibition In particular became the principal stage on which Americans confronted public health issues, long before public health became a field of professional endeavor.

By the beginning of the 20th century, prohibitionists agreed that a powerful liquor industry posed the greatest threat to American society and that only Prohibition could prevent Americans from falling victim to its seductive wiles. These conclusions were neither willful nor arbitrary, as they had been reached after three quarters of a century of experience. Goals short of total abstinence from all that could intoxicate and less coercive means—such as self-help, mutual support, medical treatment, and sober recreation—had been tried and, prohibitionists agreed, had been found wanting.[4]

For prohibitionists, as for other progressives, the only battleground where a meaningful victory might be won was the collective: the community, the state, or the nation. The Anti-Saloon League (ASL), which won leadership of the movement after 1905, was so focused on Prohibition that it did not even require of its members a pledge of personal abstinence. Battles fought on public ground certainly heightened popular awareness of the dangers of alcohol. In the mass media before 1920, John Barleycorn found few friends. Popular fiction, theater, and the new movies rarely represented drinking in positive terms and consistently portrayed drinkers as flawed characters. Most family magazines, and even many daily newspapers, rejected liquor ads.[5] New physiological and epidemiological studies published around the turn of the century portrayed alcohol as a depressant and plausibly associated its use with crime, mental illness, and disease. The American Medical Association went on record in opposition to the use of alcohol for either beverage or therapeutic purposes.[6] But most public discourse on alcohol centered on its social, not individual, effects.[7]

The only significant exception was temperance education in the schools. By 1901, every state required that its schools incorporate "Scientific Temperance Instruction" into the curriculum, and one half of the nation's school districts further mandated use of a textbook that portrayed liquor as invariably an addictive poison. But even as it swept through legislative chambers, the movement to indoctrinate children in temperance ideology failed to carry with it the educators on whose cooperation its success in the classrooms depended; teachers tended to regard Scientific Temperance Instruction as neither scientific nor temperate. After 1906, temperance instruction became subsumed within more general lessons on hygiene, and hygiene classes taught that the greatest threats to health were environmental and the proper responses were correspondingly social, not individual.[8]

By the time large numbers of voters were confronted with a choice whether or not to support a prohibitionist measure or candidate for office, public discourse over alcohol had produced a number of prohibitionist supporters who were not themselves abstainers. That is, they believed that it was a good idea to control someone else's drinking (perhaps everyone else's), but not their own. A new study of cookbooks and etiquette manuals suggests that this was likely the case for middle-class women,

the most eager recruits to the prohibition cause, who were gaining the vote in states where prohibition referenda were boosting the case for National Prohibition. In addition to the considerable alcoholic content of patent medicines, which women and men (and children) were unknowingly ingesting, women were apparently serving liquor in their recipes and with meals. In doing so, they were forging a model of domestic consumption in contrast to the mode of public drinking adopted by men in saloons and clubs.[9]

Self-control lay at the heart of the middle-class self-image, and middle-class prohibitionists simply acted on the prejudices of their class when they voted to close saloons while allowing drinking to continue in settings they considered to be respectable. Some state prohibition laws catered to such sentiments when they prohibited the manufacture and sale of alcoholic beverages, but allowed importation and consumption.[10] A brisk mail-order trade flourished in many dry communities. Before 1913, federal law and judicial decisions in fact prevented states from interfering with the flow of liquor across their borders. When Congress acted in 1913, the Webb–Kenyon Act only forbade importation of liquor into a dry state when such commerce was banned by the law of that state.[11]

# Why National Prohibition?

At the beginning of the 20th century, wet and dry forces had reached a stalemate. Only a handful of states maintained statewide prohibition, and enforcement of prohibitory law was lax in some of those. Dry territory expanded through local option, especially in the South, but this did not mean that drinking came to a halt in towns or counties that adopted local prohibition; such laws aimed to stop manufacture or sale (or both), not consumption.[12] During the previous half-century, beer's popularity had soared, surpassing spirits as the principal source of alcohol in American beverages, but, because of beer's lower alcohol content, ethanol consumption per capita had changed hardly at all.[13] Both drinking behavior and the politics of drink, however, changed significantly after the turn of the century when the ASL assumed leadership of the prohibition movement.

Between 1900 and 1913, Americans began to drink more and more. Beer production jumped from 1.2 billion to 2 billion gallons (4.6 billion to 7.6 billion liters), and the volume of tax-paid spirits grew from 97 million to 147 million gallons (367 million to 556 million liters). Per capita consumption of ethanol increased by nearly a third, a significant spike over such a short period of time.[14]

Meanwhile, the area under prohibition steadily expanded as a result of local-option and statewide prohibition campaigns. Between 1907 and 1909, 6 states entered the dry column. By 1912, however, prohibitionist momentum on these fronts slowed, as the liquor industry began a political counteroffensive. In the following year, the ASL, encouraged by congressional submission to its demands in passing the Webb–Kenyon Act. launched a campaign for a prohibition constitutional amendment.

The best explanation for this decision is simply that National Prohibition had long been the movement's goal. The process of constitutional amendment in the same year the ASL launched its campaign both opened the way to a federal income tax and mandated direct election of US senators (the Sixteenth and Seventeenth Amendments), seemed to be the most direct path to that goal.[15] Its supporters expected that the campaign for and amendment would be long and that the interval between achievement of the amendment and their eventual object would also be lengthy. Ultimately, drinkers with entrenched habits would die off, while a new generation would grow up abstinent under the salubrious influence of prohibition.[16] ASL leaders also needed to demonstrate their militance to ward off challenges from intramovement rivals, and the route to a constitutional amendment lay through state and national legislatures, where their method of pressuring candidates promised better results than seeking popular approval through a referendum in every state.[17]

Once the prohibition movement decided to push for a constitutional amendment it had to negotiate the tortuous path to ratification. The fundamental requirement was sufficient popular support to convince federal and state legislators that voting for the amendment would help rather than hurt their electoral chances.

---

**"Between 1900 and 1913, Americans began to drink more and more. Beer production jumped from 1.2 billion to 2 billion gallons, and the volume of tax-paid spirits grew from 97 million to 147 million gallons."**

---

The historical context of the Progressive Era provided 4 levers with which that support might be engineered, and prohibitionists manipulated them effectively. First the rise in annual ethanol consumption to 2.6 US gallons (9.8 liters) per capita of the drinking-age population, the highest level since the Civil War, did create a real public health problem.[18] Rates of death diagnosed as caused by liver cirrhosis (15 per 100,000 total population) and chronic alcoholism (10 per 100,000 adult population) were high during the early years of the 20th century.[19]

Second, the political turbulence of the period—a growing socialist movement and bitter struggles between capitalists and workers—made prohibition seem less radical by contrast.[20] Third, popular belief in moral law and material progress, trust in science, support for humanitarian causes and for "uplift" of the disadvantaged, and opposition to "plutocracy" offered opportunities to align prohibitionism with progressivism.[21] Concern for public health formed a central strand of the progressive ethos, and, as one historian notes, "the temperance and prohibition movements can . . . be understood as part of a larger public health and welfare movement active at that time that viewed environmental interventions as an important means of promoting the public health and safety."[22] Finally, after a fleeting moment of unity, the alliance between brewers and distillers to repel prohibitionist attacks fell apart.[23] The widespread local battles fought over the previous 20 years brought new support to

the cause, and the ASL's nonpartisan, balance-of-power method worked effectively.[24]

The wartime atmosphere during the relatively brief period of American participation in World War I played a minor role in bringing on National Prohibition. Anti-German sentiment shamelessly whipped up and exploited by the federal government to rally support for the war effort discredited a key and prohibitionist organization, the German-American Alliance. A federal ban on distilling, adopted to conserve grain, sapped the strength of another major wet player, the spirits Industry.[25] But most prohibition victories at the state level and in congressional elections were won before the United States entered the war, and the crucial ratification votes occurred after the war's end.[26]

In sum, although the temperance movement was a century old when the Eighteenth Amendment was adopted, and National Prohibition had been a goal for many prohibitionists for half that long, its achievement came about as a product of a specific milieu. Few reform movements manage to win a constitutional amendment. Nevertheless, that achievement, which seemed at the time so permanent—no constitutional amendment had ever before been repealed—was vulnerable to shifts in the context on which it depended.

## Public Health Consequences of Prohibition

We forget too easily that Prohibition wiped out an industry. In 1916, there were 1300 breweries producing full-strength beer in the United States; 10 years later there were none. Over the same period, the number of distilleries was cut by 85%, and most of the survivors produced little but industrial alcohol. Legal production of near beer used less than one tenth the amount of malt, one twelfth the rice and hops, and one thirtieth the corn used to make full-strength beer before National Prohibition. The 318 wineries of 1914 became the 27 of 1925.[27] The number of liquor wholesalers was cut by 96% and the number of legal retailers by 90%. From 1919 to 1929, federal tax revenues from distilled spirits dropped from $365 million to less than $13 million, and revenue from fermented liquors from $117 million to virtually nothing.[28]

The Coors Brewing Company turned to making near beer, porcelain products, and malted milk. Miller and Anheuser-Busch took a similar route.[29] Most breweries, wineries, and distilleries, however, closed their doors forever. Historically, the federal government has played a key role in creating new industries, such as chemicals and aerospace, but very rarely has it acted decisively to shut down an industry.[30] The dosing of so many large commercial operations left liquor production, if it were to continue, in the hands of small-scale domestic producers, a dramatic reversal of the normal course of industrialization.

Such industrial and economic devastation was unexpected before the introduction of the Volstead Act, which followed adoption of the Eighteenth Amendment The amendment forbade the manufacture, transportation, sale, importation, and exportation of "intoxicating" beverages, but without defining the term. The Volstead Act defined "intoxicating" as containing 0.5% or more alcohol by volume, thereby prohibiting virtually all alcoholic drinks. The brewers, who had expected beer of moderate strength to remain legal, were stunned, but their efforts to overturn the definition were unavailing.[31] The act also forbade possession of intoxicating beverages, but included a significant exemption for custody in one's private dwelling for the sole use of the owner, his or her family, and guests. In addition to private consumption, sacramental wine and medicinal liquor were also permitted.

The brewers were probably not the only Americans to be surprised at the severity of the regime thus created. Voters who considered their own drinking habits blameless, but who supported prohibition to discipline others, also received a rude shock. That shock came with the realization that federal prohibition went much farther in the direction of banning personal consumption than all local prohibition ordinances and many state prohibition statutes. National Prohibition turned out to be quite a different beast than its local and state cousins.

Nevertheless, once Prohibition became the law of the land, many citizens decided to obey it. Referendum results in the immediate post-Volstead period showed widespread support, and the Supreme Court quickly fended off challenges to the new law. Death rates from cirrhosis and alcoholism, alcoholic psychosis hospital admissions, and drunkenness arrests all declined steeply during the latter years of the 1910s, when both the cultural and the legal climate were increasingly inhospitable to drink, and in the early years after National Prohibition went into effect. They rose after that, but generally did not reach the peaks recorded during the period 1900 to 1915. After Repeal, when tax data permit better-founded consumption estimates than we have for the Prohibition Era, per capita annual consumption stood at 1.2 US gallons (4.5 liters), less than half the level of the pre-Prohibition period.[32]

Prohibition affected alcoholic beverages differently. Beer consumption dropped precipitously. Distilled spirits made a dramatic comeback in American drinking patterns, reversing a three-quarters-of-a-century decline, although in volume spirits did not reach its pre-Prohibition level. Small-scale domestic producers gave wine its first noticeable, though small, contribution to overall alcohol intake, as wine-grape growers discovered that the Volstead Act failed to ban the production and sale of grape concentrate (sugary pulp that could be rehydrated and fermented to make wine).[33]

## Unintended and Unexpected Consequences

Unexpected prosperity for wine-grape growers was not the only unintended consequence of National Prohibition. Before reviewing other unexpected outcomes, however, it is important to list the ways in which National Prohibition did fulfill prohibitionists' expectations. The liquor industry was virtually destroyed, and this created an historic opportunity to socialize rising generations in a lifestyle in which alcohol had no place. To some degree, such socialization did take place, and the lessened consumption of the Prohibition Era reflects that. Although other forces contributed to its decline, Prohibition finished off the old-time saloon, with its macho culture and links to urban machine politics.[34] To wipe out a long-established and well-entrenched industry, to change drinking habits on a large scale, and to sweep away such a central urban and rural social institution as the saloon are no small achievements.

Nevertheless, prohibitionists did not fully capitalize on their opportunity to bring up a new generation in abstemious habits. Inspired and led by the talented writers of the Lost Generation, the shapers of mass culture—first in novels, then in films, and finally in newspapers and magazines—altered the popular media's, previously negative attitude toward drink. In the eyes of many young people, especially the increasing numbers who populated colleges and universities. Prohibition was transformed from progressive reform to an emblem of a suffocating status quo.[35] The intransigence of the dominant wing of the ASL, which insisted on zero tolerance in law enforcement, gave substance to this perception and, in addition, aligned the league with the Ku Klux Klan and other forces promoting intolerance.[36] Thus, the work of attracting new drinkers to alcohol, which had been laid down by the dying liquor industry, was taken up by new hands.

One group of new drinkers—or newly public drinkers—whose emergence in that role was particularly surprising to contemporary observers was women. Such surprise, however, was a product of the prior invisibility of women's domestic consumption: women had in fact never been as abstemious as the Woman's Christian Temperance Union's activism had made them appear.[37] Women's new willingness to drink in public—or at least in the semipublic atmosphere of the speakeasy—owed much to Prohibition's achievement the death of the saloon, whose masculine culture no longer governed norms of public drinking. The saloon's demise also made it possible for women to band together to oppose Prohibition, as hundreds of thousands did in the Women's Organization for National Prohibition Reform (WONPR).[38]

Public drinking by women and college youth and wet attitudes disseminated by cultural media pushed along a process that social scientists call the "normalization of drinking"—that is, the breakdown of cultural proscriptions against liquor. Normalization, part of the long history of decay in Victorian social mores, began before the Prohibition Era and did not fully bear fruit until long afterward, but the process gained impetus from both the achievements and the failures of National Prohibition.[39]

Other unintended and unexpected consequences of Prohibition included flourishing criminal activity centered on smuggling and bootlegging and the consequent clogging of the courts with drink-related prosecutions.[40] Prohibition also forced federal courts to take on the role of overseer of government regulatory agencies, and the zeal of government agents stimulated new concern for individual rights as opposed to the power of the state.[41] The bans on liquor importation and exportation crippled American ocean liners in the competition for transatlantic passenger service, thus contributing to the ongoing decline of the US merchant marine, and created an irritant in diplomatic relations with Great Britain and Canada.[42] Contrary to politicians' hopes that the Eighteenth Amendment would finally take the liquor issue out of politics, Prohibition continued to boil the political waters even in the presidential seas, helping to carry Herbert Hoover first across the finish line in 1928 and to sink him 4 years later.[43]

# Why Repeal?

All prohibitions are coercive, but their effects can vary across populations and banned articles. We have no estimates of the size of the drinking population on the eve of National Prohibition (or on the eve of wartime prohibition, which preceded it by several months), but because of the phenomenon of "drinking drys" it was probably larger than the total of votes cast in referenda against state prohibition measures, and many of the larger states did not even hold such referenda. So Prohibition's implicit goal of teetotalism meant changing the drinking behavior of a substantial number of Americans, possibly a majority.

Because the Volstead Act was drafted only after ratification of the Eighteenth Amendment was completed, neither the congressmen and state legislators who approved submission and ratification, nor the voters who elected them, knew what kind of prohibition they were voting for.[44] The absolutism of the act's definition of intoxicating liquors made national alcohol prohibition a stringent ban, and the gap between what voters thought they were voting for and what they got made this sweeping interdict appear undemocratic. Nevertheless, support for prohibition in post-ratification state referenda and the boost given to Herbert Hoover's 1928 campaign by his dry stance indicate continued electoral approval of Prohibition before the stock-market crash of 1929.

Historians agree that enforcement of the Volstead Act constituted National Prohibition's Achilles' heel. A fatal flaw resided in the amendment's second clause, which mandated "concurrent power" to enforce Prohibition by the federal government and the states. ASL strategists expected that the states' existing criminal-justice machinery would carry out the lion's share of the work of enforcement. Consequently, the league did not insist on creating adequate forces or funding for federal enforcement, thereby avoiding conflict with Southern officials determined to protect states' rights. The concurrent-power provision, however, allowed states to minimize their often politically divisive enforcement activity, and the state prohibition statutes gave wets an obvious target, because repeal of a state law was easier than repeal of a federal law or constitutional amendment, and repeal's success would leave enforcement in the crippled hands of the federal government.[45] Even if enforcement is regarded as a failure, however, it does not follow that such a lapse undermined political support for Prohibition. Depending on the number of drinking drys, the failure of enforcement could have produced the opposite effect, by allowing voters to gain access to alcohol themselves while voting to deny it to others.

Two other possible reasons also fall short of explaining Repeal. The leading antiprohibitionist organization throughout the 1920s was the Association Against the Prohibition Amendment (AAPA), which drew its support mainly from conservative businessmen, who objected to the increased power given to the federal government by National Prohibition. Their well-funded arguments, however, fell on deaf ears among the voters throughout the era, most tellingly in the presidential election of 1928. Both the AAPA and the more widely supported WONPR also focused attention on the lawlessness that Prohibition allegedly fostered. This argument, too, gained little traction in the electoral politics of the 1920s. When American voters changed their minds about Prohibition, the AAPA and WONPR, together with other repeal organizations, played a key role in focusing and channeling sentiment through an innovative path to Repeal, the use of specially elected state conventions.[46] But they did not create that sentiment.

> **"Thus, the arguments for Repeal that seemed to have greatest resonance with voters in 1932 and 1933 centered not on indulgence but on economic recovery. Repeal, it was argued, would replace the tax revenues foregone under Prohibition, thereby allowing governments to provide relief to suffering families."**

Finally, historians are fond of invoking widespread cultural change to explain the failure of National Prohibition. Decaying Victorian social mores allowed the normalization of drinking, which was given a significant boost by the cultural trendsetters of the Jazz Age. In such an atmosphere, Prohibition could not survive.[47] But it did. At the height of the Jazz Age, American voters in a hard-fought contest elected a staunch upholder of Prohibition in Herbert Hoover over Al Smith, an avowed foe of the Eighteenth Amendment. Repeal took place, not in the free-flowing good times of the Jazz Age, but rather in the austere gloom 4 years into America's worst economic depression.

Thus, the arguments for Repeal that seemed to have greatest resonance with voters in 1932 and 1933 centered not on indulgence but on economic recovery. Repeal, it was argued, would replace the tax revenues foregone under Prohibition, thereby allowing governments to provide relief to suffering families.[48] It would put unemployed workers back to work. Prohibitionists had long encouraged voters to believe in a link between Prohibition and prosperity, and after the onset of the Depression they abundantly reaped what they had sown.[49] Voters who had ignored claims that Prohibition excessively centralized power, failed to stop drinking, and fostered crime when they elected the dry Hoover now voted for the wet Franklin Roosevelt. They then turned out to elect delegates pledged to Repeal in the whirlwind series of state conventions that ratified the Twenty-First Amendment, Thus, it was not the stringent nature of National Prohibition, which set a goal that was probably impossible to reach and that thereby foredoomed enforcement, that played the leading role in discrediting alcohol prohibition. Instead, an abrupt and radical shift in context killed Prohibition.

# Legacies of Prohibition

The legacies of National Prohibition are too numerous to discuss in detail; besides, so many of them live on today and continue to affect Americans' everyday lives that it is even difficult to realize that they are Prohibition's byproducts. I will briefly mention the principal ones, in ascending order from shortest-lived to longest. The shortest-lived child of Prohibition actually survived to adulthood. This was the change in drinking patterns that depressed the level of consumption compared with the pre-Prohibition years. Straitened family finances during the Depression of course kept the annual per capita consumption rate low, hovering around 1.5 US gallons. The true results of Prohibition's success in socializing Americans in temperate habits became apparent during World War II, when the federal government turned a more cordial face toward the liquor industry than it had during World War I, and they became even more evident during the prosperous years that followed.[50] Although annual consumption rose, to about 2 gallons per capita in the 1950s and 2.4 gallons in the 1960s, it did not surpass the pre-Prohibition peak until the early 1970s.[51]

The death rate from liver cirrhosis followed a corresponding pattern.[52] In 1939, 42% of respondents told pollsters that they did not use alcohol at all. If that figure reflected stability in the proportionate size of the non-drinking population since the pre-Prohibition years, and if new cohorts—youths and women—had begun drinking during Prohibition, then the numbers of new drinkers had been offset by Prohibition's socializing effect. By 1960, the proportion of abstainers had fallen only to 38%.[53]

The Prohibition Era was unkind to habitual drunkards, not because their supply was cut off, but because it was not. Those who wanted liquor badly enough could still find it. But those who recognized their drinking as destructive were not so lucky in finding help. The inebriety asylums had closed, and the self-help societies had withered away. In 1935, these conditions gave birth to a new self-help group, Alcoholics Anonymous (AA), and the approach taken by these innovative reformers, while drawing from the old self-help tradition, was profoundly influenced by the experience of Prohibition.

AA rejected the prohibitionists' claim that anyone could become a slave to alcohol, the fundamental assumption behind the sweeping approach of the Volstead Act. There were several reasons for this decision, but one of the primary ones was a perception that Prohibition had failed and a belief that battles already lost should not be refought. Instead, AA drew a rigid line between normal drinkers, who could keep their consumption within the limits of moderation, and compulsive drinkers, who could not. Thus was born the disease concept of alcoholism. Although the concept's principal aim was to encourage sympathy for alcoholics, its result was to open the door to drinking by everyone else.[54] Influenced by Repeal to reject temperance ideology, medical researchers held the door open by denying previously accepted links between drinking and disease.[55]

Another force energized by Prohibition also promoted drinking: the liquor industry's fear that Prohibition might return. Those fears were not unjustified, because during the late 1930s two fifths of Americans surveyed still supported national Prohibition.[56] Brewers and distillers trod carefully, to be sure, attempting to surround liquor with an aura of "glamour, wealth, and sophistication," rather than evoke the rough culture of the saloon. To target women, whom the industry perceived as the largest group of abstainers, liquor ads customarily placed drinking in a domestic context giving hostesses a central role in dispensing their products.[57] Too much can easily be made of the "cocktail culture" of the 1940s and 1950s, because the drinking population grew only slightly and per capita consumption rose only gradually during those years. The most significant result of the industry's campaign was to lay the foundation for a substantial increase in drinking during the 1960s and 1970s.

By the end of the 20th century, two thirds of the alcohol consumed by Americans was drunk in the home or at private parties.[58] In other words, the model of drinking within a framework of domestic sociability, which had been shaped by women, had largely superseded the style of public drinking men had created in their saloons and clubs.[59] Prohibition helped to bring about this major change in American drinking patterns by killing the saloon, but it also had an indirect influence in the same direction, by way of the state. When Prohibition ended, and experiments in economic regulation—including regulation of alcohol—under the National Recovery Administration were declared unconstitutional, the federal government banished public health concerns from its alcohol policy, which thereafter revolved around economic considerations.[60]

Some states retained their prohibition laws—the last repeal occurring only in 1966—but most created pervasive systems of liquor control that affected drinking in every aspect.[61] Licensing was generally taken out of the hands of localities and put under the control of state administrative bodies, in an attempt to replace the impassioned struggles that had heated local politics since the 19th century with the cool, impersonal processes of bureaucracy. Licensing policy favored outlets selling for off-premise consumption, a category that eventually included grocery stores. With the invention of the aluminum beer can and the spread of home refrigeration after the 1930s, the way was cleared for the home to become the prime drinking site.

## Lessons for Other Drug Prohibitions

Perhaps the most powerful legacy of National Prohibition is the widely held belief that it did not work. I agree with other historians who have argued that this belief is false: Prohibition did work in lowering per capita consumption. The lowered level of consumption during the quarter century following Repeal, together with the large minority of abstainers, suggests that Prohibition did socialize or maintain a significant portion of the population in temperate or abstemious habits.[62] That is, it was partly successful as a public health innovation. Its political failure is attributable more to a changing context than to characteristics of the innovation itself.

Today, it is easy to say that the goal of total prohibition was impossible and the means therefore were unnecessarily severe—that, for example, National Prohibition could have survived had the drys been willing to compromise by permitting beer and light wine[63]—but from the perspective of 1913 the rejection of alternate modes of liquor control makes more sense. Furthermore, American voters continued to support Prohibition politically even in its stringent form, at least in national politics, until their economy crashed and forcefully turned their concerns in other directions. Nevertheless, the possibility remains that in 1933 a less restrictive form of Prohibition could have satisfied the economic concerns that drove Repeal while still controlling the use of alcohol in its most dangerous forms.

Scholars have readied no consensus on the implications of National Prohibition for other forms of prohibition, and public discourse in the United States mirrors our collective ambivalence.[64] Arguments that assume that Prohibition was a failure have been deployed most effectively against laws prohibiting tobacco and guns, but they have been ignored by those waging the war on other drugs since the 1980s, which is directed toward the same teetotal goal as National Prohibition.[65] Simplistic assumptions about government's ability to legislate morals, whether pro or con, find no support in the historical record. As historian Ian Tyrell writes, "each drug subject to restrictions needs to be carefully investigated in terms of its conditions of production, its value to an illicit trade, the ability to conceal the substance, and its effects on both the individual and society at large."[66] From a historical perspective, no prediction is certain, and no path is forever barred—not even the return of alcohol prohibition in some form. Historical context matters.

---

*Acknowledgments*—Tom Pegram and led Brown provided helpful comments on an earlier version of the article.

# References

1. Esa Õsterberg, "Finland," in *Alcohol and Temperance in Modern History: An International Encyclopedia*, vol 1, ed. Jack S. Blocker Jr, David M. Fahey, and Ian R. Tyrrell (Santa Barbara, Calif: ABC-Clio, 2003). 240–243: Sturla Nordlund, "Norway," in *Alcohol and Temperance in Modern History*, vol 2, 458–463: William Lahey, "Provincial Prohibition (Canada), in *Alcohol and Temperance in Modern History*, vol 2, 496–499: Daniel J. Malleck, "Federal Prohibition (Canada)," in *Alcohol and Temperance in Modern History*, vol 1, 229: Laura L. Phillips, *Bolsheviks and the Bottle: Drink and Worker Culture in St. Petersburg. 1900–1920* (Dekalb: Northern Illinois University Press, 2000).

2. Thomas R. Pegram, *Battling Demon Rum: The Struggle for a Dry America. 1800–1933* (Chicago: Ivan R. Dee, 1998): Jack S. Blocker Jr, *American Temperance Movements: Cycles of Reform* (Boston: Twayne, 1989), 106–129: W. J. Rorabaugh, "Reexamining the Prohibition Amendment," *Yale Journal of Law and the Humanities* 8 (1996): 285–294; Ian Tyrell, "The US Prohibition Experiment: Myths, History and Implications," *Addiction* 92 (1997): 1405–1409.

3. Ian R. Tyrrell, *Sobering Up: From Temperance to Prohibition in Antebellum America. 1800–1860* (Westport, Conn: Greenwood Press, 1979), 89–90 and passim: Jack S. Blocker Jr, *Retreat From Reform The Prohibition Movement in the United States, 1890–1913* (Westport, Conn: Greenwood Press, 1976), 83; Blocker, *American Temperance Movements*, 24–25; Edward J. Wheeler, *Prohibition: The Principle, the Policy, and the Party* (New York: Funk & Wagnalls, 1889), 39–49, 57–66.

4. Blocker, *American Temperance Movements*, 21–27, 69–70; Tyrell, *Sobering Up*, 135–145, 227–245; K. Austin Kerr, *Organized for Prohibition: A New History of the Anti-Saloon League* (New Haven, Conn: Yale University Press, 1985), 35–138; Anne-Marie E. Szymanski, *Pathways to Prohibition:*

*Radicals, Moderates, and Social Movement Outcomes* (Durham, NC: Duke University Press, 2003); Sarah W. Tracy, *Alcoholism in America: From Reconstruction to Prohibition* (Baltimore, Md: Johns Hopkins University Press, 2005).

5. Joan L. Silverman, "I'll Never Touch Another Drop": *Images of Alcohol and Temperance in American Popular Culture, 1874–1919* [PhD dissertation] (New York: New York University, 1979), 338–340, and "The Birth of a Nation: Prohibition Propaganda," *Southern Quarterly* 19 (1981): 23–30.

6. James H. Timberlake, *Prohibition and the Progressive Movement, 1900–1920* (Cambridge. Mass: Harvard University Press, 1963). 39–66, Denise Herd, "Ideology, History and Changing Models of Liver Cirrhosis Epidemiology," *British Journal of Addiction* 87 (1992): 1113–1126; Brian S. Katcher, "The Post-Repeal Eclipse in Knowledge About the Harmful Effects of Alcohol," *Addiction* 88 (June 1993): 729–744.

7. Harry Gene Levine, "The Discovery of Addiction: Changing Conceptions of Habitual Drunkenness in America," *Journal of Studies on Alcohol* 39 (January 1978): 161–162.

8. Jonathan Zimmerman, *Distilling Democracy: Alcohol Education in America's Public Schools, 1880–1925* (Lawrence: University Press of Kansas, 1999).

9. Catherine Gilbert Murdock, *Domesticating Drink: Women, Men, and Alcohol in America, 1870–1940* (Baltimore: Johns Hopkins University Press, 1998). For studies of saloon culture, see Madelon Powers, *Faces Along the Bar: Lore and Order in the Workingman's Saloon, 1870–1920* (Chicago: University of Chicago Press, 1998); Craig Heron, *Booze: A Distilled History* (Toronto: Between the Lines, 2003), 105–121; Perry Duis, *The Saloon: Public Drinking in Chicago and Boston, 1880–1920* (Urbana: University of Illinois Press, 1983), 172–197; Elaine Frantz Parsons, *Manhood Lost: Fallen Drunkards and Redeeming Women in the 19th-century United States* (Baltimore: Johns Hopkins University Press, 2003).

10 Local option, through which many areas in states lacking prohibition statutes were rendered "dry," of course affected only the sale of liquor within the local jurisdiction; it could not, nor did it attempt to, prevent local drinkers from importing alcohol from wet areas, either by bringing it themselves or through mail order. Pegram, *Battling Demon Rum*, 141–142.

11. Richard F. Hamm, *Shaping the Eighteenth Amendment: Temperance Reform, Legal Culture, and the Polity, 1880–1920* (Chapel Hill: University of North Carolina Press, 1995), 56–91, 212–226.

12. Szymanski, *Pathways to Prohibition*, 100–121, 131–140.

13. Jack S. Blocker Jr, "Consumption and Availability of Alcoholic Beverages in the United States, 1863–1920," *Contemporary Drug Problems* 21(1994): 631–666.

14. Ibid.

15. David E. Kyvig, *Explicit and Authentic Acts: Amending the US Constitution, 1776–1995* (Lawrence: University Press of Kansas, 1996), 216–218. Creation of a national income tax also provided an alternative source of revenue for the federal government, thereby freeing Congress from reliance on liquor excise taxes. Donald J. Boudreaux and A. C. Pritchard, "The Price of Prohibition," *Arizona Law Review* 10 (1994): 1–10.

16. Kerr, *Organized for Prohibition*, 139–147.

17. Blocker, *Retreat From Reform*, 228; Kerr, *Organized for Prohibition*, 140–141; Thomas R. Pegram, "Prohibition," in *The American Congress: The Building of Democracy*, ed. Julian E. Zelizer (Boston: Houghton Mifflin, 2004), 411–427.

18. National Institute for Alcohol Abuse and Alcoholism (NIAAA), "Apparent per Capita Ethanol Consumption for the United States, 1850–2000," available at http://www.niaaa. nih.gov/databases/consum01.htm, accessed August 2004; Blocker, "Consumption and Availability," 652. All statistics given in this article for per capita consumption are for US gallons of ethanol per capita of population 15 years of age and older prior to 1970 and population 14 years of age and older thereafter.

19. Angela K. Dills and Jeffrey A. Miron, "Alcohol Prohibition and Cirrhosis," *American Law and Economics Review* 6 (2004): 285–318, esp. Figure 3; E. M. Jellinek, "Recent Trends in Alcoholism and in Alcohol Consumption," *Quarterly Journal of Studies on Alcohol*, 8 (1947): 40.

20. Blocker, *American Temperance Movements*, 117.

21. Timberlake, *Prohibition and the Progressive Movement*.

22. Robert G. LaForge, *Misplaced Priorities: A History of Federal Alcohol Regulation and Public Health Policy* [PhD dissertation] (Baltimore: Johns Hopkins University, 1987), 56.

23. Kerr, *Organized for Prohibition*, 181–184.

24. Szymanski, *Pathways to Prohibition*, LaForge, *Misplaced Priorities*; Kerr, *Organized for Prohibition*, 181–184.

25. Pegram, *Battling Demon Rum*, 144–147.

26. Blocker, *American Temperance Movements*, 118; Kyvig, *Explicit and Authentic Acts*, 224.

27. *Statistical Abstract of the United States: 1928* (Washington, DC: US Bureau of the Census, 1928), 767.

28. *Statistics Concerning Intoxicating Liquors* (Washington, DC: Bureau of Industrial Alcohol, US Treasury Department, 1930), 3, 60, 64, 72.

29. William H. Mulligan Jr, "Coors, Adolph, Brewing Company," in *Alcohol and Temperance in Modern History*, vol 1, 174; Mulligan, "Miller Brewing Company," in *Alcohol and Temperance in Modern History*, vol 2. 418; Amy Mittelman, "Anheuser-Busch," in *Alcohol and Temperance in Modern History*, vol 1, 43–45.

30. Even the death of slavery, although it put an end to the domestic slave trade, did not hinder cotton culture.

31. Pegram, *Battling Demon Rum*, 149.

32. Jeffrey A. Miron and Jeffrey Zwiebel, "Alcohol Consumption During Prohibition," *American Economic Review* 81 (1991): 242–247; Dills and Miron, "Alcohol Prohibition and Cirrhosis"; NIAAA, "Apparent per Capita Ethanol Consumption." The figure is for 1935.

33. John R. Meers, "The California Wine and Grape Industry and Prohibition," *California Historical Society Quarterly* 46 (1967): 19–32.

34. Norman H. Clark, *Deliver Us From Evil: An Interpretation of American Prohibition* (New York: W. W. Norton, 1976), 143–146; Powers, *Faces Along the Bar*, 234–236; Duis, *The Saloon* 274–303; Pegram, *Battling Demon Rum*, 163.

35. Robin Room, "'A Reverence for Strong Drink': The Lost Generation and the Elevation of Alcohol in American Culture," *Journal of Studies on Alcohol* 45 (1984): 540–546; John C. Burnham, *Bad Habits: Drinking, Smoking, Taking Drugs, Gambling, Sexual Misbehavior, and Swearing in American History* (New York: New York University Press, 1993), 34–38; Paula Fass, *The Damned and the Beautiful: American Youth in the 1920's* (New York: Oxford University Press, 1977); Murdock, *Domesticating Drink*, 93–94.

36. Thomas R. Pegram, "Kluxing the Eighteenth Amendment: The Anti-Saloon League, the Ku Klux Klan, and the Fate of Prohibition in the 1920s," in *American Public Life and the Historical Imagination*, ed. Wendy Gamber, Michael Grossberg, and Hendrik Hartog (Notre Dame, Ind: University of Notre Dame Press, 2003), 240–261.

37. Murdock, *Domesticating Drink*.

38. Ibid, 134–158; Kenneth D. Rose, *American Women and the Repeal of Prohibition* (New York: New York University Press, 1996).

39. Burnham, *Bad Habits*, 34–49; Room, "A Reverence for Strong Drink": Room, The Movies and the Wettening of America: The Media as Amplifiers of Cultural Change," *British Journal of Addiction* 83 (1988): 11–18; David E. Kyvig, *Repealing National Prohibition* (Chicago: University of Chicago Press, 1979), 28–29.

40. Andrew Sinclair, *Prohibition: The Era of Excess* (New York: Harper & Row, 1962), 211–212, 220–230; Kyvig, *Repealing National Inhibition*, 30.

41. Paul L. Murphy, "Societal Morality and Individual Freedom," in *Law, Alcohol, and Order: Perspectives on National Prohibition*, ed. David E. Kyvig (Westport, Conn: Greenwood Press, 1985), 67–80; Rayman L. Solomon, "Regulating the Regulators: Prohibition Enforcement in the Seventh Circuit," in *Law, Alcohol, and Order*, 81–96.

42. Lawrence Spinelli, *Dry Diplomacy: The United States, Great Britain, and Prohibition* (Wilmington, Del: Scholarly Resources, 1989).

43. Kyvig, *Repealing National Prohibition*, 147–168; Alan P. Grimes, *Democracy and the Amendments to the Constitution* (Lexington, Mass: Lexington Books, 1978), 109–112.

44. Kerr, *Organized for Prohibition*, 222.

45. Hamm, *Shaping the Eighteenth Amendment*, 266–269; Pegram, *Battling Demon Rum*, 156–160.

46. Kyvig, *Repealing National Prohibition*.

47. Kerr, *Organized for Prohibition*, 279; Hamm, *Shaping the Eighteenth Amendment*, 269; Pegram, *Battling Demon Rum*, 175–176.

48. Boudreaux and Pritchard, "Price of Prohibition," 5–10.

49. Sinclair, *Prohibition*, 387–399.

50. Jay L. Rubin, "The Wet War: American Liquor Control, 1941–1945," in *Alcohol, Reform and Society: The Liquor Issue in Social Context*, ed. Jack S. Blocker Jr (Westport, Conn: Greenwood Press, 1979), 235–258.

51. NIAAA, "Apparent per Capita Ethanol Consumption."

52. Dills and Miron, "Alcohol Prohibition and Cirrhosis," Figure 3.

53. Blocker, *American Temperance Movements*, 138. The United States continues to be distinguished among societies where temperance ideology was once influential by its high proportion of abstainers. Michael H. Hilton, "Trends in US Drinking Patterns: Further Evidence From the Past 20 Years," *British Journal of Addiction* 83 (1988): 269–278; Klaus Mäkelä, Robin Room, Eric Single, Pekka Sulkunen, and Brendan Walsh, *A Comparative Study of Alcohol Control*, vol 1 of Alcohol, Society, and the State (Toronto: Addiction Research Foundation, 1981), 21–24.

54. Ernest Kurtz, *Not-God: A History of Alcoholics Anonymous*, rev ed (Center City, Minn: Hazelden, 1991); Bruce H. Johnson, *The Alcoholism Movement in America: A Study in Cultural Innovation* [PhD dissertation] (University of Illinois at Urbana-Champaign, 1973); Blocker, *American Temperance Movements*, 139–154.

55. Herd, "Ideology, History and Changing Models of Liver Cirrhosis Epidemiology"; Katcher, "Post-Repeal Eclipse in Knowledge"; Philip J. Pauly, "How Did the Effects of Alcohol on Reproduction Become Scientifically Uninteresting?" *Journal of the History of Biology* 29 (1996): 1–28.

56. Blocker, *American Temperance Movements*, 136.

57. Cheryl Krasnick Warsh, "Smoke and Mirrors: Gender Representation in North American Tobacco and Alcohol Advertisements Before 1950," *Histoire sociale/Social History* 31 (1998): 183–222 (quote from p. 220); Lori Rotskoff, *Love on the Rocks: Men, Women, and Alcohol in Post-World War II America* (Chapel Hill: University of North Carolina Press, 2002), 194–210; Burnham, *Bad Habits*, 47.

58. Stephen R Byers, "Home, as Drinking Site," in *Alcohol and Temperance in Modern History*, vol 1, 296.

59. Murdock, *Domesticating Drink*.

60. LaForge, *Misplaced Priorities*.

61. Harry Gene Levine, "The Birth of American Alcohol Control: Prohibition, the Power Elite, and the Problem of Lawlessness," *Contemporary Drug Problems* 12 (1985): 63–115; David Fogarty. "From Saloon to Supermarket: Packaged Beer and the Reshaping of the US Brewing Industry," *Contemporary Drug Problems* 12 (1985): 541–592.

62. John C. Burnham, "New Perspectives on the Prohibition 'Experiment' of the 1920's," *Journal of Social History* 2 (1968): 51–68; Clark, *Deliver Us From Evil*, 145–158; Kerr, *Organizing for Prohibition*. 276–277; Tyrrell, "US Prohibition Experiment," 1406.

63. Murdock, *Domesticating Drink*, 170.

64. Burnham, *Bad Habits*, 293–297; Jeffrey A. Miron, "An Economic Analysis of Alcohol Prohibition," *Journal of Drug Issues* 28 (1998): 741–762; Harry G. Levine and Craig Reinarman, "From Prohibition to Regulation: Lessons From Alcohol Policy to Drug Policy," *Milbank Quarterly* 69 (1991): 461–494.

65. James A. Morone, *Hellfire Nation: The Politics of Sin in American History* (New Haven, Conn: Yale University Press, 2003), 343.

66. Tyrrell, "US Prohibition Experiment" 1407; Robin Room, "Alcohol Control and Public Health," *Annual Review of Public Health* 5 (1984): 293–317.

The author is with the Department of History, Huron University College, University of Western Ontario, London, Ontario.

Requests for reprints should be sent to Jack S. Blocker Jr, PhD, Huron University College, 1349 Western Road, London. Ontario N6G 1H3 Canada (e–mail: **jblocker@uwo.ca**).

# UNIT 2

# Understanding How Drugs Work—Use, Dependency, and Addiction

## Unit Selection

## Key Points to Consider

• Why do some people become dependent on certain drugs far sooner than other people?

• How is it possible to predict one's own liability for becoming drug dependent?

• Is it possible for a person to say that he or she intends to be only a recreational user of drugs like cocaine or methamphetamine?

• Of all of the influences that combine to create one's liability for addiction, which ones do you believe to be the most significant?

## Student Website
www.mhcls.com/online

## Internet References
Further information regarding these websites may be found in this book's preface or online.

**AddictionSearch.com**
*www.addictionsearch.com*

**Addiction Treatment Forum**
*www.atforum.com*

**APA Help Center from the American Psychological Association**
*http://www.apahelpcenter.org/articles/article.php?id=45*

**British Broadcasting Company Understanding Drugs**
*http://www.bbc.co.uk/health/conditions/mental_health/drugs_use.shtml*

**Centre for Addiction and Mental Health (CAMH)**
*http://www.camh.net*

**Dealing with Addictions**
*http://kidshealth.org/teen/your_mind/problems/addictions.html*

**Drugs and the Body: How Drugs Work**
*http://www.doitnow.org/pdfs/223.pdf*

**The National Center on Addiction and Substance Abuse at Columbia University**
*http://www.casacolumbia.org*

**National Institute on Drug Abuse (NIDA)**
*http://www.nida.nih.gov*

**Public Agenda**
*http://www.publicagenda.org/issues/frontdoor.cfm?issue_type=illegal_drugs*

**Understanding Addiction-Regret, Addiction and Death**
*http://teenadvice.about.com/library/weekly/aa011501a.htm*

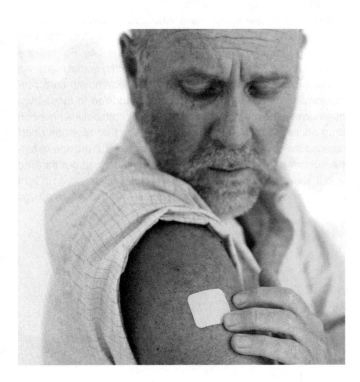

**U**nderstanding how drugs act upon the human mind and body is a critical component to the resolution of issues concerning drug use and abuse. An understanding of basic pharmacology is requisite for informed discussion on practically every drug-related issue and controversy. One does not have to look far to find misinformed debate, much of which surrounds the basic lack of knowledge of how drugs work.

Different drugs produce different bodily effects and consequences. All psychoactive drugs influence the central nervous system, which, in turn, sits at the center of how we physiologically and psychologically interpret and react to the world around us. Some drugs, such as methamphetamine and LSD, have great immediate influence on the nervous system, while others, such as tobacco and marijuana, elicit less-pronounced reactions. Almost all psychoactive drugs have their effects on the body mitigated by the dosage level of the drug taken, the manner in which it is ingested, and the physiological and emotional state of the user. Cocaine smoked in the form of crack versus snorted as powder produces profoundly different physical and emotional effects on the user. However, even though illegal drugs often provide the most sensational perspective from which to view these relationships, the abuse of prescription drugs is being reported as an exploding new component of the addiction problem. Currently, the non-medical use of pain-relievers such as oxycodone and hydrocodone is continuing at rates not observed since the mid-1970s. Forty percent of the 119,000 mentions of narcotic pain medications in emer-

gency rooms involved either oxycodone or hydrocodone. This trend has been increasing steadily since 1994, and it currently competes with methamphetamine abuse as the most alarming national trend of drug abuse.

Molecular properties of certain drugs allow them to imitate and artificially reproduce certain naturally-occurring brain chemicals that provide the basis for the drug's influence. The continued use of certain drugs and their repeated alteration of the body's biochemical structure provide one explanation for the physiological consequences of drug use. For example, heroin use replicates the natural brain chemical endorphin, which supports the body's biochemical defense to pain and stress. The continued use of heroin is believed to deplete natural endorphins, causing the nervous system to produce a painful physical and emotional reaction when heroin is withdrawn.

A word of caution is in order, however, when proceeding through the various explanations for what drugs do and why they do it. Many people, because of an emotional and/or political relationship to the world of drugs, assert a subjective predisposition when interpreting certain drugs' effects and consequences. One person's alcoholic is another's social drinker. People often argue, rationalize, and explain the perceived nature of drugs' effects based upon an extremely superficial understanding of diverse pharmacological properties of different drugs. A detached and scientifically sophisticated awareness of drug pharmacology may help strengthen the platform from which to interpret the various consequences of drug use.

Drug dependence and addiction is usually a continuum comprised of experimentation, recreational use, regular use, and abuse. The process is influenced by a plethora of physiological, psychological, and environmental factors. Although some still argue that drug dependence is largely a matter of individual behavior—something to be chosen or rejected—most experts assert that new scientific discoveries clearly define the roots of addiction to live within molecular levels of the brain. Powerful drugs, upon repeated administration, easily compromise the brain's ability to make decisions about its best interests.

Largely, drugs are described as more addictive or less addictive due to a process described as "reinforcement." Simply explained, reinforcement results from a drug's physiological and psychological influence on a person's behavior to such a degree that it causes that person to repeatedly introduce the drug to the body. Cocaine and the amphetamines are known as drugs with high reinforcement potential. Persons addicted to drugs known to be strongly reinforcing typically report that they care more about getting the drug than about anything else. Reinforcement does not, however, provide "the" basis for understanding addiction.

Drug addiction and the rate at which it occurs must compete with certain physiological and psychological, as well as environmental variables that are unique to individuals. A drug user with a greater number of biological markers known to be associated with drug addiction, such as mental illness, alcoholism, and poor physical health, may encourage drug dependency sooner than a person with fewer biological markers. Similarly, a person's positive environmental associations, or 'natural reinforcers,' such as a strong family structure, and healthy personal and professional relationships may not only make experimentation unappealing, it may delay a user's developing drug addiction. Subsequently, one's liability for drug addiction is closely associated with genetics, environment, and the use of psychoactive drugs. Understanding the concept of addiction requires an awareness of these factors. For many people, drug addiction and the reasons that contribute to it are murky concepts.

The articles in Unit 2 illustrate some of the current research and viewpoints on the ways that drugs act upon the human body. New science is suggesting that a new era has begun relative to understanding drugs and their pharmacological influence on the human body. This new science is critical to understanding the assorted consequences of drug use and abuse. Science has taken us closer to understanding that acute drug use changes brain function profoundly, and that these changes may remain with the user long after the drug has left the system. Subsequently, many new issues have emerged for drug and health-related public policy. Increasingly, drug abuse competes with other social maladies as public enemy number one. Further, the need for a combined biological, behavioral, and social response to this problem becomes more evident. Many health care professionals and health care educators, in addition to those from other diverse backgrounds, argue that research dollars spent on drug abuse and addiction should approach that spent on heart disease, cancer, and AIDS. The articles in Unit 2 provide examples of how some new discoveries have influenced our thinking about addiction. They also provide examples of how, even in light of new knowledge, breaking addictions is so very hard to do.

# Addiction Is a Brain Disease

**Greater progress will be made against drug abuse when our strategies reflect the full complexities of the latest scientific understanding.**

ALAN I. LESHNER

The United States is stuck in its drug abuse metaphors and in polarized arguments about them. Everyone has an opinion. One side insists that we must control supply, the other that we must reduce demand. People see addiction as either a disease or as a failure of will. None of this bumpersticker analysis moves us forward. The truth is that we will make progress in dealing with drug issues only when our national discourse and our strategies are as complex and comprehensive as the problem itself.

A core concept that has been evolving with scientific advances over the past decade is that drug addiction is a brain disease that develops over time as a result of the initially voluntary behavior of using drugs. The consequence is virtually uncontrollable compulsive drug craving, seeking, and use that interferes with, if not destroys, an individual's functioning in the family and in society. This medical condition demands formal treatment.

We now know in great detail the brain mechanisms through which drugs acutely modify mood, memory, perception, and emotional states. Using drugs repeatedly over time changes brain structure and function in fundamental and long-lasting ways that can persist long after the individual stops using them. Addiction comes about through an array of neuroadaptive changes and the laying down and strengthening of new memory connections in various circuits in the brain. We do not yet know all the relevant mechanisms, but the evidence suggests that those long-lasting brain changes are responsible for the distortions of cognitive and emotional functioning that characterize addicts, particularly including the compulsion to use drugs that is the essence of addiction. It is as if drugs have highjacked the brain's natural motivational control circuits, resulting in drug use becoming the sole, or at least the top, motivational priority for the individual. Thus, the majority of the biomedical community now considers addiction, in its essence, to be a brain disease: a condition caused by persistent changes in brain structure and function.

This brain-based view of addiction has generated substantial controversy, particularly among people who seem able to think only in polarized ways. Many people erroneously still believe that biological and behavioral explanations are alternative or competing ways to understand phenomena, when in fact they are complementary and integratable. Modern science has taught that it is much too simplistic to set biology in opposition to behavior or to pit willpower against brain chemistry. Addiction involves inseparable biological and behavioral components. It is the quintessential biobehavioral disorder.

Many people also erroneously still believe that drug addiction is simply a failure of will or of strength of character. Research contradicts that position. However, the recognition that addiction is a brain disease does not mean that the addict is simply a hapless victim. Addiction begins with the voluntary behavior of using drugs, and addicts must participate in and take some significant responsibility for their recovery. Thus, having this brain disease does not absolve the addict of responsibility for his or her behavior, but it does explain why an addict cannot simply stop using drugs by sheer force of will alone. It also dictates a much more sophisticated approach to dealing with the array of problems surrounding drug abuse and addiction in our society.

## The Essence of Addiction

The entire concept of addiction has suffered greatly from imprecision and misconception. In fact, if it were possible, it would be best to start all over with some new, more neutral term. The confusion comes about in part because of a now archaic distinction between whether specific drugs are "physically" or "psychologically" addicting. The distinction historically revolved around whether or not dramatic physical withdrawal symptoms occur when an individual stops taking a drug; what we in the field now call "physical dependence."

However, 20 years of scientific research has taught that focusing on this physical versus psychological distinction is off the mark and a distraction from the real issues. From both clinical and policy perspectives, it actually does not matter very much what physical withdrawal symptoms occur. Physical dependence is not that important, because even the dramatic withdrawal symptoms of heroin and alcohol addiction can now be easily managed with appropriate medications. Even more important, many of the most dangerous and addicting drugs, including methamphetamine and crack cocaine, do not produce very severe physical dependence symptoms upon withdrawal.

What really matters most is whether or not a drug causes what we now know to be the essence of addiction: uncontrollable, compulsive drug craving, seeking, and use, even in the face of negative health and social consequences. This is the crux of how the Institute of Medicine, the American Psychiatric Association, and the American Medical Association define addiction and how we all should use the term. It is really only this compulsive quality of addiction that matters in the long run to the addict and to his or her family and that should matter to society as a whole. Compulsive craving that overwhelms all other motivations is the root cause of the massive health and social problems associated with drug addiction. In updating our national discourse on drug abuse, we should keep in mind this simple definition: Addiction is a brain disease expressed in the form of compulsive behavior. Both developing and recovering from it depend on biology, behavior, and social context.

It is also important to correct the common misimpression that drug use, abuse, and addiction are points on a single continuum along which one slides back and forth over time, moving from user to addict, then back to occasional user, then back to addict. Clinical observation and more formal research studies support the view that, once addicted, the individual has moved into a different state of being. It is as if a threshold has been crossed. Very few people appear able to successfully return to occasional use after having been truly addicted. Unfortunately, we do not yet have a clear biological or behavioral marker of that transition from voluntary drug use to addiction. However, a body of scientific evidence is rapidly developing that points to an array of cellular and molecular changes in specific brain circuits. Moreover, many of these brain changes are common to all chemical addictions, and some also are typical of other compulsive behaviors such as pathological overeating.

Addiction should be understood as a chronic recurring illness. Although some addicts do gain full control over their drug use after a single treatment episode, many have relapses. Repeated treatments become necessary to increase the intervals between and diminish the intensity of relapses, until the individual achieves abstinence.

The complexity of this brain disease is not atypical, because virtually no brain diseases are simply biological in nature and expression. All, including stroke, Alzheimer's disease, schizophrenia, and clinical depression, include some behavioral and social aspects. What may make addiction seem unique among brain diseases, however, is that it

does begin with a clearly voluntary behavior—the initial decision to use drugs. Moreover, not everyone who ever uses drugs goes on to become addicted. Individuals differ substantially in how easily and quickly they become addicted and in their preferences for particular substances. Consistent with the biobehavioral nature of addiction, these individual differences result from a combination of environmental and biological, particularly genetic, factors. In fact, estimates are that between 50 and 70 percent of the variability in susceptibility to becoming addicted can be accounted for by genetic factors.

## Although genetic characteristics may predispose individuals to be more or less susceptible to becoming addicted, genes do not doom one to become an addict.

Over time the addict loses substantial control over his or her initially voluntary behavior, and it becomes compulsive. For many people these behaviors are truly uncontrollable, just like the behavioral expression of any other brain disease. Schizophrenics cannot control their hallucinations and delusions. Parkinson's patients cannot control their trembling. Clinically depressed patients cannot voluntarily control their moods. Thus, once one is addicted, the characteristics of the illness—and the treatment approaches—are not that different from most other brain diseases. No matter how one develops an illness, once one has it, one is in the diseased state and needs treatment.

Moreover, voluntary behavior patterns are, of course, involved in the etiology and progression of many other illnesses, albeit not all brain diseases. Examples abound, including hypertension, arteriosclerosis and other cardiovascular diseases, diabetes, and forms of cancer in which the onset is heavily influenced by the individual's eating, exercise, smoking, and other behaviors.

Addictive behaviors do have special characteristics related to the social contexts in which they originate. All of the environmental cues surrounding initial drug use and development of the addiction actually become "conditioned" to that drug use and are thus critical to the development and expression of addiction. Environmental cues are paired in time with an individual's initial drug use experiences and, through classical conditioning, take on conditioned stimulus properties. When those cues are present at a later time, they elicit anticipation of a drug experience and thus generate tremendous drug craving. Cue-induced craving is one of the most frequent causes of drug use relapses, even after long periods of abstinence, independently of whether drugs are available.

The salience of environmental or contextual cues helps explain why reentry to one's community can be so difficult for addicts leaving the controlled environments of treatment or correctional settings and why aftercare is so essential to successful recovery. The person who became addicted in the home environment is constantly exposed to the cues conditioned to his or her initial drug use, such as the neighborhood where he or she hung out, drug-using buddies, or the lamppost where he or she bought drugs. Simple exposure to those cues automatically triggers craving and can lead rapidly to relapses. This is one reason why someone who apparently overcame drug cravings while in prison or residential treatment could quickly revert to drug use upon returning home. In fact, one of the major goals of drug addiction treatment is to teach addicts how to deal with the cravings caused by inevitable exposure to these conditioned cues.

# Implications

Understanding addiction as a brain disease has broad and significant implications for the public perception of addicts and their families, for addiction treatment practice, and for some aspects of public policy. On the other hand, this biomedical view of addiction does not speak directly to and is unlikely to bear significantly on many other issues, including specific strategies for controlling the supply of drugs and whether initial drug use should be legal or not. Moreover, the brain disease model of addiction does not address the question of whether specific drugs of abuse can also be potential medicines. Examples abound of drugs that can be both highly addicting and extremely effective medicines. The best-known example is the appropriate use of morphine as a treatment for pain. Nevertheless, a number of practical lessons can be drawn from the scientific understanding of addiction.

**It is no wonder addicts cannot simply quit on their own.** They have an illness that requires biomedical treatment. People often assume that because addiction begins with a voluntary behavior and is expressed in the form of excess behavior, people should just be able to quit by force of will alone. However, it is essential to understand when dealing with addicts that we are dealing with individuals whose brains have been altered by drug use. They need drug addiction treatment. We know that, contrary to common belief, very few addicts actually do just stop on their own. Observing that there are very few heroin addicts in their 50 or 60s, people frequently ask what happened to those who were heroin addicts 30 years ago, assuming that they must have quit on their own. However, longitudinal studies find that only a very small fraction actually quit on their own. The rest have either been successfully treated, are currently in maintenance treatment, or (for about half) are dead. Consider the example of smoking cigarettes: Various studies have found that between 3 and 7 percent of people who try to quit on their own each year actually succeed. Science has at last convinced the public that depression is not just a lot of sadness; that depressed individuals are in a different brain state and thus require treatment to get their symptoms under

control. The same is true for schizophrenic patients. It is time to recognize that this is also the case for addicts.

**The role of personal responsibility is undiminished but clarified.** Does having a brain disease mean that people who are addicted no longer have any responsibility for their behavior or that they are simply victims of their own genetics and brain chemistry? Of course not. Addiction begins with the voluntary behavior of drug use, and although genetic characteristics may predispose individuals to be more or less susceptible to becoming addicted, genes do not doom one to become an addict. This is one major reason why efforts to prevent drug use are so vital to any comprehensive strategy to deal with the nation's drug problems. Initial drug use is a voluntary, and therefore preventable, behavior.

Moreover, as with any illness, behavior becomes a critical part of recovery. At a minimum, one must comply with the treatment regimen, which is harder than it sounds. Treatment compliance is the biggest cause of relapses for all chronic illnesses, including asthma, diabetes, hypertension, and addiction. Moreover, treatment compliance rates are no worse for addiction than for these other illnesses, ranging from 30 to 50 percent. Thus, for drug addiction as well as for other chronic diseases, the individual's motivation and behavior are clearly important parts of success in treatment and recovery.

**Implications for treatment approaches and treatment expectations.** Maintaining this comprehensive biobehavioral understanding of addiction also speaks to what needs to be provided in drug treatment programs. Again, we must be careful not to pit biology against behavior. The National Institute on Drug Abuse's recently published Principles of Effective Drug Addiction Treatment provides a detailed discussion of how we must treat all aspects of the individual, not just the biological component or the behavioral component. As with other brain diseases such as schizophrenia and depression, the data show that the best drug addiction treatment approaches attend to the entire individual, combining the use of medications, behavioral therapies, and attention to necessary social services and rehabilitation. These might include such services as family therapy to enable the patient to return to successful family life, mental health services, education and vocational training, and housing services.

That does not mean, of course, that all individuals need all components of treatment and all rehabilitation services. Another principle of effective addiction treatment is that the array of services included in an individual's treatment plan must be matched to his or her particular set of needs. Moreover, since those needs will surely change over the course of recovery, the array of services provided will need to be continually reassessed and adjusted.

**Entry into drug treatment need not be completely voluntary in order for it to work.**

**What to do with addicted criminal offenders.** One obvious conclusion is that we need to stop simplistically viewing criminal justice and health approaches as incompatible opposites. The practical reality is that crime and drug addiction often occur in tandem: Between 50 and 70 percent of arrestees are addicted to illegal drugs. Few citizens would be willing to relinquish criminal justice system control over individuals, whether they are addicted or not, who have committed crimes against others. Moreover, extensive real-life experience shows that if we simply incarcerate addicted offenders without treating them, their return to both drug use and criminality is virtually guaranteed.

A growing body of scientific evidence points to a much more rational and effective blended public health/public safety approach to dealing with the addicted offender. Simply summarized, the data show that if addicted offenders are provided with well-structured drug treatment while under criminal justice control, their recidivism rates can be reduced by 50 to 60 percent for subsequent drug use and by more than 40 percent for further criminal behavior. Moreover, entry into drug treatment need not be completely voluntary in order for it to work. In fact, studies suggest that increased pressure to stay in treatment—whether from the legal system or from family members or employers—actually increases the amount of time patients remain in treatment and improves their treatment outcomes.

Findings such as these are the underpinning of a very important trend in drug control strategies now being implemented in the United States and many foreign countries. For example, some 40 percent of prisons and jails in this country now claim to provide some form of drug treatment to their addicted inmates, although we do not know the quality of the treatment provided. Diversion to drug treatment programs as an alternative to incarceration is gaining popularity across the United States. The widely applauded growth in drug treatment courts over the past five years—to more than 400—is another successful example of the blending of public health and public safety approaches. These drug courts use a combination of criminal justice sanctions and drug use monitoring and treatment tools to manage addicted offenders.

# Updating the Discussion

Understanding drug abuse and addiction in all their complexity demands that we rise above simplistic polarized thinking about drug issues. Addiction is both a public health and a public safety issue, not one or the other. We must deal with both the supply and the demand issues with equal vigor. Drug abuse and addiction are about both biology and behavior. One can have a disease and not be a hapless victim of it.

We also need to abandon our attraction to simplistic metaphors that only distract us from developing appropriate strategies. I, for one, will be in some ways sorry to see the War on Drugs metaphor go away, but go away it must. At some level, the notion of waging war is as appropriate for the illness of addiction as it is for our War on Cancer, which simply means bringing all forces to bear on the problem in a focused and energized way. But, sadly, this concept has been badly distorted and misused over time, and the War on Drugs never became what it should have been: the War on Drug Abuse and Addiction. Moreover, worrying about whether we are winning or losing this war has deteriorated to using simplistic and inappropriate measures such as counting drug addicts. In the end, it has only fueled discord. The War on Drugs metaphor has done nothing to advance the real conceptual challenges that need to be worked through.

I hope, though, that we will all resist the temptation to replace it with another catchy phrase that inevitably will devolve into a search for quick or easy-seeming solutions to our drug problems. We do not rely on simple metaphors or strategies to deal with our other major national problems such as education, health care, or national security. We are, after all, trying to solve truly monumental, multidimensional problems on a national or even international scale. To devalue them to the level of slogans does our public an injustice and dooms us to failure.

Understanding the health aspects of addiction is in no way incompatible with the need to control the supply of drugs. In fact, a public health approach to stemming an epidemic or spread of a disease always focuses comprehensively on the agent, the vector, and the host. In the case of drugs of abuse, the agent is the drug, the host is the abuser or addict, and the vector for transmitting the illness is clearly the drug suppliers and dealers that keep the agent flowing so readily. Prevention and treatment are the strategies to help protect the host. But just as we must deal with the flies and mosquitoes that spread infectious diseases, we must directly address all the vectors in the drug-supply system.

In order to be truly effective, the blended public health/public safety approaches advocated here must be implemented at all levels of society—local, state, and national. All drug problems are ultimately local in character and impact, since they differ so much across geographic settings and cultural contexts, and the most effective solutions are implemented at the local level. Each community must work through its own locally appropriate antidrug implementation strategies, and those strategies must be just as comprehensive and science-based as those instituted at the state or national level.

The message from the now very broad and deep array of scientific evidence is absolutely clear. If we as a society ever hope to make any real progress in dealing with our drug problems, we are going to have to rise above moral outrage that addicts have "done it to themselves" and develop strategies that are as sophisticated and as complex as the problem itself. Whether addicts are "victims" or not, once addicted they must be seen as "brain disease patients."

Moreover, although our national traditions do argue for compassion for those who are sick, no matter how they contracted their illnesses, I recognize that many addicts have disrupted not only their own lives but those of their families and their broader communities, and thus do not easily generate compassion. However, no matter how one may feel about addicts and their behavioral histories, an extensive body of scientific evidence shows that approaching addiction as a treatable illness is extremely cost-effective, both financially and in terms of broader societal impacts such as family violence, crime, and other forms of social upheaval. Thus, it is clearly in everyone's interest to get past the hurt and indignation and slow the drain of drugs on society by enhancing drug use prevention efforts and providing treatment to all who need it.

**ALAN I. LESHNER** is director of the National Institute on Drug Abuse at the National Institutes of Health.

From California Society of Addiction Medicine Legislative Day Information Book, February 1, 2006, pp. 92–98. Published by the National Institute on Drug Abuse.

# Predicting Addiction

**Behavioral genetics uses twins and time to decipher the origins of addiction and learn who is most vulnerable.**

Lisa N. Legrand, William G. Iacono and Matt McGue

In 1994, the 45-year-old daughter of Senator and former presidential nominee George McGovern froze to death outside a bar in Madison, Wisconsin. Terry McGovern's death followed a night of heavy drinking and a lifetime of battling alcohol addiction. The Senator's middle child had been talented and charismatic, but also rebellious. She started drinking at 13, became pregnant at 15 and experimented with marijuana and LSD in high school. She was sober during much of her 30s but eventually relapsed. By the time she died, Terry had been through many treatment programs and more than 60 detoxifications.

Her story is not unique. Even with strong family support, failure to overcome an addiction is common. Success rates vary by treatment type, severity of the condition and the criteria for success. But typically, fewer than a third of alcoholics are recovered a year or two after treatment. Thus, addiction may be thought of as a chronic, relapsing illness. Like other serious psychiatric conditions, it can cause a lifetime of recurrent episodes and treatments.

Given these somber prospects, the best strategy for fighting addiction may be to prevent it in the first place. But warning young people about the dangers of addiction carries little force when many adults drink openly without apparent consequences. Would specific warnings for individuals with a strong genetic vulnerability to alcoholism be more effective? Senator McGovern became convinced that his daughter possessed such a vulnerability, as other family members also struggled with dependency. Perhaps Terry would have taken a different approach to alcohol, or avoided it altogether, if she had known that something about her biology made drinking particularly dangerous for her.

How can we identify people—at a young enough age to intervene—who have a high, inherent risk of becoming addicted? Does unusual susceptibility arise from differences at the biochemical level? And what social or environmental factors might tip the scales for kids at greatest risk? That is, what kind of parenting, or peer group, or neighborhood conditions might encourage—or inhibit—the expression of "addiction" genes? These questions are the focus of our research.

## Minnesota Twins

We have been able to answer some of these questions by examining the life histories of almost 1,400 pairs of twins. Our study of addictive behavior is part of a larger project, the Minnesota Center for Twin Family Research (MCTFR), which has studied the health and development of twins from their pre-teen years through adolescence and into adulthood. Beginning at age 11 (or 17 for a second group), the participants and their parents cooperated with a barrage of questionnaires, interviews, brainwave analyses and blood tests every three years. The twin cohorts are now 23 and 29, respectively, so we have been able to observe them as children before exposure to addictive substances, as teenagers who were often experimenting and as young adults who had passed through the stage of greatest risk for addiction.

Studies of twins are particularly useful for analyzing the origins of a behavior like addiction. Our twin pairs have grown up in the same family environment but have different degrees of genetic similarity. Monozygotic or identical twins have identical genes, but dizygotic or fraternal twins share on average only half of their segregating genes. If the two types of twins are equally similar for a trait, we know that genes are unimportant for that trait. But when monozygotic twins are more similar than dizygotic twins, we conclude that genes have an effect.

This article reviews some of what we know about the development of addiction, including some recent findings from the MCTFR about early substance abuse. Several established markers can predict later addiction and, together with recent research, suggest a provocative conclusion: that addiction may be only one of many related behaviors that stem from the same genetic root. In other words, much of the heritable risk may be nonspecific. Instead, what is passed from parent to child is a tendency toward a group of behaviors, of which addiction is only one of several possible outcomes.

# Markers of Risk

**Personality.** Psychologists can distinguish at-risk youth by their personality, family history, brainwave patterns and behavior. For example, certain personality traits do not distribute equally among addicts and nonaddicts: The addiction vulnerable tend to be more impulsive, unruly and easily bored. They're generally outgoing, sociable, expressive and rebellious, and they enjoy taking risks. They are more likely to question authority and challenge tradition.

Some addicts defy these categories, and having a certain personality type doesn't doom one to addiction. But such traits do place individuals at elevated risk. For reasons not completely understood, they accompany addiction much more frequently than the traits of being shy, cautious and conventional.

Although these characteristics do not directly cause addiction, neither are they simply the consequences of addiction. In fact, teachers' impressions of their 11-year-old students predicted alcohol problems 16 years later, according to a Swedish study led by C. Robert Cloninger (now at Washington University in St. Louis). Boys low in "harm avoidance" (ones who lacked fear and inhibition) and high in "novelty seeking" (in other words, impulsive, disorderly, easily bored and distracted) were almost 20 times more likely to have future alcohol problems than boys without these traits. Other studies of children in separate countries at different ages confirm that personality is predictive.

**Family Background.** Having a parent with a substance-abuse disorder is another established predictor of a child's future addiction. One recent and intriguing discovery from the MCTFR is that assessing this risk can be surprisingly straightforward, particularly for alcoholism. The father's answer to "What is the largest amount of alcohol you ever consumed in a 24-hour period?" is highly informative: The greater the amount, the greater his children's risk. More than 24 drinks in 24 hours places his children in an especially risky category.

How can one simple question be so predictive? Its answer is laden with information, including tolerance—the ability, typically developed over many drinking episodes, to consume larger quantities of alcohol before becoming intoxicated—and the loss of control that mark problematic drinking. It is also possible that a father who equivocates on other questions that can formally diagnose alcoholism—such as whether he has been unsuccessful at cutting down on his drinking or whether his drinking has affected family and work—may give a frank answer to this question. In our society, episodes of binge drinking, of being able to "hold your liquor," are sometimes a source of male pride.

**Brainwaves.** A third predictor comes directly from the brain itself. By using scalp electrodes to detect the electrical signals of groups of neurons, we can record characteristic patterns of brain activity generated by specific visual stimuli. In the complex squiggle of evoked brainwaves, the relative size of one peak, called P300, indicates addiction risk. Having a smaller P300 at age 17 predicts the development of an alcohol or drug problem by age 20. Prior differences in consumption don't explain this observation, as the reduced-amplitude P300 (P3-AR) is not a consequence of alcohol or drug ingestion. Rather, genes strongly influence this trait: P3-AR is often detectable in the children of fathers with substance-use disorders even before these problems emerge in the offspring. The physiological nature of P300 makes it an especially interesting marker, as it may originate from "addiction" genes more directly than any behavior.

**Precocious Experimentation.** Lastly, at-risk youth are distinguished by the young age at which they first try alcohol without parental permission. Although the vast majority of people try alcohol at some point during their life, it's relatively unusual to try alcohol *before* the age of 15. In the MCTFR sample of over 2,600 parents who had tried alcohol, only 12 percent of the mothers and 22 percent of the fathers did so before the age of 15. In this subset, 52 percent of the men and 25 percent of the women were alcoholics. For parents who first tried alcohol after age 19, the comparable rates were 13 percent and 2 percent, respectively. So, what distinguishes alcoholism risk is not *whether* a person tries alcohol during their teen years, but *when* they try it.

In light of these data, we cannot regard very early experimentation with alcohol as simply a normal rite of passage. Moreover, drinking at a young age often co-occurs with sex, the use of tobacco and illicit drugs, and rulebreaking behaviors. This precocious experimentation could indicate that the individual has inherited the type of freewheeling, impulsive personality that elevates the risk of addiction. But early experimentation may be a problem all by itself. It, and the behaviors that tend to co-occur with it, decrease the likelihood of sobriety-encouraging experiences and increase the chances of mixing with troubled peers and clashing with authority figures.

# A General, Inherited Risk

Some of these hallmarks of risk are unsurprising. Most people know that addiction runs in families, and they may intuit that certain brain functions could differ in addiction-prone individuals. But how can people's gregariousness or their loathing of dull tasks or the age at which they first had sex show a vulnerability to addiction? The answer seems to be that although addiction risk is strongly heritable, the inheritance is fairly nonspecific. The inherited risk corresponds to a certain temperament or disposition that goes along with so-called *extertializing* tendencies. Addiction is only one of several ways this disposition may be expressed.

Externalizing behaviors include substance abuse, but also "acting out" and other indicators of behavioral under control or disinhibition. In childhood, externalizing traits include hyperactivity, "oppositionality" (negative and defiant behavior) and antisocial behavior, which breaks institutional and social rules. An antisocial child may lie, get in fights, steal, vandalize or skip school. In adulthood, externalizing tendencies may lead to a personality marked by low constraint, drug or alcohol abuse, and antisocial behaviors, including irresponsibility, dishonesty, impulsivity, lawlessness and aggression. Antisociality, like most traits, falls on a continuum. A moderately antisocial person may never intentionally hurt someone, but he might make impulsive decisions, take physical and financial risks or shirk responsibility.

It's worth reiterating that an externalizing disposition simply increases the risk of demonstrating problematic behavior. An individual with such tendencies could express them in ways that are not harmful to themselves and actually help society: Fire fighters, rescue workers, test pilots, surgeons and entrepreneurs are often gregarious, relatively uninhibited sensation-seekers— that is, moderate externalizers.

So a genetic inclination for externalizing can lead to addiction, hyperactivity, acting-out behavior, criminality, a sensation-seeking personality or *all* of these things. Although the contents of this list may seem haphazard, psychologists combine them into a single group because they all stem from the same *latent factor*. Latent factors are hypothesized constructs that help explain the observed correlations between various traits or behaviors.

For example, grades in school generally correlate with one another. People who do well in English tend to get good marks in art history, algebra and geology. Why? Because academic ability affects grades, regardless of the subject matter. In statistical lingo, academic ability is the "general, latent factor" and the course grades are the "observed indicators" of that factor. Academic ability is latent because it is not directly measured; rather, the statistician concludes that it exists and causes the grades to vary systematically between people.

Statistical analyses consistently show that externalizing is a general, latent factor—a common denominator—for a suite of behaviors that includes addiction. Furthermore, the various markers of risk support this conclusion: Childhood characteristics that indicate later problems with alcohol also point to the full spectrum of externalizing behaviors and traits. Thus, drinking alcohol before 15 doesn't just predict future alcohol and drug problems, but also future antisocial behavior. A parent with a history of excessive binge drinking is apt to have children not only with substance-use problems, but with behavioral problems as well. And a reduced-amplitude P300 not only appears in children with a familial risk for alcoholism, but in kids with a familial risk for hyperactivity, antisocial behavior or illicit drug disorders.

The associations between externalizing behaviors aren't surprising to clinicians. Comorbidity—the increased chance of having other disorders if you have one of them—is the norm, not the exception, for individuals and families. A father with a cocaine habit is more likely to find that his daughter is getting into trouble for stealing or breaking school rules. At first glance, the child's behavioral problems look like products of the stress, conflict and dysfunction that go with having an addict in the family. These are certainly aggravating factors. However, the familial and genetically informative MCTFR data have allowed us to piece together a more precise explanation.

Environment has a strong influence on a child's behavior—living with an addict is rife with challenges—but genes also play a substantial role. Estimates of the genetic effect on externalizing behaviors vary by indicator and age, but among older adolescents and adults, well over half of the differences between

people's externalizing tendencies result from inheriting different genes.

Our analysis of the MCTFR data indicates that children inherit the general, latent factor of externalizing rather than specific behavioral factors. Thus, an antisocial mother does not pass on genes that code simply for antisocial behavior, but they do confer vulnerability to a range of adolescent disorders and behaviors. Instead of encounters with the law, her adolescent son may have problems with alcohol or drugs. The outcomes are different, but the same genes—expressed differently under different environmental conditions—predispose them both.

# The Role of the Environment

Even traits with a strong genetic component may be influenced by environmental factors. Monozygotic twins exemplify this principle. Despite their matching DNA, their height, need for glasses, disease susceptibility or personality (just to name a few) may differ.

When one member of a monozygotic pair is alcoholic, the likelihood of alcoholism in the other is only about 50 percent. The high heritability of externalizing behaviors suggests that the second twin, if not alcoholic, may be antisocial or dependent on another substance. But sometimes the second twin is problem free. DNA is never destiny.

Behavioral geneticists have worked to quantify the role of the environment in addiction, but as a group we have done much less to specify it. Although we know that 50 percent of the variance in alcohol dependence comes from the environment, we are still in the early stages of determining what those environmental factors are. This ignorance may seem surprising, as scientists have spent decades identifying the environmental precursors to addiction and antisocial behavior. But only a small percentage of that research incorporated genetic controls.

Instead, many studies simply related environmental variation to children's eventual problems or accomplishments. A classic example of this failure to consider genetic influence is the repeated observation that children who grow up with lots of books in their home tend to do better in school. But concluding that books create an academic child assumes (falsely) that children are born randomly into families—that parent-child resemblance is purely social. Of course, parents actually contribute to their children's environment *and* their genes. Moreover, parents tend to provide environments that complement their children's genotypes: Smart parents often deliver both "smart" genes and an enriched environment. Athletic parents usually provide "athletic" genes and many opportunities to express them. And, unfortunately, parents with addiction problems tend to provide a genetic vulnerability coupled with a home in which alcohol or drugs are available and abusing them is normal.

To understand the true experiential origins of a behavior, one must first disentangle the influence of genes. By using genetically informative samples, we can subtract genetic influences and conclude with greater confidence that a particular environmental factor affects behavior. Using this approach, our data suggest that deviant peers and poor parent-child relationships exert true environmental influences that promote substance use and externalizing behaviors during early adolescence.

When considering the effect of environment on behavior, or any complex trait, it's helpful to imagine a continuum of liability. Inherited vulnerability determines where a person begins on the continuum (high versus low risk). From that point, psychosocial or environmental stressors such as peer pressure or excessive conflict with parents can push an individual along the continuum and over a disease threshold.

However, sometimes the environment actually modifies gene expression. In other words, the relative influence of genes on a behavior can vary by setting. We see this context-dependent gene expression in recent, unpublished work comparing study participants from rural areas (population less than 10,000) with those from more urban settings. Within cities of 10,000 or more, genes substantially influence which adolescents use illicit substances or show other aspects of the externalizing continuum—just as earlier research indicated. But in very rural areas, environmental (rather than genetic) factors overwhelmingly account for differences in externalizing behavior.

One way to interpret this finding is that urban environments, with their wider variety of social niches, allow for a more complete expression of genetically influenced traits. Whether a person's genes nudge her to substance use and rule-breaking, or abstinence and obedience, the city may offer more opportunities to follow those urges. At the same time, finite social prospects in the country may allow more rural parents to monitor and control their adolescents' activities and peer-group selection, thereby minimizing the impact of genes. This rural-urban difference is especially interesting because it represents a gene-by-environment interaction. The genes that are important determinants of behavior in one group of people are just not as important in another.

# The Future of Addiction Research

This complex interplay of genes and environments makes progress slow. But investigators have the data and statistical tools to answer many important addiction-related questions. Moreover, the tempo of discovery will increase with advances in molecular genetics.

In the last fifteen years, geneticists have identified a handful of specific genes related to alcohol metabolism and synapse function that occur more often in alcoholics. But the task of accumulating the entire list of contributing genes is daunting. Many genes influence behavior, and the relative importance of a single gene may differ across ethnic or racial populations. As a result, alcoholism-associated genes in one population may not exert a measurable influence in a different group, even in well-controlled studies. There are also different pathways to addiction, and some people's alcoholism may be more environmental than genetic in origin. Consequently, not only is any one gene apt to have small effects on behavior, but that gene may be absent in a substantial number of addicts.

Nonetheless, some day scientists should be able to estimate risk by reading the sequence of a person's DNA. Setting aside

the possibility of a futuristic dystopia, this advance will usher in a new type of psychology. Investigators will be able to observe those individuals with especially high (or low) genetic risks for externalizing as they respond, over a lifetime, to different types of environmental stressors.

This type of research is already beginning. Avshalom Caspi, now at the University of Wisconsin, and his colleagues divided a large group of males from New Zealand based on the expression level of a gene that encodes a neurotransmitter-metabolizing enzyme, monoamine oxidase A or MAOA. In combination with the life histories of these men, the investigators demonstrated that the consequences of an abusive home varied by genotype. The gene associated with high levels of MAOA was protective—those men were less likely to show antisocial behaviors after childhood maltreatment than the low-MAOA group.

Further advances in molecular genetics will bring opportunities for more studies of this type. When investigators can accurately rank experimental participants by their genetic liability to externalizing, they will gain insight into the complexities of gene-environment interplay and answer several intriguing questions: What type of family environments are most at-risk children born into? When children with different genetic risks grow up in the same family, do they create unique environments by seeking distinct friends and experiences? Do they elicit different parenting styles from the same parents? Could a low-risk sibling keep a high-risk child from trouble if they share a close friendship? Is one type of psychosocial stressor more apt to lead to substance use while another leads to antisocial behavior?

Molecular genetics will eventually deepen our understanding of the biochemistry and biosocial genesis of addiction. In the interim, quantitative geneticists such as ourselves continue to characterize the development of behavior in ways that will assist molecular geneticists in their work. For example, if there is genetic overlap between alcoholism, drug dependence and antisocial behavior—as the MCTFR data suggest—then it may help to examine extreme externalizers, rather than simply alcoholics, when searching for the genes that produce alcoholism vulnerability.

# Much Left to Learn

Although the MCTFR data have resolved some addiction-related questions, many others remain, and our team has just begun to scratch the surface of possible research. Our work with teenagers indicates that externalizing is a key factor in early-onset substance-use problems, but the path to later-life addiction may be distinct. Some evidence suggests that genes play a lesser role in later-onset addiction. Moreover, the markers of risk may vary. Being prone to worry, becoming upset easily and tending toward negative moods may, with age, become more important indicators. We don't yet know. However, the MCTFR continues to gather information about its participants as they approach their 30s, and we hope to keep following this group into their 40s and beyond.

Meanwhile, the evidence suggests that for early-onset addiction, most relevant genes are not specific to alcoholism or drug dependence. Instead, the same genes predispose an overlapping set of disorders within the externalizing spectrum. This conclusion has significant implications for prevention: Some impulsive risk-takers, frequent rule-breakers and oppositional children may be just as much at risk as early users.

At the same time, many kids with a genetic risk for externalizing don't seem to require any sort of special intervention; as it is, they turn out just fine. DNA may nudge someone in a certain direction, but it doesn't force them to go there.

# Bibliography

Burt, S. A., M. McGue, R. F. Krueger and W. G. Iacono. 2005. How are parent-child conflict and childhood externalizing symptoms related over time? Results from a genetically informative cross-tagged study. *Development and Psychopathology* 17:1–21.

Caspi, A., J. McClay, T. E. Moffitt, J. Mill, J. Martin, I. W. Craig, A. Taylor and R. Poulton. 2002. Role of genotype in the cycle of violence in maltreated children. *Science* 297:851–854.

Cloninger, C. R., S. Sigvardsson and M. Bohman. 1988. Childhood personality predicts alcohol abuse in young adults. *Alcoholism: Clinical and Experimental Research* 12:494–505.

Hicks, B. M., R. F. Krueger, W. G. Iacono, M. McGue and C. J. Patrick. 2004. Family transmission and heritability of externalizing disorders: A twin-family study. *Archives of General Psychiatry* 61:922–928.

Iacono, W. G., S. M. Malone and M. McGue. 2003. Substance use disorders, externalizing psychopathology, and P300 event-related potential amplitude. *International Journal of Psychophysiology* 48:147–178.

Krueger, R. F., B. M. Hicks, C. J. Patrick, S. R. Carlson, W. G. Iacono and M. McGue. 2002. Etiologic connections among substance dependence, antisocial behavior, and personality: Modeling the externalizing spectrum. *Journal of Abnormal Psychology* 111:411–424.

Malone, S. M., W. G. Iacono and M. McGue. 2002. Drinks of the father: Father's maximum number of drinks consumed predicts externalizing disorders, substance use, and substance use disorders in preadolescent and adolescent offspring. *Alcoholism: Clinical and Experimental Research* 26:1823–1832.

McGovern, G. 1996. *Terry: My Daughter's Life-and-Death Struggle With Alcoholism.* New York: Random House.

McGue, M., W. G. Iacono, L. N. Legrand, S. Malone and I. Elkins. 2001. The origins and consequences of age at first drink. I. Associations with substance-abuse disorders, disinhibitory behavior and psychopathology, and P3 amplitude. *Alcoholism: Clinical and Experimental Research* 25:1156–1165.

Porjesz, B., and H. Begleiter. 2003. Alcoholism and human electrophysiology. *Alcohol Research & Health* 27:153–160.

Turkheimer, E., H. H. Goldsmith and I. I. Gottesman. 1995. Some conceptual deficiencies in "developmental" behavioral genetics: Comment. *Human Development* 38:142–153.

Walden, B., M. McGue, W. G. Iacono, S. A. Burt and I. Elkins. 2004. Identifying shared environmental contributions to early substance use: The respective roles of peers and parents. *Journal of Abnormal Psychology* 113:440–450.

**LISA N. LEGRAND** received her Ph.D. in behavioral genetics and clinical psychology from the University of Minnesota in 2003 and is currently a research associate at the Minnesota Center for Twin and Family Research (MCTFR). **WILLIAM G. IACONO** is a Distinguished McKnight University Professor at the University of Minnesota and a past president of the Society for Psychophysiological Research. **MATT McGUE** is a professor of psychology at the University of Minnesota and a past president of the Behavior Genetics Association. He and William Iacono have co-directed the MCTFR for the last dozen years. Address for Legrand: MCTFR, 75 East River Road, Minneapolis, MN 55455-0344. Internet: **legra002@umn.edu**

# Staying Sober

## Better understanding of how alcohol alters brain chemistry reveals mechanisms for beating dependency

Andreas Heinz

Former alcoholics have a tough time resisting the urge to drink in two particularly trying situations. Analysis of what is happening in their heads under these circumstances is greatly improving neurobiologists' understanding of how chronic alcohol use changes the brain. And their findings suggest measures that could help people abstain.

The following case illustrates one of the most tempting situations. Hank had been dry for several weeks thanks to a radical withdrawal program, but a simple walk past Pete's Tavern on any given night almost erased his will to abstain. During the daytime he did not feel a craving for alcohol, but when he passed the bar in the evening—when he saw the warm light through the windows and heard the glasses clinking—he would be sorely tempted to run inside for a beer. Addiction researchers call this phenomenon "conditioned desire." If a person had always consumed alcohol in the same situation, an encounter with the familiar stimuli will make the feeling of need for the substance almost irresistible. Then, even after years of abstinence, consuming a single drink can set off a powerful longing to imbibe more and more.

Ken's story illustrates the other common temptation. Ken had given up alcohol and was doing fine, even after he had lost his job and had begun collecting unemployment. But on one visit to the unemployment office downtown, a bureaucrat refused to approve his benefits. After a fruitless argument, Ken left. While standing on the subway platform for a train home, he suddenly began to sweat, twitch and feel sick. What he really wanted was a bottle. Before he had given up drinking, he would have automatically taken a swig whenever he faced a tense situation. After the argument, his brain—shaped by experience—expected the calming effect of alcohol. When the drug did not come, he began to suffer what experts call "conditioned withdrawal" symptoms.

**The very people who can drink others under the table are the ones who are especially at risk.**

Conditioned desire and conditioned withdrawal are produced in the brain by different mechanisms. In recent years, neuroscientists have investigated both phenomena thoroughly. They now feel comfortable explaining how routine alcohol consumption changes circuitry in the brain in ways that lead to addiction, and they are beginning to develop new medications that could dramatically reduce the chances of falling off the wagon.

## High Tolerance Is Bad

For centuries, societies have labeled alcoholics as self-indulgent people who lack willpower. Although the decision to drink in the first place does rest with each individual, traits inherent in a person's brain cells can strongly influence the slippery slope into addiction. Furthermore, once a person is addicted, simple willpower may be insufficient to break the grip; drugs that can reverse the brain's alcohol-altered chemistry may be necessary.

An individual's sensitivity to alcohol's effects on neurons significantly influences the chance that he or she can become addicted. According to Marc A. Schuckit, a psychiatry professor at the University of California, San Diego, and director of the VA San Diego Healthcare System's Alcohol and Drug Treatment Program, one of the best protections against addiction is nausea; people who readily get sick as they drink are less likely to consume enough, consistently, to the point that they become addicted. The very people who can drink others under the table are the ones who are especially at risk. Inhibitory and excitatory messenger substances in the brain become unbalanced in response to excessive alcohol doses. The people who can handle more drinking send more alcohol to the brain, thereby increasing over time the chance that a permanent imbalance will develop.

This brain chemistry was partially worked out in rhesus monkeys that had to grow up without their mothers, some in the laboratory and some in the wild. James Dee Higley, a research psychologist at the National Institute on Alcohol Abuse and Alcoholism, learned that these monkeys reacted less to drinks of high-proof alcohol than normal monkeys did. The motherless monkeys were similarly insensitive to other substances that, like alcohol, increase the impact of the neurotransmitter GABA (gamma aminobutyric acid), which inhibits signals between neurons so the cells do not get overexcited. As a result of this reduced sensitivity, the rhesus monkeys raised in isolation could drink an unusually large quantity of alcohol—and they sought to do so when researchers provided free access to the drug. Human studies have revealed similar changes in people's brains.Altered brain chemistry resulting from experience is just one factor that contributes to individual differences in susceptibility. Genes play a role, too. Schuckit maintains that up to half the causal factors for reduced sensitivity to alcohol are inherited. In a small-scale study that tracked people for 15 years, Schuckit's research group found that a variation in the gene that codes for a part of the GABA receptor may be related to low sensitivity to alcohol. Although high tolerance to alcohol from adjusted brain chemistry or genetics may seem like a protective trait, it is ultimately damning. If such an individual consumes quantities of alcohol regularly, his or her brain and body will gradually become accustomed to the poison, almost assuring the person will become addicted.

# Dangerous Accommodation

Tinkering with the GABA system could perhaps offer a fix, but alcohol's effects on brain chemistry depend on more than just GABA uptake. The drug does not merely boost the inhibitory function of GABA on neurons; it also blocks the excitatory effects of their NMDA (N-methyl-D-aspartate) receptors. These receptors bind glutamate, which comes from neighboring neurons and enables the receiving neuron to forward signals on to others in the network. Guochuan Tsai, now at the University of California, Los Angeles, and Joseph T. Coyle of Harvard Medical School have discovered that the brain, when exposed to chronic alcohol consumption, creates additional NMDA receptors to compensate for the blocking effect. The brain is trying to find a new balance between the underexcitatory action of glutamate and the overinhibitory action of GABA.

The repercussions come, however, when alcohol is withdrawn for a few days or, for hard-core drinkers, even overnight. The NMDA receptors maintain their increased sensitivity, and the GABA receptors maintain their reduced sensitivity. Yet without the alcohol that this new balance is attempting to counter, the brain's networks fire erratically, causing withdrawal symptoms. Anyone who wakes up with tremors, sweating or nausea and immediately needs alcohol is already critically dependent. The victim's brain is so utterly adapted to the drug that even the few nighttime hours without it are enough to throw the new chemistry into a tailspin.

Such withdrawal symptoms can be combated with agents such as chlormethiazol or a benzodiazepine, which restore the sensitivity of GABA receptors and calm the patient. Acamprosate suppresses NMDA receptors and seems especially helpful for persons suffering from conditioned withdrawal. Clinical studies show that 30 to 40 percent of patients remain dry for the first year after detoxification while taking acamprosate. The drug is particularly effective during the first few hard months

of abstinence, when relapse rates are the highest. The results still leave a high failure rate, however, necessitating additional therapeutic measures such as self-help groups and individual counseling.

## Drugs can reduce the alcoholic brain's oversensitivity to glutamate and oversupply of dopamine.

One reason medication can be insufficient is that alcohol also works on dopamine, the neurotransmitter that runs the motivation and reward system. Normally, stimuli that are important to survival—related, for example, to feeding and sex—trigger the release of dopamine. The neurotransmitter increases our anticipation of happiness and makes us want these things. The pleasant reward feelings, in turn, make us seek the sensations again and again, and we engage more strongly in the behaviors that cause dopamine to be released. Addictive drugs such as heroin unleash the same mechanisms.

As it does for GABA and NMDA, brain chemistry related to the reward system also adapts to fit the constant presence of alcohol. The brain reduces the number of dopamine binding sites on neurons, called D2 receptors, to protect itself from a persistent oversupply of the neurotransmitter. Alcohol affects other aspects of the motivation system as well. When alcoholics look at photographs of beer or wine, the regions of their brain that control attention are aroused more than they are for nonalcoholics, according to MRI imaging studies done in my lab. The fewer the D2 receptors they have, the more activity is elicited in their attention centers by the sight of alcohol.

This predilection explains why it is so difficult for alcoholics to find other stimuli pleasant and rewarding. It seems almost impossible for them to become interested in anything new that might bring satisfaction—be it a relationship, a hobby or even good food. The more serious the damage to the dopamine system, the more fixated attention becomes on the familiar images of alcohol—even when the person is lying inside the narrow, noisy tube of an MRI machine, when the brain knows it is not about to receive beer or whiskey.

The extent to which the attention centers can be activated in this lab situation highlights the severe problems recovering alcoholics have ignoring the advertising all around them. About a third of the subjects in our studies complain about the powerful effects of television commercials, especially when they are broadcast in situations in which patients would previously have been drinking, such as while watching a football game.

## Tainted Pleasure

Although dopamine directs desire, the actual feeling of pleasure comes from endorphins—the body's own opiatelike substances. Once again, regular drug use changes the system. Alcoholics develop a higher number of binding sites for endorphins. When they drink, their neurons bind more endorphins, producing a greater feeling of pleasure.

Certain medications have been designed to alter this interchange. Naltrexone, for example, blocks the receptors and can reduce the risk of relapse considerably. Recovering alcoholics say that if they are taking naltrexone and have a drink, the taste is foreign, to the point of being terrible. Yet the drug alone, without psychosocial care, is not enough, because for some patients the second or third drink will start to taste good again. A patient must want to live abstinently; then, naltrexone will help him or her avoid that first sip.

With the expanding understanding of how alcohol alters the action of neurotransmitters, it is becoming clear that people addicted to alcohol are suffering from dramatic changes in brain activity. No particular personality type is prone to becoming dependent. The culprit is excessive alcohol consumption itself, which changes the brain so that victims can no longer free themselves from the bottle. It is time to destigmatize alcoholism and to develop better methods of breaking dependency and preventing relapse. The knowledge gained from research certainly opens avenues for creating new drugs. Still, alcoholics need one aid above all: people who will listen to and stand by them as they strive to recover.

---

MANDREAS HEINZ is director of the Clinic for Psychiatry and Psychotherapy at Charité University in Berlin.

# The Effects of Alcohol on Physiological Processes and Biological Development

Adolescence is a period of rapid growth and physical change; a central question is whether consuming alcohol during this stage can disrupt development in ways that have long-term consequences. In general, the existing evidence suggests that adolescents rarely exhibit the more severe chronic disorders associated with alcohol dependence such as liver cirrhosis, hepatitis, gastritis, and pancreatitis. Adolescents who drink heavily, however, may experience some adverse effects on the liver, bone, growth, and endocrine development. Evidence also is mounting, at least in animal models, that early alcohol use may have detrimental effects on the developing brain, perhaps leading to problems with cognition later in life. This article summarizes the physiological effects of alcohol on adolescents, including a look at the long-term behavioral and physiological consequences of early drinking.

## Overview

The damage that long-term heavy alcohol consumption can do to the health of adults is well documented. Some research suggests that, even over the shorter time frame of adolescence, drinking alcohol can harm the liver, bones, endocrine system, and brain, and interfere with growth. Adolescence is a period of rapid growth and physical change; a central question is whether consuming alcohol during this stage can disrupt development in ways that have long-term consequences.

Liver disease is a common consequence of heavy drinking. More severe alcohol-related liver disease typically reflects years of heavy alcohol use. However, elevated liver enzymes that are markers of harm have been found in adolescents with alcohol use disorders and in overweight adolescents who consume more modest amounts of alcohol.

During puberty, accelerating cascades of growth factors and sex hormones set off sexual maturation, growth in stature and muscle mass, and bone development. Studies in humans have found that alcohol can lower the levels of growth and sex hormones in both adolescent boys and girls. In animals, alcohol has been found to disrupt the interaction between the brain, the pituitary gland (which regulates secretion of sex hormones), and the ovaries, as well as systems within the ovaries that are involved in regulating sex hormones. In adolescent male animals, both short- and long-term alcohol administration suppresses testosterone; alcohol use also alters growth hormone levels, the effects of which differ with age.

Studies on alcohol and adolescent bone development are limited. In studies of male and female rats, chronic alcohol consumption (an alcohol diet) for the length of adolescence was to stunt limb growth. One study found that feeding female rats alcohol in a way that mimics binge drinking resulted in either increases in bone length and density or in no change with more frequent bingeing. In human adolescent males but not females, studies have found that alcohol consumption decreases bone density.

The brain also is changing during adolescence. Adolescents tend to drink larger quantities on each drinking occasion than adults; this may in part be because adolescents are less sensitive to some of the unpleasant effects of intoxication. However, research suggests that adolescents may be more sensitive to some of alcohol's harmful effects on brain function. Studies in rats found that alcohol impairs the ability of adolescent animals more than adult animals to learn a task that requires spatial memory. Research also suggests a mechanism for this effect; in adolescents more than adults, alcohol inhibits the process in which, with repeated experience, nerve impulses travel more easily across the gap between nerve cells (i.e., neurons) involved in the task being learned. The reasons for these differences in sensitivity to alcohol remain unclear.

Research also has found differences in the effects of binge-like drinking in adolescents compared with adults. Normally, as people age from adolescence to adulthood, they become more sensitive to alcohol's effects on motor coordination. In one study, however, adolescent rats exposed to intermittent alcohol never developed this increased sensitivity. Other studies in both human subjects and animals suggest that the adolescent brain may be more vulnerable than the adult brain to chronic alcohol abuse.

Young people who reported beginning to drink at age 14 or younger also were four times more likely to report meeting the criteria for alcohol dependence at some point in their lives than were those who began drinking after age 21. Although it is possible that early alcohol use may be a marker for those who are at risk for alcohol disorders, an important question is whether early alcohol exposure may alter neurodevelopment in a way that increases risk of later abuse. Research in rats has found that prenatal or early postnatal exposure to alcohol results in a greater preference for the odor and consumption of alcohol later in life. Social experiences associated with youthful drinking also may influence drinking later in life. Additional research is needed to resolve the question of whether and how early alcohol exposure might contribute to drinking problems years down the road.

# Alcohol's Effects on the Liver, The Neuroendocrine System, and Bone

The medical consequences of chronic alcohol abuse and dependence have been well documented in adults. They include liver disease, lung disease, compromised immune function, endocrine disorders, and brain changes. Investigations of the health problems associated with adolescent alcohol abuse are sparse and rely mainly on self-report (see Clark et al. 2001; Aarons et al. 1999; Brown and Tapert 2004). In general, the existing evidence suggests that adolescents rarely exhibit the more severe chronic disorders associated with alcohol dependence, such as liver cirrhosis, hepatitis, gastritis, and pancreatitis. However, more research is needed to determine whether severe alcohol-induced organ damage is strictly a cumulative process that begins in adolescence and culminates in adulthood as a result of long-term chronic heavy drinking or whether serious alcohol-related health problems can emerge during the teenage years. The few studies available indicate that adolescents who drink heavily experience adverse effects on the liver, bones, growth, and endocrine development, as summarized below. The effects of chronic alcohol consumption on the adolescent brain are discussed in the section "Long-Term Behavioral and Physiological Consequences of Early Drinking."

## Liver Effects

Elevated liver enzymes have been found in some adolescents who drink alcohol. Clark and colleagues (2001) found that adolescent alcohol use disorders were associated with higher gamma-glutamyl transpeptidase (GGT) and alanine amino transferase (ALT). Moreover, young drinkers who also are overweight or obese exhibit elevated levels of serum ALT with even modest amounts of alcohol intake (Strauss et al. 2000).

## Growth and Endocrine Effects

In general, there has been a gradual decline in the onset of female puberty over the last century, at least when puberty is defined by age at menarche (Tanner 1989). Whether initiation of female puberty is continuing to decline and at what rate are the subjects of some debate (Lee et al. 2001; Herman-Giddens et al. 1997). Much less information exists on pubertal development in males because of the greater difficulty in assessing developmental milestones. However, a recent study comparing data from two national surveys, one conducted between 1988 and 1994 and the other between 1963 and 1970, found that American boys from the later generation had earlier onset of some pubertal stages as measured by standard Tanner staging (Herman-Giddens et al. 2001; Karpati et al. 2002). Perhaps not surprisingly, early puberty—especially among girls—is associated with early use of alcohol, tobacco, and other drugs (Wilson et al. 1994; Dick et al. 2000). In addition, alcohol use in early maturing adolescents has implications for normal growth and neuroendocrine development.

In both males and females, puberty is a period of activation of the hypothalamic-pituitary-gonadal (HPG) axis. Pulsatile secretion of gonadotrophin-releasing hormone (GnRH) from the hypothalamus stimulates pituitary secretion of follicle-stimulating hormone (FSH) and luteinizing hormone (LH) pulses, followed by marked increases in gonadal sex steroid output (estrogen and testosterone), which in turn increases growth hormone (GH) and insulin-like growth factor-1 (IGF-1) production (see Mauras et al. 1996). Data from several studies suggest that both androgens and estrogens stimulate GH production, but that estrogen controls the feedback mechanism of GH production during puberty even in males (Mauras et al. 1996; Dees et al. 2001). The increase in these hormones not only promotes maturation of the gonads but also affects growth, muscle mass, and mineralization of the skeleton. Thus, alcohol consumed during rapid development (i.e., prior to or during puberty) has the potential to disrupt normal growth and endocrine development through its effects on the hypothalamus, the pituitary gland, and the various target organs such as the ovaries and testes.

Most human and animal research on alcohol and endocrine development has been conducted in females, but the limited data on both genders suggest that alcohol can have substantial effects on neuroendocrine function (see Dees et al. 2001; Emanuele et al. 1998; Emanuele et al. 2002a,b). Human studies have found that alcohol ingestion can lower estrogen levels in adolescent girls (Block et al. 1993) and lower both LH and testosterone levels in midpubertal boys (Diamond et al. 1986; Frias et al. 2000a). In both genders, acute alcohol intoxication produces a decrease in GH levels without significant change in either IGF-1 or insulin-like growth factor binding protein-3 (IGFBP3) (Frias et al. 2000$b$).

In female rats, alcohol has been shown to suppress the secretion of specific female reproductive hormones, thereby delaying the onset of puberty (see Dees et al. 2001 and Emanuele et al). Dees and colleagues (2000) found that immature female rhesus macaques exposed daily to alcohol (2 g/kg via nasogastric tube) exhibit lower levels of GH, FSH, LH, estradiol (E$_2$), and IGF-1 (but not FSH or Leptin) compared with control subjects. Moreover, even though there was no effect on age of menarche in these animals, the interval between subsequent menstruations was lengthened, thereby interfering with the development of regular monthly cycles. Additional studies in rats have found that alcohol interferes with intraovarian systems, including IGF-1 and IGF-1 receptors; the nitric oxide (NO) system (Dees et al. 2001; Srivastava et al. 2001$a$), and the steroidogenic acute regulatory protein (StAR) (Srivastava et al. 2001$b$), all of which combine to decrease estradiol secretion. Thus, alcohol not only disrupts the interaction between the brain, pituitary gland, and ovaries, it also directly impairs the regulatory systems within the ovaries (see Dees et al. 2001 for review).

**Alcohol exposure during adolescence actually may alter neurodevelopmental processes in such a way that the likelihood of later abuse is increased.**

In male rats, both acute and chronic alcohol exposure during adolescence results in a reversible suppression of serum testosterone (Little et al. 1992; Cicero et al. 1990; Tentler et al. 1997; Emanuele et al. 1998, 1999a,b; Steiner et al. 1997). Evidence exists for involvement at the hypothalamic, pituitary, and gonadal levels, although the testes appear to be the prime target of alcohol's actions (Emanuele et al. 1999a). Furthermore, GH levels are affected by acute and chronic alcohol exposure in male adolescent rats, whereas IGF-1, growth hormone releasing factor (GRF), and GRF mRNA content are variable, depending on the type of administration (Steiner et al. 1997; Tentler et al. 1997).

Thus, the data so far indicate that females who consume alcohol during early adolescence may be at risk for adverse effects on maturation of the reproductive system. Although in males the long-term effects of alcohol on reproductive function are unclear, the fact that GH as well as testosterone and/or estrogen levels are altered by alcohol in both genders may have serious implications for normal development because these hormones play a critical role in organ maturation during this stage of development.

## Bone Density and Growth Effects

Only a handful of studies have examined the effects of adolescent drinking on bone development, with the most informative data thus far coming from animal research. Male rats chronically fed an alcohol liquid diet for 60 days encompassing the adolescent period (postnatal days 35 to 90) display limb length reduction and reduced metaphyseal and cortical bone growth in the limbs (Wezeman et al. 1999). These skeletal effects may be mediated through a reduction in osteoblast formation, which is associated with a decline in testosterone but not IGF-1. In addition, with abstinence, normal bone metabolism is not completely restored. Similarly, in female rats, Sampson and colleagues (Sampson et al. 1996; Sampson and Spears 1999) found that chronic alcohol consumption (4 weeks on an ethanol liquid diet) produces decreased limb length and reductions in cortical and cancellous bone, which are not fully reversed following cessation of drinking. Interestingly, female adolescent animals administered a binge model of drinking (i.e., 5 percent alcohol by gavage for either 2 or 5 consecutive days per week) show increased bone length, weight, and density, or no change, respectively (Sampson et al. 1999). Human studies indicate an inverse relationship between alcohol consumption and bone mineral density in adolescent males, but not females (Fehily et al. 1992; Neville et al. 2002; Elgan et al. 2002; Fujita et al. 1999). However, more studies are needed in humans and animals to get a clearer picture of alcohol's effects on bone growth in adolescents, particularly with respect to dose and pattern of consumption.

# Long-Term Behavioral and Physiological Consequences of Early Drinking

Although increased tolerance to alcohol's sedative effects may enable greater intake in adolescents, repeated exposure to alcohol may produce increased sensitivity to alcohol's harmful effects. Studies in rats show that ethanol-induced inhibition of synaptic potentials mediated by N-methyl-D-aspartate (NMDA) and long-term potentiation (LTP) is greater in adolescents than in adults (Swartzwelder et al. 1995a,b; see White and Swartzwelder 2005 for review). Initially, the developmental sensitivity of NMDA currents to alcohol was observed in the hippocampus, but more recently this effect was found outside the hippocampus in pyramidal cells in the posterior cingulate cortex (Li et al. 2002). Behaviorally, adolescent rats show greater impairment than adults in acquisition of a spatial memory task after acute ethanol exposure (Markwiese et al. 1998) in support of greater LTP sensitivity to alcohol in adolescents. Behavioral and neurobiological mechanisms for the ontogenetic differences in alcohol tolerance and sensitivity are unclear, as is the relationship between differential sensitivity to ethanol and onset of alcohol abuse and alcoholism.

Binge alcohol exposure (i.e., chronic intermittent exposure to high alcohol doses) in rats during adolescence produces long-lasting changes in memory function (White et al. 2000) and interferes with the normal development of sensitivity to alcohol-induced motor impairments (White et al. 2002). In addition, prolonged alcohol exposure during adolescence, but not adulthood, produces alterations in neurophysiological response to ethanol challenge, tolerance to the sedative effects of ethanol, enhanced expression of withdrawal-related behavior, and long-lasting neurophysiological changes in the cortex and hippocampus in rats (Slawecki et al. 2001; Slawecki 2002; Slawecki and Roth 2004). Furthermore, chronic ethanol treatment in rats may lead to increased NMDA-mediated neurotoxicity, which could be exacerbated by repeated withdrawals (Hunt 1993). Consistent with this hypothesis is the finding that severity of alcohol and drug withdrawal symptoms may be a powerful marker of neuropsychological impairments in detoxified older human adolescents and young adults (Brown et al. 2000; Tapert and Brown 1999; Tapert et al. 2002). Moreover, one recent study found reduced hippocampal volumes in human adolescents with a history of alcohol abuse/dependence disorder (De Bellis et al. 2000), and another preliminary investigation of alcohol-abusing teenagers observed subtle white-matter microstructure abnormalities in the corpus callosum (Tapert et al. 2003), which may be a precursor of more severe damage produced by long-term chronic drinking (Pfefferbaum and Sullivan 2002). Juvenile rats exposed to heavy bingelike episodes of ethanol have greater damage than adults in frontal-anterior cortical regions, including the olfactory frontal cortex, anterior perirhinal, and piriform cortex (Crews et al. 2000). Thus, the immature brain may be more susceptible to binge ethanol-induced neurotoxicity, although the mechanisms are unknown.

Because teenagers are likely to engage in binge drinking, it is important to study the effects of chronic binge patterns of ethanol exposure on brain structure, neurochemistry, and cognitive functioning. Care must be taken in extrapolating from the described animal studies to the binge-drinking adolescent. Because binge drinking does not usually entail withdrawal, it is important to distinguish between damage caused by the alcohol itself and that caused by repeated withdrawals. In addition, primate models may be a better choice for studying the long-term consequences

**Table 1** A Snapshot of Findings on Alcohol's Physiological Effects in Adolescent Humans and Animals

| | Findings | Study |
|---|---|---|
| **On the Liver** | | |
| In humans | Levels of enzymes that indicate liver damage are higher in adolescents with alcohol use disorders | Clark et al. 2001 |
| | And in obese adolescents who drink more moderate amounts. | Strauss et al. 2000 |
| **On the Endocrine System** | | |
| In humans | Drinking alcohol can lower estrogen levels in adolescent girls. | Block et al. 1993 |
| | Drinking alcohol can lower luteinizing hormone and testosterone levels in adolescent boys. | Diamond et al. 1986; Frias et al. 2000*a* |
| | In both sexes, acute intoxication reduces levels of growth hormones. | Frias et al. 2000*b* |
| In rats | In female rats, ingesting alcohol during adolescence is associated with adverse effects on maturation of the reproductive system. | Dees et al. 2001 |
| | Alcohol suppresses the secretion of certain female reproductive hormones, delaying the start of puberty. | Emanuelle et al. 2002*a,b* |
| | Alcohol not only disrupts the interaction between the brain, pituitary gland, and ovaries, but also impairs regulatory systems within the ovaries. | Dees et al. 2001 |
| | In male rats, alcohol consumption alters growth hormone and testosterone levels, which may have serious consequences for normal development. | Little et al. 1992; Cicero et al. 1990; Tentler et al. 1997; Emanuelle et al. 1998, 1999*a*, 1999*b*; Steiner et al. 1997 |
| In rhesus macaques | In immature female monkeys, daily exposure to alcohol lowered levels of female hormones and affected the development of regular monthly cycles. | Dees et al. 2000 |
| **On Bone Density** | | |
| In humans | Increased alcohol consumption is associated with lowered bone mineral density in adolescent males but not females. | Fehily et al. 1992; Neville et al. 2002; Elgan et al. 2002; Fujita et al. 1999 |
| In rats | In adolescent female rats, chronic alcohol consumption produced shorter limb lengths and reductions in bone growth, neither of which was fully reversed with abstinence. | Sampson et al. 1996; Sampson and Spears 1999 |
| | In adolescent male rats, chronic alcohol ingestion was associated with shorter limb length and reduced bone growth, which are not fully reversed with abstinence. | Wezeman et al. 1999 |
| **On the Brain** | | |
| In humans | A history of alcohol abuse or dependence in adolescents was associated with reduced hippocampal volumes | De Bellis et al. 2000 |
| | And with subtle white-matter microstructure abnormalities in the corpus callosum. | Tapert et al. 2003 |
| In rats | Chronic intermittent exposure to high alcohol doses (i.e., bingeing) results in long-lasting changes in memory in adolescent rats | White et al. 2000 |
| | And to more damage to the frontal-anterior cortical regions of the brain than are produced in adult rats. | Crews et al. 2000 |
| | Prolonged alcohol exposure during adolescence produces:<br>• Neurophysiological changes in the response to alcohol challenge and in the tolerance to alcohol's sedative effects;<br>• Enhanced expression of withdrawal behaviors; and<br>• Long-lasting neurophysiological effects in the cortex and hippocampus. | Slawecki et al. 2001; Slawecki 2002; Slawecki and Roth 2004 |

of alcohol exposure because of primates' prolonged adolescent period, which allows extensive manipulation of different types and lengths of exposure. These models, coupled with new neuroanatomical and neuroimaging techniques, offer a unique opportunity to study the brain changes associated with adolescent drinking and determine whether adolescent brains are able to recover more easily because of greater plasticity.

## Early Exposure as a Predictor of Later Alcohol Abuse

Early exposure to alcohol—at or before age 14—is strongly associated with later alcohol abuse and dependence (Grant and Dawson 1998). Two possible explanations for this effect are obvious. First, early alcohol use may simply be a marker for later alcohol abuse rather than a causative factor. A good deal of evidence indicates that at least one behavioral factor, behavioral undercontrol, is measurable very early in life and is a consistently robust predictor of earlier alcohol use as well as of elevated risk for later alcohol use disorder (NIAAA 2000; Zucker and Wong 2005; Caspi et al. 1996).

Second, it is possible that alcohol exposure during adolescence actually may alter neurodevelopmental processes in such a way that the likelihood of later abuse is increased. For example, alcohol use could promote rewiring or alter normal maturation and pruning within the nervous system. Ample evidence exists that exposing rats to low or moderate doses of alcohol during the prenatal or early postnatal period yields a greater preference for ethanol's odor and its consumption later in life (Abate et al. 2000; Honey and Galef 2003; see Molina et al. 1999 and Spear and Molina 2001 for reviews). The young rat's response to alcohol also is mediated by social factors such as maternal interactions and/or nursing from an intoxicated dam (e.g., Hunt et al. 2001; Pepino et al. 2001, 2002; Spear and Molina 2001). Recent evidence shows that prior nursing experience from an ethanol-intoxicated dam heightens ethanol consumption in infant and adolescent rats (Ponce et al. 2004; Pepino et al. 2004). In contrast, relatively few reports using animal models to study the effects of adolescent alcohol exposure on later alcohol consumption exist, and the results are conflicting (see Spear and Varlinskaya 2005). Yet, as is the case with younger animals, social experiences associated with adolescent drinking may influence future drinking behaviors (Hunt et al. 2001; Varlinskaya and Spear 2002). More studies are needed, however, to explore whether a causal relationship between early chronic exposure to alcohol and later alcohol problems exists, as well as to discover the underlying mechanisms for this effect. Nonhuman primates, because of their extended adolescent period, offer a good opportunity to study the effects of early exposure to alcohol.

# References

Aarons, G.A.; Brown, S.A.; Coe, M.T.; et al. Adolescent alcohol and drug abuse and health. *Journal of Adolescent Health* 24:412–421, 1999. PMID: 10401969

Abate, P.; Pepino, M.Y.; Dominguez, H.D.; et al. Fetal associative learning mediated through maternal alcohol intoxication. *Alcoholism: Clinical and Experimental Research* 24:39–47, 2000. PMID: 10656191

Block, G.D.; Yamamoto, M.E.; Mallick, E.; and Styche, A. Effects on pubertal hormones by ethanol abuse in adolescents. *Alcoholism: Clinical and Experimental Research* 17:505, 1993.

Brown, S.A., and Tapert, S.F. Health consequences of adolescent alcohol involvement. In: NRC and IOM. Bonnie, R.J., and O'Connell, M.E., eds. *Reducing Underage Drinking: A Collective Responsibility*. Washington, DC: National Academies Press, 2004. pp. 383–401. Available online at: http://www.nap.edu/books/0309089352/html.

Brown, S.A.; Tapert, S.F.; Granholm, E.; and Dellis, D.C. Neurocognitive functioning of adolescents: Effects of protracted alcohol use. *Alcoholism: Clinical and Experimental Research* 24:164–171, 2000. PMID: 10698367

Caspi, A.; Moffitt, T.E.; Newman, D.L.; and Silva, E.P.A. Behavioral observations at age 3 years predict adult psychiatric disorders: Longitudinal evidence from a birth cohort. *Archives of General Psychiatry* 53:1033–1039, 1996. PMID: 8911226

Cicero, T.J.; Adams, M.L.; O'Connor, L.; et al. Influence of chronic alcohol administration on representative indices of puberty and sexual maturation in male rats and the development of their progeny. *Journal of Pharmacology and Experimental Therapeutics* 255:707–715, 1990. PMID: 2243349

Clark, D.B.; Lynch, K.G.; Donovan, J.E.; and Block, G.D. Health problems in adolescents with alcohol use disorders: Self-report, liver injury, and physical examination findings and correlates. *Alcoholism: Clinical and Experimental Research* 25:1350–1359, 2001. PMID: 11584156

Crews, F.T.; Braun, C.J.; Hoplight, B.; et al. Binge ethanol consumption causes differential brain damage in young adolescent rats compared with adult rats. *Alcoholism: Clinical and Experimental Research* 24:1712–1723, 2000. PMID: 11104119

De Bellis, M.D.; Clark, D.B.; Beers, S.R.; et al. Hippocampal volume in adolescent-onset alcohol use disorders. *American Journal of Psychiatry* 157:737–744, 2000. PMID: 10784466

Dees, W.L.; Dissen, G.A.; Hiney, J.K.; et al. Alcohol ingestion inhibits the increased secretion of puberty-related hormones in the developing female rhesus monkey. *Endocrinology* 141:1325–1331, 2000. PMID: 10746635

Dees, W.L.; Srivastava, V.K.; and Hiney, J.K. Alcohol and female puberty: The role of intraovarian systems. *Alcohol Research & Health* 25(4):271–275, 2001. PMID: 11910704

Diamond, F., Jr.; Ringenberg, L.; MacDonald, D.; et al. Effects of drug and alcohol abuse upon pituitary-testicular function in adolescent males. *Journal of Adolescent Health Care* 7:28–33, 1986. PMID: 2935515

Dick, D.M.; Rose, R.J.; Viken, R.J.; and Kaprio, J. Pubertal timing and substance use: Associations between and within families across late adolescence. *Developmental Psychology* 36:180–189, 2000. PMID: 10749075

Elgan, C.; Dykes, A.K.; and Samsioe, G. Bone mineral density and lifestyle among female students aged 16–24 years. *Gynecological Endocrinology* 16:91–98, 2002. PMID: 12012629

Emanuele, M.A.; LaPaglia, N.; Steiner, J.; et al. Reversal of ethanol-induced testosterone suppression in peripubertal male rats by opiate blockade. *Alcoholism: Clinical and Experimental Research* 22:1199–1204, 1998. PMID: 9756033

Emanuele, M.A.; Wezeman, F.; and Emanuele, N.V. Alcohol's effects on female reproductive function. *Alcohol Research & Health* 26(4):274–281, 2002a. PMID: 12875037

Emanuele, N.; Ren, J.; LaPaglia, N.; et al. EtOH disrupts female mammalian puberty: Age and opiate dependence. *Endocrine* 18:247–254, 2002b. PMID: 12450316

Emanuele, N.V.; LaPaglia, N.; Vogl, W.; et al. Impact and reversibility of chronic ethanol feeding on the reproductive axis in the peripubertal male rat. *Endocrine* 11:277–284, 1999a. PMID: 10786824

Emanuele, N.V.; Lapaglia, N.; Steiner, J.; et al. Reversal of chronic ethanol-induced testosterone suppression in peripubertal male rats by opiate blockade. *Alcoholism: Clinical and Experimental Research* 23:60–66, 1999b. PMID: 10029204

Fehily, A.M.; Coles, R.J.; Evans, W.D.; and Elwood, P.C. Factors affecting bone density in young adults. *American Journal of Clinical Nutrition* 56:579–586, 1992. PMID: 1503072

Frias, J.; Rodriguez, R.; Torres, J.M.; et al. Effects of acute alcohol intoxication on pituitary-gonadal axis hormones, pituitary-adrenal axis hormones, β -endorphin and prolactin in human adolescents of both sexes. *Life Sciences* 67:1081–1086, 2000a. PMID: 10954041

Frias, J.; Torres, J.M.; Rodriguez, R.; et al. Effects of acute alcohol intoxication on growth axis in human adolescents of both sexes. *Life Sciences* 67:2691–2697, 2000b. PMID: 11105985

Fujita, Y.; Katsumata, K.; Unno, A.; et al. Factors affecting peak bone density in Japanese women. *Calcified Tissue International* 64:107–111, 1999. PMID: 9914316

Grant, B.F., and Dawson, D.A. Age at onset of alcohol use and its association with DSM–IV alcohol abuse and dependence: Results from the National Longitudinal Alcohol Epidemiologic Survey. *Journal of Substance Abuse* 9:103–110, 1998. PMID: 9494942

Herman-Giddens, M.E.; Slora, E.J.; Wasserman, R.C.; et al. Secondary sexual characteristics and menses in young girls seen in office practice: A study from the Pediatric Research in Office Settings Network. *Pediatrics* 99:505–512, 1997. PMID: 9093289

Herman-Giddens, M.E.; Wang, L.; and Koch, G. Secondary sexual characteristics in boys: Estimates from the National Health and Nutrition Examination Survey III, 1988–1994. *Archives of Pediatric & Adolescent Medicine* 155:1022–1028, 2001. PMID: 11529804

Honey, P.L., and Galef, B.G., Jr. Ethanol consumption by rat dams during gestation, lactation and weaning increases ethanol consumption by their adolescent young. *Developmental Psychobiology* 42:252– 260, 2003. PMID: 12621651

Hunt, W.A. Are binge drinkers more at risk of developing brain damage? *Alcohol* 10:559–561, 1993. PMID: 8123218

Hunt, P.S.; Holloway, J.L.; and Scordalakes, E.M. Social interaction with an intoxicated sibling can result in increased intake of ethanol by periadolescent rats. *Developmental Psychobiology* 38:101–109, 2001. PMID: 11223802

Karpati, A.M.; Rubin, C.H.; Kieszak, S.M.; et al. Stature and pubertal stage assessment in American boys: The 1988–1994 Third National Health and Nutrition Examination Survey. *Journal of Adolescent Health* 30:205–212, 2002. PMID: 11869928

Lee, P.A.; Guo, S.S.; and Kulin, H.E. Age of puberty: Data from the United States of America. *APMIS (Acta Pathologica, Microbiologica, et Immunologica Scandinavica)* 109:81–88, 2001. PMID: 11398998

Li, Q.; Wilson, W.A.; and Swartzwelder, H.S. Differential effect of ethanol on NMDA EPSCs in pyramidal cells in the posterior cingulate cortex of juvenile and adult rats. *Journal of Neurophysiology* 87:705–711, 2002. PMID: 11826039

Little, P.J.; Adams, M.L.; and Cicero, T.J. Effects of alcohol on the hypothalamic-pituitary-gonadal axis in the developing male rat. *Journal of Pharmacology and Experimental Therapeutics* 263:1056–1061, 1992. PMID: 1469619

Markwiese, B.J.; Acheson, S.K.; Levin, E.D.; et al. Differential effects of ethanol on memory in adolescent and adult rats. *Alcoholism: Clinical and Experimental Research* 22:416–421, 1998. PMID: 9581648

Mauras, N.; Rogol, A.D.; Haymond, M.W.; and Veldhuis, J.D. Sex steroids, growth hormone, insulin-like growth factor-1: Neuroendocrine and metabolic regulation in puberty. *Hormone Research* 45:74–80, 1996. PMID: 8742123

Molina, J.C.; Dominguez, H.D.; Lopez, M.F.; et al. The role of fetal and infantile experience with alcohol in later recognition and acceptance patterns of the drug. In: Hannigan, J.; Goodlett, C.; Spear, L.; Spear, N., eds. *Alcohol and Alcoholism: Brain and Development.* Hillsdale, NJ: Erlbaum, 1999, pp. 199–227.

National Institute on Alcohol Abuse and Alcoholism (NIAAA). Alcohol involvement over the life course. In: *Tenth Special Report to the U.S. Congress on Alcohol and Health: Highlights from Current Research.* Bethesda, MD: Dept. of Health and Human Services, NIAAA, 2000. pp. 28–53. Available online at: http://pubs.niaaa.nih.gov/publications/10report/intro.pdf.

Neville, C.E.; Murray, L.J.; Boreham, C.A.G.; et al. Relationship between physical activity and bone mineral status in young adults: The Northern Ireland Young Hearts Project. *Bone* 30:792–798, 2002. PMID: 11996922

Pepino, M.Y.; Spear, N.E.; and Molina, J.C. Nursing experiences with an alcohol-intoxicated rat dam counteract appetitive conditioned responses toward alcohol. *Alcoholism: Clinical and Experimental Research* 25:18–24, 2001. PMID: 11198710

Pepino, M.Y.; Abate, P.; Spear, N.E.; and Molina, J.C. Disruption of maternal behavior by alcohol intoxication in the lactating rat: A behavioral and metabolic analysis. *Alcoholism: Clinical and Experimental Research* 26:1205–1214, 2002. PMID: 12198395

Pepino, M.Y.; Abate, P.; Spear, N.E.; and Molina, J.C. Heightened ethanol intake in infant and adolescent rats after nursing experiences with an ethanol-intoxicated dam. *Alcoholism: Clinical and Experimental Research* 28:895–905, 2004. PMID: 15201632

Pfefferbaum, A., and Sullivan, E.V. Micro structural but not macrostructural disruption of white matter in women with chronic alcoholism. *Neuroimage* 15:708–718, 2002. PMID: 11848714

Ponce, L.F.; Pautassi, R.M.; Spear, N.E.; and Molina, J.C. Nursing from an ethanol-intoxicated dam induces short- and long-term disruptions in motor performance and enhances later self-administration of the drug. *Alcoholism: Clinical and Experimental Research* 28:1039–1050, 2004. PMID: 15252290

Sampson, H.W., and Spears, H. Osteopenia due to chronic alcohol consumption by young actively growing rats is not completely reversible. *Alcoholism: Clinical and Experimental Research* 23: 324–327, 1999. PMID: 10069563

Sampson, H.W.; Perks, N.; Champney, T.H.; and Defee, B., 2nd. Alcohol consumption inhibits bone growth and development in young actively growing rats. *Alcoholism: Clinical and Experimental Research* 20:1375–1384, 1996. PMID: 8947313

Sampson, H.W.; Gallager, S.; Lange, J.; et al. Binge drinking and bone metabolism in a young actively growing rat model. *Alcoholism: Clinical and Experimental Research* 23:1228–1231, 1999. PMID: 10443990

Slawecki, C.J. Altered EEG responses to ethanol in adult rats exposed to ethanol during adolescence. *Alcoholism: Clinical and Experimental Research* 26:246–254, 2002. PMID: 11964565

Slawecki, C.J., and Roth, J. Comparison of the onset of hypoactivity and anxiety-like behavior during alcohol withdrawal in adolescent and adult rats. *Alcoholism: Clinical and Experimental Research* 28:598–607, 2004. PMID: 15100611

Slawecki, C.J.; Betancourt, M.; Cole, M.; and Ehlers, C.L. Periadolescent alcohol exposure has lasting effects on adult neurophysiological function in rats. *Developmental Brain Research* 128:63–72, 2001. PMID: 11356263

Spear, L.P., and Varlinskaya, E.I. Adolescence: Alcohol sensitivity, tolerance, and intake. In: Galanter, M., ed. *Recent*

*Developments in Alcoholism, Vol. 17: Alcohol Problems in Adolescents and Young Adults: Epidemiology, Neurobiology, Prevention, Treatment.* New York: Springer, 2005. pp. 143–159. PMID: 15789864

Spear, N.E., and Molina, J.C. Consequences of early exposure to alcohol: How animal studies reveal later patterns of use and abuse in humans. In: Carroll, M.E., and Overmier, J.B., eds. *Animal Research and Human Health: Advancing Human Welfare through Behavioral Science.* Washington, DC: American Psychological Association, 2001. pp. 85–99.

Srivastava, V.K.; Hiney, J.K.; Dearth, R.K.; and Dees, W.L. Effects of alcohol on intraovarian insulin-like growth factor-1 and nitric oxide systems in prepubertal female rats. *Recent Research Developments in Endocrinology* 2(part 1):213–221, 2001a.

Srivastava, V.K.; Hiney, J.K.; Dearth, R.K.; and Dees, W.L. Acute effects of ethanol on steroidogenic acute regulatory protein (StAR) in the prepubertal rat ovary. *Alcoholism: Clinical and Experimental Research* 25:1500–1505, 2001b. PMID: 11696671

Steiner, J.C.; LaPaglia, N.; Hansen, M.; et al. Effect of chronic ethanol on reproductive and growth hormones in the peripubertal male rat. *Journal of Endocrinology* 154:363–370, 1997. PMID: 9291847

Strauss, R.S.; Barlow, S.E.; and Dietz, W.H. Prevalence of abnormal serum aminotransferase values in overweight and obese adolescents. *Journal of Pediatrics* 136:727–733, 2000. PMID: 10839867

Swartzwelder, H.S.; Wilson, W.A.; and Tayyeb, M.I. Age-dependent inhibition of long-term potentiation by ethanol in immature versus mature hippocampus. *Alcoholism: Clinical and Experimental Research* 19:1480–1485, 1995a. PMID: 8749814

Swartzwelder, H.S.; Wilson, W.A.; and Tayyeb, M.I. Differential sensitivity of NMDA receptor-mediated synaptic potentials to ethanol in immature versus mature hippocampus. *Alcoholism: Clinical and Experimental Research* 19:320–323, 1995b. PMID: 7625564

Tanner, J.M. *Foetus into Man: Physical Growth From Conception to Maturity.* Ware, Great Britain: Castlemead Publications, 1989.

Tapert, S.F., and Brown, S.A. Neuropsychological correlates of adolescent substance abuse: Four-year outcomes. *Journal of the International Neuropsychological Society* 5:481–493, 1999. PMID: 10561928

Tapert, S.F.; Granholm, E.; Leedy, N.G.; and Brown, S.A. Substance use and withdrawal: Neuropsychological functioning over 8 years in youth. *Journal of the International Neuropsychological Society* 8:873–883, 2002. PMID: 12405538

Tapert, S.F.; Theilmann, R.J.; Schweinsburg, A.D.; et al. Reduced fractional anisotropy in the splenium of adolescents with alcohol use disorder. *Proceedings of the International Society for Magnetic Resonance in Medicine* 11:8217, 2003.

Tentler, J.J.; LaPaglia, N.; Steiner, J.; et al. Ethanol, growth hormone and testosterone in peripubertal rats. *Journal of Endocrinology* 152:477–487, 1997. PMID: 9071969

Varlinskaya, E.I., and Spear, L.P. Acute effects of ethanol on social behavior of adolescent and adult rats: Role of familiarity of the test situation. *Alcoholism: Clinical and Experimental Research* 26:1502–1511, 2002. PMID: 12394283

Wezeman, F.H.; Emanuele, M.A.; Emanuele, N.V.; et al. Chronic alcohol consumption during male rat adolescence impairs skeletal development through effects on osteoblast gene expression, bone mineral density, and bone strength. *Alcoholism: Clinical and Experimental Research* 23:1534–1542, 1999. PMID: 10512321

White, A.M., and Swartzwelder, H.S. Age-related effects of alcohol on memory and memory-related brain function in adolescents and adults. In: Galanter, M., ed. *Recent Developments in Alcoholism, Vol. 17: Alcohol Problems in Adolescents and Young Adults: Epidemiology, Neurobiology, Prevention, Treatment.* New York: Springer, 2005. pp. 161–176. PMID: 15789865

White, A.M.; Ghia, A.J.; Levin, E.D.; and Swartzwelder, H.S. Binge pattern ethanol exposure in adolescent and adult rats: Differential impact on subsequent responsiveness to ethanol. *Alcoholism: Clinical and Experimental Research* 24:1251–1256, 2000. PMID: 10968665

White, A.M.; Truesdale, M.C.; Bae, J.G.; et al. Differential effects of ethanol on motor coordination in adolescent and adult rats. *Pharmacology, Biochemistry, and Behavior* 73:673–677, 2002. PMID: 12151043

Wilson, D.M.; Killen, J.D.; Hayward, C.; et al. Timing and rate of sexual maturation and the onset of cigarette and alcohol use among teenage girls. *Archives of Pediatrics and Adolescent Medicine* 148:789–795, 1994. PMID: 8044254

Zucker, R.A., and Wong, M.M. Prevention for children of alcoholics and other high risk groups. In: Galanter, M., ed. *Recent Developments in Alcoholism, Vol. 17: Alcohol Problems in Adolescents and Young Adults: Epidemiology, Neurobiology, Prevention, Treatment.* New York: Springer, 2005. pp. 299–320. PMID: 15789872

From *Alcohol Research and Health*, vol. 28, no. 3, 2004/2005, pp. 125–131. Published by National Institute on Alcohol Abuse and Alcoholism (NIAAA).

# The Toxicity of Recreational Drugs

## Alcohol is more lethal than many other commonly abused substances

ROBERT S. GABLE

The Shuar tribes in Ecuador have for centuries used native plants to induce religious intoxication and to discipline recalcitrant children. By comparison, most North Americans know little about the mood-altering potential of the wild vegetation around them. And those who think they know something on this subject are often dangerously ignorant. Over a three-week period in 1983, for example, 22 Marines wanting to get high were hospitalized because they ate too many seeds of the jimsonweed plant (*Datura stramonium*), which they found growing wild near their base, Camp Pendleton in southern California.

A dozen seeds of jimsonweed contain about 1 gram of atropine, 10 grams of which can cause nausea, severe agitation, dilation of pupils, hallucinations, headache and delirium. Tribal groups in South America refer to datura plants as the "evil eagles." Of approximately 150 hallucinogenic plants that are routinely consumed around the world, those with atropine have the most pernicious reputation—something these Marines discovered the hard way.

## Toxicity Profiles

The easier way to learn about the relation between the quantity of a substance taken and the resulting level of physiological impairment is through careful laboratory study. The first example of such an exercise, in 1927, used rodents. Research toxicologist John Trevan published an influential paper that reported the use of more than 900 mice to assess the lethality of, among other things, cocaine. As he and others have since found, a substance that is tolerated or even beneficial in small quantities often has harmful effects at higher levels. The amount of a substance that produces a beneficial effect in 50 percent of a group of animals is called the *median effective dose*. The quantity that produces mortality in 50 percent of a group of animals is termed the *median lethal dose*.

Laboratory tests with animals can give a general picture of the potency of a substance, but generalizing experimental results from, say, mice to humans is always suspect. Thus toxicologists also use two other sources of information. The first is survey data collected from poison-control centers, hospital emergency departments and coroners' offices. Another consists of published clinical and forensic reports of fatalities or near-fatalities.

But these sources, like animal studies, have their limitations. Simply tallying the number of people who die or who show up at emergency rooms is, by itself, meaningless because the number of such incidents will be influenced by the total number of people using a particular substance, something that is impossible to know. For example, atropine is more toxic than alcohol, but more deaths will be reported for alcohol than for atropine because so many more people get drunk than ingest jimsonweed. Furthermore, most overdose fatalities involve the use of two or more substances (usually including alcohol), situations for which the overall toxicity is largely unknown. In short: When psychoactive substances are combined, all bets are off.

How then does one gauge the relative risks of different recreational drugs? One way is to consider the ratio of effective dose to lethal dose. For example, a normally healthy 70-kilogram (154-pound) adult can achieve a relaxed affability from approximately 33 grams of ethyl alcohol. This effective dose can come from two 12-ounce beers, two 5-ounce glasses of wine or two 1.5-ounce shots of 80-proof vodka. The median lethal dose for such an adult is approximately 330 grams, the quantity contained in about 20 shots of vodka. A person who consumes that much (10 times the median effective dose), taken within a few minutes on an empty stomach, risks a lethal reaction. And plenty of people have died this way.

As far as toxicity goes, such deaths are quite telling. Indeed, autopsy reports from cases of fatal overdose (whether from alcohol or some other substance) provide key information linking death and drug consumption. But coroners are generally hard-pressed to determine the size of the dose because significant redistribution of a drug often occurs after death, typically from tissues of solid organs (such as the liver) into associated blood vessels. As a result, blood samples may show different concentrations at different times after death. Even if investigators had a valid way to measure the concentration of a lethal drug in a decedent's blood, they would still need to work backward to make a retrospective estimate of the quantity of the drug consumed. Although the approximate time of death is often known, the time the drug was taken and the rate at which it was metabolized are not so easily established. Lots of guesswork is typically involved. Obviously, people who want clean answers should not seek information from corpses.

## Safety Comparison

Despite these difficulties, it is evident that there are striking differences among psychoactive substances with respect to the lethality of a given quantity. The way a substance is absorbed is also a critical factor. The common routes of consumption, from the least toxic to the most toxic (in general), are eating or drinking a substance, depositing it inside the nostril, breathing or smoking it, and injecting it into a vein with a hypodermic syringe. So, for example, smoking methamphetamine (as is done with the increasingly popular illicit drug "crystal meth") is more dangerous than ingesting it.

Once a drag enters the body, physiological reactions are determined by many factors, such as absorption into various tissues and the rates of elimination and metabolism. Individuals vary enormously in how they metabolize different substances. One person's sedative can be another person's poison. This variability alone introduces unavoidable ambiguities in estimating effective and lethal doses. Still, the wide range between different substances suggests that they can be rank-ordered with reasonable confidence. One can be quite certain, for example, that the risk of death from ingesting psilocybin mushrooms is less than from injecting heroin.

The most toxic recreational drugs, such as GHB (gamma-hydroxybutyrate) and heroin, have a lethal dose less than 10 times their typical effective dose. The largest cluster of substances has a lethal dose that is 10 to 20 times the effective dose: These include cocaine, MDMA (methylenedioxymethamphetamine, often called "ecstasy") and alcohol. A less toxic group of substances, requiring 20 to 80 times the effective dose to cause death, include Rohypnol (flunitrazepam or "roofies") and mescaline (peyote cactus). The least physiologically toxic substances, those requiring 100 to 1,000 times the effective dose to cause death, include psilocybin mushrooms and marijuana, when ingested. I've found no published cases in the English language that document deaths from *smoked* marijuana, so the actual lethal dose is a mystery. My surmise is that smoking marijuana is more risky than eating it but still safer than getting drunk.

Alcohol thus ranks at the dangerous end of the toxicity spectrum. So despite the fact that about 75 percent of all adults in the United States enjoy an occasional drink, it must be remembered that alcohol is quite toxic. Indeed, if alcohol were a newly formulated beverage, its high toxicity and addiction potential would surely prevent it from being marketed as a food or drug. This conclusion runs counter to the common view that one's own use of alcohol is harmless. That mistaken impression arises for several reasons.

First, the more frequently we experience an event without a negative outcome, the lower our level of perceived danger.

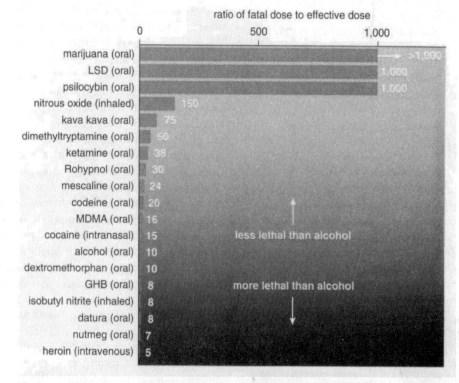

**Figure 1** Ranking psychoactive substances by their ratios of lethal dose to effective dose gives a general picture of how likely each is to precipitate an acute fatal reaction. By this measure, many illicit drugs are considerably safer than alcohol.

For example, most of us have not had a life-threatening traffic accident; thus, we feel safer in a car than in an airplane, although we are 10 to 15 times more likely to die in an automobile accident than in a plane crash. Similarly, most of us have not had a life-threatening experience with alcohol, yet statistics show that every year about 300 people die in the United States from an alcohol overdose, and for at least twice that number of overdose deaths, alcohol is considered a contributing cause.

Second, having a sense of control over a risky situation reduces fear. People drinking alcoholic beverages believe that they have reasonably good control of the quantity they intend to consume. Control of the dose of alcohol is indeed easier than with many natural or illicit substances where the active ingredients are not commercially standardized. Furthermore, alcohol is often consumed in a beverage that dilutes the alcohol to a known degree.

Consider the following: The stomach capacity of an average adult is about 1 liter; therefore, a person is unlikely to overdose after drinking beer containing 5 percent alcohol. Compare this situation to GHB (a depressant originally marketed in health food stores as a sleep aid), where stomach capacity does not place much of a limit on consumption because the effective dose is only one or two teaspoonfuls. No wonder that more than 50 percent of novice users of GHB have experienced an overdose that included involuntary loss of consciousness.

Another reason that alcohol is often thought to be safe is that popular media do not routinely report fatalities from alcohol overdoses. Deaths are usually considered newsworthy when they involve a degree of novelty. Thus a fatality caused by LSD or MDMA is thought to be more interesting than one caused by alcohol.

## Other Ways to Invite Death

A simpleminded look at the ratio of effective to lethal doses ignores many complications, some of which are well recognized, some rather subtle. Take, for example, the fact that danger generally increases with repetitive consumption. High blood levels of a drug, without rest periods between use, tend to heighten risk, because the affected organs do not have sufficient time to recover. Studies of MDMA use, for example, show that relatively small repeated doses result in disproportionately large increases of MDMA in blood plasma. Cocaine is the substance that induces the highest rate of repetitive consumption as a result of mood change. Heroin and alcohol come in second and third. Also, the tendency of a user to take a "booster" dose prematurely is greater with substances that require an hour or more to provide the full psychological effect—during the interim the user often assumes that the original dose was not sufficiently potent. This phenomenon routinely occurs with dextromethorphan (found in cough medicines), GHB and MDMA.

Overdose quantities that are based on acute toxicity also do not take into account the probability that an individual will become addicted. This probability can be cast as a drug's capture ratio: Of the people who sample a particular substance, what portion will become physiologically or psychologically dependent on the drug for some period of time? Heroin and methamphetamine are the most addictive by this measure. Cocaine, pentobarbital (a fast-acting sedative), nicotine and alcohol are next, followed by marijuana and possibly caffeine. Some hallucinogens—notably LSD, mescaline and psilocybin—have little or no potential for creating dependence.

Finally, a comparison of overdose fatalities does not take into account cognitive impairments and risky or aggressive behaviors that sometimes follow drug use. And as most people are well aware, a substantial proportion of violent confrontations, rapes, suicides, automobile accidents and AIDS-related illnesses are linked to alcohol intoxication.

Despite the health risks and social costs, consciousness-altering chemicals have been used for centuries in almost all cultures. So it would be unrealistic to expect that all types of recreational drug use will suddenly cease. Self-management of these substances is extremely difficult, yet modern Western societies have not, in general, developed positive, socially sanctioned rituals as a means of regulating the use of some of the less hazardous recreational drugs. I would argue that we need to do that. The science of toxicology may provide one step in that direction, by helping to teach members of our society what a lot of tribal people already know.

ROBERT S. GABLE is an emeritus professor of psychology at Claremont Graduate University. He receipted both a doctorate in education from Harvard and a doctorate in experimental psychology from Brandeis in 1964. Much of his professional work has centered on developing behavioral therapy for juvenile delinquents, including remote radio-frequency monitoring of physiological responses. Address: Department of Psychology, Claremont Graduate University, 150 E. 10th St., Claremont, CA 91711. Internet: **Robert.Gable@cgu.edu**

From *American Scientist*, May/June 2006, pp. 206–208. Copyright © 2006 by American Scientist, magazine of Sigma Xi, The Scientific Research Society. Reprinted by permission.

*Effects of Drug Use*

# Structural Differences Found in Brains of Heavy Marijuana Users

Heavy marijuana use may be responsible for structural alterations in the brains of heavy marijuana users, according to a study published in a recent issue of *Drug and Alcohol Dependence*. Previous imaging studies have failed to demonstrate any significant structural differences in marijuana users compared to nonusers.

Using a technique called voxel-based morphometry, researcher John A. Matochik and colleagues from the National Institute on Drug Abuse and John Hopkins University School of Medicine in Baltimore investigated brain tissue composition differences in both gray matter and white matter in a sample of heavy marijuana users, abstinent for 20 days, and a non-using comparison group. They hypothesized that heavy marijuana users would show alterations in brain tissue composition, especially in the hippocampus, an area abundant in cannabinoid receptors.

Drug use history was obtained using the Drug Survey Questionnaire, the Addiction Severity Index, and the Diagnostic Interview Schedule. All subjects had a complete medical evaluation and urine screens. Current consumption of less than seven alcoholic drinks per week was required for both groups, due to the documented effects of alcohol on brain structure.

Exclusion criteria included a past or current Axis I psychiatric diagnosis according to DSM-IV criteria, a past or current diagnosis of dependence or abuse of any substance except for marijuana including alcohol, a past or current history of neurological problems, abnormal findings on the neurological exam, or left-handedness.

Subjects in the marijuana group had smoked marijuana for at least two years, currently used the drug at least 4 times per week, and had a positive urine screen for marijuana and its metabolites at study admission. Marijuana users were housed at the NIDA Clinical Inpatient Research Unit for approximately 25 days, and had MR scans on Day 20 after admission. Subjects in the comparison group were marijuana-free, as determined by drug report scales and urine screens. These subjects were housed only on the night prior to their MR scan.

Researchers found that compared to non-users, marijuana users had lower gray matter density in a cluster of voxels in the right parahippocampal gyrus, and greater density near the left precentral gyrus, including portions of the postcentral gyrus, the right precentral gyrus, also including portions of the postcentral gyrus, and in the thalamus, including the dorsomedial nucleus, on the right side.

## Table 1 Study sample

| | Marijuana users | Non-users |
|---|---|---|
| N = 19 (100% male) | N = 11 | N = 8 |
| Mean age (years) | 25.4 ± 5.0 | 29.7 ± 4.7 |
| Mean education (years) | 12.8 ± 1.9 | 13.9 ± 2.7 |
| Marijuana use/week (joints) | 34.7 ± 17.6 | — |
| Marijuana use duration (years) | 7.5 ± 5.5 | — |
| Marijuana age at onset (years) | 15.7 ± 2.5 | — |
| Alcohol use (drinks/week) | 1.4 ± 2.2 | 1.5 ± 2.0 |

Marijuana users also had lower white matter density in the left parietal lobe and higher density around the parahippocampal and fusiform gyri on the left side, and near the lentiform nucleus and in the pons of the brainstem when compared to nonusers. In addition, researchers found a correlation between longer duration of marijuana use and higher white matter density around the left precentral gyrus.

No significant associations were identified between gray matter density and duration of use, or between either marijuana use (joints/week) or starting age of marijuana use and gray matter or white matter tissue density.

## Study Limits

The authors note that these results cannot determine if the differences identified between the two study groups existed prior to initiation of marijuana use, or if other variables may have contributed to the differences detected in tissue density. Self-reports of past drug use and small sample size may also limit the study's findings, according to the authors.

## Authors' Conclusions

This study identified brain tissue composition alterations in heavy marijuana users that have not been previously detected by image analysis. The next step, the authors say, is understanding what these structural results mean at the cellular level. Understanding the effects of these changes may yield insight into the use and abuse of this drug.

## Suggested Reading:

Bolla KI, Brown K, Eldreth D, et al.: Dose-related neurocognitive effects of marijuana use. *Neurology* 2002; 59:1337–1343.

MATOCHIK JA, ELDRETH DA, CADET JL, ET AL.: Altered brain tissue composition in heavy marijuana users. Drug and Alcohol Dependence 2005; 77:23–30. E-mail: **jmatochi@intra.nida.nih.gov**

# Does Cannabis Cause Psychosis or Schizophrenia?

**There is no shortage of studies on cannabis and its links with psychosis and schizophrenia. While most agree there is a link, causality is not clear-cut. Here we examine recent studies and invite two UK experts to comment on their findings.**

## Dutch Studies
### Cannabis Linked to Early Onset of Schizophrenia

This Dutch study speculates that cannabis use brings on schizophrenic episodes at an earlier age. They looked at schizophrenia in 133 patients in The Hague. Following assessment and interviews they found that those who smoked cannabis encountered schizophrenic episodes on average 6.9 years earlier than non-users.

They looked at three milestones in the early development of schizophrenia: 1) first social and/or occupational dysfunction; 2) first psychotic episode and 3) first negative symptoms.

Male patients were significantly younger than female patients at first social and/or occupational dysfunction, first psychotic episode and first negative symptoms. Cannabis-using patients were significantly younger at these milestones than were patients who did not use cannabis.

They conclude that there is a strong association between use of cannabis and earlier age at first psychotic episode in male schizophrenia patients.

> Veen N, Selten SP, van der Tweel I, Feller WG, Hock HW & Kahn RS (2004) Cannabis use and age at onset of Schizophrenia. *American Journal of Psychiatry* 161 501–506.

### Cannabis and psychosis reciprocally linked

Cannabis use and psychosis are shown to be inextricably linked with one preceding the other and vise versa. This Dutch study followed 1,580 young people (4 to 16-year-olds) for 14 years.

They found that people who initially did not have psychotic symptoms were more likely to develop them if they started using cannabis. Similarly, they found that those who did not take cannabis but later developed psychotic symptoms were more likely to subsequently take cannabis—suggesting cannabis is used to self-medicate.

The results imply either a common vulnerability with cannabis and psychosis or a two-way causal relationship between the two.

> Ferdinand RF, Sondeikjer F, van der Ende J, Selten J-P, Huizink A & Verhulst FC (2005) Cannabis use predicts future psychotic symptoms, and vice versa. *Addiction* 100 (5) 612–618.

## New Zealand Study
### Cannabis Almost Doubles Risk of Psychosis

New Zealand research forms much of present-day thinking on cannabis and psychosis. This one goes that step further by concluding that not only does heavy cannabis cause psychosis, but that this is one-way and not down to confounding factors.

The study is impressive, using a 25-year longitudinal study of 1,265 children. Using the usual regression analysis, they found that daily cannabis users are 1.6 to 1.8 times more likely to develop psychotic symptoms.

They suggest that these associations reflected the effects of cannabis use on symptom levels rather than the effects of symptom levels on cannabis use. In other words, cannabis is the trigger for psychosis, and not, as other studies suggest, psychosis the trigger for people to start using cannabis.

> Fergusson DM, Horwood LJ & Ridder EM (2005) Tests of casual linkages between cannabis use and psychotic symptoms. *Addiction* 100 (3) 354–366.

## Statistical Reviews
### Increase in Cannabis Use Not Matched by Increase in Psychosis

This study refutes a causal link between cannabis use and psychosis on the grounds that recent increase in cannabis use are not matched by increases in the number of people developing cannabis psychosis.

Newcombe asserts that for a causal link to exist, trends in cannabis use and cannabis psychosis should be positively correlated.

The annual rate of cannabis psychosis among English cannabis users is typically one in 10,000. However, although recent cannabis use (used in past year) climbed from 2.55 million in 1994 to 3.36 million in 2002/03, there are no clear trends in either schizophrenia. (36,000–38,500 cases annually) or cannabis psychosis cases (280–380).

Interestingly, when incidences of acute cannabis intoxication and harmful cannabis use are taken into account, there does seem to be a correlation.

The study concludes therefore that there is not support for the claim that cannabis use can cause psychosis, nor for a 'true' cannabis psychosis. Instead, cannabis psychosis cases are arguable misdiagnoses of extreme cases of acute cannabis intoxication and harmful cannabis use, and/or mental and behavioral disorders arising from other/multiple drug use.

RD Newcombe (2004) Does cannabis use cause psychosis? A study of trends in cannabis use and psychosis in England, 1995–2003. *Adiktologie* 4 (4) 492–507.

### Review Confirms Link but Not Causation

This extensive review of success studies concludes that almost all research shows that frequent use of cannabis increases the risk of subsequent psychotic symptoms. According to their figures regular cannabis use doubles the relative risk for later schizophrenia. They speculate that if cannabis use were eradicated the incidence of schizophrenia would fall by approximately 8%, assuming of course a causal relationship.

Though importantly, they rule out direct causality by saying *"cannabis use appears to be neither a sufficient nor a necessary cause for psychosis. It is a component cause, part of a complex constellation of factors lead to psychosis."*

The authors call for the identification of "vulnerable youths" and efforts to discourage use among this group.

Arsenealut L, Cannon M, Witton J & Murray RM (2004) Causal association between cannabis and psychosis: examination of the evidence. *British Journal of Psychiatry* 104 (2) 110–117.

## US study on general health
### Age of Onset Predicts Physical and Mental Health Problems

This US study predicts that the younger you are when you start using cannabis the more likely you are to develop physical and mental health problems and other "unhealthy" behaviors such as using other drugs.

However, once frequency of recent marijuana use was included in the calculations, age of initiation was only associated with other illicit drug use.

This is another longitudinal study starting in 1984 with 2,079 school-age children from various ethnical groups, such as white, African-American, Hispanic, Asian and others.

Ellickson PI, D'Anico EJ, Collins R & Klein DJ (2005) Marijuana use and later problems when frequency of recent use explains age of initiation effects (and when it does not). *Substance Use & Misuse* 40 (3) 343–359.

# UNIT 3

# The Major Drugs of Use and Abuse

## Unit Selection

## Key Points to Consider

- Why is it that some drugs have remained popular throughout history while others have not?

- How does the manner in which a drug is consumed change or influence the effects on the user?

- What influences help perpetuate the problem of binge drinking on college campuses?

- In what ways do the United States and its allies intend to disrupt heroin production in Afghanistan and Colombia?

- What are the distinct features associated with the spread of methamphetamine use across the United States?

## Student Website

www.mhcls.com/online

## Internet References

Further information regarding these websites may be found in this book's preface or online.

**National Institute on Drug Abuse**
*www.drugabuse.gov*
**Office of Applied Studies**
*www.oas.samhsa.gov*
**QuitNet**
*http://www.quitnet.org*
**The American Journal of Psychiatry**
*http://ajp.psychiatryonline.org/cgi/content/abstract/155/8/1016*

The following articles discuss those drugs that have evolved to become the most popular drugs of choice. Although pharmacological modifications emerge periodically to enhance or alter the effects produced by certain drugs or the manner in which various drugs are used, basic pharmacological properties of the drugs remain unchanged. Crack is still cocaine, ice is still methamphetamine, and black tar is still heroin. In addition, tobacco products all supply the drug nicotine, coffee and a plethora of energy drinks provide caffeine, and alcoholic beverages provide the drug ethyl alcohol. These drugs all influence how we act, think, and feel about ourselves and the world around us. They also produce markedly different effects within the body and within the mind.

To understand why certain drugs remain popular over time, and why new drugs become popular, one must be knowledgeable about the effects produced by individual drugs. Why people use drugs is a bigger question than why people use tobacco. However, understanding why certain people use tobacco, or cocaine, or marijuana, or alcohol is one way to construct a framework from which to tackle the larger question of why people use drugs in general. One of the most complex relationships is the one between Americans and their use of alcohol. More than 76 million Americans have experienced alcoholism in their families.

The most recent surveys of alcohol use estimate that 126 million Americans currently use alcohol. The use of alcohol is a powerful influence that serves to shape our national consciousness about drugs. The relationship between the use of alcohol and the use of tobacco, and the use of alcohol and illicit drugs provide long-standing statistical relationships. The majority of Americans, however, believe that alcohol is used responsibly by most people who use it, even though approximately 10 percent of users are believed to be suffering from various stages of alcoholism.

Understanding why people initially turn to the non-medical use of drugs is a huge question that is debated and discussed in a voluminous body of literature. One important reason why the major drugs of use and abuse, such as alcohol, nicotine, cocaine, heroin, marijuana, amphetamines, and a variety of prescription, designer, over-the-counter, and herbal drugs retain their popularity is because they produce certain physical and psychological effects that humans crave. They temporarily restrain our inhibitions; reduce our fears; alleviate mental and physical suffering; produce energy, confidence, and exhilaration; and allow us to relax. Tired, take a pill; have a headache, take a pill; need to lose weight, take a pill; need to increase athletic performance, the options seem almost limitless. There is a drug for everything. Some drugs even, albeit artificially, suggest a greater capacity to transcend, redefine, and seek out new levels of consciousness. And they do it upon demand. People initially use a specific drug, or class of drugs, to obtain the desirable effects historically associated with the use of that drug. Heroin and opiate-related drugs such as Oxycontin and Vicodin produce, in most people, a euphoric, dreamy state of well-being. The abuse of these prescription painkillers is one of the fastest growing (and alarming) drug trends. Methamphetamine and related stimulant drugs produce euphoria, energy, confidence, and exhilaration. Alcohol produces a loss of inhibitions and a state of well-being. Nicotine and marijuana typically serve as relaxants. Ecstasy and other "club drugs" produce stimulant as well as relaxant effects. Various over-the-counter and herbal drugs all attempt to replicate the effects of more potent and often prohibited or prescribed drugs. Although effects and side effects may vary from user to user, a general pattern of effects is predictable from most major drugs of use and their analogs. Varying the dosage and altering the manner of ingestion is one way to alter the drug's effects. Some drugs, such as LSD and certain types of designer drugs, produce effects on the user that are less predictable and more sensitive to variations in dosage level and to the user's physical and psychological makeup.

Although all major drugs of use and abuse have specific reinforcing properties perpetuating their continued use, they also produce undesirable side effects that regular drug users attempt to mitigate. Most often, users attempt to mitigate these effects with the use of other drugs. Cocaine, methamphetamine, heroin, and alcohol have long been used to mitigate each other's side effects. A good example is the classic "speedball" of heroin and cocaine. When they are combined, cocaine accelerates and intensifies the euphoric state of the heroin, while the heroin softens the comedown from cocaine.

Additionally, other powerful influences on drug taking such as advertising for alcohol, tobacco, and certain prescription drugs, significantly impact the public's drug related consciousness. The alcohol industry, for example, dissects numerous layers of society to specifically market alcoholic beverages to subpopulations of Americans, including youth. The same influences exist with tobacco advertising. What is the message in Philip Morris's advertisements about its attempts to mitigate smoking by youth? Approximately 500 thousand Americans die each year from tobacco related illness. Add to the mix advertising by prescription drug companies for innumerable human maladies and one soon realizes the enormity of the association between business and drug taking. Subsequently, any discussion of major drugs could begin and end with alcohol, tobacco, and prescription drugs.

# A More Addictive Meth Emerges as States Curb Homemade Type

KATE ZERNIKE

D es Moines, Jan. 18—In the seven months since Iowa passed a law restricting the sale of cold medicines used to make methamphetamine, seizures of home-made methamphetamine laboratories have dropped to just 20 a month from 120. People once terrified about the neighbor's house blowing up now walk up to the state's drug policy director, Marvin Van Haaften, at his local Wal-Mart to thank him for making them safer.

But Mr. Van Haaften, like officials in other states with similar restrictions, is now worried about a new problem: the drop in home-cooked methamphetamine has been met by a new flood of crystal methamphetamine coming largely from Mexico.

Sometimes called ice, crystal methamphetamine is far purer, and therefore even more highly addictive, than powdered home-cooked methamphetamine, a change that health officials say has led to greater risk of overdose. And because crystal methamphetamine costs more, the police say thefts are increasing, as people who once cooked at home now have to buy it.

The University of Iowa Burn Center, which in 2004 spent $2.8 million treating people whose skin had been scorched off by the toxic chemicals used to make methamphetamine at home, says it now sees hardly any cases of that sort. Drug treatment centers, on the other hand, say they are treating just as many or more methamphetamine addicts.

And although child welfare officials say they are removing fewer children from homes where parents are cooking the drug, the number of children being removed from homes where parents are using it has more than made up the difference.

"It's killing us, this Mexican ice," said Mr. Van Haaften, a former sheriff. "I'm not sure we can control it as well as we can the meth labs in your community."

The influx of the more potent drug shows the fierce hold of methamphetamine, which has devastated many towns once far removed from violent crime or drugs. As Congress prepares to restrict the sale of pseudoephedrine, the cold medicine ingredient that is used to make methamphetamine, officials here and in other states that have recently imposed similar restrictions caution that they fall far short of a solution.

"You can't legislate away demand," said Betty Oldenkamp, secretary of human services in South Dakota, where the governor

this month proposed tightening a law that last year restricted customers to two packs of pseudoephedrine per store. "The law enforcement aspects are tremendously important, but we also have to do something to address the demand."

Here, officials boast that their law restricting pseudoephedrine, which took effect in May, has been faster than any other state's in reducing methamphetamine laboratories. Still, when Mr. Van Haaften, director of the Governor's Office of Drug Control Policy, surveyed the local police, 74 percent said that the law had not changed demand, and 61 percent said supply had remained steady or increased.

## 'Mexican drug cartels were right there to feed that demand.'

In a survey of treatment professionals, 92 percent said they had seen as many or more methamphetamine addicts; the state treated 6,000 in 2005 and expects to treat more than 7,000 this year, based on current trends. Some health officials said abuse among women, typically the biggest users of methamphetamine, was rising particularly fast.

While seizures of powdered methamphetamine declined to 4,572 in 2005 from 6,488 in 2001, seizures of crystal methamphetamine increased, to 2,025 from one.

Federal drug agents tend to describe ice as methamphetamine that is at least 90 percent pure. Officials here say much of their crystal methamphetamine is less pure—"dirty ice," they call it. But either is far more potent than homemade powdered methamphetamine; a "good cook" yields a drug that is about 42 percent pure, but around 25 percent is more common. And in the first four months after the law took effect here, average purity went to 80 percent from 47 percent.

Other states have seen the same.

"The Mexican drug cartels were right there to feed that demand," said Tom Cunningham, the drug task force coordinator for the district attorneys council for Oklahoma, the first state to put pseudoephedrine behind pharmacy counters, in

2004. "They have always supplied marijuana, cocaine, and heroin. When we took away the local meth lab, they simply added methamphetamine to the truck."

A methamphetamine cook could make an ounce for $50 on a stovetop or in a lab in a car; that same amount now costs $800 to $1,500 on the street, the police say.

"Our burglaries have just skyrocketed," said Jerry Furness, who represents Buchanan County, 150 miles northeast of Des Moines, on the Iowa drug task force. "The state asks how the decrease in meth labs has reduced danger to citizens, and it has, as far as potential explosions. But we've had a lot of burglaries where the occupants are home at the time, and that's probably more of a risk. So it's kind of evening out."

When the state surveyed the children in state protection in southeastern Iowa four months after the law took effect, it found that 49 percent were taken from parents who had been using methamphetamine, the same percentage as two years earlier, even as police said they were removing fewer children from homes with laboratories.

Some law enforcement officials say that addicts may find the crystal form more desirable. "If they don't have to mess with precursor chemicals, it's actually a bit easier on them, and safer," said Kevin Glaser, a drug task force supervisor for the state highway patrol in Missouri, which last year led the nation in methamphetamine lab seizures.

But the switch has also increased the risks. "People are overdosing; they're not expecting it to do this much," said Darcy Jensen, director of Prairie View Prevention Services in South Dakota. "They don't realize that that fourth of a gram they're used to using is double or triple in potency."

Federal officials say there are 1.4 million methamphetamine addicts in the United States, concentrated in the West, where the drug began to take hold in the late 1980's, and the Midwest and South, where it moved in the mid- and late 1990's.

Drug enforcement officials have always said that 80 percent of the nation's supply comes from so-called super labs, those able to make 10 pounds or more. But in some counties here, officials say that all the methamphetamine came from mom-and-pop labs that made the drug by cooking pseudoephedrine with toxic farm and household chemicals.

Law enforcement focused on the laboratories because they were so destructive: the police found children who had drunk lye thinking it was water, or went without food as parents went through the long binge-and-sleep cycles of using. Laboratories in homes, motels, abandoned farm buildings or cars frequently exploded, or dumped their toxic chemicals into drains or soil. Small police departments spent much of their time attending to contaminated sites.

More than 30 states have restricted pseudoephedrine in some way. Nine have put it behind pharmacy counters, and Oregon now requires a prescription to obtain it.

Addicts and cookers have proved to be skilled at getting around the restrictions; as one state imposes a law, bordering states see an increase in laboratories. Oklahoma recently linked its pharmacies by a computer database to track sales after discovering that cooks were going county-to-county buying from several pharmacies a day.

Iowa's law passed unanimously. As in other states, officials say the number of laboratories had already begun to decline, most likely because cooks feared they would be caught because there was so much public attention on the problem.

The law resulted in a decline of at least 80 percent. Police found 138 laboratories from June to December, down from 673 for the same period the year before. The state had hit a high of 1,500 lab busts in 2004, but with the law, had 731 for 2005, and expects just 257 this year. Law enforcement says the costs of policing and cleaning up labs will drop to $528,000 next year from $2.6 million in 2004.

But here and in many of the states with recent pseudoephedrine restrictions, frustration with the stubborn rate of addiction has moved the discussion from enforcement to treatment and demand reduction.

That discussion, officials say, will be much tougher.

After listening to Mr. Van Haaften's report on the effects of the law this week, State Representative Clel Baudler, a former state trooper who now heads the public safety committee for the Iowa General Assembly, charged his committee to come back to the next meeting with strategies to reduce demand.

"My fear is, when I ask what they think we should do, they'll say 'I don't know,' " Mr. Baudler said in an interview afterward. "We've increased penalties, we've increased prison time, we're still not getting in front of it."

Officials say they never advertised the law as one that would reduce methamphetamine addiction. Still, they are surprised at how the drug has hung on.

"Things that are highly destructive, including diseases, tend to be self-limiting," said Arthur Schut, president of the Mid-Eastern Council on Chemical Abuse in Iowa City, and a member of the state's drug policy advisory council. "This has been devastating. It's remarkable how quickly people are damaged by it."

Mr. Van Haaften, too, knows that it was too much to hope that the law would reduce demand. Still, he says, "I had a little hope."

"I knew of the addictive nature, but in my heart, I believed people didn't want to deal with dealers," he said. "They have guns, it's dangerous, if you make your own it's safer. I hoped for a dip, but the availability did not allow that to happen."

# Just Say No? No Need Here

ABIGAIL SULLIVAN MOORE

Like many students enjoying the newfound freedom of college, the young man accelerated the drinking he had begun at prep school. "You go nuts," he explains, looking back, seemingly both amazed and disgusted. At 6-foot-1 and 215 pounds, he was able to put away up to 18 beers a night at weekend parties. "It was crazy," says the student, now a junior at Fairfield University, adding that afterward, "I'd feel like death all day."

At one party last spring, he drank so much rum that he doesn't remember anything that happened. Other students complained about his behavior and a graduate assistant escorted him to his room. When a campus security guard showed up to talk to him the next day, "I was still drunk at 3 p.m.," he says.

The university bans alcohol for students under the legal drinking age of 21. Twice before that worrisome blackout, university authorities had penalized him for drinking. For beer in his dormitory room on a "substance-free" floor in freshman year, he paid a $50 fine and lost his spot there. The next year, a security guard caught him smuggling a 30-pack of beer into his dorm to entertain friends from Marist College. "I was almost compelled to get it," he says. "It's a standard of a good time in college." As punishment, he paid a $75 fine and had a talk with his coach on the varsity baseball team.

But for this last violation, he was evaluated by a licensed drug and alcohol counselor, ordered to attend the university's fledgling drinking-reduction program and placed on probation. If he didn't comply, he would have to leave school and lose his academic scholarship.

The eight-session therapeutic program was life-changing, perhaps life-saving. That is why this likable, driven young man is willing to share his story, though not his name, fearing that his past will interfere with his chance of getting into law school. "I don't binge, that's the most important thing,"

he says. Binging is defined as having at least five drinks in a two-hour period, four for women. Now, he says, he has only an occasional beer and doesn't drink and drive.

The fact that he continues to drink is an acceptable part of his therapy. The program's goal is to get heavy drinkers who are not alcoholics to want to cut back, not necessarily to quit. Using a method called motivational interviewing, a counselor asks questions that nudge students, in a non-judgmental way, to examine their drinking, their ambivalence about it and its effect on their daily life and long-term ambitions.

"It's not anti-drinking; it's anti-harmful drinking," explains G. Alan Marlatt, a psychology professor who uses the techniques for the drinking reduction program he created at the University of Washington in Seattle.

In the last five years, programs using a nonjudgmental approach have been slowly spreading on college campuses. They range from Fairfield's intensive group program to an online self-assessment of drinking patterns, called e-CHUG, now used by students at some 110 colleges.

"When you sit with a person and ask them what the trouble is with their drinking, they've got a whole list of problems" like hangovers, drinking-related traffic violations and other risky behavior, says William R. Miller, a psychology professor at the University of New Mexico who developed the approach. But label the same person an alcoholic and he will deny it, he says. The nonconfrontational approach works well with college students. "Who's more oppositional than an adolescent?" Dr. Miller says.

Another element of motivational programs is to show alcohol-abusing students that they're not in step with the norm. Heavy student drinkers overestimate how much their peers typically consume by three or more drinks, according to a study last year by **H. Wesley Perkins, a sociology professor at Hobart and William Smith Colleges**. Since most students want to fit in and be "normal," educating them about the norm may help them change their behavior.

Drinking has been a part of college life—and a concern—for decades. A 2002 study by the National Institute on Alcohol Abuse and Alcoholism linked alcohol to the deaths of at least 1,400 students annually, including in car accidents, and the assault of at least 600,000 others. At least four students died this past fall from binging, the most publicized of those incidents occurring at the University of Colorado at Boulder and the University of Oklahoma. Research results are conflicting, but anywhere from 22 to 44 percent of all students drink to excess.

With students drinking regularly in high school, freshmen with deeply ingrained drinking habits are arriving at campuses in record numbers, college officials say. Over time, many moderate their drinking. In fact, only 12 percent of people who drink become alcoholics. What worries health educators and researchers on alcohol abuse is the window of time when students engage in the heaviest drinking and the perilous behavior associated with it.

The most popular approach—prevention programs that lecture students about the effects of alcohol abuse—seems to be failing, researchers say. Given the diversity of colleges, experts agree there is no one-size-fits-all solution, and programs must be comprehensive and aimed at a campus's specific student population.

Experts cite Fairfield's strategy as one of the most promising for at-risk drinkers. Three months after the program, all participants for the 2002–03 year reported less drinking, with more than 50 percent describing their reduction as considerable. In 2003–04, 25 percent of participants said they were drinking considerably less and 69 percent somewhat less.

At the University of Washington, Professor Marlatt has also documented positive results among graduates of his two-session program, which has been chosen as a national model by the Department of Health and Human Services. In his program, alcohol-abusing students meet one-on-one with counselors to assess their drinking patterns, family history and perceptions about drinking. The counselors also present students with information about their peers' lesser drinking levels and options on how to change their behavior.

"This is a big step for us," says Mark C. Reed, Fairfield's dean of students, of the university's decision to start a program aimed at reducing student drinking rather than eliminating it. Some parents say underage students should forgo all alcohol, Mr. Reed says. But "the reality to go from all to nothing is pretty unrealistic."

Most students in the program have had at least one health-threatening encounter with drinking and are mandated to attend by the university (a handful of others were referred for marijuana use). Students with a diagnosis of alcoholism are referred for more intensive help off campus. A few students in the program referred themselves. "They've been dry-heaving at the health center until they're bringing up blood—on the 21st birthday, they do 21 shots," says Lisa Arnold, the program's facilitator and an alcohol and drug counselor. The program is not a "get out of jail" free card: participants who are on probation with the university can be expelled if caught drinking again.

Initially, many of the students are resistant, seeing the program as a version of the abstinence-based Alcoholics Anonymous. Adding to their resistance is the fact that so many of their friends drink, too, although clearly not all to such extremes.

"The kids struggle most with the fact that they got in trouble but could point to 20 other kids on their floor who could be sitting in their chair," says Ms. Arnold, adding that her response is: "I understand, but let's figure out why you're sitting in this seat and they're not."

During sessions, students learn to identify internal triggers for drinking like stress and depression. They figure out the effects of certain drinking buddies, happy hours and unstructured weekends, as well as learning practical information like the importance of hydration and how to drink safely.

Students also keep drinking diaries. On Thursdays, they plan how much to drink on the weekend. "They drink more if they wing it," Ms. Arnold explains. The next session, they share their experiences, talking about the weekend and what their friends did. The biggest drinkers have a literally sobering effect. "Some of these kids get scared straight," says Deirdre Barrett, a psychologist and director of a similar program at the Addiction Institute of New York.

For many students, such programs are the first opportunity to reflect on their drinking. "Kids at this age are drinking a lot—they tolerate blackouts and fights," says Ms. Barrett, who works with students from Fordham, Columbia, Barnard, New York University and City College. "This is the first chance they've had to say maybe this isn't so good."

The varsity baseball player at Fairfield had mixed feelings about the class at first. "I wasn't embarrassed, but I felt like I should have been," he says. He also felt relieved. He began to look forward to his 90-minute sessions with Ms. Arnold and the nine or so other students. Students attend four to eight sessions, according to their need; a relapsing few have repeated the program.

"She kind of helped you along to realize that things were suffering," the young athlete says, adding that he came to understand that it was impossible to compete on the baseball team, maintain good grades and drink heavily, even if only on weekends. He was also disappointing his parents, with whom he is close. "Your parents are paying money for what, to be burned?" he says.

But it has been hard to resume a social life. "It made you realize you didn't need to go out to get plastered to have a good time," he says. Now he works off campus on Friday and Saturday nights as a waiter and saves his money for the future.

He is eager to finish college, saying he feels "kind of isolated a little bit," and he keeps apart from friends who continue to binge. "I was one of the first to start," he says. "Now, I'm one of the first to stop."

---

ABIGAIL SULLIVAN MOORE contributes regularly to the Connecticut section of *The Times*.

# A Harvest of Treachery

**Afghanistan's drug trade is threatening the stability of a nation America went to war to stabilize. What can be done?**

RON MOREAU AND SAMI YOUSAFZAI

In the privacy of his sparsely furnished house in Kabul, a veteran Afghan Interior Ministry official says the situation may already be hopeless. Although he has no authorization to speak with the press, and he could be in personal danger if his identity became known, he's nevertheless too worried to keep silent. "We are losing the fight against drug traffickers," he says. "If we don't crack down on these guys soon, it won't be long until they're in control of everything."

His pessimism is spreading. Despite the recent fanfare over the convening of Afghanistan's first elected Parliament in more than three decades, the rule of law is under attack by a ruthless organization of warlords and drug smugglers that spans the country and transcends its ethnic divisions. Narcotics trafficking isn't merely big, it's more than half the economy—amounting to $2.7 billion annually, according to the United Nations Office on Drugs and Crime (UNODC)—that is, 52 percent of the country's entire GDP. And many of the underground industry's most important figures are said to be senior government officials in Kabul and the provinces. Amanullah Paiman, a newly elected member of Parliament from the far northern province of Badakhshan, has studied the country's drug problem and says Afghan government officials are involved in at least 70 percent of the traffic. "The chain of narcodollars goes from the districts to the highest levels of government," he says.

That accusation is supported by the public complaints of Ali Jalali, a former Interior minister who quit the job this past summer. He has repeatedly said he has a list of more than 100 high-ranking Afghan officials he suspects of involvement in the drug trade. A source close to him, fearful of being killed if identified, says Jalali's unpublished list includes at least 13 former and present provincial governors and four past or present cabinet ministers. The source adds that one of the minister's chief reasons for resigning was his frustration over President Hamid Karzai's failure to sack and prosecute crooked officials.

The president, having declared a "holy war" against drugs a year ago, can claim a few victories. A successful eradication campaign reduced total poppy-growing acreage by 21 percent this past year, but exceptional weather yielded an opium harvest just 2 percent below the record crop of 2004. The price of raw opium rose anyway, from $90 a kilo to more than $100, and many former growers are said to be returning to poppies for lack of a better source of income. Gen. Mohammad Daud, the president's deputy Interior minister for counternarcotics, says the president recently gave a severe tongue-lashing to the governors of 10 major opium provinces. "I don't want to see any poppy cultivation in your provinces," Karzai reportedly told them. "It harms and defames Afghanistan"—and, he added, it could ultimately deprive the country of desperately needed international help in the war against the Taliban. That's America's worry, too: the unchecked spread of drug corruption in Afghanistan could affect the future stability and democracy of a country that U.S. troops gave their lives to stabilize and democratize.

President Karzai's name has never been linked to the drug trade. His younger brother, Ahmed Wali Karzai, a personal representative of the president based in Kandahar, is a different story. He was alleged to be a major figure by nearly every source who described the Afghan network to NEWSWEEK for this story, including past and present government officials and several minor drug traffickers. "He is the unofficial regional governor of southern Afghanistan and leads the whole trafficking structure," says the veteran Interior Ministry official. Ahmed Wali Karzai vehemently denies the allegation, telling NEWSWEEK it's "propaganda" concocted by his family's political enemies—a defense that is seconded by the presidential palace.

General Daud is also a subject of persistent reports of past involvement in trafficking. "These are false accusations," says the former Northern Alliance general. "Such rumors cannot weaken my determination." Daud says he is making steady progress against the drug gangs, arresting more than 300 traffickers in the past year and winning stiff prison sentences against most. He says the busts have included government officials and border policemen. "These traffickers are killers of humanity," he says.

All the same, the drug trade is making some Afghans rich. Many of them don't bother hiding their newfound wealth. Dozens of gleaming new multistory commercial edifices are going up amid the low-lying mud-brick architecture of old Kabul, along with scores of palatial villas where squatters used to live in makeshift huts. A prominent local building contractor, asking not to be named for fear of retribution, estimates that 70 percent of the new construction is funded by drug profits. "Here you build with ready cash," he says, "not with bank loans."

Most Afghans are far less fortunate. More than 300,000 families in Afghanistan raise opium as a cash crop, but it earns them an average of less than $1,800 a year. The remaining 80 percent of the country's total drug income goes to the traffickers and their well-connected friends. Nevertheless, almost every move to stop the traffic seems to be directed mainly at the growers. "The poor farmers who benefit least from the narcotics business are the target of the anti-drug campaign," says Ahmed Nader Nadery of the Afghan Independent Human Rights Commission. "The focus instead should be on the more important players, the Kabul officials, provincial governors and police."

The drug trade is placing terrible costs on the rest of the country. According to a recent study by the UNODC and the Ministry of Counter Narcotics, approximately 170,000 Afghans—roughly 1.4 percent of the population—now use opium or heroin. About 30,000 of those addicts are women, a shockingly high number in such a conservative Muslim society. The toll doesn't end there. "Afghanistan's main problems are all linked to drug trafficking: rampant corruption, repressive militia groups, human-rights abuses and bad governance," says a Western diplomat in Kabul who would discuss drug trafficking only on condition of anonymity.

Karzai is in the most difficult of positions. Many of the figures under suspicion were useful to the United States in the overthrow of the Taliban and continue to serve as checks against the old regime's resurgence. The president sometimes reassigns officials who have come under scrutiny, but rarely in a way that would upset the status quo. He's particularly careful with the warlords who run many of the biggest opium-growing provinces.

"His options are limited," says senior presidential adviser Javed Ludin. "These guys have been propped up by and are allied with U.S.-led Coalition forces." Now Karzai depends on the military strength and political influence of his warlord governors. Ludin says: "The same people who are being accused by some in the international community of being drug traffickers . . . are our most reliable partners in the war against terrorism."

Meanwhile the traffickers are waging a political war of their own—and winning. Diplomats and well-informed Afghans believe that up to a quarter of the new Parliament's 249 elected members are linked to narcotics production and trafficking. One especially controversial figure is Arif Noorzai, who has won the post of deputy speaker of Parliament. (He denies any wrongdoing.) In a study for the independent Afghanistan Research and Evaluation Unit, Afghan expert Andrew Wilder concludes that at least 17 newly elected M.P.s are drug traffickers themselves, 24 others are connected to criminal gangs, 40 are commanders of armed groups and 19 face serious allegations of war crimes and human-rights abuses.

There's little doubt that Afghanistan's future depends on stopping the drug lords. "It's the cornerstone of everything you want to do here," says a UNODC representative in Kabul who asks not to be identified because the subject is so sensitive. "It's linked to security, to building the justice and law-enforcement systems and to economic and political development." Western governments ought to confront Karzai directly and "name and shame" some of the worst drug offenders on the public payroll, says the diplomat. "Then the president could tell governor X and police chief Y, 'You're out—the international community is telling me you are involved in drugs, and I have to believe them'." That's easy to say. Karzai has never had much luck at telling the warlords what to do. The question is how much more help the West is prepared to give him—and whether it would be enough.

# An End to 'Power Hour'

## A tragic alcohol fatality spurs a crackdown on the time-honored custom of birthday bingeing up north.

T. TRENT GEGAX

Throwing up in the men's room might not seem much of a birthday celebration. But for Gregg Rock, and a lot of newly legal drinkers, it's the price of turning 21. For Rock, it started with "pre-drinking" a bottle of Bacardi rum with college buddies last Wednesday before walking into a University of Minnesota tavern. It was midnight, the magic hour he became legal. On the bar rail there were soon "The Three Wise Men" (Jim Beam, Johnny Walker, Jack Daniels). The sound system played the Ramones' "I Wanna Be Sedated." Rock pounded. Then his body rebelled. "Yes, I puked," said a visibly relieved Rock, a senior. "But I know my limit."

It's known as "power hour," the post-midnight drinking spree common on many campuses. Steve Johnson, a 20-year-old Minnesota student, says he's looking forward to spending his power hour in August like Rock did. "It's a rite of passage," he says, "like you got to show how much you can drink." But Johnson won't be powering up at a tavern the moment he turns 21. A stunning alcohol overdose during a "power hour" has triggered moves to end the custom in North Dakota and Minnesota.

This week Minnesota Gov. Tim Pawlenty is expected to sign a bill into law prohibiting bars from serving alcohol to 21-year-olds until 8 a.m. on their birthday. North Dakota passed the same law last month. The new legal tool is aimed at curbing binge drinking on college campuses. "We're on the verge of more kids' killing themselves," says Bob Pomplun, who conducts alcohol-safety classes for employees of bars in the Upper Midwest. "Young people don't know how to drink smartly, so we need to teach intelligent drinking."

Anne Buchanan thought she had talked through all the dangers with her son Jason Reinhardt, right up till the moment last August that he walked out the door for his power hour with friends at Minnesota State University at Moorhead. Jason said he knew how dangerous it was, but he also knew that his friends would watch out for him. "But they didn't know what to watch out for," Buchanan says. He died of acute alcohol poisoning in his sleep. Stunned by Jason's tragic passing, legislators in the northland moved quickly. Even the Minnesota Licensed Beverage Association didn't object. "Whatever we can do to limit problems, we do," says Jim Farrell, the group's executive director, "regardless of whether it makes sense."

But the trend to stop power hour will not likely catch on in next-door Wisconsin. A lot more than a river separates Minnesota (12,500 bars) and Wisconsin (30,000 bars), two states of roughly equal population. A recent Harvard study ranked Wisconsin first in the nation in binge drinking. But the legislature is considering lowering the drinking age to 19 for active-duty service members. The bipartisan bill has a dozen cosponsors and the support of a powerful congressman in U.S. Rep. James Sensenbrenner. "It's the outgrowth of the German heritage," says Bill Dixon, a Madison lawyer who ran Gary Hart's presidential campaign. "It's a state where we still do consider beer a food, and brandy's not far behind." Wisconsin is a state where even children can drink legally in bars, as long as an approving parent is on the premises.

The country's bar industry hasn't shown a taste for a nationwide power-hour ban. The tavern industry is already reeling from the no-smoking bans, and generally believes that self-policing is the most effective way to manage drinkers. It's already against the law to serve alcohol to an intoxicated customer. But anybody who has ever been inside a bar knows bartenders can be rather lenient about that rule. Raising the drinking age to 21 significantly reduced fatalities. Will the new power-hour law? "By itself I doubt it will have a major impact," says Dr. Henry Wechsler, director of college alcohol studies at the Harvard School of Public Health. "But if it saves one life, that will be good." That's something that Jason Reinhardt's mother knows all too well.

With Dirk Johnson

# Helping Students Stay Clean and Sober

## More colleges create programs for recovering alcoholics and drug addicts

Joshua Karlin-Resnick

Christopher S. Johnson was 13 when he took his first sip of beer. By 14 he was drinking three or four times a week, trying to drown his depression, and smoking marijuana with his friends. At 15 he ran away from home to a nearby town in Minnesota, where he partied every night and popped dozens of pain-killing pills per day.

For seven months he spent his days in a laundromat, sleeping at "whoever's house would take me," he says.

Then one night in November 2001, he passed out in the bathroom of a Cambodian restaurant. He says he wanted to kill himself, but that he was too drunk to do so.

When the restaurant's manager chased him outside to a pay telephone, Mr. Johnson says he received "the gift of desperation." That night he turned himself in to the police and told his parents that he wanted to stop drinking. A few days later he entered a substance-abuse treatment program.

Mr. Johnson, now a 19-year-old rising senior at Sobriety High West, a school for recovering alcoholic teenagers in Edina, Minn., has been clean for two years. He is looking for a college that will help him stay that way, and a handful of institutions have developed programs designed for just such a purpose.

As more students with drug and alcohol problems come through the doors of academe, a small but growing number of colleges are offering specialized support services for those who have received treatment for their addictions. Some substance-abuse experts say the programs are crucial for recovering alcoholics and drug addicts, who need help navigating life in the campus party zone.

Designed both for students who complete treatment before they matriculate as well as for those who overcome dependencies while they are in college, the programs create support groups and help students avoid the booze-soaked social scenes that could lead them back to bad habits. Most require weekly attendance at Alcoholics Anonymous or Narcotics Anonymous meetings on the campus. Some provide students with special housing.

Augsburg College, in Minneapolis; Dana College, in Nebraska; and Rutgers and Texas Tech Universities are among the institutions with established recovery programs. And this fall several colleges, including Case Western Reserve University; Grand Valley State University, in Michigan; and the University of Texas at Austin, plan to introduce recovery programs of their own.

Representatives of the programs met on the Rutgers campus here last month for the third annual conference of the Association of Recovery Schools, a Nashville-based organization that helps colleges and high schools develop and strengthen services for students in recovery for alcohol and drug dependence. One of the convention's guests was Mr. Johnson, who told the officials what high-school students like him are looking for: a college that will support them without exiling them to the fringes of the campus.

"We do want to be normal and do want to have some sort of tie-in with people who don't have an alcohol or drug addiction," Mr. Johnson says.

David T. Hadden, assistant director of Augsburg's recovery program and a member of the association's executive board, says the programs not only keep students who have been through exhaustive—and expensive—treatment from backsliding, but help them succeed in college and become "good, tax-paying citizens."

"If they go back to a regular college campus where they don't have support, where they don't have a community environment where it's really actually cool not to be drunk or party," says Mr. Hadden, "it makes it lonely."

## An Alcohol-Free Haven

Rutgers started the nation's first on-campus alcohol- and drug-recovery program in 1983. At first the participants attended weekly support-group meetings, and those who were having trouble staying sober received individual counseling as well.

After some of the students said they needed more than just meetings, Lisa Laitman, the program's director, developed an alcohol-free dormitory—a haven where students in recovery would not have to share rooms with their former drinking buddies.

Despite the initial apprehension of some administrators, she says, the program has been a success, involving 15 to 25 students each year.

Augsburg's program includes a dorm with spaces for more than 60 students. Dana does not set aside a separate area for recovering alcoholics but does allow them to room together. Students in most of the programs do not have to pay extra for such housing.

Officials at Case Western say they decided to build their program around a dormitory because they were dissatisfied with the results of outsourcing their recovery efforts. James E. Sellers, director of University Counseling Services and the Center for Collegiate Behavioral Health at the university, had helped counsel students with drug and alcohol problems and referred them to off-campus locations, including halfway houses in downtown Cleveland, for recovery services.

But some students came back with horror stories. One such student went through treatment and started in a recovery program, but ended up relapsing and failing to graduate. "It really moved me that this student was failing in his recovery program in the sense that he had no other place to go except home or a halfway house in the inner city, where it's quite a shockingly different reality," Mr. Sellers says.

Joseph, the resident coordinator in Case Western's recovery dorm (he asked that his last name not be published), dropped out of the University of Akron in 1996 to undergo treatment for alcoholism. He might have been able to return to college sooner, he says, if any of the colleges near him had had a recovery program.

Instead he attended a community college for three years before he felt comfortable returning to a four-year college campus. Even then he lived alone.

Now a graduate student in Case Western's academic program in chemical-dependency counseling, in the social-work school, he hopes to help students in his dorm stay sober and graduate on time. "As the RA I'm going to try to make sure we're aware of what's going on with each other and be supportive," he says.

Texas Tech has taken a different approach in its program, which began in 1985. It does not include housing, but participating students share common requirements. Each must attend at least two 12-step-program meetings on the campus every week and take a special one-credit-hour seminar on recovery each semester. The students are also eligible for academic scholarships of up to $2,000 per year, which are financed entirely by an endowment.

Kitty S. Harris, the program's director, says there is a strong sense of community among the students, even though they do not live in the same dorm. In fact, putting all recovering students in the same building can do more harm than good, she says.

"I think it stigmatizes the kids," Ms. Harris says. "At the center we help them learn to live in the real world, so they're better adjusted when they graduate."

UT-Austin's new program will also offer scholarships to participants and will require them to enroll in a course on recovery and relapse prevention, attend weekly meetings, and participate in community-service projects. The program will not have a housing component, although Laura G. Jones-Swann, director of the university's new Center for Students in Recovery, says she would consider adding one.

# Keeping a Pact

Officials who run on-campus recovery services emphasize that their programs are not punitive. Students who participate must want to be there. Many of the programs require participants to have at least six months of sobriety under their belts before they can enroll, to ensure that they are serious about cleaning up.

The screening process for most of the programs includes an interview with a university counselor. Students at Texas Tech must submit an essay and three letters of recommendation attesting to their recovery status.

The programs also usually ask students to sign agreements stating that they will stay sober and study hard. Students in the Case Western dormitory must develop recovery plans listing their academic and recovery goals, including any therapy sessions they plan to attend.

At Augsburg, each of about 60 students in the program must sign a contract developed by veterans of the program, who sit on a governing board. A student review board decides what to do with residents who violate the pact, which requires students to attend 12-step meetings, keep up with their studies, and avoid bars and keg parties.

The contract and the penalties give everyone in the program a "protective barrier," says Eric W. Maurer, a senior who heads both boards. "It's a lot easier to live somewhere where everyone's sober," he says.

The programs generally allow students to stay involved for the duration of their college careers, or until they feel confident in their sobriety.

Christin R. Crabtree-McWethy, a recovering alcoholic, participated in Augsburg's program for one year. She was so successful academically that she was chosen to deliver the commencement address at her graduation, in 2003.

"I came into Augsburg with a concern that if I was going home to a dorm where there was drinking and drug use at night, it would be just like going to a bar," she says. "What I like about it is I was still a part of the general community at Augsburg, but I had that safe environment to go home to at night."

It is difficult to measure the long-term effectiveness of on-campus recovery programs because there has not been a major study of their impact. But Augsburg officials say they have been successful: Since the college's program began, in 1997, it has attracted 365 students, only 62 of whom, or 17 percent, have relapsed.

Program officials say they compare that rate with recent statistics on high-school students in Minnesota. About 85 percent of those who go through treatment and return to regular high schools subsequently relapse, Mr. Hadden says, while high schools designed for recovering alcoholics and drug addicts report a relapse rate of about 20 percent.

Not everyone at Augsburg was convinced that the program would benefit the college when the Faculty Senate first considered the idea, in the mid-1990s, says Christopher W. Kimball, vice president for academic and student affairs and dean of the college. Mr. Kimball, who was then a faculty member, says that at first he and some of his colleagues had a "fear of the unknown."

There was some concern that the dorm would scare other students away, he recalls. Faculty members worried that prospective students or their families would think, " 'Oh, my gosh, there's a section of a dorm where everyone's in recovery.' "

But the program has become an asset to the campus, he says, attracting a diverse group of students who are among the smartest at Augsburg. The college took a chance, he says, "and it's been repaid many times over."

Mark A. Murray, president of Grand Valley State, sees a clear need for the programs.

"We've got alcohol issues in middle schools and high schools, and we certainly have them at the college and university level," he says. Mr. Murray adds that it is important to be straightforward and supportive of students who are trying to deal with their problems.

Some substance-abuse experts, however, say many of the nation's top colleges are unlikely to develop the programs anytime soon. One reason is cost: Colleges located in areas with plenty of off-campus recovery services may deem it unnecessary to add a similar program on their campus, where most funds go to prevention and treatment.

Bruce E. Donovan, who recently retired as associate dean for chemical dependency at Brown University, says elite colleges tend to "focus much more intently on the basic academic purposes of the institution" than on specialized services for students.

The program that he ran at Brown provided counseling to students who were struggling with alcohol or drugs, but it referred them to off-campus recovery programs. That approach has worked well for the college, says Mr. Donovan, himself a recovering alcoholic.

"Particularly in a time of tightened budget, the main mission is academics," he says. "Everything else is seen as a nice add-on, but decidedly add-on."

William DeJong, director of the Center for College Health and Safety, in Newton, Mass., questions the wisdom of that approach. Top colleges, he argues, tend to think that they do not need to cater to a broad range of student needs, because they get to pick the "cream of the crop."

"That's a mistake because these schools—Ivy League and others—are among those with the highest alcohol rates in the country," says Mr. DeJong, who is a member of the board of Substance Abuse Recovery on College Campuses Inc., a Minnesota-based nonprofit group that promotes a program based on Augsburg's.

Andrew J. Finch, director of the Association of Recovery Schools, says administrators may mistakenly believe that they are doing enough for students in recovery by financing counseling services.

"There's a misconception that because they may have a counselor in student health, that they're somehow addressing the pretty unique needs of someone who is new into recovery," Mr. Finch says. "When they're coming out of a treatment facility right back into the atmosphere in which they were using drugs . . . it can set them right back again into using behaviors."

## Looking Ahead

Like most high-school seniors, Mr. Johnson, the student from Minnesota, has begun his college search. He is looking for a campus with housing for students in recovery, but also one where he can major in physical therapy. After his visit to Rutgers in July, he put it at the top of his list.

If he chooses a college without a recovery program, however, Mr. Johnson's biggest concern is that he will end up sharing a room with someone who drinks. He says he would be straightforward with his roommate about his alcoholism, as he has been with his friends who drink. "Usually I don't expect a lot," he says. "I expect them to just basically know that is something that bothers me."

He is confident that he will find the right college, and that he will be able to handle the freedom of campus life.

"As long as I participate fully in my recovery program and in others' recovery programs, that's what keeps me sober," says Mr. Johnson. "That's what helps me not be so stressed out about what college to go to."

# The Power of Potent Steroids

**Hamster research raises new questions about whether the commonly abused drugs may be addictive.**

RACHEL ADELSON

As professional baseball players have been finding out, steroid use draws a lot of scrutiny. And it's not just in pro sports. Given the surge in steroid abuse, especially among young people, neuroscientists are racing to find out whether and how these drugs affect the nervous system. At the University of Southern California's Keck School of Medicine, neuroscientists Cortney Ballard, PhD, and Ruth Wood, PhD, investigated for the first time how hamsters handled four popular anabolic steroids and got a clear answer: The nervous system can find some of these drugs reinforcing.

The findings, published in the June *Behavioral Neuroscience* (Vol. 119, No. 3), also show that it's not just the drug. It's the form of the drug. The injectable anabolic androgenic steroids (AASs) appear to be more reinforcing than oral AASs.

"This highly significant study . . . helps form the groundwork for the identification and characterization of AASs as classically rewarding substances," says Richard Melloni Jr., PhD, a behavioral neuroscientist at Northeastern University. Because rodents' nervous systems are like people's, researchers say they can comfortably transfer their conclusions to humans. Testing drug reinforcement in animals also allows scientists to eliminate the impact of social factors on drug use.

Nancy Pilotte, PhD, chief of the Functional Neuroscience Research Branch at the National Institute on Drug Abuse (NIDA), which helped to fund the study, describes it as a good first step in understanding how these drugs act on the brain. The research, she says, is crucial in figuring out whether their use can result in addiction, which NIDA views as a chronic relapsing brain disease in which people will take a drug often and repeatedly in the face of negative consequences. Says Pilotte, "We know these drugs are abused; now we're exploring whether they're addictive."

Evidence that steroids affect the nervous system augments the findings of neurobiologist Marilyn Y. McGinnis, PhD, of the University of Texas at San Antonio, that long-term AAS exposure boosts aggression in rats, particularly in response to mild provocation. McGinnis says that if anabolic steroids are rewarding, "this factor may contribute to the increasing and long-term use of these drugs in humans."

## Risky Business

AASs have been classified as controlled substances since 1991, yet their potential for dependence remains largely unknown.

"AASs are not mysterious, just understudied," says Wood. As abuse—their use for nonmedical purposes—has risen, doctors have begun to report possible cases of physical and psychological dependence. According to Ballard and Wood, more than 1 million Americans have taken these synthetic hormones, mostly to build muscle.

Melloni notes that steroids—also known as roids, juice, hype, weight trainers, gym candy or pumpers—have been "typically not thought of as classically rewarding substances like many other drugs of abuse, and so they are not considered as potentially dangerous by the American psyche."

Pilotte points out that people don't take AASs for themselves, as they might with cocaine or heroin, but rather for what they produce. The new revelation about reinforcement raises new questions because, as Wood notes, "Initially, most athletes and clinicians simply assumed that AASs acted systemically, but had little impact on the central nervous system."

Known health hazards include mood swings, hallucinations and paranoia; liver damage; high blood pressure; and increased risk of heart disease, stroke and some types of cancer. There are sex-specific dangers and, from sharing injection needles, the risks of HIV and hepatitis. The Centers for Disease Control and Prevention estimate that upwards of 3 percent of high schoolers have used steroids, a rate comparable to that of crack cocaine or heroin use.

Steroid abuse, especially by adolescents and young adults, can promote aggressive behaviors and may be followed by serious depression when their use is discontinued, says Pilotte. Still, abuse may be reinforced by a culture that reveres athleticism and stresses body image. In response, most pro sports leagues have banned steroid use because of the unfair impact on competition. To assess enforcement, the U.S. House of Representatives has held public hearings on steroid use among athletes and opened subcommittee hearings in May to discuss a proposed Drug Free Sports Act. For effective regulation and consumer education, policymakers need to understand the full impact of these drugs on human health, say experts.

## Drug Testing

The four most commonly used AASs differ in their method of administration (oral versus injection), duration of action (long versus short) and potential for metabolic breakdown to estrogen or DHT, a potent androgen called dihydrotestosterone. They are:

- **Nandrolone,** a popular injectable with a longer metabolic breakdown.
- **Drostanolone,** a fast-acting injectable derived from DHT.
- **Oxymethalone,** taken orally.
- **Stanozolol,** also taken orally and popular among females because of its low androgenic potency.

Ballard and Wood hypothesized that although all these steroids are reinforcing, the male Syrian hamsters on which they have conducted other sex-hormone studies would respond the most to potent, fast-acting injectable androgens compared with lower-potency steroids with longer half-lives.

To gauge which type of steroid the hamsters would come to want the most once they had a "taste," the researchers randomly assigned the subjects into 12 groups of eight hamsters. Reward power was tested at three different concentrations: 0.1, 1.0 and 2.0 micrograms per microliter each in solution.

Ballard and Wood implanted tiny stainless-steel pipes, or cannulae, into the animals' skulls to deliver steroid infusions into brain cavities filled with cerebrospinal fluid, which allows for maximum diffusion without tissue damage. This process is called icv, for intracerebroventricular infusion. After the hamsters recovered, the researchers placed each one for four hours in a conditioning chamber that had two nose-poke holes, one-inch circles cut into the wall. A nose poking into the "active" hole broke an infrared beam positioned just on the other side, which triggered a computer to turn on a syringe pump to deliver an icv infusion. Ballard and Wood also recorded nose pokes into the "inactive" hole, which had no effect.

The researchers gave the hamsters an opening 1.0 microliter dose of the AAS solution. Then they measured what happened over the next four hours: How often did each hamster poke the active versus the inactive hole? Given that a poke into the active hole would earn the hamster another microliter of the drug, and the inactive hole would net no injection, what would leave them wanting more?

## Potency and Reinforcement

Each type of steroid presented a different pattern of results, but there was a clear dividing line between the injectables and the orally administered drugs. For the injectables, the hamsters poked the active hole significantly more times than they poked the inactive hole. Giving the hamsters the highly potent injectable drostanolone at the lowest dose had no impact. However, at the two higher concentrations, hamsters averaged twice as many responses on the active nose-poke as on the inactive nose-poke.

For the long-acting injectable nandrolone, responses on the active nose-poke increased with increasing concentrations of the drug, at least at the two higher levels (the lowest level didn't garner a reaction). At the higher concentrations, seven of the eight hamsters preferred the active nose-poke.

The picture was different for the potent oral androgen oxymethalone: The hamsters did not develop a significant preference for the active nose-poke at any dose. And the oral drug stanozolol, which also failed to induce any significant preference for the active nose-poke, produced the lowest amount of operant responding.

Thus, the authors report that the injectable androgens may be more reinforcing than the orally active steroids. However, Wood cautions that this doesn't make orally active androgens safer: First, as Melloni notes, "AAS abusers typically graduate from oral use to the [more rewarding] injectable forms." Second, oral steroids have their own serious side effects, such as liver damage.

## Game Not Over

The findings sound a warning that steroids pack an even more powerful punch than we knew. And all steroids are not the same: Ballard and Wood note that just as these drugs "differ in their potency, half-life, metabolism and mode of administration . . . the properties of different anabolic steroids also affect their reward potential." The differences may lie in how these drugs are metabolized and in their androgenic potency, the intensity with which they affect masculinization.

---

**If anabolic steroids are rewarding, "this factor may contribute to the increasing and long-term use of these drugs in humans."**

Marilyn McGinnis
University of Texas at San Antonio

---

Further research is needed, experts say. For one, Wood and her colleagues want to find the specific brain site where steroids act. She hopes that if research uncovers more about AAS reinforcement, such as permanent changes in brain and behavior, "those who may be tempted to try steroids will be more cautious, particularly high school students for whom AASs—in addition to the other hazards—can limit adult height."

Pilotte would like to see the findings replicated with closer attention to the different ways that humans get steroids into the bloodstream. Additionally, Melloni hopes that new knowledge about steroids, "will better assist us in the development of rational pharmacologic and therapeutic treatment strategies for long-term AAS users."

---

RACHEL ADELSON is a science writer in Raleigh, N.C.

# Cannabis-Related Problems and Their Management

**Despite being the most common illicit drug in the Western world, treatment for cannabis use is not readily available. Primary health care and even specialist drug treatment services have often under-recognised, and under-treated, cannabis-related problems. Australian researcher Jan Copeland is one of the few people to test cannabis treatment models. Here she outlines the most effective models for treating cannabis and how they can be applied to other services.**

DR JAN COPELAND

Cannabis affects public health in many ways. There are many users and most are young (European Monitoring Centre for Drugs and Drug Addiction, 2002; Australian Institute of Health and Welfare, 2005; Substance Abuse and Mental Health Services Administration, 2002; Anthony, Warner & Kesslet, 1994; Swift, Hall & Tesson, 2001). Though we know roughly how many use, we know less about how many are dependent and what effect this is having on physical and mental health.

In Australia a recent survey found that around 200,000 individuals met the criteria for cannabis dependence in one year (1.6% of the population). Among current cannabis smokers—defined as smoking the drug more than five times in that year—23.3% met the criteria for dependence (Swift, Hall & Tesson, 2001).

## Cannabis Health Problems

While cannabis has very low acute toxicity and mortality rates, it is associated with considerable health problems. Cannabis dependence is the most obvious harm, though there is a growing body of evidence of subtle cognitive impairment affecting attention, memory and the organization and integration of complex information as a result of cannabis use (Solowij, 1998).

As cannabis is almost always smoked, there is an obvious risk of adverse respiratory effects, such as chronic bronchitis. Some studies have also identified changes in lung tissue that may be precursors to cancer (Tashkin, 1999). Many smokers mix cannabis with tobacco, and are also regular tobacco smokers. There is evidence that some of the negative respiratory effects of cannabis and tobacco may also be additive (Taylor *et al.*, 2002).

Co-existing cannabis and tobacco use may complicate the management of smoking cessation, where cannabis use prompts relapse to tobacco use, with the reverse also reported in cannabis treatment populations.

Certain groups may be at a higher risk of developing adverse acute and chronic effects of cannabis. These include adolescents, pregnant women, those with respiratory or cardiovascular disease whose conditions may be aggravated by use, and those with a dual diagnosis (Swift, Copeland & Lenton, 2000).

The issue of dual diagnosis involving other substance use disorders (for example cannabis and alcohol use), or substance use and other mental health disorders (such as substance use disorders and anxiety or depression) is relatively common (Andrews *et al*, 1999; Degenhardt, Hall & Lynskey, 2003).

There is increasing agreement that those with schizophrenia may be particularly susceptible to the effects of cannabis and that cannabis use has a negative impact on the management of psychotic disorders (Hall & Pacula, 2003).

## Managing Cannabis Problems

Despite high levels of problematic cannabis use, only a minority seek assistance from health professionals. The demand for treatment for cannabis problems, nonetheless, is increasing across the world. Willie there have been a range of therapies applied to the treatment of drug dependence, there has been very little systematic development of interventions designed for cannabis dependence to date.

# Outline of a Brief Cannabis Intervention

The one session intervention (Copeland *et al.*, 2001) was made up of the following clinical components:

- personalised feedback from the assessment of cannabis use, dependence, cannabis-related problems and related results (eg, you meet the accepted criteria for dependence and you have told me it has these negative effects on your life)
- education on the bases of addictive behaviour (it is a drug of dependence, you have described experiencing symptoms such as loss of control, tolerance and withdrawal)
- advice on planning strategies for quitting (eg, make time and plan ahead, get rid of drug paraphernalia, avoid cannabis-using friends etc)
- goal setting (make a definite quit date, plan how to reward yourself for success)
- tips for dealing with craving and withdrawal (eg, recognise high-risk situations and how to manage them, remember urges are self-limiting etc)
- behavioural self-management (plan for a cannabis-free lifestyle).

This session took approximately 60–90 minutes and the participants received a booklet that reinforced the key points of the session. The patient booklet and clinical guidelines are available from the National Drug and Alcohol Research Centre (Copeland, Swift & Matalon, 2001).

While nicotine, alcohol and opioid dependence can be treated with drugs such as nicotine patches and agonist and antagonist drugs, there are no such drugs tried and tested for cannabis—despite current trials in this area (Copeland, 2004).

The best evidence to date has been for brief interventions similar to those successfully employed by nurses and other health care practitioners for alcohol and tobacco problems.

Most include some variant of cognitive behavioural therapy (CB1) or motivational interviewing (MI). While CBT examines the interplay between thoughts, behaviour and environment, the main aim of MI is to enhance the motivation of the participant to change.

The first two psychological intervention studies were conducted in the US and showed that even brief psychological treatments had a significant impact on the treatment outcome of cannabis-dependent adults (Stephens, Roffman & Simpson, 1994; Stephens, Roffman & Curtin, 2000).

Our own randomised controlled trial of brief cognitive behavioural interventions for cannabis use disorder also supported the efficacy of providing even one hour of individual skills-based therapy (Copeland *et al.*, 2001).

Participants in the study were randomised to either six- or one-session CBT or a delayed-treatment control group. The participants reported a variety of cannabis-related problems in the preceding six months. These include 83% with general health problems (largely respiratory-related). The most common psycho-social concerns and the percentage reporting that concern include:

## "In Australia, young people aged 14–19 years are more likely to have smoked cannabis than tobacco"

- 85% reduced motivation
- 70% went to work stoned

- 67% felt paranoid and antisocial
- 64% of those with a spouse and 36% of those with children complained about their cannabis use
- 59% had given up previously enjoyed hobbies
- 17% had trouble with the police.

Young, dependent cannabis users are heavy consumers of health care services with around a third of the participants having seen a medical practitioner in the preceding two weeks. Just under a fifth (19%) were hospitalised in the last year (Copeland, Rees & Swift, 1999).

What this shows is that nurses and other primary health care providers have high rates of contact with people experiencing severe cannabis dependence. They are therefore ideally placed for opportunistic assessment and intervention. (For a brief outline of the content of a brief intervention and issues in assessment see the accompanying textboxes).

The largest published trial of interventions for cannabis dependence was recently completed by a group in the USA (Babor *et al.*, 2004). It was a multi-site study of 450 adults seeking treatment for cannabis dependence in three US states (Connecticut, Florida and Washington).

The participants received either two sessions of a motivational intervention, nine sessions of a multi-component therapy that included motivational enhancement, CBT or case management. At four months follow-up, the nine-session treatment group had reduced cannabis smoking and associated consequences, such as dependence symptoms, significantly more than the two-session treatment, which significantly reduced cannabis use relative to a no treatment control group.

# Special Populations— Adolescents and Those with Mental Health Problems

There are two groups for whom the issue of interventions for cannabis use disorder are especially problematical. Cannabis use is most commonly initiated in adolescence, when heavy, regular use is of concern, and treatment seeking among this group is rare.

Those with psychotic disorders are also a group that are particularly vulnerable to the effects of cannabis and are difficult to engage, retain and successfully treat for cannabis dependence.

### Mental Health Problems

One of the most challenging clinical issues is the dual management of schizophrenia and cannabis dependence. Cannabis use and dependence is more common among those with schizophrenia (Cabtor-Graae, Nordstrom & McNeil, 2001). Longitudinal studies have reported that the rate of development of cannabis dependence is associated with increased rates of psychotic symptoms in young people, even when pre-existing symptoms and background factors are taken into account (Fergusson, Horwood & Swain-Campbell, 2003).

Cannabis contributes to the burden of schizophrenia through an increased relapse rate, an exacerbation of the positive symptoms of the disorder (hallucinations and delusions), non-compliance with treatment and poorer social functioning (Agosti, Nunes & Levine, 2002). Population studies have also reported higher rates of dual diagnosis among those who have previously been or are currently cannabis dependent (Drake, Essock & Shaner, 2001).

With no evidence-based pharmacotherapy for the dual diagnosis of schizophrenia and cannabis dependence, the use of psychological interventions and shared care with mental health and substance use disorder treatment services is central to their optimal management (Copeland, 2004; Drake, Essock & Shaner, 2001).

They are an especially difficult group to engage and retain in treatment. Clinician's recommendations for the management of substance use in the context of severe and persistent mental illness rests with integrated shared care or dual diagnosis services. Such services can provide staffed interventions, assertive outreach, motivational interventions, counselling, social support interventions, a comprehensive and long-term perspective and cultural sensitivity and competence (Carey et al., 2000).

### Adolescents

In Australia, young people aged 14–19 years are more likely to have smoked cannabis than tobacco (Australian Institute of Health and Welfare, 2005). Among individuals who have just started to use cannabis, the clinical features of cannabis dependence occur twice as often among adolescents than with adults (Chen & Anthony, 2003).

Longitudinal studies have reported that a positive response to cannabis use before the age of 16 years greatly increases the risk of developing dependence in adulthood (Fergusson, Horwood & Lynskey, 2003) and that weekly use marks a threshold for the increased risk of dependence (Coffey, Carlin & Lynskey, 2003).

Cannabis is now the most commonly reported illicit substance cited in adolescent treatment admissions, emergency room admissions and autopsies (Swift, Copeland & Lenton, 2000). Longitudinal studies have reported a significant, adverse impact of adolescent cannabis use on educational achievement (Copeland, Swift & Matalon, 2001).

Among adolescents there is a strong association of cannabis use with the progression of health risk factors, depression, problems with other drugs and criminal offending (Copeland, 2004).

Given these risks, it is not surprising that there is a greater range of interventions for cannabis use disorder among young people described in the literature. Among non-treatment seeking adolescents, motivational enhancement therapies have been trialled internationally, including as a 'check-up approach' (Copeland, 2004).

These intervention models are showing promise with this group. Among treatment-seeking and detained adolescents the treatment outcome of psychological interventions for cannabis-related problems are similar to those for other substance use disorders (Copeland, 2004).

## What Treatment, When?

Research into interventions for cannabis use disorders therefore supports the efficacy of assessing and treating patients who present with cannabis use disorder and associated problems.

Among daily cannabis users, 33–50% will meet criteria for cannabis dependence and should be a primary target group along with the other high-risk groups such as adolescents and those with mental health problems.

Where a cannabis use disorder is diagnosed and the patient is interested in assistance to reduce or quit, a brief intervention

## Assessment of Cannabis-Related Problems

As with other drugs of dependence there are a number of ways of assessing cannabis-related problems. There is no well-accepted screening test for cannabis problems for use in a range of clinical settings. The main issues to be considered are:

- age of first cannabis use (mitiation to use) particularly if before the age of 16 years
- years of regular use (at least weekly)
- current quantity and frequency of cannabis use
- method of cannabis use (infused, eaten or smoked in joint or bong)
- where it is difficult to ascertain reliable measures of quantity and frequency of use, the amount of money spent and/or hours of the day stoned may be an indicator of problems cannabis dependence may be quickly measured with the five-item Severity of Dependence Scale (Swift, Copeland & Hall, 1998)
- there is no accepted clinical measure of cannabis withdrawal available
- for an indicator of a range of cannabis related problems, the Cannabis Problems Questionnaire (Copeland et al., under review) may be useful.

should be provided. In a primary health care setting even firm advice to reduce or quit with a referral to a specialist alcohol and other drug worker would be of value.

Where the person is not ready for assistance, the counsellor should inform him/her of the health and psychological effects of cannabis and provide a referral to the local alcohol or other drug agency for use at a later time.

Harm reduction strategies such as the use of joints rather than bongs, not holding the smoke in the lungs for long periods of time, not mulling up with tobacco and other techniques may also be explored with this group (Swift, Copeland & Lenton, 2000).

It is important to be realistic and flexible in the approach to cannabis-related harms and to continue to incorporate evidence-based intervention strategies, where possible.

Most importantly, don't ignore concerns about the role of cannabis use in a patient's health and psychological status, as even imperfect messages about the harms of cannabis and how to avoid, or reduce them, will improve client outcomes.

Although relatively brief CBT has the strongest evidence of success for adults with cannabis dependence, among adolescents involved in the juvenile justice system and those with severe, persistent mental illness, longer and more intensive therapies provided by interdisciplinary teams may be required.

# References

Agosti V, Nunes E & Levine F (2002) Rates of psychiatric comorbidity among US residents with lifetime cannabis dependence. *American Journal of Drug and Alcohol Abuse* 28 643–652.

Andrews G, Hall W, Teeson M & Henderson S (1999) *The Mental Health of Australians. National Survey of Mental Health and Well-being Report 2*. Canberra. Mental Health Branch, Commonwealth Department of Health and Aged Care.

Anthony J, Warner L & Kessler R (1994) Comparative epidemiology of dependence on tobacco, alcohol, controlled substance and inhalants basic findings from the National Comorbidity Survey *Experimental and Clinical Psychopharmacology* 2 244–268.

Australian Institute of Health and Welfare (2005) *The 2004 National Drug Strategy Household Survey: first results* Canberra AIHW (Drug Statistics Series).

Babor T, Carroll K, Christiansen K, Kadden R, Litt M, McRee B, Miller M, Roffman R, Solowij N, Steinberg K, Stephens R, Vendetti J, Donaldson J & Herrell J (2004) Brief treatments for cannabis dependence findings from a randomised multi-site trial *Journal of Consulting and Clinical Psychology* 72 455–466.

Cabtor-Graae E, Nordstrom L, McNeil T (2001) Substance abuse in schizophrenia: a review of the literature and a study of correlates in Sweden *Schizophrenia Research* 48 69–82.

Carey K, Purnine D, Malsto S *et al.* (2000) Treating substance abuse in the context of severe and persistent mental illness clinician's perspectives *Journal of Substance Abuse Treatment* 19 189–198.

Chen C & Anthony J (2003) Possible age-associated bias in reporting of clinical features of drug dependence epidemiological evidence on adolescent onset marijuana use. *Addiction* 98 71–82.

Coffey C, Carlin J & Lynskey M (2003) Adolescent precursors of cannabis dependence findings from the Victorian Adolescent Health Cohort Study *British Journal of Psychiatry* 182 330–336.

Copeland J (2004) Interventions for cannabis use disorder *Current Opinion in Psychiatry* 17 (3) 161–167.

Copeland J, Gilmour S, Gates P & Swift W (submitted) The Cannabis Problems Questionnaire factor structure, reliability and validity.

*Drug and Alcohol Dependence* (under review—available from the author).

Copeland J, Rees V & Swift W (19991) Health concerns and help-seeking among a sample entering treatment for cannabis dependence Correspondence *Australian Family Physician* 28 540–541.

Copeland J, Swift W & Matalon E (2001) *What's the Deal on Quitting Cannabis?* Sydney: National Drug and Alcohol Research Centre Available from http://ndarc.med.unsw.edu.au (Accessed May 2005).

Copeland J, Swift W, Roffman R & Stephens R (2001) A randomised controlled trial of brief interventions for cannabis use disorder *Journal of Substance Abuse Treatment* 21 55–64.

Degenhardt L, Hall W & Lynskey M (2003) Testing hypotheses about the relationship between cannabis use and psychosis. *Drug and Alcohol Dependence* 71 37–48.

Drake R, Essock S & Shaner A (2001) Implementing dual diagnosis services for clients with severe mental illness. *Psychiatric Services* 52 469–476.

European Monitoring Centre for Drugs and Drug Addiction (2002) *Annual Report on the State of the Drugs Problem in the European Union and Norway* (pp. 16). Lisbon EMCDDA.

Fergusson DM (2004) Cannabis and psychosis accumulating evidence. *Addiction* 99 1351–1352.

Fergusson D, Horwood J & Lynskey M (2003) Early reactions to cannabis predict later dependence. *Archives of General Psychiatry* 60 1033–1039.

Fergusson D, Horwood J & Swain-Campbell N (2003) Cannabis dependence and psychotic symptoms in young people. *Psychological Medicine* 33 3–6.

Hall JA & Pacula RL (2003) *Cannabis Use and Dependence: public health and public policy.* Cambridge: Cambridge University Press.

Solowij N (1998) *Cannabis and Cognitive Functioning.* Cambridge: Cambridge University Press.

Stephens R, Roffman R & Curtin L (2000) Comparison of extended versus brief treatments for marijuana use. *Journal of Consulting and Clinical Psychology* 68 898–908.

Stephens R, Roffman R & Simpson E (1994) Treating adult marijuana dependence: a test of the relapse prevention model. *Journal of Consulting and Clinical Psychology* 62 92–99.

Substance Abuse and Mental Health Services Administration (SAMHSA) (2002) *2002 National Survey on Drug Use and Health.* Rockville, MD Office of Applied Statistics.

Swift W, Copeland J & Hall W (1998) Choosing a diagnostic cut-off for cannabis dependence. *Addiction* 93 1681–1692.

Swift W, Copeland J & Lenton S (2000) Cannabis and harm reduction (Harm Reduction Digest 8). *Drug and Alcohol Review* 19 101–112.

Swift W, Hall W & Tesson M (2001) Cannabis use and dependence among Australian adults results from the National Survey of Mental Health and Wellbeing. *Addiction* 96 737–748.

Tashkin DP (1999) Cannabis effects on the respiratory system In: Kalant H, Comgall W, Hall W & Smart R (Editors) *The Health Effects of Cannabis* (pp. 313–347). Toronto: Centre for Addiction and Mental Health.

Taylor D, Fergusson D, Milne B *et al.* (2002) A longitudinal study of the effects of tobacco and cannabis exposure on lung function in young adults. *Addiction* 97 1055–1061.

National Drug and Alcohol Research Centre, University of New South Wales, Sydney, Australia. **j.copeland@unsw.edu.au**

# Pot Farms Ravaging Park Land

## Big raid in Marin County only hints at the extent of erosive techniques by growers

CHUCK SQUATRIGLIA

The discovery of 22,740 marijuana plants growing in and around Point Reyes National Seashore last week wasn't only the biggest pot seizure ever made in Marin County. It was an environmental mess that will take several months and tens of thousands of dollars to clean up.

The crops seized on the steep hillsides overlooking Highway 1 were planted by sophisticated growers who cleared vegetation, terraced land, drew water from streams through miles of irrigation hoses and doused acres of land with hundreds of pounds of fertilizer and pesticides.

Such operations are turning up in greater numbers within state and national parks throughout California. Federal officials estimate the state produces half of all the marijuana seized on public lands nationwide.

Officials at Point Reyes National Seashore have only begun to assess the resulting damage to an area that is habitat for the spotted owl, steelhead trout and coho salmon, and they said it could be months before they know the long-term implications for the ecosystem.

"We've seen some really nasty damage," National Park Service spokesman John Dell'Osso said Tuesday. "And there's a very good possibility there are sites we haven't even found yet."

Cultivating marijuana on land managed by the Park Service, the National Forest Service and other agencies is a multibillion-dollar industry. So far this year, authorities have found more than 940,000 marijuana plants growing on state and federal land in the Golden State. With the harvest season beginning, officials expect to find more pot farms and surpass last year's haul of 1.1 million plants.

Federal officials believe as much as 80 percent of the marijuana on public land is grown by Mexican drug cartels that have turned to places like Point Reyes National Seashore, Sequoia-Kings Canyon National Park and Whiskeytown National Recreation Area in this era of tightened border security; growing the drug here is far easier than smuggling it in. The plants found in Point Reyes last week were valued at around $50 million, Dell'Osso said.

The federal Office of National Drug Control policy estimates that growing 1 acre of marijuana damages 10 acres of land. Repairing that land is a costly, time-consuming process, and because the National Park Service does not allocate money specifically for the task, the funds come from each park's operating budget—leaving less money for things like park programs and improvements.

"We have no budget for this," Dell'Osso said, noting that it is a problem "the powers-that-be need to start discussing."

The pot seized last week was growing on six sites scattered along Bolinas Ridge between Stinson Beach and the Randall Trail just south of Olema. About half of it was on land managed by the Marin Municipal Water District. Marin County sheriff's deputies discovered it during a routine aerial search. Investigators have not made any arrests.

Lt. Scott Anderson of the Marin County Sheriff's Department said the pot farm's similarities to those found in other national parks suggests it was the work of a Mexican cartel that probably employed undocumented immigrants.

The sites in Marin County are tucked away in remote canyons, sheltered beneath madrone and oak trees and surrounded by thick brush hacked away haphazardly. Trees have been stripped of their limbs to make room for the plants, leaving only a canopy of branches to hide the illicit crop.

Irrigation hoses as long as a mile each drew water from pools dug into the ground and fed by the springs and streams that course through the Tomales Bay watershed. The steep hillsides have been terraced, much like a vineyard, and are dotted with hundreds of deep holes that held as many as four marijuana plants apiece. The land is littered with empty 50-pound bags of fertilizer and gallon jugs of pesticide.

Investigators believe as many as three people tended each plot, and the amount of trash—empty soda and beer cans, food wrappers, propane canisters and clothing—suggests they'd been living there for at least several weeks but fled before officials reached the site. Authorities found animal traps, pellet guns and a rabbit hutch, leading them to believe the growers hunted for food.

With the last of the crops cleared away, park officials have begun assessing the damage. Once the trash is removed, the biggest priority will be protecting the land with straw and new ground cover to prevent the winter rains from washing it away. Beyond that, though, it's not yet known exactly what must be done to restore the land and what it will cost.

---

## "We've seen some really nasty damage. And there's a very good possibility there are sites we haven't even found yet."

John Dell'Osso
National Park Service

---

Sequoia-King's Canyon National Park has spent more than $72,000 during the past two years to clean up 81 cultivation sites that covered 10 acres, said Athena Demetry, a restoration ecologist at the park. Authorities have seized more than 100,000 marijuana plants within Sequoia-King's Canyon since 2004. The latest seizure came Aug. 9, when authorities found 2,152 marijuana plants growing within view of Moro Rock, a popular park destination.

Over the course of six weeks during the winter of 2005 and 2006, park rangers hauled almost 5 tons of trash and debris out of the park, removed 13 miles of irrigation hose, and repaired deep cuts and terraces made to 35 hillsides, Demetry said. Empty bags and bottles revealed the growers used at least 8,031 pounds of fertilizer, 15 pounds of rodenticide and 7.6 gallons of pesticide. An additional 80 grow sites still must be repaired.

"We chose the sites that are easiest to reach and did those first," she said. "The ones that are left to do are more remote, and on steeper terrain."

Demetry said the land will recover quickly as new vegetation grows but the effect on wildlife will be harder to measure. No one knows how much fertilizer and pesticide is polluting the land, or how much of it made its way into the streams that feed the East Fork of Kaweah River.

"It's got a huge impact on the stream ecology," she said. "It has the potential to ripple through the food chain."

Park rangers have for years stumbled upon small stands of marijuana, but the problem has exploded within the past five years and reached a point where they're having difficulty keeping up, Demetry said. Although individual cultivation sites are rarely cover more than an acre, the growers have taken to scattering them over hundreds of acres to evade detection. That, she said, spreads the destruction over a far broader area, with far graver results.

"When we first saw them, we thought they were pretty small," she said. "But then we realized how many there were, and it became staggering. And there's a lot more out there."

---

E-mail CHUCK SQUATRIGLIA at **csquatriglia@sfchronicle.com**.

---

# UNIT 4

# Other Trends in Drug Use

## Unit Selection

## Key Points to Consider

- Why are some drug-related trends more specific to certain subpopulations of Americans than others?

- How significant is socioeconomic status in influencing drug trends? Why?

- What influences have contributed to the dramatic spread of prescription drug abuse in the United States?

- What role do advertising and the media play in influencing drug use?

- What factors cause drug-related trends to change?

## Student Website
www.mhcls.com/online

## Internet References
Further information regarding these websites may be found in this book's preface or online.

**Drug Story.org**
*http://www.drugstory.org/drug_stats/druguse_stats.asp*
**Marijuana as a Medicine**
*http://mojo.calyx.net/ olsen/*
**Monitoring the Future**
*www.monitoringthefuture.org*
**Prescriptions Drug Use and Abuse**
*http://www.fda.gov/fdac/features/2001/501_drug.html*
**SAMHSA**
*http://www.drugabusestatistics.samhsa.gov/trends.htm*
**United States Drug Trends**
*www.usdrugtrends.com*

**R**arely do drug-related patterns and trends lend themselves to precise definition. Identifying, measuring, and predicting the consequence of these trends is an inexact science, to say the least. It is, nevertheless, a very important process.

Some of the most valuable data produced by drug-related trend analysis is the identification of subpopulations whose vulnerability to certain drug phenomena is greater than that of the wider population. These identifications may forewarn of the implications for the general population. Trend analysis may produce specific information that may otherwise be lost or obscured by general statistical indications. For example, tobacco is probably the most prominent of gateway drugs, with repeated findings pointing to the correlation between the initial use of tobacco and the use of other drugs.

The analysis of specific trends related to drug use is very important, as it provides a threshold from which educators, health care professionals, parents, and policy makers may respond to significant drug-related health threats and issues. Over 19 million Americans report the use of illegal drugs. The current rate of illicit drug use is similar to rates of the past two years. Marijuana remains as the most commonly used illicit drug at 14.6 million current users.

Historically popular depressant and stimulant drugs—such as alcohol, tobacco, heroin, and cocaine—produce statistics that identify the most visible and sometimes the most constant use patterns. Other drugs such as marijuana, LSD, Ecstasy and other "club drugs" often produce patterns widely interpreted to be associated with cultural phenomena such as youth attitudes, popular music trends, and political climate.

Another continuing concern addressed in this unit focuses on mental illness and its relationship to drug abuse. Currently, 25 million Americans are believed to suffer from Serious Psychological Distress, and of those, more than 5 million are dependent upon, or abuse illicit drugs or alcohol. Approximately 31 million American adults have suffered at least one Major Depressive Episode in their lifetime. Of those who suffered from MDE in the past year, 20 percent abused illicit drugs or alcohol. Among youth 12–17, over 2 million were diagnosed as having a MDE in the past year. Of these youth, 20 percent abused illicit drugs or alcohol. One important health controversy continues to involve and question the ways antidepressant drugs are prescribed to youth. The relationship between drug use, mental illness, and suicide among youth continues to be a major nationwide health worry.

Two other continuing trends are those that involve the abuse of prescription drugs and those that involve the use of inhalant drugs by teenagers. Americans are abusing prescription drugs more than ever before with the most frequently mentioned offenders being oxycodone and hydrocodone. There are currently 6.4 million persons who use psychotherapeutic drugs for non-medical reasons. Of these, 4.7 million used pain relievers, and 1.1 million used stimulants. Relative to the abuse of inhalant drugs, 877 thousand persons reported using in the past year and of these 72 percent were under 18. The abuse of inhalants by teenagers continues as an on-again worrisome trend. Lastly, the pandemic spread of methamphetamine through rural cities, counties, and states is suggesting abuse patterns and health issues beyond those related to cocaine.

Information concerning drug use patterns and trends obtained from a number of different investigative methods is available from a variety of sources. On the national level, the more prominent sources are the Substance Abuse and Mental Health Services Administration, the National Institute on Drug Abuse, the Drug Abuse Warning Network, the National Centers for Disease Control, the Justice Department, the Office of National Drug Control Policy, and the surgeon general. On the state level, various justice departments, including attorney generals' offices, the courts, state departments of social services, state universities and colleges, and public health offices maintain data and conduct research. On local levels, criminal justice agencies, social service departments, public hospitals, and health departments provide information. On a private level, various research institutes and universities, professional organizations such as the American Medical Association and the American Cancer Society, hospitals, and treatment centers, as well as private corporations, are tracking drug-related trends. Surveys abound with no apparent lack of available data. As a result, the need for examination of research methods and findings for reliability and accuracy is self-evident.

The articles in this unit provide information about some drug-related trends occurring within certain subpopulations of Americans. While reading the articles, it is interesting to consider how the trends and patterns described are dispersed through various subpopulations of Americans and specific geographical areas.

Additionally, much information about drugs and drug trends can be located quickly by referring to the list of websites in the front section of this book.

# Resurgence of Teen Inhalant Use

RON CHEPESIUK

The 2004 Monitoring the Future (MTF) survey showed that inhalant use ("huffing") is rising among American teenage students, particularly 8th graders. The results, released in December 2004, showed that 9.6% of 8th graders used inhalants in 2004, up from 7.7% in 2002 and 8.7% in 2003. Inhalant use was also up slightly among 10th and 12th graders in 2004. Findings from the latest MTF will be released in late December 2005, and researchers are anxious to see if the trend holds.

"These increases are disturbing because they come after a long period of decline in inhalant use by students in all three grades," says Lloyd D. Johnston, a professor at the University of Michigan Institute for Social Research and principal investigator of the MTF since it began in 1975. "We are concerned that the use of this class of drugs may be about to rebound."

Each year, the MTF, which is funded under grants from the National Institute on Drug Abuse (NIDA), asks approximately 50,000 8th-, 10th-, and 12th-grade students in some 400 schools nationwide about their use of drugs, alcohol, and cigarettes. The data gathered are used to help government officials and policy makers identify potential drug problem areas so they can target resources to deal with them.

"We know that inhalant use starts early and that long-term abusers are among the most difficult drug abuse patients to treat," says NIDA director Nora Volkow. "It is critical that research efforts to characterize the behavioral effects of inhalants intensify, so that more effective preventions, interventions, and treatments can be developed." This year, NIDA announced the continuation of a broad-based research initiative begun in 2002 to address the epidemiologic, social, behavioral, cognitive, and neurobiological consequences of inhalant abuse, as well as treatment and prevention.

More than 1,000 readily available products are used as inhalants, and they can potentially kill, according to the Office of National Drug Control Policy (ONDCP). Such products include glue, shoe polish, gasoline, lighter fluid, and the propellants in spray deodorant, hair sprays, and canned whipped cream.

The ONDCP further reports that glue, shoe polish, and toluene-containing products were the most commonly abused inhalants among users aged 12 to 17. According to the American Association of Poison Control Centers, gasoline accounted for the greatest percentage (44%) of reported inhalant deaths between 1996 and 2001, followed by air fresheners (26%) and propane/butane (11%). Other health effects of inhalant use include headache, nausea, vomiting, slurred speech, loss of motor coordination, and wheezing.

The physical and social environment both play a key role in inhalant use, says Harvey Weiss, executive director of the National Inhalant Prevention Coalition. Treatment sometimes requires removing the abuser from the environment in which he or she is abusing inhalants. "We should not view inhalant abuse [simply] as a substance abuse problem," Weiss says. "It's a public health problem, so we need to do more public health outreach to young people."

Sources believe that education is the key to preventing inhalant use from becoming a dangerous fad. When MTF data from the mid-1990s began showing a long-term gradual increase in inhalant use, the Partnership for a Drug-Free America and NIDA mounted an aggressive media campaign about the dangers of inhalants. The next round of MTF data showed a decline in inhalant use and a concurrent increase in young people viewing inhalants' use as risky, but use began climbing again after the media campaign ended.

"Of course, the evidence is circumstantial, but we've seen the same thing happen for so many other drugs," Johnston says. "A drug can have a resurgence in use among young people because of what I call 'generation forgetting'—that is, a new generation of young people comes along that hasn't heard too much about a drug, so it is naïve about the consequences of its use. That begins to change when a public education campaign is launched."

Despite the MTF findings, the U.S. government hasn't yet documented a trend indicating a rise in inhalant use among teenagers, says Terry Zobeck, deputy associate director for policy and budget at the ONDCP. But he adds, "The MTF is respected and well documented. We will be quite concerned if its next survey shows that inhalant use is up for the third year in a row." **–Ron Chepesiuk**

From *Environmental Health Perspectives*, December 2005. Published by National Institute of Environmental Health Sciences. www.ehponline.org

# New Study Shows 1.8 Million Youth Use Inhalants

## Known as 'Silent Drugs,' Inhalant Abuse Rising Significantly

Teddi Dineley Johnson

Parents who think their homes are drug-free received a wake-up call in March from the National Inhalant Prevention Coalition: Dozens of children die each year from abusing products that are purchased and brought into the home by their parents.

While overall drug use among young people has declined substantially over the past four years, inhalant abuse has increased, according to a new report from the Substance Abuse and Mental Health Services Administration. Based on data gathered from 2002–2004, approximately 598,000 children ages 12 to 17 initiated, inhalant use in the past 12 months, the report said, which translates to 1.8 million new inhalant users in the past three years.

The report, "Characteristics of Recent Adolescent Inhalant Initiates," said nearly 20 percent of youth ages 12 to 17 used inhalants for 13 or more days during their first year of abuse, even though sudden death from cardiac arrest or suffocation can occur on the first use. Products identified by the report as most often abused are solvent-based glues, shoe polish, gasoline, lighter fluid, nitrous oxide, solvent-based markers, spray paints, correction fluid, degreasers, cleaning fluids, products in aerosol cans, locker room deodorizer and paint solvents.

The term "inhalants" refers to more than 1,400 household and commercial products "that are intentionally misused, either by sniffing them directly from the container or "huffing" them through the mouth, to achieve a high. Inhalant abuse is difficult to control because the abused products are legal, serve useful purposes and are readily, available in homes.

Inhalants can harm the brain, liver, heart, kidneys and lungs and can interfere with brain development, said Nora Volkow, MD, director of the National Institute on Drug Abuse, during a March news conference in Washington, D.C., releasing the report and kicking off the 14th annual National Inhalants and Poisons Awareness Campaign.

"These products are very accessible because they are all over our homes and garages, and for that reason they have become the most frequently abused drugs by young children," Volkow said, noting that inhalants are often referred to as the "silent" drugs because they are so difficult for parents to detect.

Abuse of inhalants increased significantly between 2002 and 2005, the report said, with the largest increase noted among eighth-graders, "who may be unaware of the damage inhalants can cause," Volkow said.

Thirty percent of those initiating inhalant use during the past year were 12 or 13 years old, the report said; 39 percent were 14 or 15 and 31 percent were 16 or 17. The majority of the youth were white and from homes with incomes well above the poverty line, with girls found to be abusing inhalants more frequently than boys.

"Now is the time to marshal our collective efforts to reduce and prevent inhalant experimentation and abuse," said Harvey Weiss, MBA, founder and executive director of the National Inhalant Prevention Coalition. "Our children's future may depend on it."

Between 100 and 125 deaths from inhalant abuse are reported each year to the National Inhalant Prevention Coalition, "but many inhalant deaths go unreported or are underreported," Weiss said, noting that the coalition has developed guidelines to help medical examiners, coroners and pathologists determine inhalant deaths.

"If you don't know the signs, you can't save your children," warned Jeff Williams, a Cleveland police officer whose 14-year-old son, Kyle, died in March 2005 after huffing a can of computer dust cleaner that Williams had purchased several days earlier to clean the family's computer keyboard.

Kyle, who had started abusing inhalants about a month before his death after a friend in the neighborhood showed him how to do it, had been complaining that his tongue hurt, Williams said during the news conference. The parents also noticed that their son had been exhibiting uncharacteristic anger. At the time, however, neither Williams nor his wife, who is a nurse, were aware that the two issues—anger and a sore tongue—are common warning signs of inhalant abuse.

As he fought back tears, Williams shared the story of how his wife, upon attempting to wake their son for school, found him sitting up in bed cross-legged, the can of dust cleaner in his lap and the straw that came with the can still in his mouth. Their son had died around midnight, Williams said.

Later, Williams and his wife learned that computer dust cleaner is inhaled mostly by children ages 9 to 15.

"They even have a name for it," Williams said. "It's called 'dusting.' It gives them a slight high for about 10 seconds."

But dust cleaner is not just compressed air, Williams said. It also contains a propellant—a refrigerant similar to what is used in refrigerators—and there is no way to predict if sudden death will occur.

"It's a heavy gas," Williams said. "It decreases the oxygen to your brain, to your heart . . . the horrible part about this is there is no warning. There is no level that kills you. It's not cumulative. It's not an overdose. It can just go randomly, terribly wrong. It's Russian roulette."

For more information on inhalant abuse prevention, visit <www.inhalants.org> or call (800) 269-4237. The report, "Characteristics of Recent Adolescent Inhalant Initiates," is available at <www.oas.samhsa.gov>.

# The Changing Face of Teenage Drug Abuse—The Trend toward Prescription Drugs

RICHARD A. FRIEDMAN, M.D.

When Eric, an 18-year-old who lives in San Francisco, wants to get some Vicodin (hydrocodone–acetaminophen), it's a simple matter. "I can get prescription drugs from different places and don't ever have to see a doctor," he explained. "I have friends whose parents are pill addicts, and we 'borrow' from them. Other times I have friends who have ailments who get lots of pills and sell them for cheap. As long as prescription pills are taken right, they're much safer than street drugs."

Eric's habits reflect an emerging pattern in drug use by teenagers: illicit street drugs such as "ecstasy" (3,4-methylenedioxymethamphetamine) and cocaine are decreasing in popularity, whereas the nonmedical use of certain prescription drugs is on the rise. These findings were reported in the Monitoring the Future survey, which is sponsored by the National Institute on Drug Abuse and designed and conducted by researchers at the University of Michigan.[1] The study, which began in 1975, annually surveys a nationally representative sample of about 50,000 students in 400 public and private secondary schools in the United States.

## "We're living in a time that seems decidedly more apocalyptic. . . . Maybe we need something to slow down."

Overall, the proportion of teens who reported having used any illicit drug during the previous year has dropped by more than a third among 8th graders and by about 10 percent among 12th graders since the peaks reported in the mid-to-late 1990s, according to the 2005 survey. Alcohol use and cigarette smoking among teens are now at historic lows. In contrast, the number of high-school students who are abusing prescription pain relievers such as oxycodone (OxyContin), a potent and highly addictive opiate, or sedatives is on the rise. A total of 7.2 percent of high-school seniors reported nonmedical use of sedatives in 2005, up from a low of 2.8 percent in 1992 (see graph).

Reported use of oxycodone in this group increased from 4.0 percent in 2002 to 5.5 percent in 2005.

The survey did not ask teenagers how they obtained their prescription drugs, but there is little doubt that the medications are easy to get from a variety of sources. "Prescription drugs are a lot easier to get than street drugs," said John, a high-school sophomore in Austin, Texas. "Kids can get them on the street, from parents and friends, or on the Internet."

They can also get them all too easily from physicians, according to recent data from the National Center on Addiction and Substance Abuse at Columbia University.[2] A 2004 survey of physicians found that 43 percent did not ask about prescription-drug abuse when taking a patient's history, and one third did not regularly call or obtain records from the patient's previous physician before prescribing potentially addictive drugs. These alarming data suggest that physicians are much too lax in prescribing controlled drugs. Claire, an 18-year-old who lives in Maine, told me, "You can always find a doctor who you can convince that you have a sleeping problem to get Ambien [zolpidem] or that you have ADD [attention-deficit disorder] and get Adderall." And even if most teenagers do not seek controlled prescription drugs directly from doctors, physicians are surely the original source of much of the medication that teens use, which has been diverted from its intended recipients.

In explaining the increase in the recreational use of prescription drugs, many teenagers draw key distinctions between these drugs and illicit street drugs. Teenagers whom I interviewed said that whereas they used illicit drugs only for recreation, they often used prescription drugs for "practical" effects: hypnotic drugs for sleep, stimulants to enhance their school performance, and tranquilizers such as benzodiazepines to decrease stress. They often characterized their use of prescription drugs as "responsible," "controlled," or "safe." The growing popularity of prescription drugs also reflects the perception that these drugs are safer than street drugs. According to the Monitoring the Future survey, for example, the use of sedatives among high-school seniors has increased in tandem with a decrease in the perceived risk and an increase in peer-group approval of the use

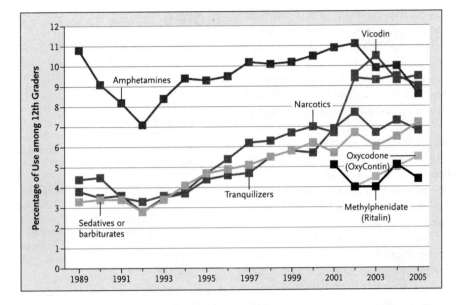

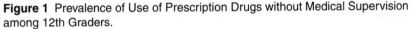

**Figure 1** Prevalence of Use of Prescription Drugs without Medical Supervision among 12th Graders.

Data are from the Monitoring the Future survey. In 2001, the text of the question regarding tranquilizers was changed in half the questionnaire forms: Miltown (meprobamate) was replaced by Xanax (alprazolam) in the list of examples. This resulted in a slight increase in the reported prevalence. In 2002, the remaining questionnaire forms were changed. Also in 2002, the text of the question about narcotics other than heroin was changed in half the questionnaire forms: Talwin (pentazocine–naloxone), laudanum, and paregoric (which all reportedly had negligible rates of use by 2001) were replaced with Vicodin (hydrocodone–acetaminophen), OxyContin (oxycodone), and Percocet (oxycodone–acetaminophen). This resulted in an increase in reported prevalence, and in 2003, the remaining questionnaire forms were changed.

of sedatives, whereas amphetamine use has steadily dropped as the perceived risk and societal disapproval have increased.

What might explain the growing confidence in the safety of prescription drugs? Negative media attention is frequently cited as a factor in the decreasing popularity of cocaine and stimulants among teenagers. The converse appears to be true regarding prescription medications. Nowadays, it is nearly impossible to open a newspaper, turn on the television, or search the Internet without encountering an advertisement for a prescription medication. Expenditures by the pharmaceutical industry for direct-to-consumer advertising increased from $1.8 billion in 1999 to $4.2 billion in 2004.[3,4] One effect has been to foster an image of prescription drugs as an integral and routine aspect of everyday life. Any adverse effects are relegated to the fine print of an advertisement or dispatched in a few seconds of rapid-fire speech.

Not all prescription drugs, however, have equal appeal among teenagers. According to the Monitoring the Future study, calming prescription drugs have become more popular, whereas the use of stimulants is decreasing. Whether this trend reflects the differential availability of sedative drugs, the selective effects of advertising, or other social factors is anyone's guess. Asked to speculate about it, teenagers said more or less what John, the teen from Austin, expressed in an e-mail message: "We're living in a time that seems decidedly more apocalyptic, especially since 9/11 and all the recent natural disasters. Maybe we need something to slow down."

The perception that prescription drugs are largely safe seems to justify the attitude that occasional use poses little risk. And indeed, there is little doubt that many more people try drugs than become serious drug abusers. For example, in the 2004 National Household Survey on Drug Abuse, 19 percent of persons between 12 and 17 years of age reported ever having used marijuana, whereas 14.5 percent reported use during the previous year, and only 7.6 percent reported use during the previous month.[5]

Still, the fact that 50 percent of students have tried an illicit drug by the time they finish high school—another finding of the Monitoring the Future survey—is nothing to be happy about, not to mention the 5.5 percent of 12th graders who have tried the highly addictive oxycodone. For a substantial number of teenagers with risk factors, such as a psychiatric illness or a family history of drug abuse, crossing the line from abstinence to exposure will be the first step toward serious substance abuse.

Moreover, even in small doses, sedatives, hypnotics, and opiates have subtle effects on cognition and motor skills that may increase the risk of injury, particularly during sports activities or driving. From a longer-term perspective, the brains of teenagers are still developing, and the effects of drug abuse may be harmful in ways that are not yet understood. Do we really want teenagers to think nothing of popping a pill to relax, get through the tedium of a long homework assignment, or relieve normal anxieties?

Clearly, physicians play an important role in this problem, given their apparent laxness in prescribing controlled drugs. Physicians should routinely assess their patients for substance use and psychiatric illness before they put pen to a prescription pad. They should also discuss with their adult patients who have teenage children the risks associated with controlled drugs and the need to restrict the availability of such drugs at home.

In order to address these problems appropriately, physicians need adequate education in substance abuse. The survey by the National Center on Addiction and Substance Abuse reveals that physicians do not feel they are well trained to spot signs of substance abuse or addiction—a skill that should be taught in all medical schools and residency programs.

Finally, educators and parents must address the potential dangers of prescription-drug abuse with teenagers. As Claire put it, "In a way, prescription drugs are more dangerous than street drugs, because we don't recognize their dangers."

(The names of the teenagers who were interviewed have been changed to protect their privacy.)

# Notes

1. Johnston LD, O'Malley PM, Bachman JG, Schulenberg JE. Monitoring the future: national results on adolescent drug use: overview of key findings, 2005. Bethesda, Md.: National Institute on Drug Abuse (in press).

2. Doe J. Under the counter: the diversion and abuse of controlled prescription drugs in the U.S. New York: National Center on Addiction and Substance Abuse of Columbia University, 2005.

3. R&D spending. In: PhRMA annual membership survey. Washington, D.C.: Pharmaceutical Research and Manufacturers of America, 2004.

4. Promotional data. In: Integrated Promotional Services and CMR. Fairfield, Conn.: IMS Health, June 2004.

5. Office of Applied Studies. Results from the 2004 National Survey on Drug Use & Health: national findings. NSDUH series H-28. Rockville, Md.: Substance Abuse and Mental Health Services Administration, 2005. (DHHS publication no. SMA 05-4062.)

**DR. FRIEDMAN** is a psychiatrist and the director of the Psychopharmacology Clinic at Weill Cornell Medical College, New York.

# OxyContin Acting as Pathway Drug for Adolescent Heroin Addiction

Reports from around the country indicate that teenagers who abuse OxyContin, a powerful prescription narcotic, are switching to heroin, either snorting it or injecting it. When they need more OxyContin than they can afford, they can find heroin, and pay less for it.

OxyContin, when swallowed whole, works as a time-release pain medication. But when crushed, the medication takes effect all at once instead of over time, causing euphoria. OxyContin in its own right led to a wave of addiction, and in some cases, tragic deaths, especially when taken with alcohol.

While chewing OxyContin does bring a rush, the biggest rush is from snorting it. "I've been told that once you snort it, you never chew again," says Massachusetts State Senator Steven A. Tolman, chair of the legislature's Mental Health and Substance Abuse Committee.

The Massachusetts Department of Public Health held a summit May in Chelsea, Mass., which was the result of a year-long research project on prescribing opiates. Doctors, pharmacists, and teens worked together on an education message on the dangers of crushing OxyContin, according to a report in the Boston Globe. The Massachusetts research project has resulted in a series of pamphlets for doctors, urging them to ask patients about alcohol use before prescribing opiates.

Teens obtain the OxyContin pills surreptitiously from a family member, and then graduate to buying them on the street. Street OxyContin is more expensive than heroin, and it's not a big jump for adolescents to buy heroin instead of OxyContin from their street source.

The concern about OxyContin and heroin is national. "OxyContin use is reported by 5 percent of high school seniors," says Wilson Compton, M.D., director of the division of epidemiology services and prevention research at the National Institute on Drug Abuse (NIDA). "That's a frightening statistic."

Compton is particularly concerned about the fact that these teens are starting with OxyContin. "The idea that people are starting with prescriptions and progressing to heroin is something that is startling to all of us," he says.

There's no clear evidence on who is getting OxyContin from where. There are reports that in Ohio, young people began with OxyContin and progressed to injecting heroin, says Compton. In other parts of the country, the progression might be to snorting heroin, and then to injecting. Or it may stop at snorting.

## A 'Pathway' to Injection

Compton is reluctant to call OxyContin a "gateway" drug because it is very unlikely that someone who didn't use any drugs previously would use this first. "They're also using marijuana, alcohol, and tobacco," he says. But it is a "new pathway" to injection drug use, he says.

For OxyContin itself, it's not unusual that drug abusers would progress from chewing to inhaling, says Compton. "Drug users are remarkably inventive and will try all sorts of routes of administration," he says.

Once someone starts using OxyContin and heroin, how fast do they move to needing heroin on a daily basis? "There is tremendous variation in these trajectories," says Compton. "Many people will use these intermittently and eventually stop on their own and not use. For full-blown addiction, it's a progression over months."

When taken as directed—swallowed whole—OxyContin has a "long duration of action," says Compton. "But when it's crushed, it has a much more rapid onset, and the period of action is just a few hours." OxyContin, even taken alone, can be fatal, he says. When combined with alcohol, this danger is even more pronounced due to respiratory depression, he says. (Compton notes that another prescription painkiller, Vicodin, is also popular with young drug users, and can also lead to heroin use.)

The problem has reached the point at which some legislators want OxyContin severely restricted or even banned. Massachusetts State Senator Tolman is extremely concerned about the OcyContin-heroin link. "I am totally convinced, from talking to people who were or are on OcyContin or heroin, that there are a lot of people out there who are addicted but not telling anyone," he says. "The hardest part is telling their mom and dad," says

Toleman has made a point of reaching out to these young people. "What I want to say to them is this: If you are addicted

# OxyContin Facts

During 2004, 1.7 percent of 8th graders, 3.5 percent of 10th graders, and 5 percent of 12th graders reported using OxyContin within the past year, according to the Monitoring the Future Survey.

According to the 2003 National Survey on Drug Use and Health, about 2.8 million people ages 12 or older had used OxyContin not pursuant to a prescription at least once in their lifetime. This was up from 1.9 million lifetime users in 2002.

OxyContin diversion and abuse emerged at 13 of the 20 Pulse Check sites, according to the November 2002 Pulse Check: Trends in Drug Abuse. These sites were Baltimore; Billings, Mont.; Boston; Chicago; Columbia, S.C.; Denver; Detroit; Memphis, Tenn.; Miami; New Orleans; Philadelphia; Portland, Ore.; and Seattle.

Source: Office of National Drug Control Policy.

to OxyContin or heroin—or any substance—we can get you the proper help." What these young people really want, he says, is to "become their old self again."

But finding treatment for these teens in treatment may not be that simple. "Where will we put them all?" is the big question raised when Tolman brings up this problem with members of Massachusetts Gov. Mitt Romney's administration, which has put OxyContin-heroin at the top of its drug prevention priorities.

# Club Drugs: Study Explores Reasons for Use by Young Adults

## Special Focus On Substance Use In Young People

Young people use club drugs—Ecstasy, GHB, ketamine, Rohypnol, methamphetamine, and LSD —to relax and to enhance their social interactions, but a large number also report negative consequences of the use of these drugs, according to a study published in the *Journal of Psychoactive Drugs*.

Kathleen A. Parks and colleagues from SUNY Buffalo surveyed a sample of 50 club drug users who were recruited through various means. Subjects completed a 60-minute individual interview during which they provided information about their sociodemographic characteristics, lifetime substance use, past year substance use, and positive and negative consequences associated with the use of club drugs. Subjects' levels of substance abuse and/or dependence were assessed using the Drug Abuse Screening Test (DAST).

Researchers note that during the past year, nearly all of the participants (98%) had used Ecstasy; the majority had used ketamine (72%), LSD (68%), and methamphetamine (58%), while the use of the other club drugs (GHB, dextromethorphan, and Rohypnol) was much lower. In addition, nearly all of the subjects reported using alcohol (98%) and marijuana (96%) in the past year, with a majority reporting use of amphetamine, cocaine, hallucinogens, opiates, and tobacco. The average number of club drugs used over the past year was 4.1, and the average number of non-club drugs used was 4.4. The majority of subjects (75%) reported using club drugs once or twice each month or less.

**The use of club drugs centers around a social context; the drugs are used to enhance or heighten positive sensory experience rather than as a means to escape negative affect. In addition, subjects reported a significant number of negative consequences associated with Ecstasy use.**

The subjects' average score on the DAST was 10.2, suggesting that on average the sample met the cut-off for abuse or dependence. The majority of subjects (72%) reported that Ecstasy was the first club drug they had ever used. The average age at first use was 18. The average duration of Ecstasy use was 2.9 years.

## Study Sample

N = 50
Average age = 21.3 years
52% were male
84% were European American, 8% African American, 8% other
40% were employed full-time, 38% were students, 4% were unemployed
84% had never been married

Subjects reported using Ecstasy at raves, bars, or at home with others. Ketamine was most often used at raves or at home with others. The use of LSD most often took place at home with others.

Subjects indicated that they used club drugs to "experiment" and to feel good or high (98%) and to have a good time with friends (90%). The majority (70%–80%) indicated using club drug for their stimulant properties, to enhance the effect of another drug, to seek insight, or to relax or relieve tension. Less than half (48%) said they used these drugs to get away from their problems, and less than 30% said they used club drugs because they were hooked, to get through the day, or because of anger or frustration.

Positive consequences of club drug use were reported by 10% or more of subjects in regard to Ecstasy, GHB, Ketamine, methamphetamine, and LSD. Feeling good and social benefits were reported as positive consequences of all five of these drugs. Subjects reported increased energy as a positive consequence of using Ecstasy, methamphetamine, and LSD. Stress relief and escape were positive consequences for Ecstasy and ketamine use. Gaining insight or great open-mindedness was reported for LSD use.

Ecstasy was the primary drug for which negative consequences were reported. Most frequent negative physical effects reported by 50% to 75% of users included profuse sweating, hot and cold flashes, tingling or numbness, and blurred vision. The most frequent negative psychological symptoms were trouble sleeping (reported by 75% of users); 20% to 46% of users also reported hallucination, depression, confusion, anxiety, irritability, paranoia, and loss of sex urge at least some of the time. Among negative life consequences reported were having trouble maintaining usual daily activities (40%) and experiencing financial and work troubles (20%).

Subjects reported few problems with aggression following club drug use. A small group of subjects reported getting into verbal arguments sometimes (14%) or half the time (2%) following Ecstasy use; 14% reported they had ever been involved in physical aggression, and 2% reported being involved in sexual aggression after taking Ecstasy.

## Study Limits

Authors note that this study was descriptive in nature and limited in size. Additional studies are needed to confirm and expand these findings.

## Authors' Conclusions

The authors conclude that the use of club drugs centers around a social context; the drugs are used to enhance or heighten positive sensory experience rather than as a means to escape negative affect. However, despite the fact that few users reported being "hooked," the average DAST score suggests that a majority of this sample would meet criteria for drug abuse or dependence. In addition, subjects reported a significant number of negative consequences associated with Ecstasy use.

Future studies are needed, in particular to tease out negative consequences of club drug use from that associated with use of other drugs.

# Rx for Trouble

Klein, Melissa

## Abusing Legal Drugs Can Destroy Lives

On a spring afternoon last year, several students at a private high school in New York became ill. They vomited, and some passed out at their desks. What first looked like a case of bad cafeteria food turned out to be a much more serious problem—drug overdoses.

The teens had taken Xanax, a powerful prescription medicine used to treat anxiety; they bought it from fellow students. And it didn't take much to get them sick. "In a couple of the cases, only one pill was taken," says Inspector Daniel Jackson of the White Plains police force.

The teenagers recovered, but those who sold the pills and some who took the drugs were arrested and charged. The incident is part of what experts say is a disturbing new trend. Teens are abusing prescription drugs and are also misusing drugs sold over the counter (OTC), such as cold medicines.

The trend is called pharming, from the word pharmaceuticals. One national study found that 18 percent of teens reported using Vicodin, a prescription painkiller. A total of 10 percent had tried Ritalin or Adderall without a prescription; both drugs are stimulants used to treat attention deficit/hyperactivity disorder (ADHD). The same percentage had misused OxyContin, which is prescribed for pain.

## The Other Drug Problem

The pharming problem has been confirmed in a study by the Partnership for a Drug-Free America. Teens in the United States are now more likely to abuse legal painkillers than to try illegal drugs such as ecstasy, cocaine, an crack. "In other words, 'Generation Rx' has arrived," Roy Bostock, the chairman of the partnership, said when the study results were announced last spring.

Anna, a 17-year-old Virginia high school senior, says trouble can be as close as the local drugstore. That's where some student she knows buy cough medicine to get high The national survey says that 9 percent of all teens have done just that. "You just go in and buy it, and nobody really cares," Anna says.

For example, few are aware of the dangers of dextromethorphan, the active ingredient in many cough medicines. "There's no doubt that this is a brain-damaging chemical when used in high doses," says Dr. Drew Pinsky. He runs chemical dependency services at a hospital in Pasadena, Calif. "How much before you get damage? We don't know."

The brain is not fully developed until about age 24, notes Ken C. Winters, who directs research at the University of Minnesota. Winters says that researchers do not know all the risks of taking drugs while the brain is still changing. "You're adding chemicals during the time when the brain is still trying to normally develop. It adds a whole other risk layer to taking any drugs," Winters says.

## Right in Your Medicine Cabinet

Why do some teens pharm? Easy access to the drugs is one reason. Prescription and OTC drugs are in the home medicine cabinet. Students know the medications from advertisements and often see parents or friends taking pills. That leads some to think that abusing prescription drugs is safer than using illegal drugs; but nothing could be farther from the truth.

More painkillers are dispensed now than 20 years ago. "When you prescribe more, then more of the drug is available, [and] not only to the people who need it. It hangs around in medicine cabinets and drawers," says Dr. Herbert Kleber of Columbia University's College of Physicians and Surgeons in New York City. One in five teens says he or she has been offered prescription painkillers to get high.

Between 1992 and 2003, the number of people who abused controlled prescription drugs—those with a high risk of abuse and addiction—rose 94 percent. Those drugs include Xanax, OxyContin, and Ritalin. Use of such drugs by teens increased a whopping 212 percent, according to a study by the National Center on Addiction and Substance Abuse. In 2003, about 15 percent of teens abused or were addicted to controlled drugs, says the same study.

Young people today have a more relaxed attitude about taking prescription drugs, says Carol Falkowski, a director at the Hazelden Foundation in Minnesota, since many teens grew up needing medication for a behavior problem, such as ADHD. "Kids learn at a very early age that if you take a pill, you get a mood change," Falkowski says. "They think very little about sharing their pills with other kids."

Jac is a 17-year-old high school senior from New York who says some students obtain Adderall from those with prescriptions for it. "Kids take it for big exams—like, some kids will take it for the SAT," he says.

Sharing pills can have tragic consequences. "Even though kids believe that if it's a pill it must somehow be safe, they don't know what they're getting. They don't know the dose," Falkowski says. An adult dose can have a "dramatically different effect on a smaller person," she adds. "Even one-time use can be fatal."

## Danger to the Mix

Trouble also comes from mixing drugs with alcohol. Poor judgment often occurs; many teens regret their actions the next day, says Russel Falck, assistant professor in community health at Wright State University in Ohio. The result could also be as bad as respiratory distress or overdose. Mixing alcohol with prescription painkillers can plunge breathing and heart rates to dangerously low levels. "Basically it's an equation for danger," Falck says.

Rob Rosenberg, a 17-year-old from New Jersey, knows well the pitfalls of being a member of Generation Rx. His mother was on disability following an accident and had a lot of pills in the house. Curious, he swallowed a few of her Xanax tablets when he was barely 10 years old.

"I liked the feeling that I couldn't feel," he says. "It made you numb." Rob swiped his mother's pills for over six years. He took the pain medications OxyContin, Vicodin, and others.

Rob was thrown out of school. When he needed money, he sold pills. Rob stopped only when he was arrested for selling drugs. He was sent to Daytop New Jersey, a drug treatment program, as an alternative to jail and spent 13 months there before getting out last summer and reenrolling in high school.

"The consequences [of prescription drug abuse] are way more harsh than you can ever imagine," Rob says.

### Table 1  Drugs and Teens Who Have Tried Them

| | |
|---|---|
| Marijuana | 37% |
| Inhalants | 19% |
| (*)Vicodin | 18% |
| (*)Ritalin/Adderall | 10% |
| (*)OxyContin | 10% |
| Cough Medicine | 9% |
| Crack/Cocaine | 9% |
| Ecstasy | 9% |
| Methamphetamine | 8% |
| LSD | 6% |
| (*)Ketamine | 5% |
| Heroin | 4% |

(*)Prescription drugs used in ways not prescribed by doctor

Source: Partnership for a Drug-Free America, Partnership Attitude Tracking Study 2004

# Studies Identify Factors Surrounding Rise in Abuse of Prescription Drugs by College Students

LORI WHITTEN

Prescription drug abuse among students in U.S. colleges and universities has been rising for several years. The 2004 Monitoring the Future (MTF) Survey of College Students and Adults—the most recent data available—estimated that 7.4 percent of college students used the painkiller hydrocodone (Vicodin) without a prescription in that year, up from 6.9 percent in 2002, with similar increases for other opioid medications, stimulants, and sedatives. Three new NIDA-funded studies reveal which students and campuses have the highest rates of abuse and connect such abuse to other unhealthy behaviors. According to the research, rates of collegiate prescription stimulant abuse are highest among men, Whites, fraternity/sorority members, and at schools in the Northeast.

## Stimulant Abuse Nationwide

Dr. Sean Esteban McCabe and colleagues at the University of Michigan and Harvard University analyzed the answers from the Harvard School of Public Health College Alcohol Study, which in 2001 surveyed 10,904 randomly selected students enrolled at 119 colleges across the United States. Overall, 4 percent of the respondents reported having taken a stimulant medication without a prescription at least once during the previous year. Men were twice as likely as women (5.8 percent versus 2.9 percent) to have abused methylphenidate (Ritalin), dextroamphetamine (Dexedrine), and amphetamine/dextroamphetamine (Adderall). Stimulant medication abuse was also more prevalent among students who were:

- White (4.9 percent versus 1.6 percent for African-Americans and 1.3 percent for Asians);
- Members of fraternities or sororities (8.6 percent versus 3.5 percent for nonmembers); and
- Earning lower grades (5.2 percent for grade point average of B or lower versus 3.3 percent for B+ or higher).

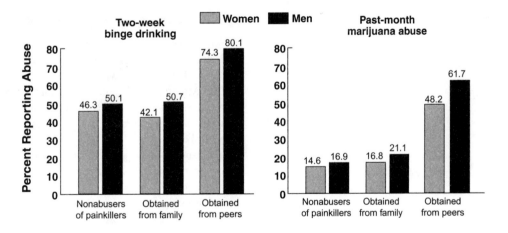

*At one university, students who obtained perscription painkillers from peers reported higher levels of binge drinking and marijuana abuse than nonabusers or those who received painkillers from family.*

**Figure 1**   Binge Drinking, Marijuana Abuse Are Elevated Among Students Who Obtain Painkillers From Peers

Students who abused prescription stimulants reported higher levels of cigarette smoking; heavy drinking; risky driving; and abuse of marijuana, MDMA (Ecstasy), and cocaine. Compared with other survey respondents, for example, they were 20 times as likely to report past-year cocaine abuse and 5 times as likely to report driving after heavy drinking. The campus prevalence of past-year stimulant abuse ranged from 0 percent at 20 colleges—including the three historically African-American institutions included in the survey—to 25 percent. The prevalence was 10 percent or higher at 12 colleges. Students attending colleges in the Northeast, schools with more competitive admission standards, and noncommuter schools reported higher rates of abuse.

# One University's Painkiller Picture

At a large Midwestern university, about 9 percent of 9,161 undergraduates surveyed had taken a prescription pain medication without a doctor's order at least once during the past year; 16 percent reported such abuse in their lifetime. Of the latter, 54 percent said they had obtained the drugs from peers, while 17 percent said their source was a family member. Dr. McCabe and colleagues at the University of Michigan Substance Abuse Research Center found that students who obtained medications from peers were more likely to smoke and drink heavily and to have abused other substances—including marijuana, cocaine, and other illegal drugs—than those who obtained them from family members.

## Table 1   Stimulant Abuse Varies by Campus Characteristics

| Selected Characteristics | Past-year Stimulant Abuse Rates, % |
|---|---|
| **Admission criteria** | |
| More competitive | 5.9 |
| Competitive | 4.5 |
| Less competitive | 1.3 |
| **Geographical region** | |
| Northeast | 6.3 |
| South | 4.6 |
| West | 3.2 |
| North Central | 2.8 |
| **Commuter Status** | |
| Noncommuter school | 4.6 |
| Commuter school | 1.2 |

Students enrolled in the most selective colleges reported relatively high levels of past-year stimulant abuse, as did those attending schools in the Northeast. Residential schools reported higher rates than commuter colleges.

The researchers found that exposure to prescription pain medication early in life increased the likelihood of abuse in college. Women who had received prescriptions for pain relievers in elementary school were more than four times as likely as those with no prescribed use to report abuse in the past year. Men with early prescribed use were twice as likely as those without to report such abuse. In addition:

- Women students were more likely to be prescribed pain medication, while men were more likely to be approached to sell or give away prescribed medication.
- More men obtained the drugs from peers while more women obtained them from family members.
- Past-year prescription painkiller abuse was higher among fraternity members than nonmembers (17 percent versus 9 percent) and among sorority members compared with nonmembers (9.6 percent versus 8.6 percent).

"Students abuse prescription drugs to get high, to self-medicate for pain episodes, to help concentrate during exam time, and to try to relieve stress. Regardless of the motivation, people need to know the risks of abuse and the dangers of mixing drugs," says Dr. Lynda Erinoff, formerly of NIDA's Division of Epidemiology, Services and Prevention Research. Most people assume that if a medication is available on the market, it must be safe—even if it has not been prescribed for them, says Dr. Erinoff, "but a drug or dose that a doctor orders for one person is not necessarily appropriate for another, and prescription abusers are potentially taking a serious risk." NIDA continues to work with doctors and pharmacists and to link prevention specialists with researchers focusing on the problem. "Educating the public remains a critical challenge," says Dr. Erinoff.

**". . . people need to know the risks of abuse and the dangers of mixing drugs."**

# Membership Matters

Based on responses from more than 5,000 young people who participated in the MTF when they were high school seniors in 1988 to 1997, and also when they were in college, Dr. McCabe and his Michigan colleagues found that active members of college fraternities or sororities engage in more heavy episodic, or "binge," drinking, cigarette smoking, and marijuana abuse than nonmembers.

The students who joined fraternities or sororities in college were the same ones who reported the highest levels of substance abuse in high school. Moreover, cigarette smoking, binge drinking, and drug abuse increased for all survey participants as they progressed through college. Fraternity and sorority members showed greater elevations in binge drinking and marijuana abuse over time compared with nonmembers. The picture that emerges is of students who are already heavy drinkers when they come to college selecting fraternities and sororities with a reputation for "partying" and then, as members, further increasing their drinking in an environment that supports the behavior.

"It's important for each student to explore, perhaps with counseling, a possible mismatch between his or her college environment and individual needs. Some students benefit from settings that emphasize socialization outside of the party scene; these might include group living arrangements based on shared academic or extracurricular interests," Dr. McCabe says.

# Sources

McCabe, S.E., et al. Non-medical use of prescription stimulants among US college students: Prevalence and correlates from a national survey. *Addiction* 100(1):96–106, 2005. [Abstract]

McCabe, S.E., et al. Selection and socialization effects of fraternities and sororities on US college student substance use: A multi-cohort national longitudinal study. *Addiction* 100(4):512–524, 2005. [Abstract]

McCabe, S.E.; Teter, C.J.; and Boyd, C.J. Illicit use of prescription pain medication among college students. *Drug and Alcohol Dependence* 77(1):37–47, 2005. [Full Text]

From *NIDA Notes*, vol. 20, no. 4. Published by The National Institute on Drug Abuse.

*The Drug War*

# 'The Best High They've Ever Had'

HILARY SHENFELD

Street users call it drop dead, executioner, flat-liner, the exorcist, Al Capone, fefe, Teflon and diesel. Cops know it as a deadly mix of heroin and fentanyl, an anesthetic and painkiller far more potent than morphine. For cancer patients racked with pain, legally prescribed fentanyl can be a godsend. But for junkies, the fentanyl-heroin cocktail has become the hot new high, as lethal as it is alluring. It is being blamed for hundreds of deaths this year in big cities in the Midwest and Northeast.

In Wayne County, Mich., home to Detroit, there have been 50 deaths in just the past two weeks, including 19 in one deadly day in May.

The problem is that cops don't know who is spreading the killer junk on the streets. It might be just one big bad batch that's been widely distributed, or it could be coming from multiple sources, say law-enforcement officials, who first began noticing a spike in fentanyl-heroin overdoses in November. One promising new lead came from the arrest of five people at an underground fentanyl lab in Mexico. "We're working to see if there's a connection, if that lab was the source," says DEA spokeswoman Rogene Waite. Federal and local police are meeting in Chicago this month to compare notes and come up with a cohesive strategy to combat the growing crisis.

Dealers are not intentionally killing their customers. Instead, it appears that in their zeal to get the new product on the street, dealers haven't perfected the recipe. Users say the blend, when snorted, injected or smoked, gives them an instant feeling of extreme euphoria. After 11 people died from the drug in one day in Chicago last month, police issued a public warning. Instead of being scared off, "people flocked to the area looking for the drug," says police spokeswoman Monique Bond. "They say," says Frank Limon, a top Chicago cop, "that it's the best high they've ever had." And the deadliest.

# Some Cold Medicines Move Behind Counter

**Some over-the-counter (OTC) cold and allergy medicines are being moved behind the counter at pharmacies nationwide as part of the fight against illegal drug production.**

LINDA BREN

Under the Patriot Act signed by President Bush on March 9, 2006, all drug products that contain the ingredient pseudoephedrine must be kept behind the pharmacy counter and must be sold in limited quantities to consumers after they show identification and sign a logbook.

Pseudoephedrine is a drug found in both OTC and prescription products used to relieve nasal or sinus congestion caused by the common cold, sinusitis, hay fever, and other respiratory allergies. The drug is also a key ingredient in making methamphetamine—a powerful, highly addictive stimulant often produced illegally by "meth cooks" in home laboratories.

The new legal provisions for selling and purchasing pseudoephedrine-containing products are part of the Combat Methamphetamine Epidemic Act of 2005, which was incorporated into the Patriot Act. These "anti-meth" provisions introduce safeguards to make certain ingredients used in methamphetamine manufacturing more difficult to obtain in bulk and easier for law enforcement to track.

According to the National Institute on Drug Abuse, methamphetamine use and abuse is associated with serious health conditions including memory loss, aggression, violence, paranoia, hallucinations, and potential heart and brain damage. The Drug Enforcement Administration says there is a direct relationship between methamphetamine abuse and increased incidents of domestic violence and child abuse.

Meth users ingest the substance by swallowing, inhaling, injecting, or smoking it. There are currently no safe and tested medications for treating methamphetamine addiction.

The new law affects several hundred OTC products for children and adults, such as Sudafed Nasal Decongestant Tablets, Advil Allergy Sinus Caplets, TheraFlu Daytime Severe Cold SoftGels, Tylenol Flu NightTime Gelcaps, and Children's Vicks NyQuil Cold/Cough Relief. "There are very few decongestants on the market that don't contain pseudoephedrine," says Charles Ganley, M.D., director of the Food and Drug Administration's Office of Nonprescription Products.

Ganley says that products containing pseudoephedrine are still available without a prescription and that they are packaged the same way as any OTC drug. "The only difference is that people will have to go to the pharmacist to buy them," he says. "They just need to ask for them and show ID, and know that there's a limit to the amount they can purchase."

Buyers must show a government-issued photo ID, such as a driver's license, and sign a logbook. Stores are required to keep a record about purchases, which includes the product name, quantity sold, name and address of purchaser, and date and time of the sale, for at least two years. Single-dose packages containing 60 milligrams or less of pseudoephedrine are excluded from the recordkeeping requirement, but must still be stored behind the counter.

The federal law limits the amount of pseudoephedrine an individual can purchase to 3.6 grams in a single day and 9 grams in a month at a retail store. For example, a person may buy Advil Allergy Sinus Caplets, which contain pseudoephedrine and other ingredients, in quantities of up to 146 tablets in one day and 366 tablets in one month. The number of pills or amount of liquid medicine allowable will vary depending on the type of product and its strength.

The limits on the amount an individual can purchase became effective April 8, 2006. The requirements to place products behind the counter and to keep a logbook take effect Sept. 30, 2006. Many drug stores are already complying voluntarily or because some state laws require similar controls.

Drug companies are reformulating some of their products to eliminate pseudoephedrine. Pfizer, for example, while still offering Sudafed nasal decongestants, which contain pseudoephedrine, also markets a line called Sudafed PE as an "on the shelf" alternative. Sudafed PE contains the active ingredient phenylephrine, which is not used to make methamphetamine, and so is not under the same restrictions as pseudoephedrine.

"Drugs that contain phenylephrine are also safe and effective," says Ganley. "The dosing is a little different—you have to take them a little more frequently than the pseudoephedrine-containing drugs because their effects are not as long-lasting."

The anti-meth provisions of the Patriot Act restrict the sale of two other drug ingredients, ephedrine and phenylpropanolamine, because of their potential to be used illegally to make methamphetamine. Like pseudoephedrine, drugs containing these ingredients must be placed behind the counter, and buyers must show identification to purchase a limited quantity.

Synthetic ephedrine is used in some topical drugs, such as nose drops, to temporarily relieve congestion due to colds, hay fever, sinusitis, or other upper respiratory allergies. It is also used orally for temporary relief of asthma symptoms.

Phenylpropanolamine was commonly used in OTC decongestants and weight-loss drugs. Today, it is unlikely that consumers will find phenylpropanolamine in their drug stores, says Ganley. In 2000, the FDA asked drug manufacturers to discontinue marketing products containing phenylpropanolamine because of an increased risk of bleeding in the brain (hemorrhagic stroke) associated with the ingredient. The FDA has taken regulatory actions to remove phenylpropanolamine from all drug products.

From *FDA Consumer*, July/August 2006, pp. 18–19. Published 2006 by U.S. Food and Drug Administration. www.fda.gov

# Facing an Uncertain Twilight

## Older addicts present a growing concern

MICHELLE BOORSTEIN
*Washington Post Staff Writer*

James Gulick looks around at the recovering drug addicts in the room and thinks: Yeah, I fit in here. He has the whole sad list of credentials: the estranged family, the drained bank account, the regrets.

But he doesn't look the part. The 62-year-old crack cocaine addict stands out among the dozens of people in his Fredericksburg treatment group, with his full head of white hair and bifocals in a sea of young men with goatees and young women in tight jeans.

Unlike many of them, Gulick, a retired food distributor, isn't here to rebuild a career or a marriage or save his house; those things went up in the smoke of a crack pipe long ago. All he wants now is a peaceful place to watch stock car racing on television and to reconcile with his son.

So Gulick is trying to get used to baring his soul in group therapy and undergoing regular drug screening. And the counselors are trying to adjust to him.

As unusual as Gulick seems—the others have nicknamed him "Gramps"—experts say he represents a larger, unseen wave of addicts who came of age before it was common to admit addiction and seek treatment. They say the numbers, growing for a decade, will swell as baby boomers—the first generation in which recreational drug use was widespread—reach old age. With age, they say, can come more isolation, more free time and changing body chemistry, all of which can help turn a weekend habit into a daily compulsion.

Although there are few geriatric addiction specialists, the subject is starting to appear on conference agendas. The National Institute of Drug Addiction held its first forum on the issue in September, and the Department of Health and Human Services recently released a study predicting that the number of seniors with substance abuse problems will rise 150 percent by 2020.

Addicts of all ages have traits in common, but seniors have some distinguishing ones. Their systems may be less tolerant of drugs than those of younger people. They have more free time, and no small children or bosses to be accountable to. And they have lost more in their lives, according to Margaret Anne Lane, a counselor at Sentara Williamsburg Community Hospital, who recently began a substance abuse counseling program for people older than 60.

But when they are ready to quit, they often have more success, according to David Oslin, a psychiatrist at the University of Pennsylvania's medical school. Although they may regard therapy with suspicion, having grown up before it was common, they are highly motivated and keep appointments. Their age often means that sessions must be tailored for them, Lane said.

"There's a greater need for respect and privacy, good manners, and logistically, things like having sessions during the day since they don't like to drive at night, shorter sessions, good lighting, people speaking louder," she said.

Generally, people older than 60 make up less than 3 percent of the millions who seek treatment each year, though the number of senior addicts is estimated to be higher. Few older addicts seek treatment, but when they do decide to quit, they are generally more successful than younger ones are, Oslin said.

"They are trying to maintain their independence and their health," he said. "They realize, 'If I want to be around for my grandkid to graduate from high school, I need to get my act together.' "

In 1992, 77 percent of people older than 50 being treated for substance abuse were alcoholics; the rest had a drug problem or an alcohol and drug problem, according to Health and Human Services. By 2002, half of people older than 50 being treated had a drug problem.

But only 2 percent of people older than 50 are considered addicts, compared with 4 percent to 5 percent of the general population, so little is known about addiction among the elderly—including whether they are more or less likely to relapse after treatment.

Gulick's counselors at the Rappahannock Area Community Services Board say they do not see enough people his age to draw conclusions about them. One case manager says some older addicts serve as mentors to the younger ones in drug courts, where 1 percent of participants nationwide are older than 60. Gulick, reluctant to preach, isn't one of them.

But he couldn't contain himself during a recent session when the counselor threw out this question: Is it worth your time to warn young people to stay off drugs?

"Maybe some of these young people should learn the hard way!" Gulick said, folding his arms across his chest and smiling a surprised smile—as though he couldn't believe he had ventured an opinion.

Gulick's voyage into treatment began the way it began for the other members of the group—in the back of a police cruiser.

After being arrested one December night two years ago as he bought cocaine at a Spotsylvania hotel, he was given a choice by prosecutors: spend six months in jail or make a commitment to drug court, a treatment program for addicts. Treatment would require him to learn things about himself that he wasn't eager to know.

"I can't think about why I've done drugs; there's no answer," Gulick said in the low drawl of his native southeastern Virginia, nervously wiping imaginary crumbs off the Denny's restaurant table for the fourth time in a half-hour.

"I just know the life I had before drugs, I know the life I had on drugs, and I know the life I have now. It was time to come off it."

Eighteen months after starting drug court, he hasn't delved very deeply into the whys. He took the first pipe from a friend when he was in his forties and, during a decade, lost his marriage, his home and contact with his son and brother. When he retired from a sales management job in 2000 with $238,000 in savings and a pension, he began pouring money into crack, spending $1,000 a day by the end, he says. He dropped 30 pounds.

He spent the first several months of treatment in denial. At weekly check-in sessions with Fredericksburg Circuit Court Judge John W. Scott Jr.—who chats briefly with each participant and often jails those who have failed surprise drug tests— Gulick would lean back in his pew and let an easy smile rest on his weathered face. He looked like the rebellious student who laughs when he is sent to the principal's office.

But in recent months, Gulick and his counselors agree, his outlook began to change. Broke and required by drug court to work or volunteer, Gulick went nearly a year ago to the local day-labor office and struggled through construction work. After a few months, a friend gave him a job at a publishing house, where he packs boxes. On weekends, he tries to stay busy, barbecuing or fishing.

Settling into a new life at his age hasn't been easy. He moved from Caroline County to Fredericksburg to be closer to drug court, and it took three months to find a roommate who wanted to live with an older man with special requirements.

"I'd say, 'Look, I don't drink, I don't do drugs.' They'd say, 'I'll call you back and let you know if you got the apartment,' and then you never hear from them," he said. "That's how you know."

If Gulick is all laid-back pragmatism, Richard Butler is the opposite, bouncing off walls one minute with tear-choked regret and the next with elation over the life he has reclaimed in his seventh decade. The burly carpenter embraces the self-examination that came with drug court, carrying self-help books and churning with analysis.

"No, no, no!" he responds to Gulick's suggestion. "If only someone would have told me that freedom comes from living life today as honestly as possible!"

With his tousle of sandy brown hair and puppylike grin, Butler, 62, looks as if he should be organizing a family touch football game, not smoking crack alone in the Fredericksburg motel where he was living when he was busted in 2003.

"It was the right time," Butler said one morning, a book about "the pursuit of happiness" on the restaurant table next to his Marlboros. "I needed to travel all those little side roads and ravines. I just wish the right time would have happened earlier."

His decades of addictions—of crack, scratch lottery cards, bowling, women—cost him four marriages and estranged him from his three children and 11 siblings.

Butler grew up in a large family in which there was a lot of drinking, violence and transience. "We'd stay somewhere as long as people could tolerate us," he said.

He joined the Navy, where he became a health worker, giving sailors information about alcohol and drugs. He smoked pot for the first time at 32 at a port in Africa, after a sailor challenged his lectures by noting that Butler had never tried drugs. "I wasn't going to accept that," he said, shaking his head at what identifies now as deep insecurity and anger.

After the Navy, Butler drifted through Ohio and Texas before winding up in the Fredericksburg area, where he was offered crack in 1991 by a man who was always accompanied by attractive women. In the three years before his arrest, he said, he smoked crack every day.

In February, Butler and Gulick are set to leave drug court for an uncertain future. Both are optimistic.

Before a recent session, Gulick was elated over what he said was a recent milestone; he had called his son for the first time in years, he said, and planned to see him over the holidays. But David Gulick, 32, of King George, Va., said he hadn't received any message from his dad. "But I'd be more than happy to talk to him," he said. "Everyone makes mistakes."

Butler was excited about plans to expand his carpentry business. Despite two heart attacks, he works seven days a week. His goal, he said, "is to get clean to the point that I can live without fear of falling back in."

With the zeal of a convert, he tells his younger peers: "Look at me, I've missed 62 years."

A 19-year-old group member said his sermons are "annoying"—but she's listening.

"That's not going to be me," said the woman, who spoke on condition of anonymity. "I wouldn't be alive if I'm still using at that age."

From *The Washington Post,* January 31/February 6, 2005. Copyright © 2005 by The Washington Post. Reprinted by permission.

# UNIT 5

# Measuring the Social Costs of Drugs

## Unit Selection

## Key Points to Consider

- Where does one look to identify the social costs associated with drug abuse?

- Determine what percentage of your class that has been the victim of a crime and determine what percentages of those crimes were related to drugs.

- How has the spread of methamphetamine use and manufacture affected children?

- In which subpopulations of Americans does fetal alcohol syndrome manifest itself differently, and why?

- What do you believe to be the greatest drug-related threat currently facing the United States?

## Student Website

www.mhcls.com/online

## Internet References

Further information regarding these websites may be found in this book's preface or online.

**BMJ.com a publishing group**
*http://bmj.bmjjournals.com/cgi/content/abridged/326/7383/242/a*
**Drug Enforcement Administration**
*http://www.usdoj.gov/dea/*
**Drug Use Cost to the Economy**
*www.ccm-drugtest.com/ntl_effcts1.htm*
**Drug Policy Alliance**
*www.drugpolicy.org/database/index.html*
**National Drug Control Policy**
*http://www.ncjrs.org/ondcppubs/publications/policy/ndcs00/chap2_10.html*
**The November Coalition**
*http://www.november.org*
**TRAC DEA Site**
*http://trac.syr.edu/tracdea/index.html*
**United Nations Chronicle - online edition**
*http://www.un.org/Pubs/chronicle/1998/issue2/0298p7.html*

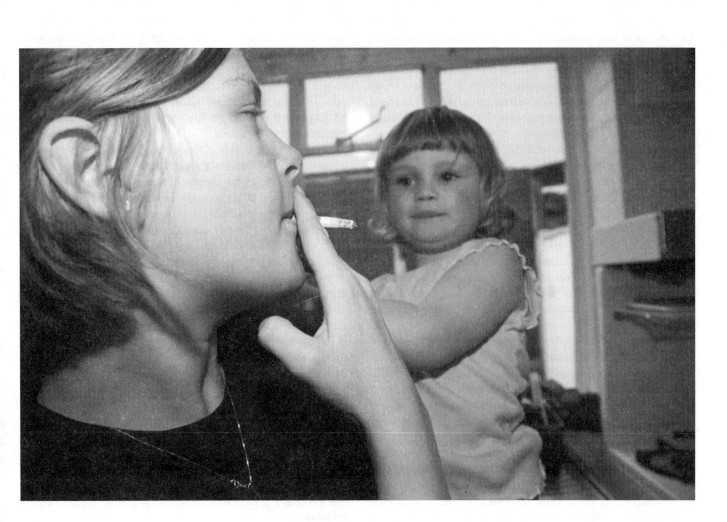

The most devastating effect of drug abuse in America is the magnitude with which it affects the way we live. Much of its influence is not measurable. What is the cost of a son or daughter lost, a parent imprisoned, a life lived in a constant state of fear? The emotional costs alone are incomprehensible.

The social legacy of this country's drug crisis could easily be the subject of this entire book. The purpose here, however, can only be a cursory portrayal of drugs' tremendous costs. More than one American president has stated that drug use threatens our national security and personal well-being. The financial costs of maintaining the federal apparatus devoted to drug interdiction, enforcement, and treatment are staggering. Although yearly expenditures vary due to changes in political influence, strategy, and tactics, examples of the tremendous effects of drugs on government and the economy abound. The federal budget for drug control exceeds $12.7 billion and includes almost $1.5 billion dedicated to drug fighting in foreign countries including Mexico, Colombia, Afghanistan, and Pakistan. The Department of Justice commits almost $3 billion to antidrug efforts, the Department of Health and Human Services almost

$3.5 billion and the Department of Homeland Security over $3.3 billion. Currently, the growing problems associated with methamphetamine use and manufacture are commanding dollars in federal, state, and local budgets. The President has dedicated specific funds to the U.S. Attorney for the high priority prosecution of meth manufacturers. The taking over of large-scale meth production by Mexican criminal syndicates who produce thousands of pounds of methamphetamine in super-labs located in California and the Southwest is a national problem. Over $20 million is committed to state and local authorities to clean up toxic methamphetamine labs, and in 2007 special research funds were again made available to study the harmful effects caused to children exposed to meth labs. Even though much effort is being dedicated to control serious visible problems with methamphetamine, there is great concern that this problem is much worse than numbers indicate. Federal seizures of methamphetamine in the West and Southwest alone number in the thousands of kilos.

Drugs *are* the business of the criminal justice system. Approximately 80 percent of the people behind bars in this country had a problem with drugs or alcohol prior to their arrest. The United States incarcerates more of its citizens than almost any other nation and the financial costs are staggering. Doing drugs and serving time produces an inescapable nexus and it doesn't end with prison. More than 36 percent of adults on parole or supervised release are classified with dependence on or abuse of a substance. Some argue that these numbers represent the fact that Americans have come to rely on the criminal justice system as an unprecedented way of responding to social problems. Regardless of the way one chooses to view various relationships, the resulting picture is numbing.

In addition to the highly visible criminal justice–related costs, numerous other institutions are affected. Housing, welfare, education, and health care provide excellent examples of critical institutions struggling to overcome the strain of drug-related impacts. In addition, annual loss of productivity in the workplace exceeds well over a $160 billion per year. Alcoholism alone causes 500 million lost workdays each year. Add to this demographic shifts caused by people fleeing drug-impacted neighborhoods, schools, and businesses and one soon realizes that there is no victimless public or private institution. Last year, almost 4 million Americans received some kind of treatment related to the abuse of alcohol or other drugs. The number of persons needing treatment for an illicit drug problem remains at over 7 million and the number of persons needing treatment for alcohol abuse remains at more than 18 million. Fetal alcohol syndrome is the leading cause of mental retardation in the United States, and still, survey data continues to report over 11 percent of pregnant women drink alcohol; of these, 4.5 percent report binge drinking. Add injured, drug-related accident and crime victims, along with demands produced by a growing population of intravenous-drug users infected with AIDS, and an overwhelmed health care system frighteningly appears. Health care costs from drug-related ills are staggering. Drug abuse continues to cost the economy $13 billion annually in health care costs alone.

It should be emphasized that the social costs exacted by drug use infiltrate every aspect of public and private life. The implications for thousands of families struggling with the adverse effects of drug-related woes may prove the greatest and most tragic of social costs. Children who lack emotional support, self-esteem, role models, a safe and secure environment, economic opportunity, and an education because of a parent on drugs suggest costs difficult to comprehend or measure. In some jurisdictions in California and Oregon, as many as 70 percent of child welfare placements are precipitated by methamphetamine abuse.

When reading Unit 5 of this book, consider the diversity of costs associated with the abuse of both legal drugs and illegal drugs. As you read the following articles, consider the historical progressions of social costs produced by drug abuse over the past century. How are the problems of the past replicating themselves and how has science, medicine and social policy changed in an attempt to mitigate these impacts?

Ample evidence informs us that there is no single approach to mitigate the diverse nature of drug related social impacts. Further, some of the most astounding scientific discoveries about how addiction develops remain mysterious when compared to the reality of the lives of millions who find drugs an end in themselves. Some have argued that the roots of drug abuse problems today seem even more elusive, complicated, and desperate. Good progress has been made in treating drug addiction, but only moderate progress has been made in preventing it in the first place. What examples exist of disproportionate ways in which some populations of Americans are harmed by drugs? Are there epidemics within epidemics? How is drug abuse expressed within different populations of Americans? How do the implications for Native American families and culture differ from those implications for other racial and ethnic groups? What are the reasons for these disparities and how should they be addressed?

# Meth Addicts' Other Habit: Online Theft

**Methamphetamine addicts skilled in identity theft are turning to computers and the Internet to expand their reach. USA TODAY examines the inner workings of one small ring of addicts who began partnering with global Internet crime groups to trade in stolen identity data and launder hijacked funds.**

BYRON ACOHIDO; JON SWARTZ

Edmonton, Alberta—Hot on the trail of identity thieves, veteran Edmonton Police Service detectives Al Vonkeman and Bob Gauthier last winter hustled to a local motel, a cinder-block establishment where rooms rent by the hour.

Twice before, police had descended on locations in Edmonton and Calgary, 200 miles away, chasing down a tip about someone accessing a dial-up Internet account linked to an e-mail folder full of stolen identity data. Each time, the user logged off and vacated the premises before police arrived.

This time the motel's manager told the detectives that the phone in Room 24 was in use. As Vonkeman and Gauthier prepared to bust down the door, out strolled a garrulous drug addict, 25, whom they'd arrested before, followed by a younger man—a 21-year-old computer whiz—both sky-high on methamphetamine.

Inside Room 24 the detectives found meth pipes, stolen credit cards, notebooks with handwritten notations about fraudulent transactions and printouts of stolen identity data. The distinctive smell of street meth pervaded the air. "They were just starting to set up," recalls Vonkeman, an economic crimes analyst.

On the motel room bed, connected to a wall phone jack, a laptop computer was downloading something. Before going to work on stolen ID data, the younger man was downloading the latest version of his favorite video game. "But it was a dial-up modem, so it was taking forever," says Gauthier, a veteran drug unit detective.

Vonkeman, 44, and Gauthier, 48, had flushed out the roving nerve center of a loose-knit ring of meth addicts running identity-theft scams. Evidence in the motel room would ultimately lead them to a much bigger revelation: The Edmonton ring had gone global.

It no longer relied solely on dumpster-diving, mailbox-pilfering street addicts to supply stolen credit cards, checks and account statements, the grist for local thefts. Instead, it had advanced to complex joint ventures, conducted over the Internet, in partnership with organized cybercrime rings outside the country.

## Intersection of Crimes

What's happening in Edmonton is happening to one degree or another in communities across the USA and Canada—anywhere meth addicts are engaging in identity theft and can get on the Internet, say police, federal law enforcement officials and Internet security experts.

Internet Relay Chat channels, private areas on the Internet where real-time text messaging takes place, are rife with communications between organized cybercrime groups and meth users and traffickers discussing how they can assist each other. "It's big time," says San Diego-based security consultant Lance James, who monitors IRC channels.

Such collaboration seems almost preordained. "This hits at the intersection of two of the more complex law enforcement investigations: computer crimes and drug crimes," says Howard Schmidt, CEO of R&H Security Consulting and former White House cyber-security adviser.

Identity theft has fast become the crime of preference among meth users for three reasons: It is non-violent, criminal penalties for first-time offenders are light—usually a few days or weeks in jail—and the use of computers and the Internet offers crooks anonymity and speed with which to work. Meth is a cheap, highly addictive street derivative of amphetamine pills; it turns users into automatons willing to take on risky, street-level crime.

Meanwhile, global cybercrime groups control e-mail phishing attacks, keystroke-stealing Trojan horse programs and insider database thefts that swell the pool of stolen personal and financial information. They also have ready access to hijacked online-banking accounts. But converting assets in compromised accounts into cash is never easy. That's where the meth users come in.

Sophisticated meth theft rings, like the one in Edmonton, control local bank accounts—and underlings who are willing to extract ill-gotten funds from such accounts. The two men at the seedy motel were helping outside crime groups link up with local accounts under their control when a tipster guided police to them in December 2004.

Edmonton police granted USA TODAY exclusive access to cases investigated by Vonkeman and Gauthier from early 2003 to the present. The newspaper examined police evidence files and interviewed two central ring members, ages 37 and 22. In this story, they are referred to as Mary and Frank.

Police set up the interviews but required that the suspects' real names, as well as the true identities of the two men arrested at the motel, be withheld for the safety of the individuals and to preserve the integrity of ongoing investigations. In this story, the two men arrested at the motel are called Martin and Socks—not their real names.

Police participated in USA TODAY'S phone interviews with Mary and Frank, then arranged for a reporter to interview Mary in person, with no police present. She took the reporter on a daylong tour of locations in Edmonton where the ring had committed ID thefts and fraud.

What emerges is the tale of how one cadre of meth addicts, from ordinary backgrounds, found extraordinary ways to steal and manipulate sensitive personal and financial data—data they discovered to be rather haphazardly protected. Here is their story:

# Dumpster Diving Summer-fall 2003

Mary had to think quickly. The security guard had appeared out of nowhere. She was sitting in her black sedan, waiting for Frank to yank garbage bags out of a dumpster behind Neiman Marcus' Edmonton call center, where the upscale U.S. retailer routes calls from customers.

A soft-spoken, attractive blonde with a friendly demeanor, Mary passed herself off as an absent-minded employee hunting for a lost day-planner. She sweet-talked the guard into helping Frank load bags into the sedan. "He says, 'Oh I'll help you, maybe it's in one of these,'" she recalled during an interview conducted while showing a reporter dumpsters she helped scope.

Mary, 37, met Frank in the summer of 2003 through her boyfriend, a meth dealer who was Frank's supplier. Up until her divorce in 2001, Mary says, she was a "model citizen": She was college-educated and had two children and a management career. But then her marriage hit the skids. Her boyfriend, the meth dealer, "was domineering, and I was vulnerable from the divorce," she says.

Frank, 22, passionate, creative but easily manipulated, says he became a meth addict at age 14. He quickly demonstrated a high aptitude for committing fraud. A fellow addict who was an employee of Canadian cellphone company Rogers Communications showed him how to open new cellphone accounts over the phone and on the Internet, using data from customer records plucked from Rogers' dumpsters.

As a high school student, Frank had possession of stolen cellphones to use and sell. He soon advanced to using stolen credit card numbers to shop online. He found that he loved manipulating data on his computer almost as much as conning customer-service reps over the phone. "I needed to feed my drug habit and make a living," Frank said in a phone interview from an Edmonton police station in October. "That's when I began to look into using my PC."

During the summer and fall of 2003, the Neiman Marcus call center was a favorite stop on a route of dumpsters Mary and Frank mined behind banks, trust companies, telecom companies, hotels, car rental agencies, restaurants, video rental stores—anywhere a business might throw out paperwork.

Neiman Marcus spokeswoman Ginger Reeder says no records of sensitive customer information are printed out at the call center. If any such information made it into the trash, "It would be a breach of company policy and an isolated incident," says Reeder.

Frank and Mary say their dumpster route yielded copies of credit card transactions, loan applications, customer-service reports, employee manuals and internal phone directories—all with potentially useful information. "Nothing was shredded," says Frank. "All the information you wanted was (in the dumpsters)."

One dumpster behind a call center in suburban Mill Woods proved to be a jackpot. In a nondescript strip mall just two blocks from the spacious three-bedroom apartment where Frank lived with his divorced dad, it brimmed with valuable data. The company using the dumpster, Convergys, often tossed out paperwork related to customer-service calls from Sprint cellphone subscribers in the USA, Mary says.

"We'd get credit check information from Equifax, credit card numbers to make payments, Social Security numbers, date of birth, addresses," Mary says. "They would make a printout, then just throw it out."

Convergys spokeswoman Lauri Roderick disputes Mary's account. The Cincinnati-based company has a "strict clean-desk policy" that requires shredding of any sensitive paperwork, she says. And Sprint customer-service calls, she says, were never handled by the 1,200 workers at the Mill Woods facility, one of 14 in Canada. "We're confident there has been no breach in security of our customers' data," Roderick says.

# Probing Systems Winter 2003–2004

Mary's management skills and Frank's computer savvy were a profitable match. By late 2003, they had delegated dumpster diving to others and concentrated on fine-tuning schemes to make the most of pilfered data. They became adept at developing what they referred to as "full profiles."

Given just a name and home address, Mary would dispatch a street addict to the residence with instructions to scour the occupant's garbage for bank statements (a big score) or even a debit card receipt (still valuable). Depending on whether the victim was a woman or man, she or Frank would phone the victim's bank and pose as the customer.

If the bank rep asked for a recent transaction as proof of identity, information from a receipt plucked from the garbage, along with a bit of improvised play acting, often sufficed to win the rep's help. They could then change a billing address, request a replacement debit card and PIN number, apply for credit cards and credit line increases, and add other account users.

Frank used stolen credit card numbers to order the tools of their trade online: computers, graphics software to manufacture fake IDs, and online services, such as Vonage phone accounts. Vonage, like other Internet-based phone services, allows subscribers to pick any area code they want. That's useful for ID thieves who want to take control of financial accounts surreptitiously. Mary could order up area codes matching those of the location of breached accounts outside of Edmonton. The numbers appeared to be local, but actually routed back to her.

Stolen credit card numbers, Social Security numbers, and Canadian Social Insurance Numbers emerged as valuable commodities. Frank progressed to buying and selling them online. He maneuvered his way onto Internet Relay Chat channels where such trading takes place, and began transacting with crime rings in Romania, Austria and Egypt. "Whatever you wanted to buy or sell, it was there," he says.

Meanwhile, Mary and Martin, a longtime fixture in the Edmonton meth crowd, focused on assembling a street-level distribution network. Martin, 25, from a well-to-do family, had a knack for recruiting underlings. "If he was in the business world, he'd be a headhunter," Detective Vonkeman says.

Soon the Edmonton ring controlled a matrix of local bank accounts, some stolen, some opened by addicts using their real names, others opened by addicts using assumed identities and fake IDs supplied by Frank.

Mary, Frank and Martin began to test financial websites. They exploited e-mail cash transfers—a service offered by Canadian banks, by which account holders can conveniently e-mail up to $1,000 to an individual.

They sent runners to withdraw cash from ATMs just before and after a unit was serviced late at night, thus getting two days' of maximum withdrawals in the same hour. They set up shell companies to exploit bill-paying services that allow online payments of up to $10,000 to business accounts.

And they tapped online payment services, like PayPal and NETeller, to bypass the 48-hour hold on international bank-to-bank cash transfers.

They stayed awake for days at a time in hotel rooms or dingy residences—called sketch pads—where meth addicts congregated. The three of them plotted intricate variations of scams or concocted wild, blockbuster capers. Sleep-deprived, they were paranoid about two things: the police and their larcenous fellow addicts.

Frank migrated from sketch pad to sketch pad, rarely going home to his father's apartment. "I stayed until the cops knocked on the door—or someone ripped me off," Frank says.

Mary often fantasized about a big score that would give her the impetus to return to a normal life.

"But nothing ever got really big," she says. "Somebody rips you off, or you never collect what you're owed. You feel like you can do anything (when high on meth). But you can't stay focused. You lose your train of thought. You have to move fast when you're doing fraud, and speeders don't move fast."

# Dark Side of the Internet
# Early 2004

By the time 2003 drew to a close, Frank had been arrested twice and released on bail. A judge ordered him to avoid contact with the meth crowd and banned him from using a computer.

Frank was trying to stay low when Mary introduced him to Socks, an acquaintance. Then 20, Socks was idle and had time on his hands. He had never used meth or committed ID theft. But he had just been laid off from his job as a computer technician.

A somewhat introverted video game fanatic, Socks began smoking crystal meth and associating with Mary, Frank and Martin. When the extroverted Frank bragged about his prowess at scams, Socks paid close attention. Then he began delving deeper than Frank ever did.

Socks began wheeling and dealing with cybercrime rings in Quebec, Romania and Egypt via Internet Relay Chat channels. "What we saw with Socks was interactions that were more with the dark side of the Internet," Vonkeman says.

The global contacts Socks developed put the Edmonton ring in a position to make a profound transition. Instead of going through the labor-intensive process of building profiles of local marks, it began to buy ready-made full profiles of identity theft victims in the USA.

Milking a victim from Tallahassee, Fla., had become as easy as bilking someone from nearby Banff. Mary could easily attach a Vonage IP phone number, say, with a Tallahassee area code, onto a hijacked account and use PayPal or Western Union to transfer funds across international borders.

Besides, going after U.S. victims seemed less risky; and the going rate for a full profile of a U.S. consumer seemed a bargain: $200 American for data that typically included the mark's bank account password, credit card number with security code, even his or her Social Security number.

It was such a good deal, Martin insisted on using clean money sent via Western Union to make the purchase. "We didn't want to screw it up and use fraud money that might get them caught," Mary says.

The Edmonton ring also began helping outside crime groups launder hijacked funds through local bank accounts. A street addict would take the last—and riskiest—step: making a cash withdrawal. Martin would use Western Union to wire some of the cash back to the crime group and divide the rest locally.

# Extra Precautions Since Late 2004

Yet, the maxim "there is no honor among thieves" has never been truer than with meth addicts. "They're very networked and quite social, but when you arrest and debrief these people, they'll give you a ton of information," Vonkeman says.

Someone ratted out Frank in the summer of 2004, leading to his third arrest—and an 11-month jail sentence. Mary and Martin got arrested multiple times at sketch pad raids. Released on bail, they'd lie low for a few weeks before starting up again. Meanwhile, copycat cells cropped up to try to imitate their success.

"It's like plugging your finger in the dike," Gauthier says. "For all the people we catch and take out of action, there could be 10 more networking and already starting to form another cell."

Socks was arrested three times in an eight-month span. He is now serving a two-year sentence for various drug and theft crimes.

Until his initial arrest at the motel in December 2004, Socks had been a mystery figure to Vonkeman and Gauthier. The detectives heard rumors about a new techie on the scene with access to thousands of credit card numbers. But Socks had no rap sheet, nothing, really, to tie him to the *meth* crowd.

He was also clever. Socks knew investigators could monitor Internet traffic going into and out of his laptop computer, so he had made it a point to move around.

For two months in early 2004, Socks, Mary and a friend of Frank's worked from inside a plush GMC camper van parked in an alley alongside a rundown, three-story apartment building a half-mile from downtown Edmonton.

Socks extended a phone cable from the van, down a stairwell to the building's telephone-access panel. When a tenant left for work or appeared to be sleeping, he'd patch into the person's phone line to get on the Internet. "We needed a safe place to use the computer, and it was so nice in there," Mary says.

As an extra precaution, Socks stored nothing of importance on his laptop's hard drive. He uploaded all incriminating stolen identity data to an e-mail folder that came with the dial-up Internet account he'd been given by a fellow addict who worked for an Internet service provider.

But when that accomplice got arrested on another criminal matter, the accomplice promptly disclosed the existence of the account. Vonkeman asked the Internet service provider to leave the account open and alert him anytime anyone logged on.

Ironically, it was that e-mail folder, Socks' protective buffer, that drew Vonkeman and Gauthier to the motel to see who had logged on.

Released on bail soon after the motel arrest, Socks skipped a court appearance and was on the run until Gauthier arrested him again last March. He had become more involved than ever with overseas cybercrooks.

On his person Socks had a slip of paper with log-ons and passwords for 15 hijacked Canadian bank accounts, which he said came from Romanian cybercrooks, including one account

---

## Where they are now

Detectives Al Vonkeman and Bob Gauthier continue to investigate meth trafficking and identity theft in Edmonton.

Among the addicts in this story, Socks, 21, last July began serving his two-year sentence on drug and fraud charges.

Here's what has happened to his compatriots:

- Frank, 22. Upon completing an 11-month jail sentence in May, Frank moved into a halfway house, got a job as a laborer and began attending Narcotics Anonymous meetings. "I'm just trying to get through each day," he said in a telephone interview in early October. At the time, he had been clean for 17 months. "It was very hard to stop using. I think about using all the time."

  Like Socks, Frank possessed skills that made him a magnet for the meth crowd. On Oct. 31, he failed a random urine test. That night, he skipped out of the halfway house. He was arrested Nov. 13 in a car in the company of a known meth trafficker. In his possession Frank had a laptop computer, a cellphone and a credit card swipe device, used to decrypt information stored on credit cards. He is back in jail.

- Mary, 37. When Mary was arrested for a third time in April, her mother declined to quickly put up bail, as she had done before. After three days in a lockup, Mary stopped using meth cold turkey.

  "Three days to me was a lifetime. It was horrible, just horrible," she says. Now out on bail and working at a job in the hospitality industry, she is awaiting a January trial for possession of stolen credit cards and possession of meth.

  She says her focus is now squarely on raising her two children, of whom she has shared custody, and disassociating herself from the meth crowd. "I've cut all ties to the old lifestyle," she says. "I pretend I'm in a different city, a different country, a different universe. I'm in my own little bubble."

- Martin, 25. Police describe Martin as an astute money manager. He is free on probation for possession of meth but remains under investigation for serious criminal fraud charges. Martin is presumed to be recruiting replacements for Mary, Frank and Socks, Gauthier says.

with access to six figures' worth of funds. Police believe the accounts served partly as a show of good faith to cement a partnership with the Edmonton ring.

Sentenced to house arrest after pleading guilty on several drug- and fraud-related counts after the March incident, Socks took off again, Gauthier says.

Then last July, an informant guided Gauthier to a north Edmonton apartment where the detective caught Socks in the act of using a laptop computer to manufacture fake IDs.

Socks reacted calmly, Gauthier says. "He says, 'Hi, Bob. I've been wondering when you were coming to get me'."

ACOHIDO reported from Edmonton, SWARTZ from San Francisco.

# Mothers Addicted to Meth Face Losing Their Children

"Crack babies" as a term stood for babies who were born to crack-addicted mothers, who with care could develop normally but who required extra services, and who overburdened the child welfare caseload tremendously in the 1980s. Additionally, these babies were stigmatized, and potential adoptive parents may have decided against adopting a baby from a crack home.

While nobody is yet bandying about the term "meth babies," methamphetamine is no longer threatening to become the "crack" of this generation of stimulant addicts—it is. But this time, researchers are learning about treatment at the same time that they're learning about the mechanics of addiction, and if that treatment can be gotten to the people who need it, more can be done to prevent the broad panoply of problems that goes along with this drug.

Still, the caseloads of children removed from the home is going up due to methamphetamine, according to a survey released last week by the National Association of Counties (NaCO). The reason is not limited to in-utero exposure; there are serious problems with the ability of parents who are addicted to meth to care for their older children, and law enforcement has found children living in these homes when they conduct drug investigations and arrests.

Parents addicted to methamphetamine become so involved in drug-seeking and drug use that they neglect their children, according to the NaCO report. Another danger is when the drug is manufactured or "cooked" in home "labs," these children are exposed to the side effects of the fumes. Finally, methamphetamine use by the mother can cause in-utero harm, resulting in birth defects, low birth weight, and other problems.

The survey focused on out of home placement, in which children are removed from their parents. These placements have increased dramatically due to methamphetamines over the past five years, and the last year in particular, the survey found.

Overall, 37 percent of the increase in out of home placements nationwide was attributable to methamphetamine, according to the NaCO survey. With counties with populations above 500,000, the increase was 54 percent, reflecting the fact that methamphetamine is no longer mainly a rural problem, but an urban one as well. More than 300 counties in 13 states participated in the survey.

The reports of increases were also dependent on geography; methamphetamine is moving eastward, but it first took hold in the west. For example, 70 percent of Colorado counties reported an increase in methamphetamine-related out-of-home placements.

Counties are concerned about the increases because they shoulder much of the responsibility for ensuring the safety of these children, many of whom have special needs due to the treatment they have received at home. Also, many of these children are eventually placed in foster care.

The parents may be in treatment, or may be waiting to get into treatment, according to the NaCO survey. Some are in jail.

---

## Who are the Friends of NIDA?

American Academy of Addiction Psychiatry
American Psychiatric Association
American Psychological Association
American Society for Pharmacology & Experimental Therapeutics
American Society of Addiction Medicine
American Sociological Association
College on Problems of Drug Dependence
Community Anti-Drug Coalitions of America
Entertainment Industries Council
International Nurses Society on Addictions
Join Together
Legal Action Center
National Association of State Alcohol and Drug Abuse Directors
National TASC
Society for Neuroscience
State Associations of Addiction Services
Therapeutic Communities of America

And while the goal is always family reunification, methamphetamine as a drug makes this particularly difficult, according to the report.

"The reality, as county officials who have experienced difficulty indicated, is that in 48 percent of these counties there are more families that cannot be reunified, 56 percent say the families take much longer to reunify than in the past, and in 27 percent of the counties, officials say recidivism is so great with meth users that the reunification of these families does not last."

We spoke to Maurice Lee, area director for WestCare in Nevada, where the program has a women and children's campus where about 20 women can be in treatment and have their children with them. "Reunification is the best case scenario, and in most cases, we're going to try to reunify," says Lee, who explains that case workers from the county help with this process. "But in some cases there is no reunification. Events may have occurred in the house and the kids can't go back." Also, sometimes the mother knows that she isn't ready to have her children back. "Part of what we do is help them come to terms with that," says Lee.

Recently, Lee observed a surrender—in which the mother gives up her parental rights—of children by a WestCare patient. "I watched the process from afar, and saw another group of women there not understanding how she could do that," he tells ADAW. "But it wasn't just selfish, with her saying, 'I want to have a life.' It was because she said, 'I'm not ready to take care of these children, and I don't know if I'll ever be ready.'" Since part of the goal of treatment at WestCare is to be a responsible member of society—working and taking care of your family—this was a responsible decision that the woman made, even if it's hard to understand, he explains.

At the same time that it released the child welfare survey, NaCO also released a survey of law enforcement, in which 58 percent of the counties said methamphetamine was their largest drug problem. Next were cocaine (19 percent of the counties said this was the biggest problem), marijuana (17 percent), and heroin (3 percent). (For copies of both NACo surveys, go to www.naco.org.)

"Right now there's a real trend with meth," says WestCare's Lee, in Nevada. "Over 50 percent of our clients that we get now are for meth." Is there something about methamphetamine addiction that makes it more difficult to treat than other addictions? "I don't think so," responds Lee. "People said the same thing about crack, and before crack they said it about heroin. As each new drug comes along, people say it's harder to treat. I think we just have to alter what we do."

## Meth Treatment Works: Friends of NIDA

In Washington, an effort is under way to counter the misconception that methampethatine addiction is untreatable. Most recently, the Friends of NIDA (National Institute on Drug Abuse) came together June 29 to discuss the dangers of the drug, and also the hope that exists for addicts. A Congressional briefing, aptly titled "Methamphetamine Addiction: Cause for Concern — Hope for the Future," featured NIDA Director Nora D. Volkow, M.D., Richard Rawson, Ph.D., associate director of UCLA's Integrated Substance Abuse Programs (and executive director of the Matrix Institute, which specializes in stimulant addictions), and Vicki Sickels, a counselor who is also in recovery for methamphetamine addiction. The focus of the hearing was on the fact that yes, brain functioning can be damaged by methamphetamine, but that with treatment, brain functioning can be recovered. Rawson presented data from a study that shows that success rates for methamphetamine addicts were comparable to success rates for other types of addiction. And Sickels, who has been in recovery for seven years, focused on the fact that methamphetamine addiction can affect anyone regardless of class, family, or education. She stressed, however, that funding is needed for treatment.

# The Role of Substance Abuse in U.S. Juvenile Justice Systems and Populations

HEATHER HOROWITZ, HUNG-EN SUNG AND SUSAN E. FOSTER

In 1998, the National Center on Addiction and Substance Abuse (CASA) at Columbia University released a study, *Behind Bars: Substance Abuse and America's Prison Population*, which revealed that substance abuse and addiction is implicated in the felony crimes of 80 percent of the adult prison inmates in America, that few of these inmates receive treatment for their substance abuse problems, and that providing treatment for this adult population would save taxpayers money within a year. CASA (1998) also found that substance-related crime runs in the family. Incarcerated adults are likely to be children of parents who were in prison. Incarcerated adults are themselves the parents of almost 2.5 million children who are more likely than children whose parents have not been incarcerated to end up in prison. About 30 percent of adult inmates admit to being arrested as juveniles.

These revelations led CASA to examine the characteristics and situations of the minors who end up in the juvenile justice population—2.4 million arrests in 2000. The result was the October 2004 report, *Criminal Neglect: Substance Abuse, Juvenile Justice and the Children Left Behind*, the first comprehensive examination of the relationship between substance abuse and juvenile delinquency (CASA, 2004). The findings sketch a bleak portrait of juvenile justice systems overwhelmed by drug and alcohol abuse and addicted adolescents. These substance-involved juveniles slip through the cracks in the nation's health, education and family support systems and exhibit many other health, education and social problems that receive little attention.

America has 51 separate juvenile justice systems with no national standards of practice or accountability. These systems often are part of the problem, not part of the solution. Although they were created to focus on prevention and rehabilitation of juvenile offenders, the trend has been to mimic adult systems of retribution and punishment. By abandoning a commitment to rehabilitation, a more punitive approach renders these juvenile justice systems a dead end for substance-involved youths rather than an opportunity to reshape their lives.

CASA analyzed data from the National Institute of Justice's Arrestee Drug Abuse Monitoring Program, the Office of Juvenile Justice and Delinquency Prevention's Juvenile Court Statistics, and arrest data from OJJDP's *Juvenile Arrests* publications. CASA also examined data from the National Survey on Drug Use and Health, the National Longitudinal Survey of Youth and the National Longitudinal Survey of Adolescent Health. Although more recent statistics are available from many data programs, 2000 data were used to assure comparability. Unless otherwise referenced, all findings reported below are from CASA's analysis of these databases.

## Substance Abuse and Juvenile Delinquency

Of the 2.4 million juvenile arrests made in 2000, 78.4 percent (1.9 million) involved children and teens who were under the influence of alcohol or drugs while committing their crime; tested positive for drugs; were arrested for committing an alcohol or drug offense, including drug or liquor law violations, drunkenness or driving under the influence; reported having substance abuse problems such as feeling dependent on alcohol or drugs or needing them at the time of their crime; or shared some combination of these characteristics. More than half of arrested juveniles (53.9 percent) tested positive for drugs at the time of their arrest (see Table 1). The main drugs of abuse among juvenile offenders are alcohol and marijuana. Of the 1.3 million juvenile arrestees who tested positive for drugs at the time of their arrest, 92.2 percent tested positive for marijuana, 14.4 percent for cocaine, 8.8 percent for amphetamines, 7.6 percent for methamphetamines and 2.3 percent for opiates (e.g., heroin, methadone and prescription opioids). Alcohol is not included in the standard drug tests, but of juveniles under the influence of some substance at the time of their crime, 37.8 percent admit being under the influence of alcohol

Forty-four percent of juveniles arrested during the previous year met the clinical DSM-1V (the fourth edition of the *Diagnostic and Statistical Manual of Mental Disorders*) criteria of substance abuse or dependence, compared with 7.4 percent of nonarrested youths; 27.8 percent met the clinical criteria of substance dependence, compared with 3.4 percent of nonarrested youths.

**Table 1** Substance Involvement Among Arrested Juveniles, 2000

| | Percentage of All Arrested Juveniles |
|---|---|
| Positive urinalysis at arrest | 53.9 |
| Under the influence during crime | 18.2 |
| Arrested for alcohol/drug offense | 12.1 |
| Reported substance abuse problems: | 62.5 |
| Tried to cut down/quit alcohol/drugs in past year | (58.0) |
| Felt dependent on alcohol/drugs in past year | (20.3) |
| Felt they could use treatment for alcohol/drugs | (17.6) |
| Currently receiving treatment for alcohol/drugs | (8.4) |
| In need of alcohol/drugs at the time of their crime | (4.6) |
| Total substance involved* | 78.4 |

*Percentages do not add up to 78.4 percent because many juveniles fall into more than one category.
Source: CASA analysis of 2000 data from the Arrestee Drug Abuse Monitoring Program (ADAM)

Juvenile substance abuse is implicated in all types of juvenile crime, including violent offenses, property offenses and other offenses such as assaults, vandalism and disorderly conduct (see Table 2). Although juvenile arrest rates overall have declined in recent years, the arrest rate for juvenile drug law violations (637.5 per 100,000 persons ages 10 to 17) is on the rise. From 1991 to 2000, the arrest rate (arrests per 100,000 persons ages 10 to 17) for all juvenile offenses decreased by 12.9 percent, but the arrest rate for drug law violations increased a staggering 105 percent. During this time, the arrest rate for property crimes decreased 38.4 percent and the arrest rate for violent crimes decreased 33.2 percent.

**Table 2** Substance-Involved Arrested Juveniles by Type of Offense, 2000

| Offense | Percentage of all Arrested Juveniles |
|---|---|
| Violent offenses | 69.3 |
| Property offenses | 72.0 |
| Other offenses | 81.2 |
| Alcohol and drug offenses | 100.0 |
| Total arrests | 78.4 |

Source: CASA analysis of 2000 ADAM data

This increase in drug law violation arrests has cascaded through juvenile justice systems, raising the number of drug law violation cases referred to juvenile court, in detention, incarcerated, in other out-of-home placement and on probation. Of the 1.6 million cases referred to juvenile courts in 2000, 40.9 percent were for property offenses, 22.9 percent for person offenses, 22.5 percent for public order offenses and 13.5 percent for drug and liquor law violations. The number of drug law violation cases referred to juvenile courts increased, however, at more than 12.5 times the rate of the total number of cases referred to juvenile courts (196.9 percent vs. 15.6 percent), from 65,400 cases in 1991 to 194,200 cases in 2000.

# The Demographics of Juvenile Crime

**Age and Gender Disparities.** While cases referred to the juvenile courts generally involve youths ages 10 to 17, most cases (57.7 percent) involve those age 15 and younger. Seventy-two percent of the 2.4 million juvenile arrests involve males; however, arrests involving females are on the rise. Between 1991 and 2000, the number of cases referred to juvenile courts involving females increased 51 percent, compared with a 7.3 percent increase for males. The largest percentage growth between 1991 and 2000 for both males and females was in drug law violation cases—these cases grew 311.4 percent for females and 181.2 percent for males.

**Racial Disparities.** Racial differences are difficult to determine since arrest rates and rates of cases referred to juvenile courts are not reported for Hispanics who may appear in either white or black racial categories. However, given this limitation, in 2000, the total arrest rate for black juveniles (11,094.2) was more than 1.5 times the rate for white juveniles (6,839.8). In 1999, while blacks comprised just 15 percent of the juvenile population (Bilchik, 1999), black juveniles represented 28 percent of all cases referred to juvenile courts and 36 percent of detained cases. Other research Finds that Hispanic juveniles are more likely than white juveniles to be detained, placed in out-of-home residential facilities and incarcerated in adult prisons (Human Rights Watch, 2002; Sickmund, 2004).

**Income Disparities.** Arrested juveniles are more likely than their nonarrested peers to come from impoverished homes. In 2002, 67.5 percent of teens ages 12 to 17 who had at least one arrest in the previous year reported an annual family income of less than $50,000, compared with 52.8 percent of teens who had not been arrested; 26.1 percent of arrested juveniles reported an annual family income of less than 820,000, compared with 17.4 percent of nonarrested youths.

# Drug Involvement Among Juvenile Offenders

Compared with juveniles who have not been arrested, those who have been arrested once in the past year are more than twice as likely to have used alcohol (69.3 percent vs. 32.7 percent), more than 3.5 times more likely to have used marijuana (49.5 percent vs. 14.1 percent), more than three times more likely to have used prescription drugs for nonmedical purposes (26.8 percent vs. 8.1 percent), more than seven times more likely to have used Ecstasy (12.1 percent vs. 1.7 percent), more than nine times more likely to have used cocaine (13 percent vs. 1.4 percent) and 20 times more likely to have used heroin (2 percent vs. 0.1 percent).

The more often juveniles are arrested, the more likely they are to drink and use drugs. Juveniles with three or more past year arrests are almost twice as likely to abuse prescription drugs, more than 2.5 times more likely to use cocaine, almost three times more likely to use Ecstasy and more than 3.5 times more likely to use heroin than youths with only one past year arrest (see Table 3).

Juveniles who drink and use drugs are more likely than those who do not to be arrested and be arrested multiple times. Each felony conviction a youth receives increases the likelihood of becoming an adult felon by 14 percent; each misdemeanor conviction increases the risk by 7 percent (Washington State Institute for Public Policy, 1997).

Substance-involved juvenile offenders are more likely to be reincarcerated than other juvenile offenders (Dembo et al., 1998) and go on to commit criminal acts as adults. In 2000, compared with nonsubstance-involved juvenile offenders, those who were substance involved were nearly 1.5 times more likely to have at least one previous arrest in the past year (58.1 percent vs. 40.6 percent) and were almost twice as likely to have two or more prior arrests in the past year (31.5 percent vs. 18 percent).

In 2002, almost 1.5 million youths ages 12 to 17 (6 percent) had been incarcerated or held in a juvenile detention center at least once in their lifetime. Compared with those who were never incarcerated or in a detention center, those who have been at least once are 1.5 times more likely to have used alcohol in the past year (49.1 percent vs. 33.7 percent), almost two times more likely to have used inhalants (8.1 percent vs. 4.1 percent), more than twice as likely to have smoked cigarettes (41.4 percent vs. 19 percent), more than twice as likely to have used marijuana (31.7 percent vs. 14.7 percent), 2.5 times more likely to have misused prescription drugs (21.2 percent vs. 8.4 percent), almost four times more likely to have used hallucinogens (12.3 percent vs. 3.3 percent), five times more likely

to have used heroin (1 percent vs. 0.2 percent), and more than six times more likely to have used cocaine (9.9 percent vs. 1.6 percent).

The earlier a young adult begins to abuse drugs, the more likely he or she is to be arrested. Juvenile alcohol and drug use also increases the risk of adult substance dependence, which increases the likelihood of criminal involvement (see Table 4).

**Table 4**  Juvenile Alcohol and Marijuana Use and Young Adult Crime, 2002

| Age of First Use | Percentage of 18- to 25-Year-Olds Arrested in Past Year | |
|---|---|---|
| | Alcohol | Marijuana |
| 11 or younger | 13.7 | 21.6 |
| 12 | 10.8 | 13.7 |
| 13 | 9.0 | 13.7 |
| 14 | 8.3 | 12.2 |
| 15 | 7.2 | 9.6 |
| 16 | 6.7 | 9.7 |
| 17 | 6.6 | 8.0 |
| 18 | 3.2 | 5.7 |
| Never used | 1.4 | 2.1 |

Source: CASA analysis of 2002 National Survey on Drug Use and Health data

# Missed Opportunities for Prevention

There are often early signs of future trouble. The more these markers are present in a young person's life and the fewer protective influences present, the greater the chances for substance abuse and crime (Lipsey, Wilson and Cothern, 2000; Lipsey, 1999).

**Off to a Troubled Start.** Children whose parents abuse drugs and alcohol are almost three times more likely to be physically or sexually assaulted and more than four times more likely to

**Table 3**  Percentage of Arrested Juveniles Who Use Alcohol and Drugs (ages 12 to 17), 2002

| Offense | Ever Arrested | | Number of Arrests in Past Year | | | |
|---|---|---|---|---|---|---|
| | Yes | No | 0 | 1 | 2 | 3 or More |
| Alcohol | 60.6 | 31.9 | 32.7 | 69.3 | 78.1 | 80.2 |
| Marijuana | 43.1 | 13.1 | 14.1 | 49.5 | 58.1 | 65.3 |
| Prescription drugs for nonmedical use | 24.1 | 7.7 | 8.1 | 26.8 | 37.0 | 50.1 |
| Cocaine/crack | 11.6 | 1.1 | 1.4 | 13.0 | 22.5 | 34.4 |
| Ecstasy | 10.4 | 1.5 | 1.7 | 12.1 | 13.9 | 32.8 |
| Heroin | 1.5 | 0.1 | 0.1 | 2.0 | 1.7 | 7.1 |

Source: CASA analysis of 2000 data from the Arrestee Drug Abuse Monitoring Program (ADAM)

be neglected than children of parents who are not substance abusers. Neglected and abused children are more likely to use drugs (43 percent vs. 32 percent) and commit juvenile crimes (42 percent vs. 33 percent) than nonmaltreated children (Kelley, Thornberry and Smith, 1997).

**Impoverished and Dangerous Neighborhoods.** Being raised in poverty or living in communities plagued by crime, drug selling, gangs, poor housing and firearms contributes to increased involvement in delinquent and violent behavior (Elliot, Huizinga and Menard, 1989; Fingerhut et al., 1991; Hawkins et al., 2000; Thornton et al., 2002).

**Disconnected From Schools.** Juveniles who test positive for multiple drugs are more than 2.5 times more likely to not be in school than nondrug-using juveniles (40.1 percent vs. 15.3 percent) and they are more likely to be truant, suspended from school and functioning below their grade level. An estimated 50 percent to 80 percent of all juveniles incarcerated in juvenile correctional facilities qualify for services designed to address learning disabilities—three to five times more than the eligible public school population (Leone and Meisel, 1999; Portner, 1996; Stephens and Arnette, 2000).

**Health Problems.** Between 50 percent and 75 percent of incarcerated youths have a diagnosable mental health disorder (Coalition for Juvenile Justice, 2000), compared with 20 percent of 9- to 17-year-olds (Office of the Surgeon General, 1999; Coalition for Juvenile Justice, 2000), and at least 80 percent of all young offenders are estimated to have conduct disorders (Cocozza and Skowyra, 2000). Female juvenile offenders have been found three times more likely to have clinical symptoms of depression or anxiety than female adolescents in the general population (Kataoka et al., 2001).

**Risky Sexual Behavior.** Incarcerated juveniles are more likely to be sexually active, to have initiated sex at an earlier age, to have had more sexual partners and to have less consistent condom use than their nonincarcerated peers (Diclemente et al., 1991). Up to 94 percent of juveniles held in detention facilities are sexually active (Morris et al., 1995), compared with 46 percent of high school students (Grunbaum et al., 2002).

**Running With the Wrong Crowd.** Children and teens who are involved with juvenile offenders and drug-using peers are more likely to be arrested and use drugs themselves (Brendgen, Vitaro and Bukowski, 2000; Svensson, 2003). Children and teens with marijuana-using peers were 10 times more likely to use marijuana than children and teens with no marijuana-using peers (70 percent vs. 7 percent). Compared with youths who are not gang members, those who are in gangs are more likely to commit assault, robbery, breaking and entering, and felony theft; indulge in binge drinking; use and sell drugs; and be arrested (Hill, Lui and Hawkins, 2001).

**Lack of Spiritual Grounding.** Teens who do not consider religious beliefs important are almost three times more likely to smoke, drink and binge drink, almost four times more likely to use marijuana and seven times more likely to use illicit drugs than teens who consider religion an important part of their lives (CASA, 2001b). Juveniles who have been arrested one or more times in the past year are almost 1.5 times more likely to never attend religious services than teens who have not been arrested (41.7 percent vs. 31 percent).

# Criminal Neglect

By the time juveniles enter juvenile justice systems, the vast majority are troubled and in need of support, health care, education, training and treatment. Limited data are available to document services provided to juveniles in juvenile justice systems. However, available data suggest that youths in custody rarely receive needed services to help them get on the track to responsible adulthood (Pfeiffer, 2004).

Nationwide, only 36.7 percent of juvenile correctional facilities provide on-site substance abuse treatment (SAMHSA, 2002). Only 20,000 (16 percent) of the estimated 122,696 substance-involved juvenile offenders in juvenile correctional facilities receive substance abuse treatment such as detoxification, individual or group counseling, rehabilitation and methadone or other pharmaceutical treatment within these facilities. Another 4,500 juvenile offenders receive substance abuse treatment through drug courts. Together, this adds up to only 24,500 juveniles of the 1.9 million substance-involved arrests for which CASA can document receipt of any form of substance abuse treatment—about 1.3 percent. Even if a full 20 percent of juveniles who received "other sanctions" (community service, restitution, fines, social services) were placed in substance abuse treatment, the percentage of substance-involved arrested juveniles who receive any form of treatment would only be 3.6 percent.

Moreover, mental health services are scarce and many education programs fail to meet even minimum state educational criteria. In 1995, which is when the latest data were available, almost 60 percent of the children admitted to secure detention found themselves in crowded facilities (Annie E. Casey Foundation, 1997). Children in crowded detention centers are more likely to be injured, spend less time in school, participate in fewer constructive programs, receive fewer family visits, have fewer opportunities to participate in religious activities and get sick more often. There are few, if any, programs that provide for the spiritual enrichment of these children and teens.

Instead of providing prevention and remediation, juvenile justice systems compound problems of juvenile offenders, pushing them toward increased substance abuse and crime. At the same time, public policy demands accountability from juvenile offenders. Demanding accountability from children while refusing to be accountable to them is criminal neglect. Because there is no model juvenile justice code or national standards of practice and accountability, states and counties respond to these issues of criminal neglect through federal, state and local investigators, and lawsuits brought by the U.S. Department of Justice under the Civil Rights of Institutionalized Persons Act (U.S. Department of Justice, 2002).

# The Cost of Substance Abuse and Delinquency

The cost of substance abuse to juvenile justice programs is at least $14.4 billion annually for law enforcement, courts, detention, residential placement, incarceration, federal formula and block grants to states and substance abuse treatment. Only 1 percent (8139 million) of this cost is for treatment (CASA, 2001a). The costs of probation, physical and mental health services, child welfare and family services, school costs and the costs to victims are impossible to determine. However, together, these costs could more than double this $14.4 billion figure.

On average, a year of incarceration costs taxpayers $43,000 per juvenile (Juvenile Justice FYI, 2004). However, if society were, for example, to invest $5,000 in substance abuse treatment and getting comprehensive services and programs like drug courts just for each of the 123,000 substance-involved juveniles who would otherwise be incarcerated, society would break even on this investment in the first year if only 12 percent of these youths stayed in school and remained drug and crime free. Further, by preventing the crimes and incarceration of just 12 percent of adults now incarcerated who had juvenile arrest records, there would be more than 60,480 fewer inmates, $18 billion in savings from reduced criminal justice and health costs and employment benefits, and at least 5.9 million fewer crimes.

# Preventing Substance Abuse and Delinquency

Juvenile crime, violence and substance use are rooted in a host of interrelated social problems, including adult substance abuse, child abuse and neglect, family violence, poor parenting, uneducated and undereducated youths, lack of appropriate health care, lack of community ties and support, increased availability of guns, gangs and poverty (Kumpfer and Alvarado, 1998). Stemming the tide of substance-involved juveniles entering juvenile justice systems will require a concerted effort on the part of parents, child welfare agencies, schools, health care providers, clergy, neighborhoods and local law enforcement officers to look for the signs and signals of risk and intervene early.

Although comprehensive prevention approaches offer the most hope for juveniles at risk for substance abuse and delinquency, few program models exist (SAMHSA, 2001). A comprehensive model would include attention to strengthening families, increasing school engagement, reinforcing positive peer groups, strengthening neighborhood resources, reducing poverty and offering spiritual guidance. The earlier prevention efforts start—whether they focus on the individual child, the family, the school or the community—the more likely they are to succeed in preventing substance abuse and delinquency (Loeber, Farrington and Petechuk, 2003).

# Treating Substance-Involved Juvenile Offenders

By the time juveniles enter juvenile justice systems, 44 percent already meet the clinical criteria of substance abuse or dependence and need treatment; up to 80 percent need intervention for learning disabilities, conduct disorders and mental illnesses (Coalition for Juvenile Justice, 2000; Cocozza and Skowyra, 2000; Portner, 1996; Stephens and Arnette, 2000). There are many points in the adjudication process where juveniles can be diagnosed and treated: at arrest, intake, detention, court processing, probation, incarceration and other out-of-home placement, and aftercare. Juvenile drug courts are a promising venue for intervention. These programs, which provide intensive treatment and monitoring for substance-abusing delinquents, have become increasingly popular in recent years and represent a collaboration among juvenile justice, substance abuse treatment and other health, education, law enforcement and social service agencies. They demonstrate that treatment and accountability are complementary rather than mutually exclusive objectives (Cooper, 2002; National Drug Court Institute, 2003).

# Opportunities and Next Steps: Policy Recommendations

A top-to-bottom overhaul of the way the nation treats juvenile offenders is required in order to address the needs of these substance-using juvenile offenders. This overhaul should be designed to achieve two fundamental goals, while assuring that juvenile offenders are held accountable for their actions:

- Ensure that each child entering the systems receives a comprehensive needs assessment; and
- Take advantage of opportunities within juvenile justice systems to divert juveniles from further substance use and crime by providing appropriate treatment and other needed services in custody and detention, during incarceration or other out-of-home placement, while on probation and in aftercare.

To accomplish these goals, the following policy recommendations are essential.

Create a model juvenile justice code, setting forth standards of practice and accountability for states in handling juvenile offenders. This model code should incorporate practice requirements, including staffing and training, screening, assessments, treatment planning, case management, substance abuse, mental health and education services, counseling, access to care and record keeping.

Train all juvenile justice system staff—law enforcement, juvenile court judges and other court personnel, prosecutors and defenders, correctional and probation officers—to recognize substance-involved offenders and know how to respond.

Divert juvenile offenders from deeper involvement with juvenile justice systems through such promising practices as comprehensive in-home services, juvenile drug courts, including reentry courts, and other drug treatment alternatives that assure comprehensive services as well as accountability.

Make available treatment, health care, education and job training programs, including spiritually based programs, to juveniles who are incarcerated.

Develop a state and national data system through which a baseline can be established to judge progress in meeting the many needs of these children.

Expand OJJDP grant programs that provide federal funds to states and localities, conditioning grants under such programs on providing appropriate services to juvenile offenders.

If these recommendations are implemented, billions of citizens' tax dollars can be saved, crime can be reduced and help can be provided to thousands of children—who would otherwise be left behind—to grow up to lead productive, law-abiding lives.

# References

Annie E. Casey Foundation. 1997. *Juvenile detention alternatives initiative: A progress report.* Baltimore: Annie E. Casey Foundation.

Bilchik, S. 1999. *Minorities in the juvenile justice system.* Washington, D.C.: Office of Justice Programs, Office of Juvenile Justice and Delinquency Prevention.

Brendgen, M., F. Vitaro and W.M. Bukowski. 2000. Deviant friends and early adolescents' emotional and behavioral adjustment. *Journal of Research on Adolescence,* 10(2):173–189.

CASA. 1998. *Behind bars: Substance abuse and America's prison population.* New York: Columbia University.

CASA. 2001a. *Shoveling up: The impact of substance abuse an state budgets.* New York: Columbia University.

CASA. 2001b. *So help me God: Substance abuse, religion and spirituality.* New York: Columbia University.

CASA. 2004. *Criminal neglect: Substance abuse, juvenile justice and the children left behind.* New York: Columbia University.

Coalition for Juvenile Justice. 2000. Coalition for Juvenile Justice 2000 annual report. Washington, D.C.: Coalition for Juvenile Justice.

Cocozza, J.J. and K.R. Skowyra. 2000. Youth with mental health disorders: Issues and emerging responses. *Juvenile Justice Journal,* 7(1):3–13.

Cooper, C.S. 2002. Juvenile drug treatment courts in the United States: Initial lessons learned and issues being addressed. *Substance Use and Misuse,* 37(12–13):1689–1722.

Dembo, R., J. Schmeidler, B. Nini-Gough, S.C. Chin, P. Borden and D. Manning. 1998. Predictors of recidivism to a juvenile assessment center: A three year study. *Journal of Child Adolescent Substance Abuse,* 7(3):57–77.

Diclemente, R.J., M.M. Lanier, P.F. Horan and M. Lodico. 1991. Comparison of MDS knowledge, attitudes, and behaviors among incarcerated adolescents and a public school sample in San Francisco. *American Journal Public Health,* 81 (5):628–630.

Elliot, D., D. Huizinga and S. Menard. 1989. *Multiple problem youth: Delinquency, substance use, and mental health problems.* New York: Springer-Verlag.

Fingerhut, L.A., J.C. Kleinman, E. Godfrey and H. Rosenberg. 1991. Firearm mortality among children, youth, and young adults: 1–34 years of age, trends and current status: United States, 1979–88. *Monthly Vital Statistics Report,* 39(11): 1–16.

Grunbaum, J.A., L. Kann, S.A. Kinchen, B. Williams, J.G. Ross, R. Lowry and L. Kolbe. 2002. Youth risk behavior surveillance: United States, 2001. *Morbidity and Mortality Weekly Report,* 51(SS-4): 1–66.

Hawkins, J.D., T.I. Herrenkohl, D.P. Farrington, D. Brewer, R.C. Catalano, T.W. Harachi and L. Cothern. 2000. *Predictors of youth violence.* Washington, D.C.: Office of Juvenile Justice and Delinquency Prevention.

Hill, K.G., C. Lui and J.D. Hawkins. 2001. *Early precursors of gang membership. A study of Seattle youth.* OJJDP juvenile justice bulletin. Washington, D.C.: Office of Juvenile Justice and Delinquency Prevention.

Human Rights Watch. 2002. *Race and incarceration in the United States: Human Rights Watch briefing,* February 27, 2002. New York: Human Rights Watch. Available at www.hrw.org/backgrounder/usa/race.

Juvenile Justice FYI. 2004. Juvenile justice FAQ. Available at www.juvenilejusticefyi.com/juvenile_justice_faqs.html.

Kataoka, S.H., B.T. Zima, D.A. Dupre, K.A. Moreno, X. Yang and J.T. McCracken. 2001. Mental health problems and service use among female juvenile offenders: Their relationship to criminal history. *Journal of the American Academy of Child and Adolescent Psychology,* 40(5):549–555.

Kelley, B.T., T.P. Thornberry and C.A. Smith. 1997. *In the wake of childhood maltreatment.* Washington, D.C.: Office of Juvenile Justice and Delinquency Prevention.

Kumpfer, K.L. and R. Alvarado. 1998. *Effective family strengthening interventions.* Washington, D.C.: Office of Juvenile Justice and Delinquency Prevention.

Leone, P.E. and S.M. Meisel. 1999. *Improving education services for students in detention and confinement facilities.* College Park, Md.: The National Center on Education, Disability and Juvenile Justice. Available at www.edjj.org/Publications/list/leone_meisel-1997.html.

Lipsey, M.W. 1999. Can intervention rehabilitate serious delinquents? *The Annals of the American Academy of Political and Social Sciences,* 564(1): 142–166.

Lipsey, M., D. Wilson and L. Cothern. 2000. *Effective intervention for serious juvenile offenders.* Washington, D.C.: Office of Juvenile Justice and Delinquency Prevention.

Loeber, R., D.P. Farrington and D. Petechuk. 2003. *Child delinquency: Early intervention and prevention.* Child delinquency bulletin series. Washington, D.C.: U.S. Government Printing Office.

Morris, R.E., E.A. Harrison, G.W. Knox, E. Tromanhauser, D.K. Marquis and L.L. Watts. 1995. Health risk behavioral survey from 39 juvenile correctional facilities in the United States. *Journal of Adolescent Health,* 17(6):334–344.

National Drug Court Institute, and National Council of Juvenile and Family Court Judges. 2003. *Juvenile drug courts: Strategies in practice.* Washington, D.C.: Bureau of Justice Assistance.

Office of the Surgeon General. 1999. *Mental health: A report of the surgeon general.* Rockville, Md.: National Institute of Mental Health.

Pfeiffer, M.B. 2004. Juvenile detention system struggles: Use of force a focal point: Boy critically hurt in Lansing. *The Ithaca Journal,* cited 2004 Feb. 17 from www.theithicajournal.com.

Portner, J. 1996. Jailed youths shortchanged on education. *Education Week,* 16(5):1.

Sickmund, M. 2004. *Juveniles in corrections.* Washington, D.C.: Office of Justice Programs, Office of Juvenile Justice and Delinquency Prevention.

Stephens, R.D. and J.L. Arnette. 2000. *From the courthouse to the schoolhouse: Making successful transitions.* OJJDP juvenile justice bulletin. Washington, D.C.: Office of Juvenile Justice and Delinquency Prevention.

Substance Abuse and Mental Health Services Administration (SAMHSA). 2001. *Youth violence: A report of the surgeon general.* Washington, D.C.: U.S. Government Printing Office.

Substance Abuse and Mental Health Services Administration (SAMHSA). 2002. *Drug and alcohol treatment in juvenile correctional facilities: The DASIS report.* Rockville, Md.: Office of Applied Studies.

Svensson R. 2003. Gender differences in adolescent drug use: The impact of parental monitoring and peer deviance. *Youth and Society,* 34(3):300–329.

Thornton, T.N., C.A. Craft, L.L Dahlberg, B.S. Lynch and K. Baer. 2002. *Best practices of youth violence prevention: A sourcebook for community action.* Atlanta: Centers for Disease Control and Prevention.

U.S. Department of Justice. 2002. *Fiscal year 2002 activities under the Civil Rights of Institutionalized Persons Act.* Washington, D.C.: U.S. Department of Justice.

Washington State Institute for Public Policy. 1997. *The class of 1988, seven years later. How a juvenile offender's crime, criminal history, and age affect the chances of becoming an adult felon in Washington State.* Olympia, Wash.: Washington State Institute for Public Policy. Available at www.wsipp.wa.gov.

Authors' Note: The research presented in this article was partially funded by the William T. Grant Foundation, the National Institute on Drug Abuse and the Abercrombie Foundation.

**HEATHER HOROWITZ, JD, MPH,** is a former research associate, **HUNG-EN SUNG, PH.D.,** is a research associate, and **SUSAN E. FOSTER, MSW,** is vice president and director of policy research and analysis for the National Center on Addiction and Substance Abuse at Columbia University in New York.

# My Spirit Lives

ROXANNE CHINOOK

The Nightmare: I close my eyes and lean my head out of the passenger window to feel the warm wind on my face. I do not know who is driving the car, as I travel down a familiar canyon road. It is a highway in Idaho—some road that I may have hitchhiked on my way to visit my mother. The car begins to slow down, and when I open my eyes I notice a row of cars with over a dozen young men standing beside them. As we come closer, I feel an overwhelming sense of fear in every cell of my body. The car moves in slow motion as it goes by the row of cars and men. From the beginning to the end of the long row, I notice their faces and recognize each and every one of them. Yet, I do not understand why I am so scared. Their faces are smug and unsmiling.

I recognize the cars, but can't remember where I've seen their faces before. Suddenly a roaring noise goes off in my head. I hear a loud popping bang and see a white light. My eyes abruptly open and I realize that I am in my bed. I am unable to move because my entire body is frozen in fear; tears emerge as I realize that all these young men were men that raped me.

Before the Relapse: I am a proud tribal member of the Confederated Tribes of the Warm Springs Indian Reservation, a professional artist, and a college graduate. In 1991, I was listed in the Fourteenth Addition of the National Dean's List for receiving a 4.0, while doing postgraduate studies at Boise State University. I am the former Exhibits Coordinator of my tribal museum, and have held several professional positions in the social service field on my reservation. I have three beautiful daughters. My oldest was taken away from me when she was just 14 months old and raised by a very loving and wonderful family in Warm Springs. I was raising my two youngest alone until my illnesses took them away from me in February 1997.

I stand proud today because I am finally healing from my primary illness, post-traumatic stress disorder (PTSD), and secondary illness, substance abuse. My spirit has been broken many times as a result of these illnesses, which are directly related to the incest and multiple rape wounds of my past. The damage caused by these traumas sought to destroy my very being.

Although I did spend a year or two in recovery since 1979, the first time I experienced true long-term recovery began in Boise, Idaho, on August 15, 1987. In 1989, I married a man I had met in the early period of my recovery and we had a child together. However, because he battered me I divorced him. In 1991, I moved back to my reservation to work, raise my two daughters, and live near my family. I had abstained from alcohol and cocaine for almost eight years before I relapsed in April 1995.

The Relapse: Since the early 1980s, I have suffered from muscle tension headaches, extreme anxiety, and depression. However, soon after I moved back to my reservation, I began to experience rape flashbacks, nightmares, insomnia, body numbness, and suicidal thoughts. These symptoms became worse and started to affect all aspects of my life. At times, I felt that I was going crazy. I finally pursued counseling, but I needed something stronger to relieve my anguish. After almost five years of suffering, I went back to my old coping behaviors and took my first drink in April 1995.

It was not long before I started using my new drug of choice, cocaine. I believe it was because the high was more intense than alcohol and I could remain alert. Despite its increased lethality, I was never raped while high on cocaine. I became addicted to cocaine again and found myself on a downhill swirl into darkness. My attempts to recover included everything from counseling, to going to church, to taking different medications.

I started to lose everything that I had gained during my years of abstinence: my self-respect, job, home, car, and my relationship with my family. Most important, my children were losing their mommy, I could not stop the path I was on, and I did not have a clue that all these symptoms were interrelated and symptomatic of rape trauma syndrome.

The Chicken or the Egg: I was diagnosed with chronic post-traumatic stress disorder in the past, and at the time I found some relief having a name for my distress. Nevertheless, my addiction was already in control. So how does one address these kinds of issues when they inevitably trigger the return of substance abuse?

Today, I realize that it does not matter which came first, the chicken or the egg. The abuse and my addictions went hand and hand. I have since learned that for me to refrain from returning to substance abuse, I must address my past traumas.

My victimization began in early childhood when our non-Native grandfather molested my sister and me. His selfish violation of our childhood directly led to the loss of my virginity on a date rape at age 19. I know today that this past trauma kept me from developing appropriate boundaries, self-worth, and basic trust of my own instincts.

I drank so I would not feel or remember. And as my alcoholism progressed, I became more vulnerable to rape. At the time, I did not know why I drank the way I did. Today I know that booze, and later cocaine, became my only means of survival.

The Rapes: Thus, my victim cycle emerged. I was raped 13 times between the ages of 19 and 28. Four of those were gang rapes. One of the rapists was Native American, another Hawaiian mixed, four were African American, and the rest were young white men. I was always extremely intoxicated before the rapes, and could only remember bits and pieces prior to each one, but had very clear memories afterwards. Three of the rapes (one of them a gang rape) happened in Madras, Oregon, a small town just outside my reservation, and the place I made my first and last attempt to seek justice in 1981.

The rape occurred after I was offered a ride to Warm Springs by a non-Native local man, who was drinking in the same bar I was. He said that he was a friend of my ex-boyfriend, and I thought he was a nice guy. On the drive home he took a detour off the road before the grade goes down to Warm Springs. He pulled the car over and raped me.

After he was done, he acted like nothing was wrong and said that no one would believe me anyway. He actually had the audacity to drop me off where I was living. I called the Warm Springs police department only because my brother was a tribal policeman at the time. This incident was the first time that I had the courage to report it. My brother, who happened to be on duty, chased and apprehended him on the flats between Madras and Warm Springs. The rapist was no longer on tribal land, so the Jefferson County police took over and held him in custody overnight.

The next day, I went to the Jefferson County police station only to pick up the evidence: my beaded belt and torn bra the officers found in his car. I decided not to press charges because while I was being questioned, the officer told me it was my word against his, and the rapist had told him that the sex was consensual. The officer also stressed that the rapist had a wife and children to support. I left the police station with my head held down in shame, and walked to the nearest bar never to pursue justice again.

The Shame: It was not long before my whole essence became a warehouse of shame. I was on a road to self-destruction, and became so expert at drowning each incident with booze that I thought no one would ever suspect what had happened to me. Deep down inside I blamed myself and felt I deserved the abuse. During periods of recovery, I told only a few therapists, counselors, and close friends. I have only recently been able to disclose the number of times I've been raped to others.

Today, when I openly share the amount of times I've been raped, it not only takes away the rapists' power, but also alleviates some of the shame. I also know in my heart that no one deserves to be raped, regardless of the shape they are in.

The Addiction: After relapsing in April 1995, I went into treatment in April 1996. But I relapsed within a month after I returned to Warm Springs. My drug of choice was very accessible at the time, and sometimes all it took was one call or an unexpected visit from one of my using buddies. In addition, one of the former gang rapists worked at the Indian Health Service, and I did not realize that he was a constant trigger of my PTSD symptoms.

The Suicide Attempt: My family eventually intervened, and my daughters were taken away from me. I do not think that I ever experienced so much shame and utter hopelessness in my life. On the evening of February 28, 1997, I unsuspectingly came home while my daughters were packing some clothes to take to my family's house next door. I silently watched as they left—full of disgust for me. I was still coming down from alcohol and cocaine, and became overwhelmed with shame and all the pain that I caused in my life and in their lives.

I truly wanted to die. The pain was so unbearable that I impulsively took all my antidepressants and called my pastor. I was comatose and hospitalized for three or four days, and was sent directly from the hospital to Oregon Science Hospital (OSH) in Portland for evaluation. I later learned that I had taken more than a lethal dose of pills.

The Overdose: I was at OSH for a few days when I found out that I could be legally held for 72 hours. I persuaded them to let me out and left the hospital on March 6, 1997, only to return two days later. When I escaped from OSH, I allowed a stranger to shoot me up with heroin, a drug that I had no resistance to. I had already consumed a combination of alcohol, cocaine, and crank, and the big hit of heroin was it all it took to overdose me. The stranger dragged my lifeless body down a few flights of stairs to the alley below and left me there to die. The paramedics later told me that someone probably saw me and called 911. I found out that I had been dead for five minutes, and by the time the ambulance arrived, my skin was blue and cold. I was injected with the drug Narcon to help neutralize the heroin, but it didn't work. The paramedics then used defibrillation to get my heart pumping. I remember how I reluctantly returned to my body. I believe my Creator sent me back to put an end to the cycle of abuse in my life, in my children's lives, and in their children's lives.

After my two-week stay at OSH, I was invited to stay in Oregon City with a loving family in long-term recovery. (This family is my oldest daughter's biological father's family, which I have since adopted.) I was able to stay clean and sober for several months. Unfortunately, as soon as I returned to my reservation, it was just a matter of days before I relapsed. I finally accepted the fact that I was not going to die using. My hell was living my addiction.

My Return: On August 18, 1997, my Creator intervened and my tribe allowed me to receive treatment at Sundown M Ranch in Selah, Washington. I was advised by my counselor to continue with treatment, and I agreed to go to a 60-day transitional treatment program at the St. Joseph Recovery House in Bellingham, Washington. I chose to leave everything, my home and the opportunity to be closer to my children, because I knew deep inside that I could not return to Warm Springs. I could not return because of all the triggers and my family's unfaltering animosity toward me, which was created by my relapse.

The guilt and shame from my relapse slowly lifted. I eventually fell in love with Bellingham—the beautiful scenery and all the new friends that I gained through treatment and support groups. After I completed the 60-day treatment program, my tribe helped me again by paying the rental deposit for the Towanda Oxford House, which is a clean and sober house for women. I then sought the services of the local Private Industry Council and was given the wonderful opportunity to work while being trained to teach art part time at the Northwest Indian College.

However, after I had made it through seven months of sobriety, the PTSD symptoms were so strong that I was again suicidal. This time the suicidal thoughts were more serious because I was not under the influence of alcohol or drugs. I found my way to the Whatcom Crisis Center and was very lucky to be the first and only recipient of a newly funded program that offered one-on-one counseling with a woman specially trained in these issues.

On the first visit, my counselor was so concerned about my obvious symptoms that she immediately contacted the Whatcom Counseling and Psychiatric Clinic to have me reevaluated. She scheduled a visit right away, and I was

finally prescribed a medication that specifically helped to control many of the PTSD symptoms.

My true healing began in the one-on-one counseling. I learned that my mind was able to dissociate during my rapes as a form of protection, but my subconscious mind still remembered, causing severe flashbacks and nightmares. I learned that my closed body language was prevalent in people who have suffered from both incest and rapes. I also learned that some compulsive behaviors I had developed over the years, from my choice of abusive men to my self-destructive substance abuse, were related to my childhood and young adult rapes.

Internalized Oppression: That my Native American heritage played a significant role in the rapes was an extremely agonizing recognition. In America's history of the colonization of Native peoples, rape has been used as a weapon of warfare, ethnic cleansing, humiliation, and oppression against us. In turn, Native peoples have internalized this oppression and passed it down through the generations. My Native grandmother's shame and oppression was passed down to my mother, who passed it on to me to the point that I blamed myself entirely for everything that happened to me.

An example of how whites use rape as a colonial tool of domination against Native women is embedded in my memory as a severe flashback. I thank my Creator for allowing me to remember the details only when I am in a safe place.

The Drunken Savage: A few days after I was admitted to the first alcohol and drug treatment center since my relapse began in 1995, a kind nurse found me wandering the halls late at night in a catatonic-like state. I had just experienced one the worst rape flashbacks, and she held me and let me cry as I explained to her what I remembered. When I was living in Hawaii, I was abducted by a group of young Caucasian military men. They took me to a warehouse building on a military base and repeatedly raped me. After they were done, they were concerned about letting me go so they inserted a tall, full bottle of beer inside me to flush out their semen. Throughout the gang rape, they called me derogatory names. One of the rapists asked what night happen if they broke the bottle inside me. An apathetic voice responded, "Who cares? She's nothing but a drunken Indian whore."

In this incident and in the one in Madras in which the police office discouraged me from pressing charges against the white male that raped me, it is clear that rape continues to be a tool of domination against Native women.

It's Not My Fault: After several months of working with my counselor, I finally gained the courage to attend

Whatcom Crisis Center's 12-week sexual assault program. This group was very empowering because, for the first time, I was able to share my story, in the absence of feeling judged or ashamed, with a group of women who were also survivors of traumatic sexual assaults. I also grew to understand that the lifetime of victimization was not my fault and, most of all, I learned that I do not have to be ashamed anymore. Then I moved into Dorothy Place, a transitional housing complex for women and children survivors of domestic violence, and was surrounded by brave women who were taking the steps needed to break their cycles of abuse and violence.

In 1999, I began the Master of Education in Art program at Western Washington University and graduated in December 2000, with a cumulative 3.8 GPA. Currently, I am the director of a nonprofit Art Marketing Program located at the Northwest Indian College.

I now know it was my Creator who sent me back to heal by sharing my story with other survivors and as a way to validate their pain. It was to let them know that they no longer have to feel the deep-rooted shame because they were drunk or high when they were raped. It was also to educate professionals in the alcohol and drug treatment field on how important it is to address these issues before the cycle escalates, as well as to be a consultant in the development of new programs that would help survivors heal through artistic expression.

The Revictimization: During this time I was also fighting to regain custody of my youngest daughter, who was placed with her father, the man I divorced in 1990 because of domestic violence. I decided to share this part of my struggle because, unfortunately, it is quite common for families to blame and re-victimize survivors. This often happens out of denial and the family's need for the survivor to maintain their social identity as the scapegoat. In addition, as the dually diagnosed family member, I constantly felt their frustration over the years.

My brother, who is a tribal judge, and his wife, who works for Children's Protective Services, had understandable contempt and anger toward me. Further, during my relapse I had exposed a past deception and, in retaliation, they used their influence to assure that my youngest daughter's father maintained custody of her, despite knowing his history of violence. I do not deny the effect my relapse had on my daughters or my family, and I take full responsibility for this. Nevertheless, professionals I contacted inform me that if I were living anywhere else when my relapse occurred, I would never have lost permanent custody of my girls.

I believe my brother's abuse of power in the tribal court system made it impossible for my voice to be heard by an objective ear. However, I did not give up. I made phone calls, sent hundreds of letters and e-mails to domestic violence, child abuse, rape, incest, civil liberties, and tribal and state law organizations nationwide. I received dozens of responses, referrals, validations, and kind words of support, but they basically referred me back to each other.

The Idaho Coalition Against Sexual and Domestic Violence asked me for permission to use part of my story when the National Organization for Women addressed Congress for the reauthorization of the Violence Against Women Act. Edna M. Frantela, from the National Coalition Against Domestic Violence, also asked permission to share my story at a Safe Child Summit, in hopes of affecting the judicial decision-making process regarding high-conflict custody disputes. I was happy that my story might be of some help to other survivors, yet time was running out as my daughter began sharing more about abuse she was experiencing from her father.

Just as I was about to give up all hope, my Creator sent my first angel. Her name is Terilynn Steele and she founded For the Children Advocacy in California. Having read one of my online messages on a tribal-law clearinghouse message board, she wrote me series of e-mail messages of care and support, which renewed my hope. Soon after, my second angel, Lynn Thompson, arrived. She, too, responded to my desperate cry for help after reading a message I had left on another tribal law message board. Miraculously, Lynn is not only a Native sister, but also a tribal legal advocate in Idaho. These two women became my angels on earth because they were the only people who were actually willing to do something beyond referring me to another agency. Lynn volunteered her services by preparing my second appeal, which was granted after the tribal court raised my child support in my absence. This allowed the Tribal Court of Appeals to finally hear my case, and these wise men and woman eventually validated me and recognized the injustice my daughters and I had endured because of my brother's influence.

Please understand that I do not blame my family for giving up on me; they witnessed my on-and-off self-destructive behaviors over the years. They were genuinely and understandably concerned for my children's safety. However, I believe their anger, lack of knowledge, and my brother's retaliation should never have taken precedence over what was in the best interest of my children.

Ending the Cycle of Violence: Though I am still estranged from my brother and his family, today I realize that for me to release victim consciousness, I must learn to embrace forgiveness. My oldest daughter, now 24, is living with me and working on her associates degree at the Northwest Indian College. She is determined to heal from the cycle of abuse and addiction that I passed down to her. No words can describe how proud I am of her courage to stop the cycles before they take over her life.

My 21-year-old daughter is now a senior at a university in Oregon. She is an honor roll student and their track team's number one pole-vaulter. I will always be grateful that my brother and his wife took care of her during her last year of high school. This decision resulted from the verbal sexual abuse she experienced from her father, whom the tribal court and Children's Protective Services earlier had recommended and granted permanent custody. Even though she was born and raised on my reservation, she is not an enrolled tribal member; unlike me, she has never received tribal financial aid for her higher education. She has worked hard to pay her own way and plans to attend nursing school after she graduates. Again, words cannot describe how proud I am of her courage and inner strength.

My youngest daughter is now 14 years old and has been with me for over two years. We are understandably very close and I am proud to say that she prefers staying at home creating art to hanging out at the mall with friends. She is my mainstay.

All my daughters are true inspirations and have endured the effects of my past cycle of violence, victimization, and substance abuse. They also bear witness to the changes I have made in my life toward my healing and recovery. I hope they will come to understand the priceless gift I have been given and how my healing will someday help them and their children.

Blaming the Victim: I ask not for sympathy, but for your willingness to understand. This understanding is not just for me, but also for the countless women and children who are sexually abused and raped. I know some people still think that women who drink and use drugs deserve to be raped. Yet the majority of the so-called hopeless alcoholics and addicts, both women and men found repeatedly in alcohol and drug treatment centers, psychiatric hospitals, and state and tribal courtrooms, are survivors of childhood traumas such as emotional and/or physical abuse, incest, and rape. It continues to horrify me about our society that rape is still tolerated and is an accepted consequence for drinking by women. A female cousin from my reservation laughed as she blamed a Native sister for being gang raped at a party, saying it was her own fault for getting so drunk.

My Healing Journey: By disclosing the many times I have been raped, I continue to erase any debris of shame left inside and pray my disclosure will help other women to break their silence. My continued recovery, the healing I have been able to accomplish with counseling and through my art, is all part of my journey toward resolution. Much work remains for me to do and I will always have remnants of these horrid traumas, but they will no longer have the power to control my life or define my being.

My Spirit Lives: Reaching this point in my life has taken me though years of self-destruction—up to 10 alcohol-induced suicide attempts, six inpatient treatment centers, four outpatient treatment centers, three psychiatric hospitals, and several relationships with abusive men. No one should ever have to suffer alone in silence and shame. My grandfather's rape of me as a child led to all the sexual assaults and abuse I experienced in my life. It all started with him, but it ends now. I am not at fault, yet I am responsible. I have returned from a living hell and have found a new purpose in life. Healing is where my spirit lives.

**Pretty Ones**

It's the pretty ones
that age so quickly,
sitting on the same barstool
day after day she tries not to remember.
At first her youth and beauty
captivate an admiring audience
but they too,
wonder what will happen
when her beauty begins to fade.
The jealous ones
try to cut her,
scar her pretty face,
but no one could imagine
the scars she already has.
It's the pretty ones,
they say are lucky,
because she has drinks all lined
up for her.
But there's no one there to protect her,
when she's drunk herself into a stupor,
blinded by all the booze.
Or when they dump her out on the highway,
after her use was put beyond human test.
She walks alone trying to forget
what just happened,
and the shame she feels from being
one of the pretty ones.
She goes back to her barstool.
(Written just before my relapse in 1995.)

ROXANNE CHINOOK (Wasco) B.F.A., M. Hd., is a tribal member of the Confederated Tribes of the Warm Springs Indian Reservation in Oregon (e-mail: Rjchinook@aol.com). She is the great, great granddaughter of Billy Chinook, her tribe's second treaty signer and an Indian scout for the legendary Kit Carson. Her grandmother, Jeanette Brunoe, was full-blooded Wasco, a gifted header, trick-rider, and rodeo princess in Indian rodeos. Roxanne is an accomplished artist, painter, and believes her art emulates a personal and cultural experience from the spirit of the trickster to help her heal from the traumas of her past. Her artwork and other Native American artists she represents can be viewed at www.ebuynativeart.com. Copyright © 2004 by Roxanne Chinook.

# When Drinking Kills

**Alcohol abuse is the number one drug problem among America's teens and in a twist, girls are more susceptible than boys**

EVITA NANCY TORRE

She suspected there would be alcohol at the party, but at 19, Samantha ("Sam") Spady thought she could hold her liquor. Or maybe she wasn't thinking at all. In an 11-hour period in September 2004, the Colorado State University sophomore downed some three dozen beers, tequila shooters, and vanilla-flavored vodka shots before passing out in a spare room of a fraternity house. By the time the former high school homecoming queen and class president was found the next evening, she was dead of acute alcohol poisoning, with a blood-alcohol level of .436—five times the legal driving limit. Samantha had been educated about the risks of underage drinking, says her father, Rick Spady, "but she didn't understand that alcohol can kill you." Rick and wife Patty have set up a foundation in their daughter's memory ('www.samspadyfoundation.org) to educate other kids and their parents about the potentially fatal dangers of binge drinking (defined as consuming more than four or five alcoholic beverages in a two-hour period). "What happened to Samantha can happen to anyone," warns Patty. Indeed, drinking contributes to an estimated 1,700 campus deaths a year and an additional 600,000 injuries.

Underage drinking is nothing new, of course, but today's teen drinkers start at an earlier age than their parents did, are likely to binge drink, and are apt to be female. Some 20 percent of eighth-graders consume at least one drink in a month. And about 30 percent of all 13-year-olds have experimented with alcohol. Nearly half of college students of both sexes binge drink, often participating in such extreme drinking games as "Power Hour" (downing a shot of beer per minute for an hour). In all, nearly 7.4 million underage drinkers binge at least once a month.

But the most notable shift in tradition is the fact that girls are now catching up with their male counterparts. In one study, 21 percent of ninth-grade girls binge drank in a month versus 19 percent of boys. The numbers only rise as kids hit college. According to the Harvard School of Public Health, 41 percent of college women admit to binge drinking.

## Girls' Greater Risk

Early drinking can injure certain areas of the brain, which continues to develop until about age 21. "An adult would have to drink twice as much as a teen to do the same amount of brain damage," says J. Edward Hill, MD, president of the American Medical Association.

Girls are even more sensitive to alcohol than boys are because, in addition to generally being physically smaller, females have a higher body ratio of fat to water, says Fulton T. Crews, PhD, director of the Bowles Center for Alcohol Studies at the University of North Carolina at Chapel Hill. "Fat does not absorb alcohol, as water does, so girls' blood-alcohol levels rise more quickly." To compound the problem, women have lower amounts of an active alcohol-metabolizing enzyme. "Female bodies are less efficient at breaking down alcohol," Dr. Crews says, "so they get drunk faster."

The fact that alcohol and sexual misbehavior often go hand in hand raises the stakes for women even higher. Alcohol is implicated in an estimated 97,000 sexual assaults annually among college students.

## The Allure of Alcohol

Given these hazards, why are young women drinking so much? Part of the answer can be chalked up to peer pressure and some girls' need to be seen as able to drink like "one of the guys." "Guys are impressed when I can drink almost as much as they can," says Polina, a 19-year-old from New Jersey. "It shows them I'm not a weak little girl. When I do shot for shot, they high-five me."

Add to this mix the fact that, bluntly put, alcohol makes kids feel good. It stimulates serotonin and dopamine, brain chemicals that trigger sensations of euphoria, a loss of inhibition, and a false sense of being in control. These effects appeal to all teens but seem especially alluring to teen girls, who often report that drinking makes them feel more confident and "less uptight."

Alcohol makers, too, are aggressively courting the female consumer. Such novel products as "alcopops," the generic name for sweet-flavored malt beverages that are packaged to resemble fruit drinks, specifically target women who find traditional liquor less than palatable.

Patty Spady is convinced that such flavored disguises were a factor in her daughter's death. "Vodka shots flavored with vanilla taste like candy," she notes, "so girls don't realize the danger and drink too much, too quickly." Perhaps, she adds, "if this poison were made to taste like gasoline, kids would drink a lot less."

# What Parents Can Do

Many parents, remembering their own youthful misadventures with alcohol, may underestimate the scope of the binge-drinking problem or feel hypocritical if they impose a zero-tolerance policy. Yet that is exactly what most experts prescribe. Here are some ways to make the policy stick.

- **Prohibit "at home" drinking.** Well-intentioned parents sometimes let their teens drink at home parties on the theory that this at least provides supervision. In fact, a recent Journal of Adolescent Health reported that these teens interpreted such permission as approval to drink and were twice as likely as their peers to binge drink or use alcohol.

- **Connect with other parents.** "Parents should band together and look after one another's kids," says Patricia Powell, PhD, health scientist administrator at the National Institute on Alcohol Abuse and Alcoholism. "When parents talk together and set the same rules for all their children, it reinforces the message that drinking is unacceptable."

- **Lobby schools.** Examine the anti-alcohol curriculum at your child's school. Although most schools have extensive anti-drug programs, alcohol abuse often gets short shrift, even though alcohol is the most commonly abused mood-altering substance.

- **Set a good example.** Your teen may seem barely to acknowledge your existence, but she is watching you, and your approach to alcohol will profoundly influence hers. "Drink only in moderation," says J. Edward Hill, MD. "If kids see that you practice what you preach, they're more likely to heed your advice."

- **Keep the door open.** Make sure that your teen knows that she should call you immediately if overconsumption of alcohol lands her in danger. A parent's job is to protect her child. The worst possible outcome is a child who dies or is injured because she was too afraid of reprisals to go to an adult for help.

# What Alcohol Does to a Child

Christine Gorman

Alcohol and pregnancy don't mix. Fortunately, most women who drink cut their consumption dramatically once they realize they are carrying, and the number of children who develop the severest alcohol-related effects is relatively small: from 0.5 to 2.0 per 1,000 live births in the U.S. But doctors still don't know what harm—if any—comes from light to moderate drinking during pregnancy, which is why they caution expectant mothers not to drink at all.

The wisdom of that advice grows with each new study on the topic, as a paper released last week reminds us. Just one drink a day (12 oz. of beer or 4 oz. of wine) during the first three months of pregnancy is associated with a 2-point drop in overall IQ by the time the child is 10, according to a report in the June issue of *Alcoholism: Clinical and Experimental Research*. The effect shows up most clearly in certain visual tasks—like fitting pieces of a puzzle into an empty space—and was strongest among African-American children.

The apparent racial gap is puzzling—and ultimately inconclusive. Although other studies had shown similar effects of moderate drinking among pregnant Caucasian women, this one did not, says Jennifer Willford, a psychologist at the University of Pittsburgh School of Medicine and co-author of the report. The gap does not appear to reflect differences in income or drinking patterns, Willford says, since the two groups were comparable in this particular population. And in her previous research, Willford says, she has found problems in learning and memory among 14-year-olds—both black and white—whose mothers drank during pregnancy.

## Even moderate drinking during pregnancy can have long-lasting effects

As you might expect, the effects on IQ and cognitive abilities became more pronounced if moms continued to drink throughout their pregnancy or consumed more alcohol. Conversely, the children of women who stopped drinking during pregnancy fared better than those of women who did not.

Of course, to stop drinking during pregnancy, you have to know that you're pregnant in the first place. But as another study in the same issue of *Alcoholism* points out, younger women are more likely to drink heavily than older women and are more fertile—and therefore more likely to become pregnant.

About 45% of pregnancies in the U.S. are unplanned, says Dr. Raul Caetano of the Dallas campus of the University of Texas School of Public Health, a co-author of the second paper. A month may pass before a woman even realizes she is pregnant. "If you want to drink and you are sexually active, the best thing to do is to use contraception," Caetano says. "That's what I say to my daughter." And the best time to quit drinking is from the moment you—and your partner—decide you would like to conceive a child.

# The Problem with Drinking

CHERYL HARRIS SHARMAN

Efraím was already drunk when he left the wedding at 2 a.m. It had been a "nice wedding," which in Costa Rica means only hard liquor was served. The 21-year-old headed to a local bar for a "sarpe," or nightcap, with some friends. At 5 a.m., one of them finally sent him home in a taxi. Shivering and wrapped in towels, he sat on the carpet near the toilet and threw up.

Hours passed before his father found him in the same spot around 6 in the evening and rushed him to the hospital. The nightmare finally ended after an emergency room doctor injected him with medication for alcohol poisoning.

Tadeo, a young Costa Rican, went to the beach with three friends for a few laughs and a lot of drinks. After eight beers each, they drove home on the dark highway. A truck sped by, its rear lights obscuring the curve ahead. Their car skidded off the road and into a tree. Pinned in the wreckage, Tadeo broke three ribs, fractured his skull, fell unconscious, and remained in a coma for a week.

In Costa Rica, as in most Latin American countries, social gatherings more often than not include alcohol. Weddings and funerals, births and baptisms rely at least in part on drinks to ease grieving or encourage celebration. Aside from special occasions, many homes keep well-stocked bars that facilitate impromptu gatherings.

The drive home, particularly in the half-year-long rainy season, can entail a mix of alcohol and slick, winding roads, with potentially catastrophic results. But no one abstains for this reason. Statistics reflect the outcome: 13 percent of emergency room consultations in 1987 and 33 percent of auto fatalities in 2003 were alcohol related. Yet only 5 percent of Costa Ricans are alcohol dependent.

"The biggest misconception people have is that the problem of alcohol is alcohol dependence, or alcoholism," says Maristela Monteiro, regional advisor on alcohol and substance abuse at the Pan American Health Organization (PAHO). "In terms of society, most public health problems come from acute intoxication."

Medical research shows that long-term alcohol abuse causes liver diseases such as cirrhosis and hepatitis, as well as memory loss, ulcers, anemia, impaired blood clotting, impaired sexual performance, malnutrition, depression, cancer and even brain damage. But from a public health perspective, alcohol's greatest impact comes from occasional high-risk drinking by normally light to moderate drinkers.

"Homicides, traffic accidents, suicides, violent behavior, domestic violence, child abuse or mistreatment, neglect—these are from heavy drinking occasions, but most of these people are not alcohol dependent," says Monteiro.

Studies in the United States show that alcohol is a factor in 25 percent of deaths among people aged 15 to 29. Its direct costs to the U.S. health care system add up to some $19 billion a year, and for the economy as a whole, some $148 billion. As a risk factor for the global burden of illness, alcohol rivals tobacco: It is ranked number five among risks to health worldwide (tobacco is number four), and number one in all but two countries—Canada and the United States—in the Americas.

## The most effective policies prevent intoxication by reducing the amount of alcohol people drink.

Experts note that alcohol takes a disproportionate toll on the poor, despite the fact that alcohol consumption tends to increase with educational levels and development. Poor people spend a greater proportion of their income on alcohol, and when drinking problems occur, they have less access to services, may lose their jobs, and bring major hardship on their families.

For all these reasons, many public health experts believe that alcohol policy should be a top priority in every country of the Americas.

Costa Rica is one of many countries that have instituted programs to reduce the toll of alcohol using a variety of measures: taxes and licensing, restrictions on advertising, minimum-age laws, and controls on the hours of operation and location of outlets that sell alcohol.

In addition, Costa Rican law bans alcohol consumption in most public buildings, at sporting events, in the workplace, in parks or on the street, within 100 meters of churches, and on public transportation.

"It is important to use various measures to be effective," says Julio Bejarano, head of research at the Instituto sobre Alcoholismo y Farmacodependencia (IAFA) in San José.

Programs like Costa Rica's are the outcome of a 30-year trend toward viewing alcohol less as an individual malady and more as a problem of public health. The shift began with the 1975 publication of *Alcohol Control Policies in Public Health Perspective* by the Finnish Foundation for Alcohol Studies. Since then, new definitions of alcohol use and abuse have emerged, including classifications for levels of drinking according to their risks to health.

According to the emerging consensus, people with what the U.S. health sector calls "alcoholism" and what the World Health Organization (WHO) calls "alcohol dependence" need to seek treatment. But those engaged in occasional overuse that causes mental or physical health problems—"alcohol abuse" in the United States and "harmful use" disorder for WHO—should be made aware of its impact on their health and urged to reduce their consumption before they become alcohol dependent. A third WHO category, "hazardous use," implies high-risk consumption, or what is sometimes referred to as "binge drinking." "You never had a car accident," Monteiro explains, "but you drink too much and drive." This is a large group of people who also need to cut back.

But the bottom line, says Monteiro, is that good public health policies must aim at preventing intoxication. And the best way to do this is by reducing consumption.

"What has been proven over and over in developed countries and more and more in developing countries, is that we need to reduce the overall consumption of the population," she says.

Monteiro says that experience shows that the most effective way of reducing overall consumption is by increasing prices and taxes on alcohol and restricting availability—that is, where it can be sold, to whom, how much, at what times and on which days.

"Once you reduce the hours of sale, for example, you also control the amount of alcohol people can access and drink. You reduce homicides, accidents, violence—many of the acute consequences decrease significantly. There are several examples—for a long time in Europe, the U.S., and Canada, and now in Latin America and elsewhere—that show that closing bars earlier reduces both accidents and violence."

A 2003 book, *Alcohol: No Ordinary Commodity*, published by Oxford and WHO, reviewed three decades of research and concluded that reducing consumption is key. Their top-10 list of specific measures includes minimum-age laws, government monopolies, restrictions on outlets and hours of sale, taxes, drunk-driving counter-measures and brief interventions for hazardous drinkers.

## Limiting Access

Raising the minimum age for purchasing alcohol has long been one of the most effective means of reducing access. Only a handful of countries have emulated the U.S. minimum age of 21, but this has proven to be an effective policy. When all 50 U.S. states raised their minimum age from 18 to 21, the country as a whole saw a 19 percent net decrease in fatalities among young drivers. The National Highway Traffic Safety Administration estimates that raising the minimum age has saved 17,359 lives since 1975.

Government monopolies on alcohol have also proven effective, but these are increasingly unpopular. Until 1968, Finland prohibited the sale of beer anywhere but in government-owned outlets. In 1968, the country began to allow grocery stores to sell beer, and alcohol consumption climbed by 46 percent overall (increasing particularly among 13- to 17-year-olds). Government monopolies today oversee production, sales or distribution (but not all three) in parts of the United States, Canada, Russia, India, southern Africa and Costa Rica. In Scandinavia, multinational companies have waged legal battles invoking international trade rules to break up longstanding government monopolies on alcohol, increasingly limiting their ability to restrict consumption.

Short of holding monopolies, governments can control where, when and to whom alcohol is sold, restricting the density of outlets through limited licensing and restricted hours of sale. They can also restrict the availability of high- and medium-strength alcoholic beverages. Before 1965, Swedish grocery stores could not sell beer with more than 3.5 percent alcohol. When 4.5 percent beer became legally available in grocery stores, total alcohol consumption increased nearly 15 percent. Twelve years later, Sweden returned to the 3.5 percent limit, and consumption dropped again by the same amount.

Hours of sales are equally important. When Norway closed bars on Saturdays, researchers noted that those most affected by the restricted access were also those deemed likely to engage in domestic violence or disruptive intoxication. An Australian Aboriginal community, Tennant Creek, closed bars on Thursdays and noted that fewer women required hospital attention for domestic injuries.

In Latin America and the Caribbean, Colombia provides one of the leading success stories of limiting alcohol consumption through restricted hours of operation. Rodrigo Guerrero, a physician and public health expert, served as mayor of the second-largest city, Calí, in the mid-1990s and dedicated much of his effort to tackling the city's surging violence problem. He commissioned surveys that found that 40 percent of violence victims and 26 percent of violent death victims in his city were intoxicated. In response, Calí passed a *ley semi seca* ("semi-dry law"), which closed bars and discotheques at 1 a.m. on weekdays and 2 a.m. on Fridays and Saturdays. These and other measures reduced homicides from 80 per 100,000 to 28 per 100,000 in eight years.

Costa Rica also limits hours and days of sale. The law prohibits selling or purchasing alcohol in public places after midnight, the day before and the day after a national election, and during Holy Week, "the period of highest alcohol consumption in Costa Rica," IAFA's Bejarano notes.

Probably the most effective policy to reduce consumption, however, is raising taxes on alcoholic beverages. Worldwide, raising the price of alcohol always reduces consumption. According to the recent WHO report *Global Status Report: Alcohol Policy*, the price of beer should always be more than the price of a soda. And because the harmful effects of alcohol use stem from alcohol content, higher-content beverages should be taxed at higher rates.

# Drinking and Driving

After restricting access, the next most effective policies are those aimed at reducing drunk driving. WHO's *Global Status Report: Alcohol Policy* lists among the most effective countermeasures sobriety checkpoints, lowered blood-alcohol limits, license suspension and graduated licensing for novice drivers. Enforcement is key. Police intervention must be visible and frequent, and lawbreakers must be punished to the extent of the law.

Blood-alcohol limits are a critical part of these efforts. "Very little alcohol impairs motor coordination," explains Monteiro. "If you drink just over a drink, you are at risk—actually, it's less than a drink."

Costa Rica sets the legal blood-alcohol limit for drivers at 0.05 percent, although many experts say that problems often begin at 0.04 percent. Belize, Guatemala, Mexico, Nicaragua, Paraguay, Canada and the United States set the limit at 0.08 percent. These limits are most effective when used with checkpoints and random breath testing, according to research.

Other effective measures include screening and "brief interventions," prevention tools that have become a cornerstone of WHO's alcohol policy recommendations. During routine visits to health facilities or the family doctor, patients are asked simple questions that screen them for behavioral risk factors—including alcohol, cigarettes, poor diet, physical inactivity and seatbelt use—and doctors provide brief counseling sessions based on the responses.

"This is the epitome of low-technology medicine," says Thomas Babor, one of the researchers who designed the Alcohol Use Disorders Identification Test, or AUDIT.

"It's not the kind of thing, like MRIs, that seem to capture the interest of clinicians. But it probably is of equal importance, because it provides a way to prevent problems before they occur and to minimize problems if they've already started to develop."

AUDIT has been tested in a variety of countries and has proven easy to use, inexpensive to implement, and effective in reducing alcohol consumption at all levels of the population. Translated into many languages (including a Spanish version available through PAHO), the test and booklet include everything a clinician needs to give the 10-question test, to score it for one of four levels of risk for alcohol use, and to talk to patients about cutting back (including scripts for doctors who are unsure of what to say).

Patients take the test in about one minute, a nurse or receptionist scores it in another minute, and the clinician takes a few minutes to talk to the patient. Those testing in the first risk level are cautioned and advised to avoid drinking at least two days a week. Clinicians tell second-level scorers to minimize the number of drinks per day or week and to cut back on heavy drinking. Those in the third level receive brief counseling with more tools and goal-setting. Only fourth-level scorers are referred to an alcohol specialist.

## To reduce drunk driving, lawbreakers must be prosecuted and punished to the full extent of the law.

A 1999 study by Michael Fleming, at the University of Wisconsin–Madison Medical School, showed that, with a single counseling session, subjects cut back on their drinking in the first six months and kept it down for four years. The study also found that every $10,000 invested in interventions saved $43,000 in health costs, with even greater savings when researchers factored in societal benefits, such as fewer auto accidents and crimes.

Other policies have been found to be somewhat less effective, but combined with the "top 10," they help minimize the burden of alcohol. These include having alcohol outlets refuse to serve intoxicated patrons; training their staff to prevent and manage aggression; promotion of alcohol-free events; community mobilization; and public service campaigns in schools and colleges, on television, and in print, including warning labels. Bans and restrictions on alcohol advertising and marketing can help reduce youth exposure to pro-alcohol messages. In Latin America, Costa Rica and Guatemala have completely banned alcohol companies from sponsoring youth and sporting events, and several other countries forbid alcohol advertising on Sundays and holidays.

The challenge ahead, says PAHO's Monteiro, is to build on the work of international alcohol policy experts, using the available scientific evidence to judge which mix of policies works best. But she offers a note of caution: "In Europe, there's almost a reversal of the gains they had before because of trade agreements. The trade agreements that opened the markets for equal opportunity for everyone mean that you cannot have higher taxes or higher prices. You have to allow advertising for everyone."

She notes that in Sweden, foreign companies have challenged laws forbidding alcohol advertising, arguing that they give local, better-known products an unfair advantage.

"That is a point that will be critical in the region," says Monteiro, "how to deal with the economic benefits of alcohol in certain countries while protecting public health and reducing its social costs."

Moving forward, Monteiro and researchers from 11 countries are embarking on a multicountry study that will show, with precision and hard data, the public health burden of alcohol in the Americas. The study will focus on alcohol use in Belize, Nicaragua, Paraguay and Peru. The results will be added to existing data from Argentina, Brazil, Costa Rica, Mexico, Uruguay, the United States and Canada.

Monteiro believes the new study is particularly timely, as several trends in the region point to a growing alcohol problem. For example, in most countries, women drink more as their educational levels rise. In Costa Rica, the percentage of children 13 to 15 who have tried alcohol rose from 16.3 percent in 1990 to 28.4 percent in 2000. In many countries, pressure from industry has been growing along with the spread of public health measures aimed at reducing alcohol sales.

All these developments call for more research and more action, says Monteiro, because "people not only die from drinking too much; they harm and kill those who don't drink, too."

---

CHERYL HARRIS SHARMAN is a freelance journalist based in New York City.

# ADHD Drugs and Cardiovascular Risk

Steven E. Nissen, M.D.

On February 9, 2006, the Drug Safety and Risk Management Advisory Committee of the Food and Drug Administration (FDA) voted by a narrow margin—eight to seven—to recommend a "black-box" warning describing the cardiovascular risks of stimulant drugs used to treat attention deficit–hyperactivity disorder (ADHD). This action was unexpected, largely because the FDA had not requested a review of current labeling for this class of drugs; it had merely asked for recommendations of approaches to studying the cardiovascular risks associated with these drugs. The committee, however, decided to take an independent course. As a consultant to this committee, I introduced two motions, one recommending the black-box warning and the other proposing the development of a guide for patients, which was approved by a vote of 15 to 0. The guides are handouts that are required to be provided at the time prescriptions are dispensed; they contain information, written in nontechnical language, about the potential hazards of the medication.

The drugs under review were primarily amphetamines (Adderall and other brands) and methylphenidate (Ritalin, Concerta, and other brands). These agents are closely related members of the class of sympathomimetic amines, the structures of several of which are shown in the diagram. These compounds exert potent stimulant effects on the cardiovascular and central nervous systems. One of the oldest such agents, methamphetamine, was originally synthesized in 1891 and first widely used during World War II in Nazi Germany to enhance the ability of Luftwaffe pilots to stay alert during extended hours of combat. Medical use of this agent is now limited, but illicit use has grown rapidly and now represents an increasing public health problem. When smoked or injected intravenously, methamphetamine ("speed") is associated with hyperthermia, rhabdomyolysis, myocardial infarction, stroke, and sudden death—effects well known to coroners in regions of the United States where abuse is common. Beginning in the 1950s, the stereoisomer dextroamphetamine and related agents were introduced as appetite suppressants.

ADHD is a disorder commonly diagnosed in school-age boys (less commonly in girls) and is characterized by increased activity, an inability to concentrate, and poor school performance. The effectiveness of stimulants in treating ADHD has been well documented in randomized clinical trials. Amphetamines and amphetamine-like stimulants were introduced to treat ADHD in the 1950s, but the frequency of this diagnosis and the use of stimulants to treat it have accelerated enormously in recent years. The FDA advisory committee heard testimony indicating that 2.5 million children now take stimulants for ADHD, including nearly 10 percent of all 10-year-old boys in the United States.[1] The committee also learned that the use of these agents is much less prevalent in European countries, where the diagnosis of ADHD is relatively uncommon. Even more strikingly, 1.5 million adults now take such stimulants on a daily basis, with 10 percent of users older than 50 years of age. The diagnosis of "adult" ADHD is a relatively recent phenomenon and has resulted in the most rapid growth in the use of such agents.[1]

The concern of the advisory committee reflected several considerations. The cardiovascular effects of the sympathomimetic amines have been thoroughly described in the medical literature. These agents substantially increase the heart rate and blood pressure. In a placebo-controlled trial, mixed amphetamine salts (Adderall) administered to adults increased systolic blood pressure by about 5 mm Hg; similar effects were found with methylphenidate formulations.[2] Blood-pressure changes of this magnitude, particularly during long-term therapy, are known to increase morbidity and mortality. In 2005, a separate FDA advisory committee that I chaired concluded that blood-pressure changes represented such a reliable predictor of cardiovascular outcomes that class labeling would be appropriate in most cases.[3] The increases in heart rate induced by sympathomimetic agents also have well-described adverse cardiovascular effects. The administration of these drugs produces persistent increases in heart rate, inducing chronic heart failure in animal models of dilated cardiomyopathy.

A review of the regulatory history of this class of drugs also helps to explain why the advisory committee took decisive action. The dietary supplement ephedra, sometimes called ma huang, contains two alkaloids, ephedrine (see diagram) and its enantiomer, pseudoephedrine. These supplements have been used by millions of Americans to assist in weight loss or to increase energy. Some athletes have advocated the use of ephedra-containing dietary supplements as performance-enhancing agents. On December 31, 2003, federal officials announced plans to ban ephedra immediately. Health and Human Services Secretary Tommy Thompson told reporters, "The time to stop using these products is now." This action followed several high-profile catastrophic outcomes linked to ephedra products, including the death of 23-year-old Baltimore Orioles pitcher Steve Bechler. Published studies reported that sales of ephedra-containing supplements represented less than 1 percent of all dietary-supplement sales but that these products accounted for 64 percent of the serious adverse reactions to supplements reported to the Centers for Disease Control and Prevention.[4] Unfortunately, in April 2005, a federal court in Utah struck down the federal ban on ephedra. Many companies that make these products are located in Utah.

Similar regulatory actions have been proposed for phenyl-propanolamine (PPA), another closely related sympathomimetic amine (see diagram). On December 22, 2005, the FDA issued a notice of "proposed rulemaking for over-the-counter nasal decongestant and weight control products" containing PPA. The notice called for a public comment period until March 22, 2006, after which the FDA would undertake regulatory action that would probably include banning the use of the agent in over-the-counter preparations. The FDA's action followed many years of concern about the potential of PPA products to cause hemorrhagic stroke. Six years ago, a case–control study published in the *Journal* reported a 16-fold increase in the risk of stroke among women taking PPA for appetite suppression.[5]

Briefing documents prepared for the February 9 advisory-committee meeting described cases of myocardial infarction, stroke, and sudden death in children and adults taking ADHD stimulants.[1] These narratives were derived from the FDA's Adverse Event Reporting System (AERS), a database containing reports of adverse events submitted by health care providers. The AERS is a voluntary reporting system that has been criticized because only 1 to 10 percent of serious adverse events are actually reported, limiting the database's usefulness for identifying emerging drug hazards. The drug-related events reviewed by the committee included 25 cases of sudden death in children or adults (see table), some with evidence on autopsy of undiagnosed congenital heart disease, such as hypertrophic obstructive cardiomyopathy. The physiology of this condition renders patients particularly vulnerable to the adverse effects of sympathomimetic drugs, because such agents increase contractility,

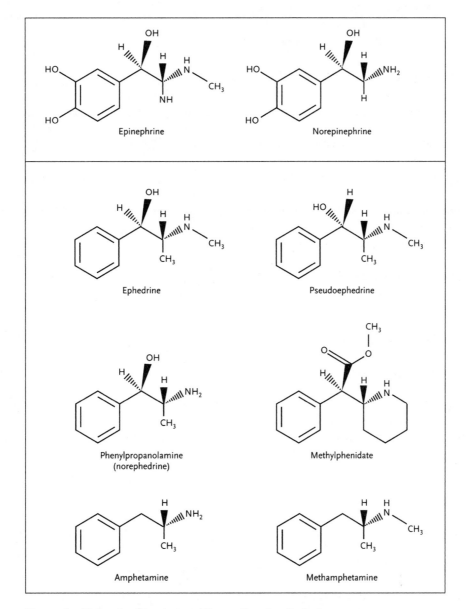

**Figure 1** Molecular Structures of Sympathomimetic Amines.

**Table 1** Cases of Sudden Death Reported to the FDA Advisory Committee from the AERS Database.*

| Patients | Amphetamines | | | Methylphenidate | |
| --- | --- | --- | --- | --- | --- |
| | Unadjudicated Sudden Deaths | Cases Meeting WHO Criteria for Sudden Death | | Unadjudicated Sudden Deaths | Cases Meeting WHO Criteria for Sudden Death |
| | | *number* | | | |
| Age, 1–18 yr | | 12 | | | 7 |
| Age, >18 yr | | 5 | | | 1 |
| Total | 28 | 17 | | 16 | 8 |

*Data are from the Adverse Event Reporting System (AERS) of the Food and Drug Administration (FDA).[1] Amphetamines include mixed amphetamine salts (Adderall), amphetamine, biphetamine, and dextroamphetamine. WHO denotes World Health Organization.

thereby increasing the pressure gradient in the left ventricular outflow tract. Many additional cases of major adverse cardiovascular events, including myocardial infarction, stroke, and serious arrhythmias, were reviewed by the committee. However, the documentation of cases was frequently incomplete, and neither the FDA reviewers nor the committee considered the AERS data to be definitive.

Despite the difficulty of interpreting these data, the advisory committee acted preemptively to recommend strong regulatory action. The majority of the group accepted my argument that the propensity of sympathomimetic agents to raise blood pressure and heart rate, the history of serious adverse effects associated with two members of the class (ephedra and PPA), and the rapid increase in exposure, particularly among adults, warranted strong and immediate action. Although the committee recognized that there are important potential benefits of these drugs for certain highly dysfunctional children, we rejected the notion that the administration of potent sympathomimetic agents to millions of Americans is appropriate. We sought to emphasize more selective and restricted use, while increasing awareness of potential hazards. We argued that the FDA should act soon, and decisively.

## Notes

1. Food and Drug Administration. Drug Safety and Risk Management Advisory Committee Meeting, February 9 and 10, 2006: table of contents. (Accessed March 16, 2006, at http://www.fda.gov/ohrms/dockets/ac/06/briefing/2006-4202_00_TOC.htm.)
2. Wilens TE, Hammerness PG, Biederman J, et al. Blood pressure changes associated with medication treatment of adults with attention-deficit/hyperactivity disorder. *J Clin Psychiatry* 2005;66:253–9.
3. Nissen SE, Cardiovascular and Renal Drugs Advisory Committee. Report from the Cardiovascular and Renal Drugs Advisory Committee: US Food and Drug Administration: June 15–16, 2005: Gaithersburg, Md. *Circulation* 2005;112:2043–6.
4. Kingston RL, Borron SW. The relative safety of ephedra compared with other herbal products. *Ann Intern Med* 2003;139:385.
5. Kernan WN, Viscoli CM, Brass LM, et al. Phenylpropanolamine and the risk of hemorrhagic stroke. *N Engl J Med* 2000;343:1826–32.

**DR. NISSEN** is the interim chairman of the Department of Cardiovascular Medicine at the Cleveland Clinic, Cleveland, and was a consultant to the FDA's Drug Safety and Risk Management Advisory Committee for the hearings on ADHD drugs.

# High on the Job

**Drug dealers and users are more savvy in workplaces today. Businesses need policies and training to counter these trends.**

MICHAEL A. GIPS

When he finally got the job he coveted with the food processing company, Jim (not his real name) was buoyant. The position offered the chance to make important contacts and earn a steady income. Jim and his girlfriend could finally begin to smell the flowers.

The problem was, the flowers came from cannabis plants, and he wasn't only smelling them, but also cutting, grinding, and selling them to his coworkers. In fact, Jim had applied for the job largely for the purpose of gaining access to the employees, to whom he could purvey marijuana, cocaine, methamphetamines, and other drugs. As one of the largest employers in the area, the food processor offered Jim a steady income and a large potential clientele.

Jim was entrepreneurial and successful. Not only did he sell to the younger crowd, but he had also cultivated many of the older workers as clients, men who had worked for the food processor for more than 25 years and had never regularly used drugs before. A convincing salesman, Jim got these workers to experiment with his wares, and he got many of them hooked.

No cash available until payday? No problem. Jim accepted credit and ATM cards, using a portable reader he borrowed from the beauty parlor operated by his girlfriend. The business thrived for more than three years, until the wife of an addicted worker placed an anonymous call to a company hotline.

The company brought in outside experts to conduct an investigation, but doing so was tricky, because of the multiple unions representing the workers and the work rules they enforced. Finally, a single investigator was approved to conduct a covert operation, systematically observing goings-on at the round-the-clock operation. When the investigator determined that he would have to buy drugs to obtain physical evidence, the company asked local law enforcement to get involved.

A four-month investigation revealed a web of drug dealing and use that startled upper management. Four dealers, including Jim, were identified, terminated, and prosecuted. Twenty other employees, who were discovered to have either used drugs at work or shared them with other workers, were also fired. Staff members who had bought and used drugs only off of company property were referred to the company's employee assistance program.

After the incident, the company realized how fortunate it had been that no drug-impaired worker had contaminated or otherwise negligently prepared food that would be distributed to the public. The company ended up completely revamping its substance abuse policy.

## Not the First Time

Cases involving sophisticated dealers who insinuate themselves into the culture of an organization aren't anomalies, says George J. Ramos Jr., vice president of Diversified Risk Management, Inc. Ramos, whose company conducted the investigation at the food processing operation, notes that drug dealers in the workplace are becoming increasingly savvy and more difficult to identify.

## Pro and Cons of Test Methods

They may be long-time workers, new hires—as in the case of Jim—or even temps. "A lot more planning goes into how they sell and how they get in to sell," Ramos says.

The growing sophistication of dealers and shifts in the types of drugs used are two trends in workplace substance abuse identified by experts in the field who provide consulting, training, policy development, testing, and investigative services. Yet many businesses—despite a rise in drug tests—lack effective policies and training to prevent workplace substance abuse.

## Drugs of Choice

Dozens of illegal drugs can be found in the workplace, but a few in particular account for most of the abuse and attendant concern. Marijuana continues to be the most prevalent.

More than half of all the positive tests conducted in the first six months of 2005 by testing lab Quest Diagnostics revealed the use of marijuana. In second and third place in the Quest Index, respectively, were cocaine (15.2 percent of all positive tests conducted for the total U.S. work force) and amphetamines (10.6 percent), which includes methamphetamine, or "meth." Depending on location, company culture, and other factors, meth and cocaine jockey for second in popularity within the United States.

**Marijuana.** As has been the case for years, marijuana continues to be far and away the most popular drug used at work. It's relatively cheap and accessible.

Problems associated with marijuana use at work include distorted perceptions of time and space, dulled physical reflexes, and reduced capacity for learning, memory, or concentration—all of which hinders performance.

**Crystal meth.** Use of methamphetamines—also called "crystal meth" when it is in crystalline form—has been surging. Crystal meth is a stimulant used to increase alertness and reduce fatigue, traits that make some workers believe it will be beneficial at work.

But what goes up must come down: when they're not high, users of the various forms of meth become mentally exhausted. The result is mental and physical sloppiness. The drug can also produce anxiety, hallucinations, psychosis, and periods of depression.

Among the general U.S. population, meth use rose from less than two percent in 1994 to more than five percent in 2004, according to the National Survey on Drug Use and Health, which is sponsored by the U.S. Substance Abuse and Mental Health Services Administration and the Department of Health and Human Services. In a recent Drug Testing Index, Quest Diagnostics reported that between 2000 and 2004, yearly growth rates in the incidence of positive drug tests attributed to methamphetamines were 16 percent, 17 percent, 44 percent, and 6 percent, respectively. For safety-sensitive U.S. workers who are federally mandated to undergo drug testing, the incidence of positive drug tests attributed to amphetamines rose 13 percent in the first half of 2005, while the positivity rate for the general U.S. work force actually dipped by 4 percent.

Ramos, whose company conducts investigations in more than 40 states, Canada, and Mexico, says that crystal meth is "the number one drug we see. It has taken over across the board." A national summit on methamphetamine abuse, held in 2005, declared the problem a "national epidemic."

Others see the methamphetamine problem as more localized. In a recently released paper titled Methamphetamine Use: Lessons Learned, Dana Hunt, Ph.D., a substance abuse expert at the University of Maine, writes that meth use varies widely across the United States.

Abuse of crystal meth, as measured by the number of people who enter treatment, is highest in western states such as Oregon and California, Hunt writes, but is being rivaled by midwestern states like Iowa and southern states like Arkansas. Hunt also cites spiraling rates of emergency room visits for crystal meth in Minneapolis, Seattle, and St. Louis.

Gene Ferraro, CPP, PCI, whose firm, Business Controls, investigates workplace drug dealing and use, says that methamphetamine production and use have percolated across the United States, but generally thrive in rural areas. He points out, however, that every organization has a unique culture in which different types of drugs may take root. His firm once did undercover investigations at companies right next door to one another. Marijuana was entrenched at one company, while coke ruled at the other.

Meth is also making headlines in Canada. Young men are flocking to Fort McMurray, a town in northern Alberta, where good money can be made in the oil extraction industry, says Barbara Butler, a Toronto-based management consultant with an expertise in workplace drug use. Anecdotal evidence and media reports suggest that meth use is spiraling there because the bored, overworked young men have money to buy drugs, like to party, and may need meth to stay awake on the job.

**Cocaine.** Despite the widespread attention received by crystal meth, cocaine use still remains strong. In fact, it registered a higher percentage of use than methamphetamine in the latest Quest index. The disparity between coke and crystal meth use is even greater when it comes to U.S. workers who are in safety-sensitive positions, and are thus federally mandated to undergo drug testing. Cocaine accounted for 23.5 percent of positive tests in the first half of 2005, compared to 14.7 percent for amphetamines.

Ferraro points out that cocaine use remains strong in African-American communities, though he thinks that it has ebbed since its heyday in the 1990s. In businesses with a high percentage of African-American workers, there is notably higher use of cocaine than other drugs among staff who test positive.

**Other illegal drugs.** Drugs producing hallucinogenic or other disabling mental or physical effects, such as heroin and LSD, tend not to be used heavily in the workplace, for a simple reason: "You can't use them consistently and still perform a job," says Ferraro.

Still, such disabling drugs do turn up in workplaces and in drug tests. Ferraro has seen some use of OxyContin at workplaces. PCP and opiates (generally, drugs derived from opium, such as heroin) appear as well. In 2004, according to the Quest index, 6.1 percent of all drugs uncovered in testing were opiates and about one-quarter of one percent was PCP. For the first half of 2005, those numbers had trended up, to 6.6 percent and four-tenths of one percent, respectively.

**Substitute drugs.** Debate has raged for decades in the United States about legalizing drugs such as marijuana. But the debate may be moot. "There are a number of substances that a committed drug user can use to substitute one high that's illegal and testable for a similar high that is legal and untestable," states Bruce R. Talbot, an instructor, trainer, and expert on substance abuse prevention and detection measures.

In some cases, a substance is legal if prescribed, but the user does not have a legitimate medical reason for obtaining a prescription, so the drug would have to be illegally obtained, and the use would be illegal. Users seek substitutes for these drugs as well. One example is kratom, a substitute for the prescription pain killer OxyContin, a popular drug with addicts seeking a high. Kratom's leaves can be smoked or put in a tea ball and brewed, and the resultant concoction drunk.

Kratom looks like marijuana and smells like sweet tea, but it produces the same effects as OxyContin: an opium-like high. "You can be actively high and still pass a drug test," Talbot says. Talbot says that most police officers aren't aware of it, and, in fact, none of the other experts interviewed for this story had heard of kratom or various other substitute drugs.

Drug users who favor marijuana and need to beat a drug test might substitute salvia divinorum, otherwise known as diviner's sage, says Talbot. Not only is it legal (and available on the Internet) and undetectable in urine, Talbot says, but it produces a more intense high than marijuana and is much cheaper. At a major state narcotics officer conference, recalls Talbot, one officer freely admitted that he smoked salvia and had done so for a long time.

The extent of use of these drugs is hard to determine because people don't get arrested for it and tests don't screen for it. The only evidence of use is anecdotal. The attractiveness of these drugs begs the question why they aren't more popular. "People are creatures of habit," replies Talbot, who adds that these drugs rarely make the front pages because "they typically don't kill people."

# Testing

All workers in safety-sensitive positions are already subject to mandatory drug testing, but most other employees are currently not asked to take drug tests. That is slowly changing, however. Companies are reevaluating their testing programs, says one executive at a large testing laboratory.

"In particular, many companies that never tested before are trying to do it," he says, pointing to a growth in testing since 2000 and a particular spike in the last year. He says the trend is part of a resurgence in background checks, partly precipitated by the events of 9-11.

Another spur to increased testing is pressure brought to bear by insurance companies. They are encouraging, and in some cases mandating, that companies set up drug testing programs, says the lab executive. "I'm inundated with small and medium-sized companies needing drug testing," he says. "Insurers are threatening rates through the roof" if a testing program is not implemented.

---

**"Some companies collect specimens from all employees, then randomly select samples to test, perhaps one in every ten."**

---

A few companies are becoming shrewder about maximizing deterrence while minimizing costs, notes Ferraro. These companies collect specimens from all employees, then randomly select samples to test, perhaps one in every ten. The money saved by not testing most of the samples is being invested in training managers in how they can better identify reasonable suspicion of drug use to determine whether there is just cause for ordering a drug test. The results have been encouraging, Ferraro says.

Nontraditional methods of drug testing have been increasing as well, for reasons ranging from efficacy to convenience. In fact, "There's been a revolution in alternative specimens," says Douglas J. Blaine, Sr., vice president of Penn Services, a Pennsylvania-based testing company.

**Urine.** "Urine is still the liquid gold standard" for testing, says Blaine. Urinalysis is the method sanctioned by the U.S. Department of Transportation for testing workers in safety-sensitive positions, "because it's easy to handle and collect, and all the work is done—the standard is there," he says.

According to the executive at the testing lab, urine tests account for more than 90 percent of the 30,000 tests the lab performs nightly.

But some companies are adding tests to accompany urinalysis or substituting for urinalysis altogether. One reason is that a whole industry of products to adulterate or substitute for urine specimens has been developed.

Other reasons are that urine doesn't show same-day drug use, which makes it less effective for detecting the presence of drugs in an employee's system when he or she is tested on reasonable suspicion of drug use or in the immediate aftermath of a workplace accident.

**Hair.** Drug testing labs report that they are doing more hair testing. One trend is the use of a combination of hair and urine testing for preemployment screening. That's proving to be a "very powerful" combination since the two complement each other well, says Blaine.

Unlike urine, hair can't be tampered with, as far as experts know. It also can detect the presence of drugs much farther back in time as compared with urine—90 days versus just a few days.

Employers, especially casino venues, want to find out, "Did he use drugs this weekend, and did he use [them] two months ago?" says Joseph Reilly, the president of Florida Drug Screening, Inc., and chairman of the Drug and Alcohol Testing Industry Association.

But it takes a hair two weeks to grow out, meaning that an analysis of hair can't be used to detect recent drug use. Also, hair testing is not an effective means of identifying marijuana, which shows up readily in urine.

Kraft Foods uses the dual-testing approach, says Ferraro. The result is a lower frequency of positive tests and fewer substance abuse issues at the company, he says.

One place where hair testing hasn't taken root is in Canada, says Butler. That country's human rights law stipulates that to conduct a drug test, employers need a bona fide reason directly related to an occupational requirement. "If your objective is to eliminate impairment, the test has to be able to do that," she says. Because hair testing doesn't identify current use, it cannot be said to be a means of testing for impairment; rather, it is only for detecting historic use.

**Oral fluids.** "Saliva testing is very exciting right now," says Talbot, though it's in its infancy. The Department of Justice (DOJ) is field-testing oral-fluid testing at police departments across the country, he says; the goal is to be able to perform a saliva test for drugs or alcohol on the roadside and have a result available in two minutes.

> ## "One frequently cited trend was the use of a combination of hair and urine testing for preemployment screening."

For the corporate world, it offers great potential for post-accident testing. Some companies are starting to use this method, because they can administer it themselves as long as they use a medical review officer.

A report funded by the DOJ, titled Evaluation of Saliva/Oral Fluid as an Alternate Drug Testing Specimen, concludes that "oral fluid is a promising specimen for drug testing and has several advantages over other testing specimens." These include simplicity of collection, the noninvasiveness of the procedure, and ease of processing. But more research is necessary on how to identify whether a sample has been diluted. And for instant tests, the technology has a long way to go, says the testing lab representative.

**Pupilometry.** Pupilometry is the measurement of the reaction of the pupil to stimuli. It is beginning to be used to test workers for drug impairment.

It works like this, according to Blaine: A person looks into a box, and a technician observes how the person's pupils react to a series of lights. Then a urinalysis is conducted. If the urine test is clean, the reaction of the pupils to the lights is established as a baseline performance of the subject when he or she isn't under the influence of drugs or alcohol. This "light test" then can be repeated at any time and checked against the baseline to determine impairment.

The method is promising, says Blaine, but the hurdles are obvious. For example, establishing a baseline depends on more factors than just the presence or absence of alcohol or drugs in a person's system. Also, legally prescribed drugs could affect the baseline pupil response. Moreover, a pupil response indicating impairment might reflect fatigue or some other factor, not necessarily the presence of drugs or alcohol.

**Blood.** As the most highly invasive measure, blood testing is still typically reserved for legal purposes or extreme cases. For example, it might be used to detect drugs in the body of a deceased worker whose family is filing a lawsuit or workers' compensation claim. It might also be used instead of urinalysis for workers who are on dialysis.

But as the basis of a regular testing program, it has too many disadvantages. For one, drugs leave the blood system quickly.

In addition, the testing process is invasive and expensive, and it requires that the specimen taker employ certain precautions that are mandated for needle use. The resultant medical waste must be properly handled and incinerated, notes Blaine.

## Subverting the Test

Countless products are available, especially over the Internet, to help workers beat drug tests. More than 400 on the market attempt to dilute or adulterate a specimen, according to the Department of Transportation (DOT). Others enable someone to substitute a different specimen. Their existence is no secret, but companies are often blasé about testing for adulterants either because they aren't familiar with them or because they don't want to incur the extra cost.

Another factor, says Reilly, is that government agencies "haven't been definitive on what labs have to do" to test for adulteration.

That's changing. In late 2004, the Department of Health and Human Services (HHS) adopted a rule requiring federal agencies to conduct so-called "specimen validity testing" to determine whether urine specimens collected under federal workplace drug testing programs had been adulterated or substituted. In an attempt to follow suit, DOT has issued a Notice of Proposed Rulemaking to make specimen validity testing mandatory.

Reluctance to screen for adulterants may also be a reaction to the statistics. Quest Diagnostics' Drug Testing Index for 2004 indicates that "oxidizing adulterants" accounted for an infinitesimal percentage—0.05 percent—of all tests of the general work force that turned up positive, and findings that a specimen was substituted accounted for only 0.49 percent. For safety-sensitive workers, those rates are 0.42 percent and 2.4 percent, respectively. The just-released figures for the first six months of 2005 show even lower rates—oxidizing adulterants turned up in less than 0.01 percent of the positive tests in the general work force and in 0.09 percent of the positive tests of safety-sensitive workers.

Asked why this should be, Quest's Dr. Barry Sample says one reason might be that the lab tests for "abnormal oxidizing activity," which is suggestive of adulteration but not a direct test for it. In other words, the tests are imperfect and may be missing occurences.

The company has seen an increase in cases where an oxidant has been found, but not in large enough quantities for the lab to conclude that a sample was adulterated. The result is an invalid specimen. Though Quest doesn't report the number of cases in which low levels of oxidants are identified, Sample says that the number of invalid specimens has risen. That could be a sign that attempts at adulteration are up. Getting an invalid specimen requires a retest, but it successfully buys time for workers.

## Policies

A drug testing program is only as effective as its policies. Unfortunately, many corporations have let their workplace substance abuse policies stagnate, says the testing lab executive. He says that of his lab's large corporate clients hasn't rewritten its policy, which runs less than a page, in years. The reason? "Substance abuse, once a hot topic at the forefront of the minds of many organizations, has slipped in importance" as other security priorities—like terrorism—have grabbed attention, says Ferraro.

Revising policies is important, says Ramos, to keep pace with changing laws and developments. For example, he says, many companies have policies prohibiting use of drugs on company property, but don't say anything about use of drugs on company time. This could provide a loophole for a worker to get high at home during lunch, for example.

Also, Ramos says, some courts have ruled that policies that use the language "under the influence" are referring to alcohol, while "impaired" refers to drug use.

Some companies have no policies at all. When companies do have policies, observes Blaine, they often fail to address what will happen to an employee who is found guilty of adulteration.

Policies should specifically equate a verified adulterated test with a positive, he says, and prescribe consequences, such as requiring the user to work with the company's employee assistance program (EAP) or referring the person to law enforcement for prosecution.

There are some companies that are strengthening their drug abuse policies. For example, companies with which Ramos has worked have been moving toward harsher sanctions in their policies. When drug abuse is accompanied by theft, more businesses have been willing to prosecute.

"Typically an employer wanted to just eliminate the problem and get on with business," he says. "Now they want to send a message to existing employees and to prosecute theft by dealers; substance abuse is secondary."

**Training.** Corporate policies should also mandate that staff and supervisors undergo training so that they will be able to identify signs of substance abuse and will know how and where to report it. "Often an employer puts in a beautiful policy, but then they don't train people on it down through the levels" of the organization, says Blaine.

An insufficiently or untrained low-level supervisor who suspects a worker of drug abuse may run afoul of proper procedures in dealing with the user or conducting a drug test. If the user is terminated on the basis of such a test, an arbitrator will reinstate that person, Blaine says.

Management consultant Butler has seen this in Canada. She has had many companies come to her because they recognized that they had to ramp up training for their supervisors to comply with demands of new clients.

Ramos's firm also does this type of work. It performs three levels of training. At the first and second levels, executives and supervisors, respectively, learn to identify behavior and patterns emblematic of drug use or sales. The third level teaches employees about the impact of substance abuse on their work and family life, and it lays out the legal ramifications. This tiered training makes sure the message gets to the whole organization, he says.

For his part, Talbot says that he teaches managers and supervisors how to document the signs and symptoms of drug impairment so that they can write a convincing fitness-for-duty report. They can use that report to impel management to order a test on the user.

The ultimate question is whether all this activity has actually led to less drug abuse on the job. One indication of progress is that since Quest began reporting the percentage of drug tests that turned up positive, the number has declined markedly, from 13.6 percent in 1988 to 4.5 percent in 2004 to 4.3 percent for the first half of 2005. Ferraro isn't so sure, however. The numbers may simply indicate that employees have gotten very good at beating the tests.

MICHAEL A. GIPS is a senior editor at Security Management.

# UNIT 6

# Creating and Sustaining Effective Drug Control Policy

## Unit Selection

## Key Points to Consider

- How do the drug policies of the United States generally differ from those of Canada and some European countries? Why?

- How does drug policy shape public opinion of drug-related events?

- What role do the media play in shaping drug policy?

- Are the problems and issues surrounding the legal use of alcohol different from those surrounding the illegal use of heroin, cocaine, or methamphetamines? How?

- To what degree would you argue that the current problems with drug abuse exist because of current drug policies, or in spite of them?

## Student Web site
www.mhcls.com/online

## Internet References
Further information regarding these websites may be found in this book's preface or online.

**Drug Policy Alliance**
*www.drugpolicy.org*
**DrugText**
*http://www.drugtext.org*
**Effective Drug Policy: Why journey's end is legalisations**
*http://www.drugscope.org.uk/wip/23/pdfs/journey.pdf*
**The Higher Education Center for Alcohol and Other Drug Prevention**
*http://www.edc.org/hec/pubs/policy.htm*
**The National Organization on Fetal Alcohol Syndrome (NOFAS)**
*http://www.nofas.org*
**National NORML Homepage**
*http://www.norml.org/*

The drug problem consistently competes with all major public policy issues, including the war in Iraq, the economy, education, and foreign policy. Drug abuse is a serious national medical issue with profound social and legal consequences. Formulating and implementing effective drug control policy is a troublesome task. Some would argue that the consequences of policy failures have been worse than the problems they were attempting to address. Others would argue that although the world of shaping drug policy is an imperfect one, the process has worked generally as well as could be expected. The majority of Americans believe that failures and breakdowns in the fight against drug abuse have occurred in spite of various drug policies, not because of them and there is an ever-increasing public pressure to rethink the get-tough, stay-tough enforcement-oriented ideas of the last 25 years.

Policy formulation is not a process of aimless wandering. Various levels of government have responsibility for responding to problems of drug abuse. At the center of most policy debate is the premise that the manufacture, possession, use, and distribution of psychoactive drugs without government authorization is illegal. The federal posture of prohibition is an important emphasis on state and local policy making. Federal drug policy is, however, significantly linked to state-by-state data which suggests that illicit drug, alcohol, and tobacco use vary substantially among states and regions. The current federal drug strategy began in 2001 and set the goals of reducing drug use by 25 percent over five years. Last year, President Bush advised Congress that the plan "is on track to meet its goals." Core priorities of the overall plan are to stop drug use before it starts, heal America's drug users, and disrupt the illegal market. These three core goals are re-enforced by specific objectives outlined in a policy statement produced by the White House Office of Drug Control Policy. All three goals reflect budget expenditures related to meeting goals of the overall policy. The current drug control policy in terms of budget allocations continues to provide for over $7 billion to reduce supply and almost $5 billion to reduce demand. In 2006, the fifth year of the plan, President Bush stated that drug use by 8th, 10th, and 12th graders dropped by 19 percent. A yearly assessment of the Federal Government's most extensive survey, however, reveals modest increases and decreases in drug use in almost all categories, including those relative to young persons. Some modifying of the present plan is occurring, such as the dedication of more federal funds to local communities for treatment options, and the dedication of major funding to address the increasing widespread cultivation of marijuana on National Park lands by Mexican criminal syndicates.

One exception to prevailing views that generally support drug prohibition is the softening of attitudes regarding criminal sanctions that historically applied to cases of simple possession and use of drugs. There is much public consensus that criminalizing use and addiction which is not related to other criminal misconduct is unjustified. The federal funding of drug court programs remains a priority with $70 million dedicated to state and local operation. Drug courts provide alternatives to incarceration by using the coercive power of the court to force abstinence and alter behavior through a process of escalating sanctions, mandatory drug testing, and out-patient programs. Successful rehabilitation accompanies the re-entry to society as a citizen, not a felon. The drug court program exists as one important example of policy directed at treating users and deterring them from further involvement in the criminal justice system. Drug courts are now in place in all 50 states.

The majority of Americans express the view that legalizing, and in some cases even decriminalizing, dangerous drugs is a bad idea. The fear of increased crime, increased drug use, and the potential threat to children are the most often stated reasons. Citing the devastating consequences of alcohol and tobacco use, most Americans question society's ability to use any addictive, mind-altering drug responsibly. Currently, the public favors both supply reduction, demand reduction, and an increased emphasis on prevention, treatment, and rehabilitation as effective strategies in combating the drug problem. Shaping public policy is a critical function that greatly relies upon public input. The policy-making apparatus is influenced by public opinion, and public opinion is in turn influenced by public policy. When the president refers to drugs as threats to national security, the impact on public opinion is tremendous.

Although the prevailing characteristic of most current drug policy still reflects a punitive, "get tough" approach to control, an added emphasis on treating and rehabilitating offenders is visible in policy changes occurring over the past 10 years. Correctional systems are reflecting with greater consistency the view that drug treatment made available to inmates is a critical component of rehabilitation. The California Department of Corrections, the largest in the nation, was recently renamed the California Department of Corrections and Rehabilitation. A prisoner with a history of drug abuse, who receives no drug treatment while in custody, is finally being recognized as a virtual guarantee to reoffend. In 2006, the National Institute of Drug Abuse published the first federal guidelines for administering drug treatment to criminal justice populations.

Another complicated aspect of creating national as well as local drug policy is consideration of the growing body of research on the subject. The past 20 years have produced numerous public and private investigations, surveys, and conclusions relative to the dynamics of drug use in American society. Most literature reflects, however, an indirect influence of research on large-scale policy decisions. There is a saying that "policy makers use research like a drunk uses a lamppost—for support, rather than illumination." One exception to the continued enforcement-oriented nature of federal policy is the consistently increasing commitment to treatment. This commitment comes as a direct result of research related to progress achieved in treating and rehabilitating users. Treatment, in terms of dollars spent, can compete with all other components of drug control policy. Over 35 percent of the current federal budget is dedicated to drug education, prevention, research, and treatment. One current example of dedicating treatment funds is NIDA's Developing New Ways to Treat Methamphetamine Addiction, which was funded with $42 million in 2007 to serve as a funding base to address the widening methamphetamine problem.

One important issue affecting and sometimes complicating the research/policy making relationship is that the policy making community, at all levels of government, is largely composed of persons of diverse backgrounds, professional capacities, and political interests. Some are elected officials, others are civil servants, and many are private citizens from the medical, educational, and research communities. In some cases, such as with alcohol and tobacco, powerful industry players assert a tremendous influence on policy. As you read on, consider the new research-related applications for drug policy, such as those related to the rehabilitation of incarcerated drug offenders.

*Drug Enforcement*

# Administration Announces Anti-Methamphetamine Plan

The Bush Administration, responding to months of criticism from Congressional leaders, has announced what it calls "a comprehensive, balanced approach to the methamphetamine challenge." The plan includes a variety of law enforcement initiatives as well as prevention and treatment programs.

A number of Republican and Democratic leaders in Congress have complained that the Bush Administration focuses too much on marijuana and has neglected the growing problem of methamphetamine abuse in the United States. For example, in an August 1 letter to John Walters, director of the Office of National Drug Control Policy (ONDCP), Sens. Chuck Grassley (R-Iowa) and Joseph R. Biden (D-Del.) demanded specifics about what Mr. Walters was doing about methamphetamine.

"We know that . . . marijuana is a much more popular drug in terms of the number of people who use it," Senators Grassley and Biden told Mr. Walters. "However, methamphetamine causes much more destruction in a much shorter period of time than marijuana. We believe that reducing drug use is not just about reducing the number of users of a drug, but reducing the overall harm to society caused by the drug."

In an August 18 event in Nashville, Administration officials outlined their new "meth" plan and made clear that they understand the harmfulness of the drug.

"Meth is a unique and deadly threat to our nation," Attorney General Alberto Gonzales said. "It is easy and cheap to produce. And it destroys lives far beyond those of just the addicts and the users. In one tragic case from Oklahoma, the parents of a five-year-old girl and an 11-month-old infant boy were 'tweaking' on meth. By the time their binge had worn off, the mother and father were out cold. Their infant, who had been left in a walker, caught a wheel in the heating grate of the home. Their daughter heard the screams of the baby trapped above the furnace grate. The mother, who slept only a few feet away from the infant, would not wake up. Several hours later the mother woke to find her son had died of severe burns. The daughter was so traumatized by the screams she could not talk."

The Administration's new meth program will include an expansion of specialized training that the federal government offers to local police officers and sheriffs' deputies, regarding how to detect meth production rings, track distribution networks, and dismantle and clean up toxic meth sites, Mr. Gonzales said.

In addition, the Drug Enforcement Administration will expand the Clandestine Lab Container Program, in which toxic waste from meth labs is transported by trained law enforcement personnel to centralized containers that meet hazardous waste storage requirements. In pilot projects, that program significantly reduced the cost of meth lab cleanups, according to the ONDCP.

The Attorney General also said he has directed U.S. Attorneys' offices to "make the prosecution of meth cooks and distributors—especially those who are repeat offenders—a high priority." The result will be that federal prosecutors will be "seeking stiff sentences for major players in the meth trade," he said.

And the Justice Department said it will now use the Organized Crime Drug Enforcement Task Force (OCDETF) program not only to fight methamphetamine traffickers, but also to identify the organizations that illegally obtain methamphetamine precursor chemicals.

Gonzales indicated that fighting methamphetamine traffickers is nothing new for the Justice Department The DEA currently spends more than $145 million a year to combat meth, he said. And "over the last three years, law enforcement has seized, on average, 45 small toxic meth labs or dump sites *each day* across America," he said—with help from Justice Department training programs.

And two weeks after announcing the new meth plan, the DEA announced that "Operation Wildfire"—the first nationally coordinated law enforcement operation designed to fight methamphetamine—had resulted in the arrest of 427 people, along with the seizure of 209 pounds of meth, 188 pounds of precursor chemicals, and $255,000 in cash. Thirty endangered children were removed from "meth environments" during the operation, the DEA said. Law enforcement agencies in more than 200 cities participated in the operation.

At the same time, the DEA announced that it had created a Web site (www.justthinktwice.com) designed to increase teenagers' awareness of the hazards of meth abuse. The Internet site "gives teens the straight facts about methamphetamine, and it's not a pretty picture," the DEA said. The site includes depictions of "meth mouth" (tooth decay caused by meth abuse) and "crank bugs" (sores caused when meth users pick at themselves because they experience the sensation of bugs crawling under their skin). The site also includes before-and-after photographs of meth users, depicting the damage the drug can cause to users' appearance.

One aspect of the Administration's meth program provoked immediate opposition from some Congressional leaders. The Administration called for certain limits on the sale of over-the-counter cold remedies and other medications containing pseudoephedrine (PSE), which is a precursor chemical for meth production, but critics of the plan said it does not go far enough.

Specifically, the Administration called for a limit of 3.6 grams in the amount of PSE a consumer could purchase in a single transaction. That is roughly the amount that would be found in 100 pills. But Sens. Jim Talent (R-Mo.) and Dianne Feinstein (D-Calif.), sponsors of the proposed Combat Meth Act, said that restrictions need to be tighter. Their bill would move all medications containing PSE behind the pharmacy counter, and would impose a limit of 7.5 grams of PSE per month.

"While the Administration should be applauded for recognizing the need for additional resources to fight meth and to provide additional funding for treatment, their plan is inadequate because it doesn't go far enough to restrict products containing pseudoephedrine," Senator Talent said. "Law enforcement across the country told us we need to relocate products with PSE behind the counter so we can keep meth cooks out of our neighborhoods and schools."

Senator Feinstein said a similar plan was enacted in Oklahoma "to great effect—resulting in an immediate drop of meth labs seized by 80 percent."

# Court Upholds Federal Authority to Reject 'Medical Marijuana'

The U.S. Supreme Court has upheld the federal government's authority to enforce marijuana possession laws regardless of state "medical marijuana" initiatives. But the ruling is expected to have little impact on day-to-day drug enforcement activities, according to experts on the issue. That is because federal agencies already focus on large-scale, for-profit marijuana operations, not individual users growing or using personal quantities of the drug.

The ruling in *Gonzales v. Raich, No. 03-1454,* decided 6-to-3 and handed down on June 6, held that the interstate commerce clause of the U.S. Constitution gave Congress the authority it needed to prohibit marijuana possession, even in the cases of individual medical marijuana users who are not involved in transporting the drug across state lines or developing it commercially.

Thus, the Supreme Court overturned a ruling by the Ninth Circuit U.S. Court of Appeals, which had held that Congress overstepped its commerce clause authority when it passed legislation banning intrastate, noncommercial cultivation and possession of marijuana.

The case involved two California women who were using marijuana for medical purposes as recommended by their physicians pursuant to California's medical marijuana law, and who sued the Attorney General after Drug Enforcement Administration agents seized one of the women's six marijuana plants.

The Supreme Court's ruling was considered a blow to advocates of medical marijuana, who would have taken a large step forward if the court had ruled that the federal government should respect the states' wishes on the medical marijuana issue. Justice Sandra Day O'Connor, in her dissenting opinion joined by Chief Justice William H. Rehnquist and Justice Clarence Thomas, said that the case "exemplifies the role of states as laboratories" for new types of policies.

In the dissenters' view, the court should have continued its recent trend of reining in the federal government's use of the interstate commerce clause to govern activities in the states.

Instead, the court essentially ratified the status quo—upholding the federal government's power to enforce its own laws against marijuana possession, but doing nothing to reverse the actions of the 11 states that have carved out medical marijuana exceptions in their drug laws.

"This ruling changes nothing," said Dan Abrahamson, director of legal affairs for the Drug Policy Alliance, a group that supports medical marijuana initiatives. "States still have the right to pass legislation that protects the rights of patients to use this life-saving medicine." (One of the litigants in the case, Angel McClary Raich, has said that marijuana saved her life because she suffers from a chronic wasting syndrome and other illnesses, and marijuana increases her appetite enough to prevent a dangerous weight loss.)

DEA agents have targeted high-profile distributors of medical marijuana in California, clashing with state Attorney General Bill Lockyer, who has called the federal crackdown on medical marijuana operations "punitive" and "petty." Me. Lockyer said he was disappointed in the Supreme Court ruling, because it means that "the conflict between state and federal law means that seriously ill Californians will continue to run the risk of arrest and prosecution under federal law when they grow or use marijuana as medicine."

However, the ACLU's Drug Law Reform Project, which supports medical marijuana efforts, said that the state laws continue to offer patients "significant protection."

"The federal government, to our knowledge, has never criminally prosecuted an individual medical marijuana patient for personally cultivating, possessing, or using medical marijuana, and we do not anticipate it will do so now," the ACLU said in a detailed analysis of the Supreme Court ruling. "Due to limited federal prosecutorial and judicial resources, the federal government generally limits marijuana prosecutions to large-scale cultivation and distribution schemes. . . . It is very unlikely that individual medical marijuana patients and caregivers will be arrested or prosecuted by federal drug agents, but high-profile patients and commercial or large-scale buyer's clubs or cooperatives are likely to be targeted once again."

The Bush Administration, which had urged the Supreme Court to rule as it did, applauded the ruling. "Today's decision marks the end of medical marijuana as a political issue," said

John Walters, director of the Office of National Drug Control Policy. "Smoking illegal drugs may make some people 'feel better.' However, civilized societies and modern day medical practices differentiate between inebriation and the safe, supervised delivery of proven medicine by legitimate doctors."

The ruling may not be the last word from the Supreme Court about medical marijuana, however. The Ninth Circuit ruled in favor of the medical marijuana users on the interstate commerce challenge, so it did not need to address other objections to the federal government's position, objections based on due process and "medical necessity" grounds. Now that the Supreme Court has reversed, the Ninth Circuit can move forward with those other legal challenges to the federal law.

Justice John Paul Stevens, who wrote the court's majority opinion, said it is "well-settled law" that the federal marijuana law "is a valid exercise of federal power, even as applied to the troubling facts of this case."

But Justice Stevens suggested that medical marijuana advocates "may one day be heard in the halls of Congress." Even though the current law has been upheld, Congress could choose to amend it.

However, nine days after the Supreme Court decision was handed down, the House of Representatives had an opportunity to vote on such a measure, and by a 264-to-161 vote it rejected an amendment that would have barred the Justice Department from using any federal funds to thwart state medical marijuana laws.

"This amendment does not encourage the recreational use of marijuana," said Rep. Maurice Hinchey (D-N.Y.), the sponsor of the measure. "It does not encourage drug use in children. It does not legalize marijuana. Our amendment is about compassion, in allowing patients the simple right of using the most effective medicine possible. Taxpayers' dollars should not be spent on sending seriously or terminally ill patients to jail."

Opponents warned that the amendment would undermine the nation's war on drugs. "If passed, this amendment would open the door for drug dealers to use medical marijuana exemptions as cover for their growing and selling operations," said Rep. John E. Peterson (R-Pa.). "I have never had a physician tell me that [marijuana] was needed in his portfolio to treat medical diseases and pain."

# Medical Marijuana, Compassionate Use, and Public Policy: *Expert Opinion or* Vox Populi?

Peter J. Cohen

A recent article in the *Hastings Center Report* reviewed the Supreme Court's current (but undoubtedly not final) delineation of the boundaries of federal power as set forth by the Constitution's commerce clause.[1] The question before the Court was straightforward: Did federal authority asserted under the Controlled Substance Act of 1970 (CSA) trump California's legalization of "medical marijuana" when these plants were grown within the state and were not bought, sold, or transported into another state?[2] By a six to three vote, the *Raich* court held that the federal Drug Enforcement Administration could enforce the CSA against two individuals who were growing marijuana for their own medical use in full compliance with California's Compassionate Use Act (Proposition 215). At the same time, the Court's holding neither struck down Proposition 215 nor demanded that California bring criminal charges against its citizens who were using marijuana on the advice of their physicians.

Unfortunately, the far more significant policy question raised by Proposition 215 was never adjudicated. In effect, Proposition 215 declared that some compounds used to treat disease could be evaluated and approved by a vote of the people rather than "by experts qualified by scientific training and experience," as mandated by the Food, Drug, and Cosmetic Act.[3] But Proposition 215 was wrong as a matter of public policy. Anecdotes, Internet blogs, and advertisements do not provide a sound basis for assessing the safety and efficacy of pharmacologic agents.[4] "Medical marijuana" should be subjected to the same scientific scrutiny as any drug proposed for use in medical therapy, rather than made legal for medical use by popular will.

In *Raich* and other cases[5] involving Proposition 215, marijuana's advocates presented this compound to the courts as a drug, a pharmaceutical agent efficacious in the treatment of serious and even life-threatening illnesses:

> Indeed, for Raich, 39, a mother of two teenagers who says she has been suffering from a litany of disabling ailments since she was a teenager herself, medical cannabis has worked where scores of other prescribed drugs have

failed. . . . It relieves pain, she said, from progressive scoliosis, endometriosis and tumors in her uterus. Raich even believes it has something to do with arresting the growth of an inoperable brain tumor.

> She is convinced that her use of medical marijuana, which began in 1997 after she had been using a wheelchair for two years, made her strong enough to stand up and learn to walk again. She said doctors could find no other explanation.[6]

These extravagant claims notwithstanding, marijuana has been used as a therapeutic agent throughout history, as Mathew W. Grey noted in a 1996 review of the use of medical marijuana:

> Cannabis, more commonly referred to as marijuana, has a long history of medical use in this country and worldwide. Accounts dating back as far as 2700 B.C. describe the Chinese using marijuana for maladies ranging from rheumatism to constipation. There are similar reports of Indians, Africans, ancient Greeks and medieval Europeans using the substance to treat fevers, dysentery and malaria. In the United States, physicians documented the therapeutic properties of the drug as early as 1840, and the drug was included in the United States Pharmacopoeia, the official list of recognized medical drugs, from 1850 through 1942. During this period, lack of appetite was one of the indications for marijuana prescription.[7]

Such anecdotal reports have been used by marijuana's adherents to support their wish to exempt the drug from the same scrutiny required for any other compound that is used to treat, ameliorate, or prevent human disease. Specifically, they have never campaigned vigorously for medical marijuana's evaluation by the Food and Drug Administration. Had those who favored the use of smoked marijuana as a drug elected not to circumvent the Food, Drug, and Cosmetic Act, and had smoked marijuana successfully traversed the same FDA regulatory process required for any drug proposed for use in medical treatment, it would have attained the status of an approved pharmaceutical. It could then have been purchased legally and used for medical purposes when prescribed by a properly licensed physician.

Why should FDA approval have been sought? Why should "medical marijuana" have been classified as a drug rather than a botanical, an herbal medication, or a folk remedy? The answer is in the Food, Drug, and Cosmetic Act itself: "The term 'drug' means articles intended for use in the diagnosis, cure, mitigation, treatment, or prevention of disease in man ... and articles (other than food) intended to affect the structure or any function of the body of man."[8] That smoked marijuana is both a "controlled substance" and a plant product is extraneous to this discussion. Controlled substances have widespread use in legitimate medical practice. As an anesthesiologist, I have legally administered more narcotics (in the course of providing medical care) than many low-level illegal drug dealers. Plants and their derivatives can be potent medications. During my internship, I used digitalis leaf (derived from the foxglove plant) to treat congestive heart failure. Botanicals are the active ingredients in tincture of opium[9] and belladonna suppositories,[10] both of which are legal and FDA approved when employed for legitimate therapeutic use. Smoked marijuana could achieve the same status were the FDA to find it safe and effective for medical use.

A Consensus Conference convened by the National Institutes of Health on February 19–20, 1997, to discuss the role of legitimate scientific research in evaluating the safety and efficacy of smoked marijuana reiterated the need for accurate and nonbiased scientific investigation of medical marijuana. The final report from the conference acknowledged that the FDA has approved a drug known as Marinol, which contains tetrahydrocannabinol (THC, the active psychotropic ingredient of *Cannabis sativa*, and a controlled substance), for oral use in treating both loss of appetite due to the AIDS-wasting syndrome and chemotherapy-induced nausea and vomiting, but then offered a caution:

> [This] does not fully satisfy the need to evaluate the potential medical utility of marijuana. The Expert Group noted that, although [THC] is the principal psychoactive component of the cannabis leaf, there may be other compounds in the leaf that have useful therapeutic properties. Furthermore, the bioavailability and pharmacokinetics of THC from smoked marijuana are substantially different than those of the oral dosage form.[11]

The Consensus Conference also observed that other pharmacologic agents had already been approved to treat many of the disorders for which marijuana's claims had not been scientifically substantiated. Yet, the report stated, "this does not mean, however, that the issue should be foreclosed. It simply means that in order to evaluate various hypotheses concerning the potential utility of marijuana in various therapeutic areas, more and better studies would be needed."[12]

Finally, the consultants felt that the evidence to date showed medical marijuana might have a significant role in the areas of appetite stimulation and cachexia (bodily wasting in the late stages of cancer), nausea and vomiting following anticancer therapy, neurological and movement disorders, analgesia, and glaucoma. At the same time, they made it clear that these possibilities would never reach fruition in the absence of scientific data:

> Until studies are done using scientifically acceptable clinical trial design and subjected to appropriate statistical analysis, the questions concerning the therapeutic utility of marijuana will likely remain much as they have to date—largely unanswered. To the extent that the NIH can facilitate the development of a scientifically rigorous and relevant database, the NIH should do so.[13]

The Food, Drug, and Cosmetic Act requires that drugs may not be advertised and sold in the absence of "evidence consisting of adequate and well controlled investigations, including clinical investigations, by experts qualified by scientific training and experience to evaluate the effectiveness of the drug involved."[14] However, the road to approval is not easy, and many investigators attempting to carry out scientific studies of marijuana have encountered political obstacles. Consider, for example, the difficulties faced by Donald Abrams, Professor of Medicine at the University of California, San Francisco, and chair of the Bay Area's Community Consortium on HIV research, in his attempts to study the effects of smoked marijuana on AIDS wasting. Abrams, a clinical pharmacologist, had proposed a study to provide objective data on whether smoked marijuana could ease the symptoms of AIDS wasting and produce gains in body weight. His university's institutional review board had approved the study, the FDA had approved it, and the university planned to fund it. Nonetheless, his request to import marijuana from the Netherlands was rejected.

Since the National Institute on Drug Abuse (NIDA) grows marijuana that is supplied to appropriate scientific investigators, the professor requested their assistance. However, because his funding had originated at his university, and not the NIH, of which NIDA is a part, he was denied access to the product. The NIH stated that its policy was to make marijuana available only to investigators who had received a peer-reviewed NIH grant to conduct the proposed study.

> In May of 1996, Dr. Abrams resubmitted his study proposal to the National Institute of Health, believing that he had addressed NIDA's concerns. At that time, the study was still approved and funded at the university level. In October 1996, four years after he had initiated requests to obtain marijuana legally, he was again informed that NIH's Mississippi marijuana "farm" would not supply the needed cannabis .... The following month, the people of California voters passed Proposition 215 by a wide margin.[15]

Political barriers to the performance of scientifically valid studies of medical marijuana do not obviate the argument that marijuana should be assessed in the same way as other drugs proposed for therapy. The sick still need medically sound treatments. In the case of Angel Raich, unfortunately, scientific evidence of this drug's efficacy in curing her inoperable brain tumor is simply nonexistent.

*Had Cannabis sativa not been proscribed by the Controlled Substances Act, every "medical marijuana" case would have been moot. As long as smoked marijuana was not advertised as an FDA-approved pharmaceutical, it would have become one of this century's premier herbal medications.*

Decades ago, the Supreme Court gave an ample argument for protecting people from the vain hope of unproven therapy:

Since the turn of the century, resourceful entrepreneurs have advertised a wide variety of purportedly simple and painless cures for cancer, including liniments of turpentine, mustard, oil, eggs, and ammonia; peat moss; arrangements of colored floodlamps; pastes made from glycerine and limburger cheese . . . . In citing these examples, we do not, of course, intend to deprecate the sincerity of Laetrile's current proponents, or to imply any opinion on whether that drug may ultimately prove safe and effective for cancer treatment. But this historical experience does suggest why Congress could reasonably have determined to protect the terminally ill, no less than other patients, from the vast range of self-styled panaceas that inventive minds can devise.[16]

Smoked marijuana ought not to be allowed to take the easy path to drug approval. Marinol, containing pure THC, has already been approved in the United States. Sativex, another formulation of THC, has been approved in Canada and is under consideration in the United States. Smoked marijuana might also be approved and legally prescribed for appropriate therapeutic uses.

I cannot resist a final thought. Had *Cannabis sativa* not been proscribed by the Controlled Substances Act (and been taxed and regulated, as are alcohol and tobacco, two substances that cause far more "societal pathology"), every "medical marijuana" case would have been moot. And under this scenario, as long as smoked marijuana was not advertised as an FDA-approved pharmaceutical (which would hardly have been necessary), it would undoubtedly have become one of this century's premier herbal medications.

**Acknowledgment**

I wish to acknowledge Cynthia B. Cohen, senior research fellow at the Kennedy Institute of Ethics, Georgetown University, for her help, encouragement, and insightful comments and suggestions.

# References

1. C.E. Schneider, "A Government of Limited Powers," *Hastings Center Report* 35, no. 4 (2005): 11–12.
2. *Ashcroft v. Raich*, 124 S. Ct. 2909 (2004). "Medical marijuana" refers to any form of *Cannabis sativa* used to treat a wide variety of pathologic states and diseases. Its adherents claim (with pharmacologic justification) that smoking allows easy titration and rapid onset of its pharmacologic effects.
3. Section 505(d) of the Federal Food, Drug, and Cosmetic Act, United States Code, Title 21, as amended, sec. 321 et. seq. (2000).
4. See P.J. Cohen, "Science, Politics, and the Regulation of Dietary Supplements: It's Time to Repeal DSHEA," *American Journal of Law & Medicine* 31, nos. 2 and 3 (2005): 175–214.
5. See *United States v. Oakland Cannabis Buyers' Cooperative*, 121 S. Ct. 1711 (2001).
6. E. Nieves, "User of Medical Marijuana Says She'll Continue to Fight," *The Washington Post*, June 7, 2005.
7. M.W. Grey, "Medical Use of Marijuana: Legal and Ethical Conflicts in the Patient/Physician Relationship," *University of Richmond Law Review* 30, no. 1 (1996): 249–74.
8. Food, Drug, and Cosmetic Act, United States Code, Title 21, as amended, sec. 201(g)(1)(B) and (C).
9. J.H. Jaffe and W.R. Martin, "Opioid Analgesics and Antagonists," in *The Pharmacological Basis of Therapeutics*, ed. A.G. Gilman, L.S. Goodman, and A. Gilman (New York: Macmillan, 1980), 494–534: Paregoric, U.S.P. (camphorated opium tincture) is a hydroalcoholic preparation in which there is also benzoic acid, camphor, and anise oil. The usual adult dose is 5 to 10 ml, which corresponds to 2 to 4 mg of morphine.
10. *Physicians' Desk Reference* (Montvale, N.J.: Thompson PDR, 2005), 2816.
11. National Institutes of Health, "Workshop on the Medical Utility of Marijuana," February 19–20, 1997, Executive Summary; available at http://www.nih.gov/news/medmarijuana/MedicalMarijuana.htm, p. 2.
12. Ibid., 4.
13. Ibid., 4.
14. Section 505(d) of the Federal Food, Drug, and Cosmetic Act.
15. P.J. Cohen, "The Politics of Marijuana," in *Drugs, Addiction, and the Law: Policy, Politics, and Public Health* (Durham, N.C.: Carolina Academic Press, 2004), 290–92.
16. *United States v. Rutherford*, 442 U.S. 544, 558 (1979).

PETER J. COHEN, "Medical Marijuana, Compassionate Use, and Public Policy: *Expert Opinion or* Vox Populi?" *Hastings Center Report* 36, no. 3 (2006): 19–22.

# Is Drug Testing of Athletes Necessary?

**"Rather than imposing an external drug-testing program on sports organizations, the Federal government should focus on preventing access to performance-enhancing drugs that pose health risks and prosecuting persons who distribute these substances illegally."**

MATTHEW J. MITTEN

In today's society, the economic and intangible rewards for extraordinary athletic achievements and winning performances are substantial. Therefore, there is a significant incentive for athletes to maximize their on-field performance, which is the paramount objective of sports competition. Virtually all athletes use various artificial means to enhance their body's natural performance while playing their respective sports.

Some substances and training techniques are not characterized as "unfair" competitive advantages, even if they are not universally available to all athletes because of their differing economic resources. It generally is permissible for athletes to ingest nonmuscle building dietary supplements that facilitate athletic performance such as carbohydrates, electrolyte drinks, energy bars, vitamins, and minerals—and they often are encouraged to do so. Even the use of creatine as a muscle-building substance currently is not considered to be "doping" or an improper means of athletic performance enhancement.

However, athletes' usage of federally controlled substances such as anabolic androgenic steroids, which include "designer steroids" such as THC (*i.e.*, tetrahydrogestrinone), and steroid precursors is characterized as doping by sports governing bodies and, if detected, punishable by sanctions. Anabolic androgenic steroids are synthetic variations of the male hormone testosterone that mimic its effects by having muscle-building (anabolic) and masculinizing (androgenic) characteristics with potentially harmful health consequences.

Steroids are a legitimate, therapeutic treatment for muscle-wasting conditions, but sports organizations prohibit their usage by athletes to enhance on-field performance. Also generally banned are steroid precursors such as androstenedione, which was admittedly used by former Major League Baseball player Mark McGwire. These substances function like steroids after being ingested and metabolized by the body. Sports organizations also ban and test for stimulants such as ephedrine and caffeine, which are contained in some over-the-counter products, because of their potential usage for "unfair" athletic performance enhancement.

## Risking severe sanctions

Some athletes at all levels of sports competition are willing to use banned performance-enhancing drugs, even though doing so violates the rules of the game and exposes them to sanctions, could adversely affect their health, and may violate Federal or state laws. Several former Major League Baseball and National Football League players such as Jose Canseco, Ken Caminiti (deceased). Bill Romanowski, and Steve Courson have admitted using anabolic steroids to enhance their on-field performances. Prominent Olympic athletes (*e.g.,* Ben Johnson and Jerome Young) have tested positive for steroid use, and other Olympians are suspected or accused of using steroids. Approximately one percent of the 11,000 National Collegiate Athletic Association student-athletes who randomly are tested each year come up positive for usage of banned performance-enhancing substances. According to a 2003 Centers for Disease Control and Prevention survey of ninth to 12th graders, steroid use by high school students has more than doubled from 1991 to 2003—to more than six percent.

Anabolic steroids, when combined with vigorous physical training, do enhance athletic performance by making users bigger, stronger, and faster—while also speeding up their recovery time after strenuous exercise. If steroids effectively enhance performance, what is wrong with allowing athletes to take advantage of modem medicine and pharmacology? After all, athletes frequently are given painkillers and are fitted with artificial devices designed to enable continued participation in a sport despite an injury, and these generally are considered to be acceptable practices. Although there is concern about potential health risks, libertarians point to the current lack of compelling medical evidence that steroid usage by adult athletes causes serious health risks beyond those already inherent in competitive sports. Some commentators, including physicians, advocate allowing athletes to use steroids with medical supervision after full disclosure regarding their known health risks rather than banning and imposing sanctions for their usage.

Is there really an appropriate line that can be drawn between legitimate athletic performance enhancement through artificial means and unethical doping to achieve an unfair competitive advantage? For example, athletes' usage of artificially created low-oxygen living environments in low-altitude training areas currently is permitted, whereas their use of erythropoietin (EPO) to achieve similar effects are prohibited by sports governing bodies. Moreover, who is the appropriate entity to draw this line?

Perhaps it is easier to answer both questions by considering the second question first. Sports governing bodies have a legitimate interest in establishing uniform rules necessary to maintain the sport's integrity and image, ensure competitive balance, and protect athletes' health and safety. Although achieving maximum individual performance and winning is the objective of athletic competition, the essence of sports is that all participants play by the same rules. Antidoping regulations are an integral part of the "rules of the game," similar to those regulating playing equipment, scoring competition results, and penalizing infractions. Even if a sport's rules of play are arbitrary (and they often are), the sport's governing body has the inherent authority to promulgate clearly defined boundaries to ensure fair play and enforce them in a uniform, nondiscriminatory manner.

Moreover, anabolic steroids are a Federally controlled substance. Medical experts have identified several potential negative side effects of using them. Clinical experiments involving athletes' use of steroids solely to improve on-field performance would raise serious ethical issues. For example, East German athletes who were given steroids under medical supervision, which enabled them to win Olympic medals during the Cold War era, now are suffering serious adverse health effects.

Courts and arbitration panels have upheld the legal authority of sports governing bodies (and educational institutions) to use random urinalysis drug testing of high school, college, and Olympic athletes. These tribunals generally conclude that protecting the integrity of athletic competition and sports participants' health and safety outweigh athletes' legitimate privacy interests. An athlete who uses these banned substances is a "cheater" whose unethical conduct may be punished.

Athletes who use prohibited substances directly expose themselves to potential adverse health consequences and indirectly subject others to similar risks. By nature, many athletes are risk-takers who will adopt their counterparts' successful training methods—even dangerous ones—if doing so enhances their performance. Thus, other athletes' actual or perceived usage of steroids creates a strong incentive to "level the playing field," which may cause an individual who would not otherwise ingest or inject steroids to do so.

Pharmacological performance-enhancing substances are banned because of their adverse effects on both athletes' health and competitive integrity. For example, the World Anti-Doping Agency (WADA) Code only prohibits usage of a substance that satisfies at least two of the following criteria: it enhances or has the potential to enhance sports performance; it creates an actual or potential health risk; or it violates the spirit of sport. No single criteria is a sufficient reason for prohibiting usage. For example, the first criteria includes the use of creatine and artificial low-oxygen living environments, which are permitted because neither of the other criteria presently are deemed to be satisfied. Conversely, the use of anabolic steroids is prohibited because at least two, and arguably all three, of these criteria have been met.

The WADA Code governs Olympic sports competition. It generally provides for strict liability and mandatory minimum suspensions for athletes' usage of banned substances. Pursuant to a contract with the United States Olympic Committee, the United States Anti-Doping Agency (USADA), an independent entity, administers and oversees the drug-testing program for American Olympic athletes. An individual has the right to appeal USADA's finding of a doping violation to an arbitral tribunal and to seek a reduced sanction because of mitigating circumstances.

The NCAA has a random drug-testing protocol applicable to all student-athletes participating in its member institutions' intercollegiate athletics program. It provides for strict liability and a one-year suspension from participation in all NCAA sports (along with a loss of one year of eligibility) for testing positive for a banned substance, with the right to an administrative appeal before members of the NCAA's Competitive Safeguards and Medical Aspects of Sports' drug education and testing subcommittee. Effective Aug. 1, 2005, the NCAA's drug-testing protocol was modified to make it more consistent with the WADA Code by withholding an athlete from NCAA competition who is under a doping suspension by a national or international sports governing body that has adopted the WADA Code, and by allowing consideration of a reduced penalty for a positive test in extenuating circumstances.

Because of the large number of students participating in interscholastic athletics and the high cost of testing ($50–100 per test), no state high school athletics governing body presently requires testing for performance-enhancing drugs. For the same reasons, very few school districts test for anabolic steroids. The California Interscholastic Federation, which regulates the state's high school athletics, recently adopted a policy to curb steroid use. It requires a student and his or her parents to agree in writing that the athlete will not use steroids without a physician's prescription and that coaches complete a certification program having a significant component regarding steroids and performance-enhancing dietary supplements. It also prohibits school-related personnel and groups from selling, distributing, or advocating the use of muscle-building dietary supplements.

Professional team sport athletes such as Major League Baseball, National Basketball Association, National Football League, and National Hockey League players generally have chosen to unionize, and drug-testing programs are a mandatory subject of collective bargaining. Thus, unlike the USOC, NCAA, and the governing bodies for nonunionized professional sports, MLB and the NBA, NFL, and NHL cannot unilaterally impose drug-testing programs on their players. The NFL and NBA have had collectively bargained mandatory drug-testing programs for several years.

As part of the Bay Area Laboratory Co-Operative (BALCO) grand jury investigation into the illegal sale and distribution of THC, several prominent baseball players were called to testify in December, 2003, regarding whether they used anabolic steroids to enhance their athletic performance, to the wake of this scandal, Pres. Bush, in his 2004 State of the Union Address, urged professional sports leagues to adopt voluntarily more stringent drug policies that effectively will eliminate steroid use and set a better example for America's youth. In January, 2005, Major League Baseball and its players union established their first testing program for performance-enhancing drugs.

Current penalties for a first drug testing violation are unpaid suspensions of 10 days for MLB players, four games for NFL players, and 10 games for NBA players. Meanwhile, the NHL's new policy, negotiated through collective bargaining after last year's lockout (non)season, has yet to be made public.

To protect public health and safety, the Federal government recently has taken steps to restrict access to performance-enhancing drugs and prevent their usage by athletes (particularly youthful ones). Anabolic steroids have been federally regulated since 1990. However, many athletes used steroid precursors, which were sold as legal over-the-counter dietary supplements under the Dietary Supplement Health and Education Act of 1994. Except for dehydroepiandrosterone (DHEA), steroid precursors now are regulated by the Anabolic Steroid Control Act of 2004, which became effective Jan. 20, 2005. As reflected by the BALCO grand jury proceeding, the Federal government also is actively prosecuting those who illegally provide performance-enhancing drugs to athletes.

In addition to these measures, there have been several 2005 Congressional committee hearings regarding professional athletes' use of steroids and proposed Federal laws to reduce their demand for these substances. These bills would establish a uniform random drug testing policy for professional athletes, with substantial fines imposed on sports organizations for failing to implement and comply with this policy.

The Clean Sports Act of 2005—which by no means is guaranteed to become law—is intended "to protect the integrity of professional sports and the health and safety of athletes generally," with the objectives of eliminating performance-enhancing substances. This proposed legislation would apply only to the NFL, NBA, NHL, MLB, Major League Soccer, Arena Football, and the United States Boxing Commission, which must develop drug-testing policies and procedures as stringent as those of USADA. However, the proposed bill provides the sense of Congress that all professional sports leagues should comply with these standards. Each athlete would be tested five times annually. There would be a mandatory two-year suspension for a first offense and a lifetime ban for a second offense, with the possibility of a reduced penalty for unknown or unsuspected usage of a banned substance.

The Director of the Office of National Drug Control Policy would be empowered to include other professional sports leagues or NCAA colleges and athletes within the Act's coverage based on a determination that doing so would prevent the use of performance-enhancing substances by high school, college, or professional athletes. Noncompliance with the Act's substantive provisions would constitute unfair or deceptive acts or practices in violation of the Federal Trade Commission Act with a potential civil penalty of $1,000,000 per violation.

# A $5,000,000 fine

The Secretary of Commerce would be directed to promulgate regulations requiring testing for steroids and other performance-enhancing substances and may fine a professional sports league $5,000,000 for failing to adopt testing policies and procedures consistent with the regulations.

With some variations, similar bills titled the Professional Sports Integrity and Accountability Act and the Professional Sports Integrity Act of 2005 have been introduced in the Senate and House, respectively. Do not be surprised if more legislative proposals are on the way.

Congress clearly has jurisdiction to establish a drug-testing program for professional leagues based on its authority to regulate interstate commerce, and there are other potential bases for enacting such legislation. Nevertheless, professional athletes and their unions may assert that federally mandated drug testing violates their rights under the Constitution. Targeted drug testing of professional athletes, but not other private employees, is inconsistent treatment. However, the Federal equal protection clause requires only a rational basis to justify treating professional athletes differently, which is satisfied by their prominence in American society and imitation by youngsters.

A more interesting issue is whether mandatory drug testing of adult professional athletes without an individualized suspicion of illegal drug usage constitutes an unreasonable "search" in violation of the Fourth Amendment. In recent years, the Supreme Court has upheld mandatory random drug testing of high school athletes for recreational drugs by public educational institutions to protect their health and safety. Other courts have rejected college athletes' legal challenges to mandatory random drug testing for performance-enhancing and recreational drugs as a condition of participation in intercollegiate athletics. This judicial precedent, which holds that random drug testing is an appropriate means of maintaining the integrity of amateur athletic competition and protecting athletes' health, also may be applied to professional sports.

Although Congress may have valid regulatory authority, this proposed Federal legislation inappropriately would interfere with the internal governance of professional sports, which historically have not been subject to direct government regulation. Athletic governing bodies are in the best position to establish appropriate drug-testing programs in order to regulate the permissible bounds of competition and to protect athletes' health and safety. The primary harm that results from athletes' usage of banned performance-enhancing substances is to the sport's integrity. Thus, the sport's governing body should have the exclusive authority to establish sanctions that effectively reduce athletes' incentives to engage in doping. Market considerations, combined with political pressure, should provide a strong economic incentive for a professional sports league and its players union to establish an effective drug-testing program. For example, MLB recently adopted its first testing program for performance-enhancing substances in response to these factors. Its program appears to be reducing steroid usage by its players, although Baseball Commissioner Bud Selig has called for more severe penalties than befell the Baltimore Orioles' Rafael Palmiero, a first-time offender who tested positive for steroids after testifying under oath at a Congressional hearing in March that he does not used banned or illegal substances.

Rather than imposing an external drug-testing program on sports organizations, the Federal government should focus on preventing access to performance-enhancing drugs that pose health risks and prosecuting persons who distribute these substances illegally. The government potentially could fine and imprison athletes for violating controlled substances laws by knowingly using illegal performance-enhancing substances,

which would penalize them for the indirect harm caused to American youths who view professional athletes as role models and emulate their conduct. (However, the International Olympic Committee is opposed to using criminal law to punish sports doping.) Both the Federal government and sports governing bodies have important roles to play in eradicating the use of banned performance-enhancing substances by athletes. However, their respective roles should be complementary rather than overlapping.

**MATTHEW J. MITTEN** is professor of law and director, National Sports Law Institute, Marquette University Law School, Milwaukee, Wisc., and chair of the National Collegiate Athletic Association's Competitive Safeguards and Medical Aspects of Sports Committee, which oversees the NCAA's drug education and testing program for student-athletes.

# Meth Madness

**Methamphetamine drug use is soaring throughout the country, to the detriment of users and employers. Here's what to do about it.**

SUSAN LADIKA

Merv Lopes was the ideal worker to handle the constant hum of life on the docks. The strength and agility gained from his years as a standout wide receiver at the University of Hawaii made him ideally suited for his $60,000-a-year job as a longshoreman, and he could work for hours without wearing out.

But it was more than his athletic ability that kept Lopes moving. It was his reliance on methamphetamines, known on the street as "ice" or "crank," which can make users stay awake for days on end. While it may seem like the ideal drug for those who need to pack 28 hours worth of work into a 24-hour day, there's a steep price to pay: Long-term use can cause everything from hallucinations to violence to irreparable brain damage.

In his case, Lopes immersed himself in the whirl of activity of moving cargo and driving heavy equipment around the docks. But in hindsight, he realizes the danger into which he was putting himself and others. "Staying up for days, you're not quick to react," he says. "On the waterfront it's a very, very life-threatening situation. You could die, or you could hurt somebody else."

When his employer confronted Lopes about his drug use and offered him help, he chose instead to walk off the job.

Lopes' story is not an aberration. Across the country methamphetamine use is soaring. This highly addictive stimulant, once used primarily by blue-collar workers to stay awake on the job, is to time-strapped soccer moms, lawyers, accountants and salespeople as a way to heighten productivity and focus.

As a result, no workplace is immune from meth. White-collar or blue-collar, service industry or manufacturing, in rural or urban locations—methamphetamine does not discriminate. HR's primary weapons against this highly addictive stimulant are awareness and prevention.

## The Highs and the Lows

What's unique about methamphetamine is the broad appeal to white-collar professionals—especially first-time drug users over the age of 30, according to law enforcement officials. What would make a highly educated, highly paid professional try such a dangerous drug? Meth initially makes users more productive,

and its use is, at first, easy to disguise. That also makes it more alarming to employers.

"Meth initially heightens concentration and increases alertness and all of the other things that are desirable characteristics of employees. It also makes it harder to spot on the job," says Carol Falkowski, director of research communications at Hazelden, a private alcohol and drug rehabilitation facility in Center City, Minn. "After a fairly short honeymoon period, many people move into addiction. They initially think they can control meth. In short order, meth starts to control them" (See "From Superman to Addict" below.)

---

### From Superman to Addict

Part of the lure of meth, says Carol Falkowski, director of research communications at Hazelden, an alcohol and drug rehabilitation facility, is that from the first time people try it, they feel "plugged in." First-time users will say methamphetamine "made me feel like I was Superman, like I could accomplish anything."

The problem is, nothing is as powerful as that first high. Users "start needing more and more to get that same effect, and they can never achieve it," Falkowski says. But the drug can quickly turn destructive and soon nothing matters more than meth to its users.

Jerry Gjesvold can attest to that Gjesvold has worked with hundreds of businesses in his job as manager of employer services at Serenity Lane, a rehabilitation facility headquartered in Eugene, Ore. One of the most dramatic cases involved a paper mill machine operator who was called into her boss's office for suspected meth use. There, the woman had a panic attack and curled up in the corner in a fetal position.

"The person wasn't fit to operate a piece of machinery. She could have done a lot of damage," Gjesvold says. Yet the woman refused to take a drug test, and the company's only choice was to fire her for insubordination. "That's how important the drug becomes to some people," he says.

---

Doug Coleman, a Drug Enforcement Administration (DEA) special agent in Washington, D.C., says that in the short term, employees may demonstrate an increased attention to detail and decreased fatigue. "They're going to be bouncing off the walls," he says. Users might be able to stay up for several days, then crash and sleep for a couple of days. "Sometimes they crash and you can't wake them up."

The drug also can take a physical toll. Personal hygiene may decline. Meth decreases users' blood flow, causing an itching sensation that causes users to scratch themselves repeatedly, leading to skin lesions. Decreased blood supply also damages the soft tissue of the gums, and chemicals attack the tooth enamel, causing "meth mouth," with teeth decayed down to the gum line.

Long-term effects can be even more dramatic. A UCLA study using high-resolution MRIs found that meth destroys the areas of the brain that control memory, emotion and reward systems. Regular meth users lose about 1 percent of their brain cells each year, which is comparable to the effects of Alzheimer's disease.

The drug also can cause mood swings, paranoia and anxiety, and can increase the chance for stroke and high blood pressure.

The effects "are hard things to control in the workplace, let alone in society," says Tim Dimoff, president of SACS Consulting & Investigative Services Inc. in Akron, Ohio. Some users steal from their job to support their habit, says the former narcotics detective, who has carved out a niche for himself specializing in high-risk workplace issues.

The link between meth and crime is perhaps most clear in Hawaii, where methamphetamine is "by far the most significant drug threat," and where experts unanimously blame the high crime rate on drugs, according to the DEA.

## Stress On the Workplace

The costs of meth use to employers can be staggering, driving up everything from absenteeism to workers' compensation claims to employee turnover.

Lopes recalls going days without sleep, then stepping into a pothole at work and tearing the ligaments in his knee. "If I was together and sharp, I could have caught myself better," he says. Instead, he wound up with a workers' comp claim.

In one Arkansas county alone, methamphetamine use costs employers $20 million to $25 million per year, according to a study by Katherine Deck, a researcher at the University of Arkansas in Fayetteville. The study, conducted in Benton County, a place with slightly more than 100,000 workers, found that after they become addicted it takes four methamphetamine users to do the work of three nonusers. In addition, a meth user is five times more likely to be absent from work than a nonusing co-worker.

What's more, the study found meth users in all industries and walks of life, from the government to doctors' offices to poultry processing facilities. "There is no industry or occupation that is exempt," Deck says.

### Meth Use Speeding Up

Barry Sample, director of science and technology for the Employer Solutions division of Quest Diagnostics, which conducted more than 7 million workplace drug tests in 2004, can attest to the growing use of methamphetamine. In 2004, amphetamines were found in 0.52 percent, or 364,000, of all drug tests conducted by Quest. This is double the rate of 2000. Methamphetamine is the most commonly abused form of amphetamine.

In contrast, cocaine results held steady during those four years, found in about 0.70 percent of drug tests, while positive marijuana results fell from 3.29 percent to 2.88 percent.

The study was based on 3,000 surveys, to which nearly 600 workers responded. Of those surveyed, about 1.7 percent said they were using or had used meth—matching the national estimate of meth users. But the study numbers may have been low. "We were told again and again by law enforcement officers that we had underestimated the number of users," Deck says.

Regardless, even a few cases of meth abuse can cause problems.

In Portland, Ore., Precision Castparts Corp., a manufacturer of metal products and components, has fired two people this year who tested positive for methamphetamine usage.

Both employees had bid on job promotions and were drug tested as part of that process. One of the workers completed his initial inpatient rehabilitation but failed the first random drug test, while the other "decided doing meth was a lot more fun than coming to work. The meth had totally taken control of his life," says Dave Coates, Precision Castparts' senior HR manager.

Coates says the experience has taught the company that it needs "to pay a lot closer attention to this and not be dependent on testing policies [alone] to catch the problem."

To bolster its efforts, Precision Castparts plans to improve supervisory training. "We really need to educate our front-line supervisors on precursor behavior" Coates says. For example, the company closely monitors performance over time, and does a lot of comparisons between individual and team performance. With one of the workers who was fired for meth use, "for a couple of weeks his productivity went through the roof." Then that was followed by absenteeism.

But not all employers are as focused on prevention as Precision Castparts. Jerry Gjesvold, who has worked with hundreds of businesses as manager of employer services at Serenity Lane, a rehabilitation facility headquartered in Eugene, Ore., says some industries turn a blind eye to the problem. He cited the manufactured home industry in particular, where bonuses are paid based on productivity. Those who churn out more units can make more money.

In some industries, employees can't pass drug screen tests. Rather than get rid of the workers, the companies have gotten rid of the testing, Gjesvold says, and have adopted a "don't ask, don't tell" policy.

## An Ounce of Prevention

If some employers are ignoring meth abuse, many others are facing the situation head-on. That is certainly the case in Hawaii, where the high cost of living drives many employees to work two jobs simply to make ends meet. Little wonder, then, that the state has the highest per capita population of meth users, according to the DEA—or that companies are finding innovative ways to educate their workers on the drug's dangers.

For example, filmmaker Edgy Lee of FilmWorks Pacific, which produces films and other projects in Hawaii, hooked up with Jeff Mueller, who runs a drug education and prevention program called Recovery Works Inc. Lee and Mueller produced a documentary on Hawaii's meth problem that was simulcast during prime time on all the state's television stations in 2004. That was followed this year by a film on meth and Hawaii's youth.

Now the team's efforts are moving into the workplace. It began at the request of the maritime industry, which wanted to educate its workforce about the dangers of meth. Films also are being produced for employees of other industries, such as hotel workers and agricultural workers, Lee says.

Gary North, senior vice president of Matson Navigation Co., a shipping company in Honolulu, says the idea originally developed as the Hawaiian Legislature was considering a bill last year that would have mandated annual drug-related education for employees. Although the bill didn't pass, the maritime industry decided to proceed with its plans to have a training film produced specifically for its workers.

The short film, which was shown to Matson employees in September, features maritime workers who use meth. "It's really helpful when someone can hear from a face they can identify with," Mueller says.

The film is designed to trigger employee discussion. Mueller serves as facilitator during the training sessions, with the aim of educating those who don't use drugs about the perils of methamphetamine, and encouraging those who use it to admit they have a problem.

"It's education. It's awareness. And I think this is unique," says North, who doesn't believe the maritime industry has a bigger problem with meth than any other industry in the state. Hawaii's five shipping companies employ about 675 longshoremen. At Matson, a "handful" of employees are treated for methamphetamine use. "It's who we don't know [about] that we're concerned about," North says.

Currently, the industry has a "three-strike" program, and if someone is caught using drugs three times, they're out of a job. But the industry wants to "create an environment in the workplace where if someone has a problem, they can step forward and not be penalized," North says.

Because many longshoremen are quite experienced and take time to train properly, North says, "it's a cheaper thing to have this preventive program than to have to replace people."

## Where the Problem Is Most Acute

Today, about two-thirds of methamphetamine sold in the United States comes from large-scale operations in Mexico and California, which may produce 100 pounds at a time, says Doug Coleman, a DEA special agent.

The remainder comes from smaller labs in the United States, which make an ounce or less in places like homes, hotel rooms and RVs.

Missouri led the nation with 2,788 meth lab seizures in 2004. That was more than 15 percent of the U.S. total. Iowa, Illinois, Indiana and Tennessee each had more than 1,000 seizures.

Carol Falkowski of Hazelden, a drug rehabilitation center, says that in 1992 there were 10 methamphetamine addicts treated for every 100,000 patients undergoing treatment in the United States. By 2002, that number had jumped to 52 of every 100,000 patients. Treatment rates are highest in Oregon at 324 per 100,000, followed by California at 200 per 100,000 and Iowa at 198 per 100,000.

According to the National Institute on Drug Abuse, which is part of the National Institutes of Health, 40 percent of the adult males arrested in Honolulu tested positive for methamphetamine, the highest percentage in the nation. This was followed by Phoenix at 38 percent and San Diego at 36 percent.

In Hawaii, the DEA says, methamphetamine is "by far the most significant drug threat. Per capita, Hawaii has the highest population of ice users in the nation."

Hawaii is far from an anomaly. Congress and law enforcement officials have called methamphetamine abuse a national epidemic. What started in the West has quickly spread to the Midwest. And the DEA classifies methamphetamine as the primary drug threat in such diverse places as California, Kansas and Arkansas.

The 2003 National Survey on Drug Use and Health, done by the U.S. Department of Health and Human Services, found that 12.3 million Americans age 12 and older, or 5.2 percent of the population, had tried methamphetamine at least once. About 600,000 people reported using it in the previous month.

Meth "appeals to anyone who has too much to do and too little time," Falkowski says. And it can be found anywhere from trailer parks to million-dollar homes.

—Susan Ladika

But the effort doesn't come without its costs. North plans to show the film twice a year during work hours. The 100 men at Matson earn an average of $70 an hour, and the training takes 45 minutes.

## Testing

While education can be important, former narcotics detective Dimoff says the best way to counter drug use in the workplace is to set up drug testing programs. In the state of Ohio, for

# How Meth Works

Methamphetamine is a derivative of amphetamine and serves as a stimulant affecting the central nervous system. It can be smoked, snorted, infected or taken orally and can cost as little as $20 a hit.

As meth use grows, use of cocaine and marijuana declines. In a recent survey of 500 law enforcement agencies in 45 states by the National Association of Counties, 58 percent said meth is their biggest drug problem, compared with only 19 percent for cocaine, 17 percent for marijuana and 3 percent for heroin. The study also found that 87 percent have seen Increases in meth-related arrests in the past three years.

Unlike cocaine and marijuana, which are derived from plants, methamphetamine is synthetic, manufactured using chemicals from readily available household products like over-the-counter cold medications, lithium camera batteries and hydrogen peroxide. Products such as gasoline, sulfuric acid and sodium hydroxide from drain cleaners also may be used. The toxic mix is cooked over high heat and leaves behind an environmental catastrophe.

To limit access to the pseudoephedrine found in cold medicine and used to make meth, some retailers are moving products like Sudafed behind the counter. In Oklahoma, consumers are limited as to how much pseudoephedrine they can buy, and they must show a photo ID and sign for every purchase. And Oregon's governor signed a law in August requiring prescriptions for cold and allergy medication. The new regulations could be in place before year's end.

example, companies can't bid on state construction contracts unless they have a drug testing program in place.

Larry Hellie, SPHR, who runs HHRC2, a management consultancy firm in Vancouver, Wash., says the ingredients in methamphetamine are water soluble, so they quickly pass through the body. As a result, testing days after meth use won't catch the drug. But if someone does test positive, it's difficult for users to claim that they were taking only over-the-counter cold remedies. "Medical review officers are pretty knowledgeable about meth. They're hard to fake out."

One company that has set up drug testing is Solon, Ohio-based Zircoa Inc., which produces industrial ceramics. New hires must take drug tests, and all employees are trained annually about drug abuse, says plant manager Scott Abel.

"People working next to a person with a drug problem know it before we do," Abel says. Zircoa urges employees to come forward if they have a problem and get treatment. "We provide whatever they need to get back on their feet."

While Ohio isn't a hotbed for meth, the drug may very well be present, Abel says. Of job applicants selected for hire, he says, 20 percent to 25 percent don't pass the initial drug screening test. Leading Abel to ask sarcastically, "Do I have a meth problem?"

SUSAN LADIKA has been a journalist for more than 90 years, working in both the United States and Europe. Now based in Tampa, Fla., her freelance work has appeared in such publications as The Wall Street Journal-Europe and The Economist.

# How to Stand Up to Big Tobacco

Noreena Hertz

A satirical film, *Thank You for Smoking*, looking at the power of Big Tobacco, hits our cinema screens on 16 June. It's a sharp reminder of just how sinister tobacco companies are. Five hundred million people will die of smoking-related illnesses over the next 50 years, yet the tobacco lobby continues to do all it can to keep up its sales.

Despite the tobacco industry's zeal, however, its efforts in developed countries have been somewhat thwarted. In the developed world, smoking rates are on the decline, thanks in large part to the hike in tobacco taxes that has taken place–on average, in high-income countries, two-thirds of the price of a packet of cigarettes is now tax.

In low-income countries the story is very different. Tax rates on tobacco products are often as low as one-third: in a quarter of developing countries examined in a recent study, tobacco was actually becoming more affordable in 2000 than it was in 1990, owing to increased wages. The upshot is that by 2030, if nothing changes, 70 per cent of smoking-related deaths will stem from low- and middle-income countries.

Why are low- and middle-income countries so reluctant to raise taxes, given that it is a policy measure proven to save lives? The evidence is now clear that, for every 10 per cent increase in price, ten million lives would be saved. The spin of the tobacco lobby goes a long way in explaining this. "Increased taxes would mean less revenue" is the main line the lobbyists peddle. Their evidence is typically cobbled together from research published by economists and academics they have funded. Yet any economist worth her salt knows that when the demand for a product is as price-inelastic as it is for tobacco, increases in taxes will generate net gains in tax take, not losses.

Other objections to raising taxation favoured by the tobacco lobby are similarly false. Lobbyists claim that taxes "are the main cause of large-scale smuggling." But smuggling is a function of corruption. And anyway, smugglers don't seek out tax arbitrage opportunities: they try to avoid paying any taxes at all, a commercial benefit that has led some tobacco companies to support and participate in the illicit tobacco trade themselves.

As for the line that raising taxes is "inequitable" because the taxes hit the poor more, although it is true that smokers from lower-income groups are more likely to quit in response to price rises, that doesn't mean the policy is unfair. The poor spend disproportionate amounts of their income on tobacco. In Morocco, for example, poor households spend more on tobacco than on health and education combined. If this group of smokers stopped smoking, we would see a reduction in health and educational inequalities in that country.

## Poor households in Morocco spend more on tobacco than on health and education combined

But if the spin is so transparent, why aren't developing countries ignoring it and raising their taxes? Put yourself in the shoes of a cash-starved government faced with a big multinational company dangling billions of pounds'-worth of potential investment if only the terms of engagement are just "right." Wouldn't you, too, perhaps be swayed?

Which means that if hundreds of millions of lives are to be saved, governments in the developed world will have to help their developing-country counterparts to stand up better to Big Tobacco. This will involve helping them create alternative investment opportunities, doing something real to help them export their products and break the deadlock on trade, and also dangling their own carrot to developing countries—if you raise your tax on tobacco, we will increase your aid. A controversial one, that, as it implies an endorsement of the micromanagement of policies chosen be another state. But to hell with political correctness here. If additional resources could be raised, and especially if those additional resources would be earmarked for health, then everyone would be better off. Everyone except the tobacco companies, that is.

The earmarking of tobacco taxes for health is not an unrealistic goal. Earmarking is very much in vogue. Only this past week a group of 14 nations announced a new mechanism to provide greater access to drugs in Africa, funded by a tax on airline tickets. Nor is it unrealistic to believe that governments in the developed world might actively support such tax measures. Almost all developed countries have now ratified the World Health Organisation's Framework Convention on Tobacco Control. This requires them to support anti-smoking measures in developing countries. And active support for higher tobacco taxes would be a tangible way to make good that pledge.

So come on, Tony Blair, run with this one. It fits with your concern for developing countries. It fits with the mandate you chose for your G8 presidency, It is in keeping with Labour's great success in reducing the numbers dying of smoking-related diseases at home. Britain itself earmarked some of its tobacco taxes for the National Health Service, and is one of the 14 countries that is going to impose the airline tax.

With Kenneth Clarke the chairman of British American Tobacco, and the Tories having voted against the ban on smoking in public places, this is one of the few areas where Blair could still secure the moral high ground.

# Cigarette Trafficking: Expanding Criminal Activity Attracts Law Enforcement Attention

**Cigarettes have been the focus of intense discussion in offices, homes, bars and restaurants, courtrooms, legislatures and other public gathering places. Holleran summarizes his key points on cigarettes and smoking.**

Jack Holleran

At the JAWP Annual Training Conference in Boston, Mr. Holleran explained how criminals and terrorist organizations are profiting from illegal trade in contraband cigarettes at a great cost to society. Women Police asked Mr. Holleran to summarize his key points in a guest column for this issue.)

For decades, cigarettes have been the focus of intense discussion in offices, homes, bars and restaurants, courtrooms, legislatures and other public gathering places. Nearly everyone has an opinion on cigarettes and smoking. At this point, you might ask, what is left to say about cigarettes?

From a law enforcement perspective, the answer is: plenty.

Criminal activity involving cigarettes is growing across the nation. Trade in illegal cigarettes is generating huge profits for criminals at great cost to society. Trafficking in contraband cigarettes increases the overall incidence of criminal activity—which is clearly bad for society and our communities.

Government sources estimate that cigarette-related crime prevents local, state and federal government from collecting billions—that's BILLIONS of dollars in badly-needed tax revenue. The underground cigarette trade hurts law-abiding retailers, wholesalers and suppliers, who lose legitimate sales and see their businesses undercut by illegal activity. When contraband cigarettes are available, sales of legitimate cigarettes decrease. That can be devastating to small shop owners who rely heavily on income from cigarette sales. Sellers of counterfeit and illegally-imported cigarettes also deceive adult smokers, who may think they're getting a good deal—but really get a raw deal.

Cigarette-related crimes often do not make high-profile headlines. However, as awareness of the problem grows—largely through the efforts of Philip Morris USA and our Brand Integrity department—law enforcement organizations are gaining greater understanding of the problem.

Of course, Philip Morris USA is well aware of the problem that criminals pose to our business and our valuable, high-quality, trademarked brands. We have taken a strong stand against cigarette-related crime, and we support law enforcement efforts across the nation to address the problem.

In the past, some people viewed illegal cigarette trafficking as a "victimless crime"—but that's certainly not the case today. Traffickers in contraband cigarettes are also often engaged in other illegal activities that may include money laundering, wire fraud, credit card fraud, check and mail fraud, immigration violations, financial crime schemes, funding of organized crime and terrorist groups, and Internet stores that operate outside the law.

Starting with consumer complaints, the story grew . . . and grew.

In the fall of 2001, after noting a sharp rise in consumer complaints, Philip Morris USA conducted investigations that revealed a problem involving counterfeit versions of Marlboro cigarettes. We have subsequently learned that criminals were operating nationwide, and that illegal cigarette trafficking takes many forms.

In the U.S., criminals buy truckloads of cigarettes in low-excise-tax states, drive them to high-excise-tax states and sell them at market prices, pocketing the difference. Others duplicate highly sophisticated state tax stamps and apply them to packs of illegal cigarettes to make them look legitimate. Cigarettes are stolen and re-sold. Billions of counterfeit cigarettes, most of them made in China and elsewhere in Asia, are smuggled into the United States every year. And cigarettes intended for sale outside of the U.S. are illegally imported into, and illegally sold, in this country.

We believe that most of this criminal activity has been driven by a desire to profit from overall rising prices and the discrepancies in selling price among the states. As cigarette excise taxes rise and the selling price of cigarettes increases, the higher profit potential spawned an illicit global cigarette trade. Criminal "entrepreneurs" counterfeiters and organized crime groups began to see illegal cigarette trafficking as a high-profit, low-risk proposition with far lesser penalties than, for example, drug-related crimes.

The contraband cigarette trade attracts a wide range of criminals, from shoplifters, smash-and-grab thieves and armed robbers to sophisticated counterfeiters and large-scale smugglers. The enormous profits gained from contraband cigarettes help criminal enterprises prosper. In some cases, criminals involved in illegal cigarette trafficking have used the profits from such activities to contribute to terrorist groups.

Cigarettes are also used in "bust-out" schemes. In a recent case in Lexington, Kentucky, a defendant purchased hundreds of thousands of dollars worth of cigarettes with fraudulent bank accounts and credit cards. In these schemes, cigarettes are illegally diverted from low-tax states to high-tax states and resold illegally—causing a great revenue loss for state governments and taxpayers.

- Contraband cigarettes

"Contraband cigarettes" is an umbrella term that we use to describe several different types of illegal activity.

- **Counterfeit cigarette** Counterfeit cigarette packaging is very similar to genuine Philip Morris USA packaging. However, the cigarettes are not genuine; they are fakes, or "knock-offs" of genuine PM USA cigarettes. Most counterfeit packs carry counterfeit tax stamps.

Between 100 billion and 150 billion counterfeit cigarettes are produced annually, mainly in China and the Far East. A container of cigarettes can be manufactured in China for less than $50,000 and sold in the U.S. for more than $1 million.

That's big business if a criminal can get away with importing and selling containers of cigarettes—and big losses to governments and legitimate businesses. The problem is very real—if the counterfeit cigarette trade were a legitimate business, its output would rank as the fifth largest cigarette manufacturer in the world.

We have also learned that counterfeiters rarely limit their activities to cigarettes. Many also deal in counterfeit currency, apparel, pharmaceutical and other "black market" merchandise.

- Diverted genuine cigarettes

These are cigarettes purchased in low-tax states or localities, smuggled to high-tax states or localities, and illegally re-sold at market prices. The difference between the buying and selling price is the difference in excise taxes, which translates into lost tax revenues for governments and illegal profits for criminals.

Some of you may watch the popular television series "The Sopranos." Earlier this year the program featured scenes of vans filled with diverted genuine Marlboro cigarettes. This illegal activity was portrayed as an easy way for the fictional organized crime family to earn money. As we all know, life mirrors

art. And, as cigarette excise tax discrepancies among the states increase—the fictitious "Sopranos" script is not far from the reality that we live every day.

In 2003, two men in Charlotte, North Carolina were convicted of providing material support to the terrorist group Hezbollah. These contributions, totaling hundreds of thousands of dollars, were funded by the illegal transportation of cigarettes from North Carolina to Michigan.

- Illegally imported cigarettes

Illegal imports are cigarettes made by Philip Morris USA, exported for sale overseas and then illegally re-imported to be sold in the United States. They can also be made by overseas subsidiaries of Philip Morris and illegally imported into the U.S.

Philip Morris does not import any cigarettes into the U.S., but our company has seen a greater incidence of cigarettes intended for foreign markets appearing in the United States. Recently, we have found Marlboro cigarettes produced in Europe, Mexico, Russia and the Philippines sold here in the U.S., predominantly over the Internet.

Like counterfeit cigarettes and diverted genuine cigarettes, illegal imports are sold outside the legitimate distribution system and profit criminals at the expense of governments and society.

- Internet sales: a growing problem

Philip Morris USA does not sell cigarettes directly to consumers, and does not sell cigarettes over the Internet.

However, we have identified more than 1,600 U.S. and foreign websites that are selling cigarettes into the United States, and most of them are selling Marlboro.

Philip Morris USA policy prohibits our direct customers—wholesalers—from selling cigarettes over the Internet unless they (1) comply with all applicable laws and tax requirements, and (2) use age verification processes that meet Philip Morris USA requirements—both at the point of ordering and at the point of delivery.

According to a 2002 report by the U.S. General Accounting Office (GAO), Internet cigarette sellers are not paying or collecting excise taxes on their sales, and they don't report cigarette sales to the state tax authorities, as they are required to do under the Jenkins Act. In the course of purchasing cigarettes from more than 400 different Internet websites, Philip Morris USA found only one website that reported sales—and to only one state. And virtually none of the websites out there have effective age verification controls in place to prevent kids from purchasing cigarettes.

The GAO estimates that, between 2002 and 2005, U.S. states will lose $1.4 billion in uncollected excise tax revenues from Internet sales alone.

- Fighting cigarette crimes in the courts

One weapon Philip Morris USA uses is litigation—suing people who we find selling counterfeit cigarettes and cigarettes that infringe on our trademarks and intellectual property rights. The goals of our litigation are to shut down the illegal activity at the point of sale, and to gather information so that we can take aggressive actions at every step of the illegal supply chain. We're making good progress.

So far, we have filed lawsuits against more than 2,800 retail defendants, four wholesalers, 23 importers, and 67 Internet site owners and operators dealing in contraband Philip Morris USA products. We have filed lawsuits in 13 states to date—and we haven't lost a single case. At last count, we had generated 218 court-ordered injunctions or seizures. A total of 2,084 cases were settled or had judgments entered. And we recently won a decision that awarded PM USA the Internet domain names that had been used by the world's largest illegal Internet cigarette seller, based in Switzerland.

We will continue to pursue this aggressive litigation strategy as long as the problem persists.

- PM USA supports tough legislation to help law enforcement address contraband cigarettes

In addition to litigation, we actively support tough anti-contraband and Internet legislation at both the federal and state levels. The legislation we are supporting—most notably the federal Prevent All Cigarette Trafficking Act, or PACT Act, includes tougher penalties for contraband trafficking; more and better tools for law enforcement to address contraband; and tough regulation of Internet sales to make sure they take place lawfully.

That means enforcing collection of all applicable taxes on Internet cigarette sales, and ensuring that effective age verification controls are in place to keep kids from getting access to cigarettes over the Internet.

- Philip Morris USA's Brand Integrity Department

Our Brand Integrity Department was created in early 2002 to disrupt, reduce and eliminate contraband PM USA cigarettes and related activities. The team includes seven former career law enforcement officials who had worked for the U.S. Secret Service; the Bureau of Alcohol, Tobacco, Firearms and Explosives; U.S. Customs; or the Federal Bureau of Investigation.

Stationed across the country, a team of regional security managers greatly strengthened our ability to engage with, and support, law enforcement efforts to address this serious issue and demonstrated the company's commitment to fight contraband cigarettes.

In coordination with local, state and federal law enforcement and regulatory agencies across the country, our Brand Integrity team collects and evaluates information about contraband cigarette activity and individuals engaged in that activity. Brand Integrity often provides this information to government agencies and prosecutors to help them build cases against criminals and illegal enterprises.

Engaging with, and supporting, law enforcement agencies and officials at all levels is one of the most important activities for Brand Integrity. How are we doing this?

We support law enforcement by providing information, by providing cigarettes for use in investigations, and by providing funding to support investigations. We also provide training

on the legitimate cigarette distribution system, contraband awareness training and counterfeit product recognition training. During 2003, we designed and conducted a series of regional law enforcement conferences to provide information to federal, state and local agencies and officials across the country.

- Success stories show that we're making progress working together

Last year, we developed information provided by a source in China that he had contacts who wanted to move counterfeit Marlboro cigarettes into the United States. We put him in touch with two law enforcement agencies, which worked together and introduced their own undercover agent into the operation. Earlier this year, the authorities broke up a sizeable counterfeit importation ring, arresting five individuals and seizing $250,000 in cash.

In another case, we supplied a considerable quantity of cigarettes to a state agency in the Northeast to set up a sting wholesaler operation in Virginia. They ran advertisements for cheap, out-of-state cigarettes in foreign-language newspapers; and when the orders started coming in, they were filled out of this mock warehouse. As people left Virginia with large quantities of cigarettes, headed north, they were followed. As a result, a. smuggling ring was dismantled, and several men are now in jail.

At the request of the New York Attorney General's Office's Organized Crime Task Force, we provided $9,000 for the purchase of some counterfeit cigarettes. A few days later, they had arrested three men and seized close to 200 cases of counterfeit Marlboro cigarettes with a street value of over $800,000. So, for a $9,000 investment, we helped law enforcement take $800,000 worth of counterfeit off the street—money well spent.

We are proud of the partnerships we have built with law enforcement and are pleased to play an important role in supporting your efforts to address contraband. However, if excise taxes and the selling price of cigarettes continue to rise, it is unlikely that contraband cigarette activity will be eliminated in the near future. We look forward to supporting you in your continued efforts to fight cigarette-related crime and its corrosive impact on society.

- What to look for on the street

Women Police requested some tips to help police officers identify possible illegal cigarette activity. Here are some indicators of potential criminal activity involving cigarettes:

- After-hours cigarette deliveries
- Loose cartons of cigarettes, or loose packs in unmarked vehicles
- Hidden caches of cigarettes
- Packs with out-of-state or missing tax stamps (be sure you are familiar with the tax stamps that should be applied to cigarettes sold in your state)
- Brand name cigarettes made outside the U.S.
- Large amounts of cigarettes possessed by known criminals and members of organized crime groups

If you find cigarette packages without required state stamps—or with stamps from other states—they may be contraband.

According to federal law, cigarettes intended for sale outside the U.S. may not be imported back into the country and sold here without the manufacturer's consent.

Packaging can also indicate whether cigarettes may be contraband. Philip Morris USA prints its shipping cases with graphics that identify the brand and manufacturing date codes. Each case of legitimate cigarettes contains 60 cartons packed in two tiers of 30 cartons.

Several factors may indicate potential contraband packaging:

- A shipping case concealed inside an outer case
- Cigarettes in plain, unmarked cases
- Full cases containing fewer than 60 cartons
- Cartons over-wrapped with clear film
- Cartons and packs stored or wrapped in plastic bags are not likely to be genuine product that can be legally sold

**JACK HOLLERAN** Senior Vice President, Compliance and Brand Integrity, Philip Morris USA

(Editor's note: Philip Morris USA is the nations largest cigarette company, with nearly 50% of the retail cigarette market in the United States. The company's Marlboro brand, with nearly 40% of the domestic market, is the best-selling cigarette brand among adult smokers in the United States, as well as the largest selling cigarette brand in the world.

**"Oh to be in England now that
And whoever wakes in England sees,
some morning unaware,
That the lowest boughs and the
brushwood sheaf
I Round the elm tree hole are in tiny leaf,
While the chaffinch sings on the
orchard bough in England-now!"**
*Robert Browning*

# Battles Won, a War Still Lost

## New and Dangerous Trends in the Andean Drug Business

Looked at in one way, these are good times for America's drug warriors, at least with regard to cocaine. Traditionally, some 70% of the white powder has come from Colombia. The $3 billion in aid that the United States has spent there since 2000 under Plan Colombia has produced what American officials present as some spectacular numbers—especially since Álvaro Uribe became president two years later and allowed large-scale aerial eradication of drug crops.

At the last count by the United Nations, in 2003, land under coca in Colombia was down to 86,300 hectares (213,200 acres) from a peak of 163,300 hectares in 2000. In 2004, contractors working for the United States sprayed herbicide on 136,555 hectares of coca, a similar amount to the previous year. That points to a further decline in cocaine production last year, according to John Walters, who heads the United States Office of National *Drug Control* Policy (ONDCP).

In 2004, almost 150 tonnes of cocaine were seized in the country, a third more than in 2003, while 1,900 cocaine labs were destroyed, 40% more than in 2002. Mr Uribe has extradited 166 Colombians to face drug charges—and probably a life behind bars—in the United States. They include Gilberto Rodríguez Orejuela, who as head of the Cali drug mob ruled the trade a decade ago. American officials say that they have squeezed the drug revenues of the FARC guerrillas and their right-wing opponents, the AUC. "We're moving in one direction. The bad guys are losing and the people in Colombia are winning," says Mr Walters. Those who see it otherwise "want this thing to fail."

Yet to many people across and beyond Latin America, the Andean drug trade seems as effective and dangerous as ever. The most telling evidence is the price of cocaine. According to the Washington Office on Latin America,

an NGO, the ONDCP's own figures, released to Congress but not yet to the public, show that in the United States a gram of cocaine wholesaled for $38 in 2003, down from $48 in 2000 and from $100 in 1986, with no fall in purity. In Britain, cocaine is cheaper than ever: in 2003 it retailed for about £46 per gram ($75), down from £57 ten years ago, according to the Independent Drug Monitoring Unit, a consultancy. Prices have fallen even as world demand has risen: consumption is broadly flat in North America, according to the UN, but rising in Europe. It is rising, too, in Brazil, Mexico and Central America, mainly because smuggling gangs are being paid in product.

## An Evolving Trade

What is the explanation? Bigger-than-anticipated stocks along the supply chain mean that there is a lag between a fall in output and its effect on prices, say American officials. Just wait to see the effect of Plan Colombia, they say. But others argue that the headline figures for hectares sprayed do not tell the full story. An alternative explanation is that coca has spread to new areas, some undetected, and that yields and productivity are rising.

According to the UN, Plan Colombia produced a modest displacement of coca to other countries: by 2003, cultivation was up slightly in Bolivia but stable in Peru. Even so, land under coca in both these countries was far below its peak of a decade ago. Overall, the UN calculated that the total potential output of Andean cocaine was 655 tonnes in 2003—a big fall from a peak of 950 tonnes in 1996.

Yet in both Peru and Bolivia, the drug warriors now face troubling new trends. In Peru, the second-biggest producer, coca is spreading to new areas, such as San Gabán, close to the border with Bolivia, and Putumayo, across the river from Colombia. Between them, these may account for up to 10,000 hectares of new coca. Local-market prices for coca leaves are rising. In the distorted economics of an illegal business, that is a sure sign that repression is failing to restrict effective demand. In December 2004, the price of a kilo of coca leaves on the illegal market had risen to $5 from a low of 50 cents, according to the Peruvian government's anti-drug agency, DEVIDA. This will lure farmers into planting more coca, says Nils Ericsson, DEVIDA's director. At current prices, a hectare of coca yields an annual income of up to $7,500, compared with $600 from coffee or $1,000 from cocoa.

Peru's cocaine industry is vertically integrating. A decade ago, small aircraft ferried semi-processed coca paste for refining in Colombia. Now, Peru's output of refined cocaine is soaring. Last year, for the first time, police seized more powder than paste. They have destroyed more than 1,700 cocaine laboratories in the past two years. This switch to refining is being pushed by Mexican drug groups which, according to prosecutors, were helped by Vladimiro Montesinos, Peru's jailed former spy chief. For the Mexican gangs, buying finished cocaine is cheaper and involves less risk, says Fernando Rospigliosi, a former interior minister. Much of the refined product is now going straight to Mexico or Spain on cargo ships, concealed in Peru's booming legal exports. In November, 700 kilos were found stuffed inside frozen giant squid. Other shipments have been found in planks of wood, carrots, guano and even votive candles.

Peru's government says it wants to eradicate all but 10,000 hectares of coca, which are reserved for traditional use, by the end of 2006. But there are signs that the drug trade is once again spreading its trail of corruption to the security forces. According to testimony from some of those arrested for the shipment of stuffed squid, the deal was planned at a club for army officers and the drugs packed at a naval base near the northern port of Paita.

Peru does not allow chemical spraying of coca. Instead, it has mixed manual eradication with schemes to encourage farmers to pull the crop up and plant legal alternatives. This approach suffered a setback last year when angry coca farmers expelled UN agronomists from Monzón, one of the main coca valleys. The United States' draft budget for next year includes a cut of $18m in aid for "alternative development" in Peru. That puts more onus on forcible eradication—a challenge for a weak and unpopular government.

## A Setback in Bolivia

Political fragility has complicated the drug war in Bolivia, too. An aggressive American-backed campaign of manual eradication in the late 1990s wiped out most of the country's illegal coca. But this contributed to a slowdown in the economy and discontent, which culminated in the overthrow of Gonzalo Sánchez de Lozada, a pro-American president, in 2003. Since then, the United States has adopted a softer approach. In October, Carlos Mesa, the new president, reached an agreement with the coca growers of the Chapare, allowing them for the first time to keep 3,200 hectares of coca legally in return for eradicating the rest. Governments have refused to allow eradication in the Yungas, the main area of legal cultivation, where illegal coca is reported to be expanding.

Curiously, Ecuador has never grown much coca. But it has become a transport and service hub for the drug industry. Since it adopted the dollar as its currency in 2000, Ecuador has become even more convenient for laundering drug profits (though most of this still happens in the United States and Europe). Around a third of Colombia's cocaine is now reckoned to be exported through Ecuador, mainly through the port of Guayaquil. Seizures of drugs in outbound shipping from Ecuador's ports fell to just 4 tonnes last year, from 12 tonnes in 2003. Nobody believes that is because less is being exported.

Mexico, too, is feeling the ripple effect of the drug trade as never before. A surge in drug-related violence along the northern border with the United States has included the kidnapping and killing of several American citizens. That prompted America's State Department last month to issue a travel warning. "Exaggerated," said Mexico's government, which recently sent several hundred troops to the border state of Tamaulipas to try to restore confidence.

Behind the violence lie turf wars. A decade or so ago, three or four big Mexican smuggling syndicates became equal partners with Colombians in the supply route to the western United States. The government of President Vicente Fox has made much bigger efforts than its predecessors to tackle these syndicates, clean up the security forces and collaborate with American drug fighters. Several notorious drug barons, such as Benjamín Arellano Félix, have been jailed.

One consequence is to transfer the drug business and its feuds to prisons. "Lawyers" relay orders from jailed bosses.

In January, the army took over a maximum-security prison near Mexico City after the murder of the brother of a fugitive drug boss sparked a riot. The government has since sent several inmates to other jails. Six warders were murdered at another prison, this one at Matamoros in Tamaulipas.

As in Colombia a decade ago, the weakening of the big syndicates in Mexico has merely resulted in them being replaced by scores of smaller, nimbler outfits, which are harder to detect. As always, the drug business appears to be one step ahead of its pursuers.

# The War on Thugs

**They were the jump-out boys—masked, black-clad narcs who busted dealers and jailed junkies all over rural Texas. Then came Tulia. Now the state's drug task forces are fighting for their own survival. And that's a good thing.**

NATE BLAKESLEE

At the annual convention of Texas narcotics officers, held this year in El Paso in August, narcs in search of continuing education were offered seminars with titles like "Hidden Compartments" "Body Language," "Risk Management" and—new for this year—"Narcotraffickers and the Spiritual World," in which a retired El Paso cop explained how to identify the image of Jesús Malverde, the patron saint of drug dealers, during traffic stops. Next year, conference organizers may have to add another seminar: "How to Find a New Career." Over the past four years, close to a quarter of all narcs in Texas have been laid off, victims of a severe contraction in the state's biggest anti-drug bureaucracy. Even more cuts may be on the way, depending on the outcome of a budget fight currently going on in Washington, D.C. The writing on the wall is easy to read: After almost two decades of lavish funding, the drug war is no longer a growth industry in Texas.

More than one hundred people are sent to prison in Texas every day, and one in three is convicted of a drug crime. Until recently, chances were good that the bust was made by a narc from one of the state's multijurisdictional drug task forces, or DTFs, which handle the lion's share of drug enforcement in rural and suburban areas. The "jump-out boys," as they are commonly called, are known for their black tactical uniforms and the masks they sometimes wear during raids. They specialize in "buy busts," undercover purchases of modest amounts of drugs—usually cocaine or marijuana—from street-level dealers. The money for the task forces comes from a U.S. Department of Justice program known as the Byrne grant, which was hatched in the late eighties, at the height of the drug war. Over a ten-year period, the DTFs grew into Texas's largest narcotics enforcement effort, accounting for roughly 12,000 arrests every year.

Then came Tulia. In 1999 a Byrne grant-funded narc named Tom Coleman set up dozens of people, most of them black, in the small Panhandle town, allegedly for dealing cocaine. In the four-year legal battle that followed, Coleman was exposed as a liar, and Governor Rick Perry eventually pardoned almost all of his victims. The scandal put the task force program—and the diminished standards of drug enforcement that it had come

to represent—in the national spotlight. Coleman had a terrible track record in law enforcement and no previous narcotics experience, yet he was allowed to do undercover work with virtually no controls—no wire, no corroborating officer, no video. But what was most embarrassing about Tulia was how common such irresponsibility and amateurism had become among task forces across the state.

The Tulia fiasco could not have come at a worse time for narcs. After September 11, the Byrne grant was one of many funding streams targeted by a Bush administration looking to free up resources for homeland security. Drastic cuts in Washington in 2003 and 2004, coupled with fears of liability for Tulia-like scandals, have led to a rapid decline in the number of task forces nationwide. Nowhere has this trend been more pronounced than in Texas. By June 2005, more than half of the state's task forces had dissolved. This year the president has once again proposed cutting the program's funding, and the mood among narcs nationwide is grim. "There's not going to be anybody out there in rural or suburban America to work that stuff," said Ron Brooks, of the National Narcotics Officers' Associations' Coalition. "We'll go back to 1978."

Critics of the Byrne program say the cuts are long overdue. In 2002 the Heritage Foundation, a conservative Washington think tank, published a paper on the Byrne grant noting that it had made no discernible impact on drug crime. In the Texas Legislature, the main detractors of the program have been an unlikely pair: Senator Juan "Chuy" Hinojosa, a Democrat from the Valley with strong law-and-order credentials, and Representative Terry Keel, a Republican from the Austin suburbs. Keel, a former sheriff who once served on the board of a drug task force, has advocated ending the program in Texas altogether. It has been an uphill fight. "Let me tell you what the political reality is," he said. "You've got a whole bunch of these brother-in-law types out there running around with ninja suits and sunglasses, cars and guns and cash. That is a valued law enforcement lifestyle for those persons, and there are lots of them. And they tend to turn up the political heat on their local elected officials, including legislators, who they lead to believe that the sky is gonna fall if their job is eliminated."

Launched in 1988, the Edward Byrne Memorial State and Local Law Enforcement Assistance Program was named in memory of a New York City police officer shot dead by drug dealers that year, when crack and inner-city violence was the hottest story in America. In a ceremony shortly after Byrne's death, Vice President George H. W. Bush, on a visit to New York in the last stages of his bitter presidential race against Massachusetts governor Michael Dukakis, held the dead officer's badge in his hand and challenged Dukakis to come out in support of a bill before Congress that would allow the death penalty for high-volume drug dealers. For months Bush had been hammering away at his opponent for being soft on crime, and the Democrats, who then controlled Congress, took up the gauntlet. The result was the Anti-Drug Abuse Act of 1988, which was passed into law just before the election with shamefully little debate. "It is the declared policy of the United States to create a drug free America by 1995," the preamble read. As preposterous as that language sounds in retrospect, by creating the Byrne grant, the bill did in fact have a drastic impact on the lives of hundreds of thousands of Americans, though not in the way most members of Congress had envisioned.

By the late nineties, the Byrne task force program had been eclipsed by better-funded and more-publicized endeavors, such as crop eradication in Colombia and interdiction along the nation's borders. Yet the Byrne money never stopped flowing and the task forces quietly flourished. There were more than eight hundred at the beginning of 2003, employing between 5,000 to 7,000 narcs. (The Justice Department does not know the exact number.) For comparison, the U.S. Drug Enforcement Administration, the nation's premier anti-drug bureaucracy, has about 5,300 agents. In a relatively short span of time, the Byrne grant, an ambitious experiment conceived in the heat of a political campaign, created an entirely new tier of law enforcement nationwide.

In Texas, drug enforcement outside the major cities was traditionally handled by the Department of Public Safety, which has maintained a narcotics unit since the early seventies. But DPS Narcotics was bypassed entirely when Texas established its first Byrne grant task forces, which were administered by the Texas Narcotics Control Program (TNCP), a new entity created inside the governor's office. This was no accident: Byrne money was seen from the beginning as a form of pork, a valuable way for the governor to seek favor with rural and suburban voters. By federal standards, the amount of money involved was modest; in the late nineties roughly $500 million per year in Byrne money was allocated nationwide, a little less than half of which was spent on drug task forces. (Though Texas spends almost all of its Byrne funding on task forces, the money can also be used for a variety of other law enforcement purposes, including drug treatment programs.) In cash-strapped rural Texas, the Byrne money was a gold mine. Many rural sheriff's deputies and police officers earn less than $20,000 per year and are forced to moonlight at second jobs. Some even qualify for food stamps. Turnover is very high.

The governor's office was flooded with applications for the new source of funds. Ambitious sheriffs and district attorneys vied with one another to recruit neighboring counties into their new outfits. The program required the task forces to come up with matching funds equal to one quarter of the total budget; federal grant money, passed through the TNCP, covered the remaining three quarters. The more counties a task force project director could sign up, the more sources of matching funds he had access to and the bigger the potential grant from Washington. The program received a huge boost in 1989, when the Texas Legislature allowed law enforcement agencies to keep cash and other assets they recovered in the course of their operations, providing an alternate source of revenue for the all-important cash match. By the late nineties, almost every county in the state was in a task force, and task force narcs outnumbered DPS narcs almost three to one.

The jump-out boys were not like state police narcs. The DPS has always prided itself on its professionalism. Applicants must pass written, physical, and psychological tests, and officers are relatively well compensated. An assignment to the narcotics division is a highly sought-after promotion and carries a certain prestige. For task force agents, by contrast, the trip from patrol deputy in a one-stoplight town to undercover narc might involve a single two-week training course. As a result, the standards of narcotics enforcement across the state gradually eroded.

"These narcotics task forces are the antithesis of every good law enforcement management technique," said Representative Keel. "The officers in the narcotics task forces do not have a chain of command that watches them carefully. They are left undercover and loosely supervised in some cases. They have unbridled discretion often on their interdiction decisions, and they deal with large amounts of cash. Now all of that is a formula for disaster."

Because the task forces often operate in rural areas, far from major media markets, stories of malfeasance tend to stay beneath the radar. Read enough clips from small-town papers, however, and a pattern begins to emerge. Rogue officers, missing drugs, stolen cash, fabricated cases, failed drug tests: Every small town in Texas seems to have a story of corruption involving the jump-out boys. "People don't understand," said Barbara Markham, a task-force-narc-turned-whistle-blower, in the wake of the Tulia scandal. "Everybody's talking about Tom Coleman: Well, there are whole task forces of Tom Colemans out there."

In April 2001 the Texas chapter of the American Civil Liberties Union announced that it had found "another Tulia" in the Central Texas town of Hearne, where dozens of indictments were dismissed after a task force snitch admitted to fabricating cases. Attorneys from the national ACLU's Drug Policy Litigation Project filed suit, making Hearne, and Byrne grant-funded task forces generally, one of their top priorities. As in Tulia, the defendants in Hearne were almost all black, and the cases were mostly for delivery of cocaine. The informant was a young black man with a history of drug abuse and mental illness. The local district attorney, who was also the head of the task force, was warned by his own polygraph examiner that the man was dishonest. But he pressed ahead with the prosecutions, until the snitch's poor performance on the stand in the first case resulted in a mistrial. The snitch later claimed that task force officers coerced him into fabricating cases. Before the scandal broke, the district attorney abruptly resigned from the task force; later, the commander and several agents left as well. The eventual settlement of the ACLU suit in Hearne this past May, like the multimillion-dollar settlement in Tulia the year before, set the precedent that all counties and municipalities belonging to a task force would be financially liable for misdeeds perpetrated by task force officers, regardless of where they took place and who actually hired the officer in question. That got the attention of rural commissioner's courts—and their insurance carriers—across Texas, hastening the statewide exodus from the program.

In Texas, as in many states, the scramble for Byrne money is a competitive, zero-sum game: One task force's funding increase is another's loss. The TNCP developed a complex system of rating the relative success of the various outfits, weighing such indicators as number of cases opened, buys made, suspects arrested, drugs confiscated, and assets forfeited. In 1999, for example, thanks in large measure to Coleman's bust in Tulia, the Panhandle Regional Narcotics Trafficking Task Force was the top-ranked task force in the state.

## "Law enforcement is about money," said defense attorney Ed Lieck. "Anybody who tells you different is lying."

This statistics-driven model of law enforcement has meant a dramatic increase in drug arrests. Not surprisingly, the growth of the task force system in Texas has also coincided with a massive acceleration in prison construction. In what amounted to the largest public-works project in modern Texas history, the state more than tripled its prison capacity—from 40,000 to 150,000 beds—in just ten years. (Texas now has more inmates than California, even though Texas has 40 percent fewer people. Only Louisiana and Mississippi incarcerate a greater percentage of their populations.) There were many factors driving this expansion, including stricter parole guidelines and overcrowding lawsuits, but the task forces were central by any reckoning. According to civil rights advocates like Texas ACLU executive director Will Harrell, the emphasis on statistics has overshadowed more-pressing questions. "Nobody is looking at quality control. We're simply looking for quantity," he said. "That's what the drug war is about: How many people have you arrested and locked up today?"

A focus on street-level buys more often than not means targeting black suspects, which helps explain a couple of striking statistics in Texas. African Americans account for 12 percent of the state's population but 40 percent of prison inmates. On any given day, roughly one in three black men between the ages of 20 and 29 is in jail, on probation, or on parole. "It's just too easy.

They never go up the chain," defense attorney Walter Fontenot, of Liberty, a small town in East Texas, said of the task forces. "If you dig into this stuff, you will find that most people are black, most people are poor, and they just cop out and get probation. A couple of years later the probation is revoked, because they go back to the same thing because that's all they know," he said. "It's all about numbers," said Anahuac defense attorney Ed Lieck, who has battled his local drug task force for years. "More numbers means more money."

In 2002 Governor Perry announced that he was assigning supervision of the state's Byrne grant drug task forces to the DPS. The transition has been a bumpy one. When DPS Narcotics captains made preliminary visits to their new charges, they discovered many of them in disarray. At one outfit in the San Antonio area, for example, evidence was missing from 20 percent of the unit's case files, forfeiture cash was not properly accounted for, and commanders had "little contact or supervisory control" over some of their agents.

The DPS crafted new rules for the task forces, bringing them more in line with established policy for state police narcs. The use of masks in the serving of arrest warrants was banned, and procedures for control of evidence and use of confidential informants were tightened. Some task forces refused to accept the new command structure and chose to shut down rather than change their ways. A few announced that they would forgo Byrne grant money to avoid DPS oversight. These "renegade" operations subsisted for a couple of years on their own asset forfeiture accounts—some had accumulated huge hoards prior to the takeover—until this summer, when the Legislature finally forced them to comply with DPS supervision or fold altogether.

The task force program has been on the ropes before; President Bill Clinton tried unsuccessfully to pare the Byrne grant down in 1994. But this time might be different. It has always been politically easier for Republicans to cut law enforcement programs, and violent crime is now at a thirty-year low. Last February, in testimony before Congress, even national drug czar John Walters said it was time to focus attention higher up the supply chain. "Otherwise, you are chasing primarily small people," he said, "putting them in jail, year after year, generation after generation."

For those who have become addicted to the annual grants, however, keeping the Byrne program alive has become an end in itself. Sensing the shift in the prevailing winds in Washington, task force directors have lately begun including "homeland security goals" in their grant applications, struggling to make a connection between combating drug abuse and fighting Al Qaeda. (The Waco-area task force, for its part, announced that it would be providing some unsolicited extra security for the Bush ranch in Crawford.)

"I've been doing this for ten years, and law enforcement is about money," said Lieck, the Anahuac defense attorney. "Anybody who tells you different is lying." After seventeen years, some veterans of the task force experiment in Texas are not shy about this fact. A former prosecutor affiliated with a Denton-based task force freely admitted that he offered lighter sentences to suspects who agreed not to fight forfeiture of cars, cash, or other items of value confiscated during drug investigations. "If we don't have enough money by the end of the grant year, we're all out of a job," he told the *Dallas Morning News* in 2003. His candid remarks earned the ire of the task force's director, Denton County sheriff Weldon Lucas. There's no need to be embarrassed now, however: Late last year, the task force folded.

# Arresting the Drug Laws

DAVID SILVERBERG

In March, Howard Woolridge set out on horseback from Los Angeles to New York City wearing a T-shirt blaring the capitalized declaration: "COPS SAY LEGALIZE POT, ASK ME WHY" The former Michigan police officer, who plans to reach New York in November, is a member of Law Enforcement Against Prohibition (LEAP), a group that wants to change our country's drug laws.

Peter Christ and Jack Cole, both former cops, founded the three-year-old LEAP with the assistance of a $50,000 grant from the Marijuana Policy Project. More than 2,000 members, including prison wardens, judges, and mayors, have since joined the organization. Some believe in drug decriminalization, others in full-out legalization, but their collective mandate is to highlight the failure of the current drug policy.

Cole wants to remove the profit motive from the equation by legalizing drugs and having them supplied by the government. "Organized criminals and world terrorists would be monetarily crippled for many years to come," Cole says.

Bob Owens, a former police chief in Oxnard, California, regards soft drugs such as marijuana "as too unimportant to use manpower" on. He calls the war on drugs "a strawman that can distract people and stir the hysteria that accompanies it."

But Owens admits LEAP won't move mountains. Yet, "The purpose of LEAP is to create more of an attitude change than to potentially change legislation," he says.

California Superior Court Judge James Gray, author of *Why Our Drug Laws Have Failed and What We Can Do About It: A Judicial Indictment of the War on Drugs,* wants to decriminalize marijuana. That would generate $2 billion annually in tax revenues that could be spent on education and drug treatment, he says. The government should regulate the quality of marijuana, he says, so tokers would know their weed won't be laced with poisons.

"Would it result in more marijuana usage?" Cray asks himself. "Yes, at least for six months, but then rates would be more like Holland's." That country's reported lifetime cannabis use is at 17 percent, according to a 2001 survey from the European Monitoring Centre for Drugs and Drug Addiction. In the United States, the 2003 National Survey on Drug Use and Health found that 40 percent of respondents reported using marijuana once in their lifetimes.

Prison wardens are usually stereotyped as drawing the hardest line. But don't say that to Richard Watkins, former warden of the Holliday Unit in Huntsville, Texas. "What's happening now is not working," says Watkins, who retired in February. "I think the war on drugs is responsible for the massive increase of prisoners in Texas."

He goes on to wonder why so many one-time drug users are imprisoned for crimes that didn't harm a third party. "What the public doesn't realize is that when you take a breadwinner out of the family and incarcerate him, it has a ripple effect," he says. "There is nothing but negative about jailing people."

After his lone-ranger travels, Woolridge plans on heading to Washington, where he hopes to become a Congressional lobbyist for LEAP.

Marijuana will be the first issue he tackles. "Eighty percent of Americans say legalize and tax it today," Woolridge says. "We're losing focus on public safety as law enforcement chases Willie Nelson and Willie Nelson's supplier." When Woolridge discusses this issue with rational Americans in any state, he says he soon hears three satisfying words: "That makes sense."

**DAVID SILVERBERG** is a freelance writer based in Toronto, Canada, who contributes to High Times, Seed Magazine, Digital Journal, Saturday Night, and Pound Magazine.

# State's Evidence

WILL BAUDE

Yesterday the Supreme Court issued its long-awaited decision in *Gonzalez v. Raich*, upholding a federal ban on marijuana possession despite California's efforts to legalize medical marijuana. The plaintiffs, Angel Raich and Diane Monson, were two seriously ill women in California who used marijuana on the advice of their doctors, pursuant to a 1996 California law, the Compassionate Use Act. After officials decided that their conduct was legal under local law, they were targeted by federal agents for violating the nationwide Controlled Substances Act. Raich and Monson argued that the federal government had exceeded its constitutional authority under the Commerce Clause and therefore could not preempt California's medical marijuana law; but a majority of the Supreme Court ruled against them, while Justices O'Connor, Rehnquist, and Thomas dissented. The Court's decision exposes the major flaw in its recent Commerce Clause jurisprudence: an unwillingness to take states seriously and an unwillingness to admit that the constitutionality of a federal law sometimes depends on what laws states adopt.

Between 1937—when Roosevelt won Supreme Court support for the New Deal—and 1995, the Court was very reluctant to enforce general limits on congressional power. The recent line of Commerce Clause cases began in *United States v. Lopez,* when the conservative majority of the Court struck down a ban on handguns near schools because the ban threatened to obliterate "the distinction between what is truly national and what is truly local." In *United States v. Morrison* in 2000, the same five justices struck down the controversial Violence Against Women Act, which created a federal rape law, and held that once again Congress was exceeding its powers to reach areas traditionally governed by the states. Advocates of federalism and decentralization hoped that *Raich* would be the next case in that line. But yesterday six members of the Court voted to uphold the federal law.

All of the justices on the court agreed (or professed to agree) that Congress can only enact a law if it is "necessary and proper" to one of its other powers enumerated in the Constitution, like the power to "regulate commerce among the several states." They all also conceded that Congress can clearly regulate interstate marijuana trade. The argument in *Raich* therefore should have been over whether it really is "necessary and proper" for the federal government to preempt California's medical marijuana laws—in other words, is there some flaw in California's regulation that jeopardizes the federal prohibition of the interstate drug trade? Whether the federal government has constitutional power to regulate herbs that are never bought, never sold, and never leave California, depends—has to depend—to some extent on what the regulatory scheme would look like without federal intervention. But the Court emphatically rejected this notion, suggesting that it "would turn the Supremacy Clause on its head" to let state laws have any effect on the scope of federal power; and the majority offered barely any analysis along these lines, writing instead that Congress was entitled to preempt California's scheme as a matter of "common sense."

As an empirical matter, it is far from common sense that California's laws would undermine the enforcement of drug laws elsewhere. The state regulatory scheme would have required all medical marijuana users to carry identification cards with security measures and the ability to be checked against a statewide database, required a doctor's approval to get marijuana, imposed sanctions on erroneous recommendations, and levied further criminal penalties on those who diverted their medical marijuana to the black market. This may explain why three strongly anti-marijuana states nonetheless wrote a brief to the Court arguing that the federal ban on intrastate medical marijuana was unnecessary and that "the States are ready, willing, and able to police and prosecute local drug crimes." There was no evidence or argument that California would enforce its regulations or restrictions in bad faith.

Indeed, the Court's invocation of the Supremacy Clause of the Constitution—which says that federal laws that are not unconstitutional are "the supreme law of the land"—is misleading. Nobody doubts that when a valid federal law and a valid state law conflict, the federal law prevails. But to determine whether the federal law is valid in the first place, state law is relevant. The federal law is valid only if it is necessary for the interstate drug laws to work, so one has to look at whether the interstate drug laws would work if California's scheme were in place. It is possible, of course, to imagine that having a haven to grow medical marijuana would make it much easier to smuggle marijuana into the interstate market. But given that California continues to police unlawful marijuana production (seizing *a record-setting* $2.5 billion worth of plants last year), and given the program's relatively modest scope, the state law should have been entitled to more than being summarily dismissed.

The Court is probably reluctant to give the presence of state laws any weight in its constitutional analysis at all because it is difficult to establish exactly when a state law has failed at keeping intrastate activity separate, and because different approaches in different states could make a lot more work for the Court and for Congress. It is far easier to leave Congress to be the judge of its own powers, an approach that is sometimes called "process federalism." But the Court's opinions shape that process, and help determine what concerns Congress must address when it wishes to regulate. As University of Texas law professor Ernest Young has pointed out, because the Controlled Substances Act was enacted years before California's medical marijuana initiative, Congress never passed judgment on California's regulation scheme one way or the other; only the lawyers in the Justice Department did. The Court could at least make sure that Congress preempts state regulations only when it actually examines them and decides they do not work. As it stands, the only democratic body to even make a judgment about California's regulations was California itself. The Court does not have to second-guess Congress in every case so long as it retains the possibility of meaningful judicial review.

This problem is not unique to the Court's decision in this case. Since 1995, the Court has struck down a few federal statutes that it saw as outliers but without serious investigation of whether the state had managed to create a class of activity with minimal interstate spillovers. This Congress-centered view has meant that the Court is unable to create a Commerce Clause jurisprudence that works—one that would spur a dialogue between state and federal governments.

To be sure, states sometimes fail to live up to their constitutional obligations, and sometimes lax enforcement or misguided regulation can cause one state's laws to jeopardize a federal regulatory scheme. But federal courts analyze constitutional and legal claims against state and local governments all the time, and by providing some meaningful review, they both give governments an incentive to behave well and help sustain the balance of power between local and national governments. When it is actually necessary for the federal government to take over local regulations to solve a national problem, nobody doubts that it can. But the fact that the federal government's power is supreme does not make it unlimited or unreviewable; and it should not mean that the states have no say in the matter either.

---

**WILL BAUDE** is a student at Yale Law School.

# UNIT 7

# Prevention, Treatment, and Education

## Unit Selection

## Key Points to Consider

- What three goals exist as the primary guidelines for federal drug policy?

- Can you impact the drug problem by targeting demand and not supply? Why?

- Explain the concept of 'denial' and explain why it is a critical obstacle to providing successful drug treatment.

- What is the association between drug abuse and mental illness?

- Should it be the job of correctional systems to be involved in treating drug dependency of prisoners? Why?

## Student Website
www.mhcls.com/online

## Internet References
Further information regarding these websites may be found in this book's preface or online.

**American Council for Drug Education**
   *www.acde.org*
**D.A.R.E.**
   *http://www.dare-america.com*
**Drug Watch International**
   *http://www.drugwatch.org*
**Join Together**
   *www.jointogether.org*
**Marijuana Policy Project**
   *http://www.mpp.org*
**National Institute on Drug Abuse**
   *http://www.nida.nih.gov/Infofacts/TreatMeth.html*
**Office of National Drug Control Policy (ONDCP)**
   *http://www.whitehousedrugpolicy.gov*
**Hazelden**
   *http://www.hazelden.org*
**KCI (Koch Crime Institute) The Anit-Meth Site**
   *http://www.kci.org/meth_info/faq_meth.htm*
**The Drug Reform Coordination Network (DRC)**
   *http://www.drcnet.org*
**United Nations International Drug Control Program (UNDCP)**
   *http://www.undcp.org*

There are no magic bullets for preventing drug abuse and treating drug-dependent persons. Currently, 22.2 million American are classified as drug dependent on illicit drugs and/or alcohol. Of those, 15.4 million abuse alcohol, and 6.8 million were dependent on or abused illicit drugs. Of those who abused illicit drugs, 4.1 million were dependent on marijuana followed by those dependent on cocaine. Males continue to be twice as likely to be classified as drug dependent as females. Research continues to establish and strengthen the role of treatment as a critical component in the fight against drug abuse. Some drug treatment programs have been shown to dramatically reduce the costs associated with high-risk populations of users. For example, recidivism associated with drug related criminal justice populations has been shown to decrease 50 percent after treatment. Treatment is a critical component in the fight against drug abuse but it is not a panacea. Society cannot "treat" drug abuse

away just as it cannot "arrest" it away. It is estimated that there are over 23 million persons in the United States today who are in need of drug treatment.

Drug prevention and treatment philosophies subscribe to a multitude of modalities. Everything seems to work a little and nothing seems to work completely. The articles in this unit illustrate the diversity of methods utilized in prevention and treatment programs. Special emphasis is given to treating the drug problems of those who are under the supervision of the criminal justice system. All education, prevention, and treatment programs compete for local, state, and federal resources.

*Education:* One critical component of drug education is the ability to rapidly translate research findings into practice, and today's drug policy continues to emphasize this in its overall budget allocations. Funding for educational research and grants is generally strong with the trend being toward administering funds to local communities and schools to fund local proposals. For example, in 2007, $52 million dollars were made available to schools for research based assistance for drug prevention and school safety programs. Another is the $120 million National Youth Media Campaign designed to help coach parents in processes of early recognition and intervention. Parenting is one primary emphasis in current federal drug policy. Other significant continuing research efforts support important education, prevention, and treatment programs such as The National Prevention Research Initiative; Interventions and Treatment for Current Drug Users Who Are Not Yet Addicted; the National Drug Abuse Treatment Clinical Trial Network; and Research Based Treatment Approaches for Drug Abusing Criminal Offenders. In 2007 federal research related grants totaling almost $100 million were made available to local and state school jurisdictions.

*Prevention:* A primary strategy of drug prevention programs is to prevent and/or delay initial drug use. A secondary strategy is to discourage use by persons minimally involved with drugs. Both strategies include (1) educating users and potential users, (2) teaching adolescents how to resist peer pressure, (3) addressing problems associated with drug abuse such as teen pregnancy, failure in school, and lawbreaking, (4) creating community support and involvement for prevention activities, and (5) involving parents in deterring drug use by children.

Prevention and education programs are administered through a variety of mechanisms, typically amidst controversy relative to what works best. Schools have been an important delivery apparatus. In 2007, the Substance Abuse and Mental Health Administration announced that drug use by youth was down 19 percent since 2002. Funding for school prevention programs is an important emphasis within the efforts to reduce the demand for drugs. Subsequently, an increase of $4.7 million in federal money was dedicated to expanding the number of high school programs that implement student drug testing. Drug testing in high schools has produced a positive deterrent despite its controversy and is promoted as a positive way to reinforce actions of parents to educate and deter their children from use. The testing program provides for subsequent assessment, referral, and intervention process in situations where parents and educators deem it necessary.

Additionally, in 2007 $72 million in grant funds have continued to support the federal Drug-Free Communities Program which provides funds at the community level to anti-drug coalitions working to prevent substance abuse among young people and in local neighborhoods. There are currently 709 local community coalitions working under this program nationwide. Also there are community-based drug prevention programs sponsored by civic organizations, church groups, and private corporations. All programs pursue funding through public grants and private endowments. Federal grants to local, state, and private programs are critical components to program solvency.

The multifaceted nature of prevention programs makes them difficult to assess categorically. School programs that emphasize the development of skills to resist social and peer pressure produce generally varying degrees of positive results. Research continues to make more evident the need to focus prevention programs with specific populations in mind.

*Treatment:* Like prevention programs, drug treatment programs enlist a variety of methods to treat persons dependent upon legal and illegal drugs. There is no single-pronged approach to treatment for drug abuse. Treatment modality may differ radically from one user to the next. The user's background, physical and mental health, personal motivation, and support structure all have serious implications for treatment type. Lumping together the diverse needs of chemically dependent persons for purposes of applying a generic treatment process does not work. In addition, most persons needing and seeking treatment have problems with more than one drug—polydrug use. Current research also correlates drug use with serious mental illness (SMI). Current research by the federal Substance Abuse and Mental Health Services Admin-

istration (SAMHSA) reports that adults with a drug problem are three times more likely to suffer from a serious mental illness. The existing harmful drug use and mental health nexus is exacerbated by the fact that using certain powerful drugs such as methamphetamine push otherwise functioning persons into the dysfunctional realm of mental illness. Subsequently in 2007, one new federally funded treatment program dedicated $41.6 million dollars to enhance research on methamphetamine addiction. Methamphetamine's mechanism of action, behavioral and physical effects, and prevention and intervention processes are being examined in research grants and contracts, and clinical trials in geographical areas where methamphetamine abuse is highest. This research, in collaboration with the National Synthetic Drug Action Plan hopes to initiate state and local interventions related to the latest research and science.

Although treatment programs differ in methods, most provide a combination of key services. These include drug counseling, drug education, pharmacological therapy, psychotherapy, relapse prevention, and assistance with support structures. Treatment programs may be outpatient-oriented or residential in nature. Residential programs require patients to live at the facility for a prescribed period of time. These residential programs, often described as therapeutic communities, emphasize the development of social, vocational, and educational skills.

The current trend is to increase the availability of treatment programs. One key component of federal drug strategy is to continue to fund the Access to Recovery treatment initiative which began in 2004. This program funds drug treatment for individuals otherwise unable to obtain it through a voucher system. In 2007, over $98 million was committed to this program, which allows dependent persons to personally choose care providers, including faith-based care providers. It is hoped that this program will encourage states to provide a wider array of treatment and recovery options. As one example, the State of Missouri has transformed all public drug treatment within the state to an 'Access to Recovery-Like' program in which involved persons choose their providers and pay with state vouchers. It is hoped that this and similar programs will allow a more flexible delivery of services that will target large populations of dependent persons not reached through other treatment efforts.

# How to Quit the Cure

RAINA KELLEY

Two years ago, Kimberly Koehlinger of Ft. Wayne, Ind., quit the Prozac she'd been taking for 15 years to treat anxiety and depression. She hated side effects like night sweats and insomnia. So when her doctor told her she could stop, she weaned herself off over two to three weeks. But the withdrawal symptoms, according to Koehlinger, were brutal. "You're full of rage, you're delirious, you're dizzy," she says.

Millions of Americans (as many as one in 10 adults by some estimates) take antidepressants for reasons that range from social anxiety to severe depression. The vast majority of these antidepressants are SSRIs, or selective serotonin reuptake inhibitors, including Prozac, Paxil, Lexapro and Zoloft. But many people who are prescribed these drugs won't need them forever. Some will navigate a difficult situation in their lives and feel better. Others will seek alternate treatment because of the common side effects of SSRIs, such as sexual dysfunction and weight gain.

But getting off this class of antidepressants can be tricky. Withdrawal symptoms can range from the bewildering (vivid dreaming) to the debilitating (dizziness, diarrhea) to the life-threatening (suicidal thoughts). And while most people will not suffer as badly as Koehlinger did, as many as 50 percent of the people who stop using antidepressants will have some withdrawal symptoms. Manufacturers of the major drug brands acknowledge that the drugs can have withdrawal symptoms, but say in most cases they are mild.

They're widespread enough, however, that an active online community has sprung up offering advice to people who want to quit SSRIs. Paxilprogress.org, a Web site offering advice on how to manage withdrawal from all major SSRIs, gets about 2 million hits a month, according to founder Darcy Baston.

If you are trying to stop, here are some tips for minimizing your discomfort:

**Talk to your doctor.** No one should adjust his meds on his own. Just because you feel better doesn't mean your depression is gone for good. Remission from depression isn't just a reduction of symptoms, it means a wholehearted return to your normal activities.

**Don't quit cold turkey.** Drugmakers recommend tapering off SSRIs (and always under a doctor's care). The rules for tapering vary depending on the dose and drug you're taking. (If you're taking Prozac, you can find information about tapering at Prozac.com.) But your doctor will probably suggest cutting your dose by 25 to 50 percent at first. If you tolerate this reduction for two or four weeks, ask your doctor if you can reduce further. If you begin to experience unbearable withdrawal symptoms, talk to your physician about temporarily upping your dose a bit, says Nada Stotland, vice president of the American Psychiatric Association.

## No one should adjust his meds on his own.

**Look out for relapse.** Withdrawal symptoms appear shortly after anti-depressants are stopped; depression develops slowly, over months. Keep a list in your mind of what your depression felt like and make a resolution to go to your doctor if you feel it's returning.

Dr. Matthew Rudorfer, from the National Institute of Mental Health (www.nimh.nih.gov), has successfully helped many of his patients to stop taking SSRIs. And though they often experience withdrawal symptoms, he uses small, incremental changes in dosage to ease the transition. And he's quick to add that the risk of not treating depression is far greater than the risk of potential adverse effects. These pills can help you break out of the depression trap, but you don't have to feel trapped by them, either.

With Karen Springen

# Drug Treatment and Reentry for Incarcerated Women

Doris Wells and Laurie Bright

For many years, corrections officials applied the same drug addiction treatment programs to women as they did to men. During the past several years, the number of women inmates has increased (and continues to increase at a faster rate than that of men).[1] Research now indicates that many female inmates and parolees have physical, emotional and social needs that are different from men and thus may require different treatment programs. For example, women tend to have stronger attachments to their children (thus more separation anxiety), more childcare responsibilities and parenting issues, and have histories of sexual and physical abuse more often than men.

Two recent National Institute of Justice studies of drug addiction treatment and rehabilitation programs for female inmates, KEY/CREST[2] and Forever Free,[3] found that a much higher percentage of participants in these two programs remained drug-free and arrest-free at three- and one-year follow-up periods, respectively, than the comparison groups. Results from both studies show that treatment programs that provide aftercare, and recognize and address issues unique to female inmates can help to reduce recidivism.

## KEY/CREST in Delaware

KEY is a women-only residential therapeutic community drug rehabilitation program at Baylor's Women's Correctional Institute in New Castle, Del. CREST is a coed work release therapeutic community (TC) at Sussex Correctional Institute in Georgetown, Del. Prison TCs separate participants from the general prison population and place them in an environment where they can develop positive behavioral, mental and emotional changes that can help them reduce or stop drug use.

Prior research has demonstrated that the therapeutic community model, which was originally designed for men, can be effective for treating women if redesigned in a more female-oriented format that, for example, helps build trust and is less confrontational.[4] Women respond to a program that emphasizes repairing their abusive relationships with men and teaches them how to build positive ones, shows them how to deal with family relationships and child care responsibilities,

and helps them sort out their histories of sexual and/or physical abuse and other personal issues, including mental-health problems such as depression.

The process evaluation of KEY/CREST showed that the environment and curriculum of both programs addressed the physical, emotional and social needs of women, but the researchers recommended changing CREST to a single-sex program. They suggested that the presence of men and the confrontational methods used in the program could combine to provide a psychologically threatening environment for women.

However, CREST participants expressed mixed views about the proposed change. Some women said that the program was gender appropriate and that they did not feel unsafe or threatened by the presence of men. Some women wanted less hostility in the encounter groups, others wanted more female-only encounter groups, and still others wanted to keep parts of the program coed to help them learn how to relate to the opposite sex in nonsexual ways. Although some participants saw a need for male involvement, they all seemed to indicate a preference for a program that focused more on female issues.

A three-year follow-up study of KEY/CREST produced positive results. The study found that 69 percent of inmates completing KEY/CREST and aftercare remained arrest-free, compared with 55 percent of those completing CREST only, 28 percent of CREST dropouts and 29 percent of the control group. The study also found that 35 percent of inmates completing CREST and aftercare remained drug-free, compared to 27 percent who completed CREST only, 17 percent who dropped out and 5 percent of the comparison group.[5]

## Forever Free in Calif.

Forever Free is a four-to six-month residential drug addiction treatment and reentry program for women at the California Institution for Women in Frontera. Women participate in Forever Free for four to six months while they are incarcerated and for up to six months while under supervised parole. It offers a cognitive-behavioral curriculum that emphasizes preventing relapse and views addiction as a disease. It teaches women how to identify and confront withdrawal symptoms. Like KEY/CREST, Forever Free addresses issues especially important to women such as self-esteem and addiction, anger management, assertiveness training, healthy relationships, physical and psychological abuse, post-traumatic stress disorder, co-dependency, parenting, and sex and health.

The Forever Free study showed that the program had positive results. Participants had fewer arrests and convictions during the one-year post-release evaluation period than those in the comparison group who attended an eight-week, three-hour per-day substance abuse education course.

Forever Free participants also reported significantly lower drug use, better psychological functioning, better parenting experiences, better use of community services and improved treatment readiness scores. The program successfully treated women's drug addiction and criminal offense issues and also effectively addressed other important areas of their lives, including employment and relationships with children.

## Aftercare and Community Services

Both studies built on previous research that has verified the need to continue the progress made through in-prison drug treatment programs by providing female inmates with aftercare services during parole. For example, the KEY program staff observed that their graduates needed help to continue and maintain the positive changes acquired during the program. So they established the CREST work release program. The researchers found that addicts who attended both programs had lower recidivism rates than those who have been in only one of the programs.

Likewise, the Forever Free program found that continued treatment during parole was extremely important to success. As inmates progressed from receiving no residential treatment to receiving treatment both in prison and during parole, their reincarceration significantly decreased during the one-year follow-up period. In addition, the study found that the Forever Free program had a positive impact on post-release drug use, parenting and psychological functioning, and that women who were in community residential treatment were 15 times more likely to be employed at the follow-up period. Therefore, the researchers recommended that criminal justice policy makers should encourage, if not mandate, community aftercare for women enrolled in prison-based treatment programs.

Providing links to services such as transportation, employment assistance, and medical/dental health care, improves treatment outcomes. The researchers found large gaps between the services needed and received by both the Forever Free participants and the comparison group, but the gaps were greater among the comparison subjects. Results also showed that female inmates who have children have difficulty finding suitable family residential aftercare services, and they also have a great need for vocational and educational services.

The high levels of unmet service needs probably contributed to the failures of those women who were reincarcerated at the follow-up period. The researchers suggested that one way to increase the success rate would be to identify a woman's needs before she leaves prison and then connect her to community-based programs that offer those services.

## Counselors and Staff

The KEY/CREST program study also looked at training of staff and counselors, and noted that in a therapeutic community designed for women, the staff must have expertise in all areas of women's health care and health needs, be knowledgeable and experienced in working with the kinds of emotional, physical and psychological abuse that incarcerated women experience, and be able to reach these women and understand their lives on the streets. The researchers recommended that KEY/CREST give women greater direct access to program counselors and provide more outside training for the staff—a recommendation that could be useful for the Forever Free program and other therapeutic programs as well.

## Agreeing on the Differences

The KEY/CREST and Forever Free programs varied in their approaches, but they both recognized the many ways in which the treatment needs of female inmates differ from those of male inmates. Results from both studies show that rehabilitation programs that recognize these differences and focus on women-specific issues can help female inmates successfully reenter society. They add to the continuing research effort to show "that investments in gender-responsive policy and procedures will likely produce long-term dividends for the criminal justice system and the community as well as for women offenders and their families."[6] Additional resources and publications about reentry can be downloaded from NIJ's Web site at www.ojp.usdoj.gov/nij.

## Notes

1. Bloom, B., B. Owen and S. Covington. 2003. *Gender-Responsive Strategies: Research, Practice, and Guiding Principles for Women Offenders.* Washington, D.C.: U.S. Department of Justice, National Institute of Corrections, Table 1, pp. 2. Available at www.nicic.org/pubs/2003/018017.pdf.

2. Garrison, A., A. Rose, W. Rosenbauer, D. Lockwood-Dillard and B. Haslett. 2002. *Process Evaluation Assessing the Gender Appropriateness of the KEY/CREST Program, Final Report.* Available at www.ncjrs.org/pdffiles1/nij/grants/195788.pdf.

3. Prendergast, M., E. Hall and J. Wellisch. 2002. *Outcome Evaluation of the Forever Free Substance Abuse Treatment Program: One Year Postrelease Outcomes.* Available at www.ncjrs.org/pdffiles1/nij/grants/199685.pdf.

4. Lockwood, D., J. McCorkel and J. Inciardi. 1998. Developing comprehensive prison-based therapeutic community treatment for women, *Drugs and Society*, 13(1–2):193–212, 195. See also, McCorkel, J., L. Harrison and J. Inciardi. 1998. How

treatment is constructed among graduates and dropouts in a prison therapeutic community for women, *Journal of Offender Rehabilitation*, 27(3/4):37–59.

5. Martin, S.S., C.A. Butzin, C.A. Saum and J.A. Inciardi. 1999. Three-year outcomes of therapeutic community treatment for drug-involved offenders in Delaware: From prison to work release to aftercare, *The Prison Journal*, 79(3):294–320.

6. Bloom, B., B. Owen and S. Covington. 2003.

**DORIS WELLS** is a writer and editor for the National Institute of Justice. **LAURIE BRIGHT,** a senior social science analyst in NIJ's Office of Research and Evaluation, monitors the prisoner reentry evaluations for NIJ.

Author's Note: Points of view expressed in this article do not represent the official position or policies of the U.S. Department of Justice.

# Combination Treatment for One Year Doubles Smokers' Quit Rate

PATRICK ZICKLER
*NIDA NOTES* Staff Writer

Most smokers understand the health risks associated with tobacco use and want to stop, but the addictive grip of nicotine makes quitting difficult; nearly 80 percent of smokers who try relapse within a year. Those poor odds can be improved, NIDA-supported investigators say, by extending the length of smoking cessation therapy to at least 1 year.

Among smokers who received medication and counseling for 12 months rather than the conventional 12 weeks, half were abstinent a year after quitting. This is more than double the success rate of other treatment programs, says Dr. Sharon Hall, who investigated the extended treatment approach at the University of California, San Francisco. "Smoking is not just a bad habit; it is a powerful and deadly addiction," Dr. Hall says. "It has to be treated with methods that are commensurate with its addictive properties, which are extensive and long term."

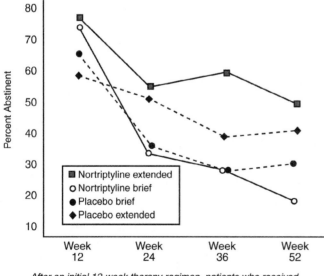

*After an initial 12-week therapy regimen, patients who received monthly counseling for 40 more weeks maintained higher abstinence rates than patients who did not.*
*Concurrent nortriptyline therapy enhanced the advantage of extended counseling.*

**Figure 1** Smoking Cessation Rates Improve With Year-Long Treatment

Dr. Hall and her colleagues assigned each of 160 trial participants who smoked 10 or more cigarettes daily to one of four regimens. All the participants received nicotine replacement therapy (transdermal patch) and took part in five group counseling sessions during the first 12 weeks of the study. These 90-minute sessions concentrated on understanding health issues associated with smoking and quitting, developing personalized quit strategies, and avoiding relapse. The investigators gave half the participants a placebo and half nortriptyline, an antidepressant that Dr. Hall's research group had previously found helps smokers to quit. The researchers adjusted participants' medication doses to maintain blood concentrations of 50 to 150 ng/L.

At the end of 12 weeks, treatment ended for half of the participants. The rest continued their regimens of nortriptyline (40) or placebo (41) for 40 more weeks. During this time, they continued to participate in monthly 30-minute group counseling sessions and were contacted by phone 2 weeks after each session to reinforce counseling lessons.

At the end of weeks 24, 36, and 52, far fewer of the participants in extended treatment were smoking than were participants whose treatment ended after 12 weeks. At the end of 1 year, 50 percent of patients who had received nortriptyline and counseling throughout were abstinent, compared with 18 percent who got this treatment for only 12 weeks. Forty-two percent of patients who received extended counseling and placebo were abstinent at 1 year, compared with 30 percent of those who got them for 12 weeks.

"The highest success rate was with nortriptyline and counseling for 52 weeks," Dr. Hall says. "Extended treatment with placebo and counseling came in a very close second, suggesting that prolonged psychological support and counseling are important components in improved treatment outcomes." The mix of long-term combination treatment with both pharmacological and behavioral therapies reflects the complexity and power of smoking addiction, says Dr. Hall. "Smoking is more complex than just the physical addiction. There are psychological factors such as stress that can trigger a desire to smoke. There are social and environmental factors—a certain group of friends or a certain kind of meal or a certain type of gathering—that make a contribution, too," Dr. Hall says. "Simply treating the physical addiction doesn't address these psychological influences, which can trigger a relapse to smoking months or years after a person has quit."

"These findings are significant because they show that a combination treatment provided over an extended period has great potential to improve smoking cessation rates," says Ms. Debra Grossman of NIDA's Division of Neuroscience and Behavioral Research. "Dr. Hall has shown that providing smokers with a comprehensive extended treatment can achieve better abstinence rates than have ever previously been reported from a controlled trial."

Dr. Hall and her colleagues are continuing to test long-term treatments in two other studies. One involves smokers older than 50, a group with markedly poorer outcomes than younger smokers. The second will evaluate bupropion, a prescription medication specifically approved for smoking cessation treatment, in combination with counseling.

For some smokers, the prospect of a year-long course of treatment is daunting, Dr. Hall acknowledges. "But this may be what you need to do if you want to be successful. Smokers, as well as the practitioners who treat them, need to know that it is possible to achieve high rates of long-term abstinence. It is not a simple process because it's not a simple addiction. But it is worth it to stop doing something that can kill you."

From *NIDA Notes*, March 2006. Published by The National Institute on Drug Abuse.

# Medications + Counseling: The 'New Paradigm' in Alcoholism Treatment

Alcoholism treatment works, and when the treatment includes medications aimed at reducing relapse, it works long-term, according to researchers. There are already medications currently approved for alcoholism treatment which alleviate craving: acamprosate (Campral) and long-acting injectable naltrexone (Vivitrex). "And we have many new medications in the pipeline," says Mark L. Willenbring, M.D., director of the Division of Treatment and Recovery Research at the National Institute on Alcohol Abuse and Alcoholism (NIAAA). "We have this scientific base of understanding that's new," Willenbring told *ADAW*. "That leads to rational development of medications."

Willenbring was a speaker at a July 21st American Medical Association media briefing in New York City entitled "Alcohol Dependence: From Science to Solutions." Sponsored by David R. Gastfriend, M.D., vice president for medical affairs at Alkermes (the Cambridge, Mass-based manufacturer of Vivitrex), the briefing had as an overarching theme the new era emerging in alcoholism treatment in which pharmacotherapy plays an increasingly important role. The two most exciting areas of alcoholism treatment research are neurotransmitters and genetics, Willenbring told *ADAW*.

## Drugs to Reduce Craving

With Vivitrex, patients get one injection a month. According to the main study on the drug, 64 percent of patients received all six injections and were still in treatment at the end of six months. Of these, 88 percent signed on to continue getting injections for another year.

Naltrexone, whether in the injectable form of Vivitrex or in oral form (ReVia), works on the brain's opioid system. "Its main effect is on reducing heavy drinking by blocking the reward," explains Willenbring. "If an alcoholic is in recovery and takes a drink, it's like priming the pump—the craving increases as a result, and the drinking continues." But naltrexone blocks the reward, diminishing the craving.

Says Willenbring of naltrexone, "It's not unusual for me to hear someone, say a middle-aged guy who had been an

---

### The Genetics of Alcoholism

The gene or genes for alcoholism aren't clearly delineated. And they may never be. "There's been considerable progress is quantifying the genetic contribution to the development of alcoholism," says Willenbring. In 50 to 60 percent of alcoholics, there is a familial factor. "But there won't be one gene." The fact is that the genetics of alcoholism are much more complicated that were originally thought—in fact, genetics are more complicated. "You need the environment, you need genes, the environment turns the genes on and off, the genes turn each other on and off."

Marc Schuckit, M.D., professor of psychiatry at the Veterans Affairs San Diego Healthcare System and an expert in inherited traits related to alcoholism, compares it to heart disease. Heart attacks run in families, but there is no "heart attack gene." Rather, there are conditions such as high blood pressure, which increases the risk for a heart attack. Schuckit also spoke at the July 21 media briefing in New York City.

---

alcoholic for years before recovery, say, 'I did have a slip, I did drink but after two or three drinks, I didn't feel like having any more—that's never happened to me in my life'"

The benefit of the injectable form—Vivitrex—is that it enhances compliance, says Willenbring. Instead of having to take a naltrexone pill every day, the patient only needs to go to the doctor (or nurse) once a month for an injection. "In psychiatry, where we've used long acting injectables primarily with antipsychotics, it's been a real boon to compliance," he says.

Acamprosate (Campral) appears to have activity on glutamate receptors rather than the opioid system. "This is the other main system, and these neurotransmitters produce dysphoria, anxiety, insomnia—the icky feeling many people have in abstinence," says Willenbring. People may start out drinking because it feels good—that's the reward system. But they continue drinking to seek relief from the negative feelings. "Sometimes we call these feelings protracted abstinence syndrome or subacute withdrawal." The dysphoria—a stressed, anxious, vaguely depressed feeling—can be countered by acamprosate. Then, the patient no longer feels the need to drink to make these feelings go away. "Acamprosate, our speculation is, it works to normalize that system," says Willenbring.

There are other medications under study as well, including topiramate (Topamax), an anticonvulsant which is currently in clinical trials for alcoholism. Like naltrexone and acamprosate, topiramate focuses on reducing relapse and heavy drinking. Other drugs under study include gabapentin, ondansetron, and baclofen.

Medications are based in science. They can help treat alcoholism because they are aimed at treating the neurotransmitter system that is at the root of craving and relapse, says Willenbring. Through animal studies with rats who have been bred to become "alcoholic," and wild rats who are not alcoholic, researchers have learned that neurotransmitter systems involved in heavy drinking may be different than those involved in continued drinking for someone who is a chronic alcoholic. "These animal studies show why a patient of mine could be sober for 20 years, go to a party and have a drink, and end up in the gutter five days later," he says. "The alcohol dependence hasn't gone away, even though the alcohol has. The brain systems get hijacked by the chemical."

## Medications Helping Counselors

But what does the world of science—whether it's rats bred to drink alcohol or neurotransmitters in the brain—have to do with the hard work counselors do face to face with people? "Science provides an understanding for what we're doing clinically," says Willenbring. "These aren't just findings in rats. When counselors hear patients talk about craving and being preoccupied, someone who walks past a liquor store and suddenly is consumed by an urge to drink, there's a scientific basis for it. When someone feels grumpy, gloomy, and anxious in the weeks and months of abstinence, there's a scientific basis. And that is why counselors ought to be excited about medications—they'll help patients."

Willenbring adds that after 30 years as a clinician working with alcoholics, he knows every treatment tool is needed. "This is a tough illness," he says. "We can't afford to be arguing over different kinds of treatment—we need them all."

Some alcoholism treatment professionals, especially those who took charge of their own recovery without the help of medications, may have doubts about the use of

---

## Health Insurance and Alcoholism Treatment

At the July 21 meeting, Eric Goplerud, Ph.D., director of Ensuring Solutions to Alcohol Problems at the George Washington University Medical Center in Washington, D.C., revealed results of a new employer survey showing that only 16 percent of employees in health plans who are referred to alcoholism treatment get 3 or more services within 30 days. This is based on 64 health plans reporting in to the 2005 eValue8 project sponsored by the National Business Coalition on Health, a membership group of employers concerned about health care. "Why is this happening?" is what the employers want to know, Goplerud told *ADAW*. "This needs to be addressed to the employers who are paying the bills for the employees and who are writing the contracts with the health plans. What's important is not a gotcha. What's important is fixing the system."

The danger of medications is that they can be seen as a substitute for counseling, something that would jeopardize the success of treatment, says Goplerud, whose group has looked at how antidepressant medication has affected mental health treatment. "We see there has been a substantial shift towards medication and away from psychotherapy in depression," he says. "We also have seen lots of research that shows if you don't accompany medications with counseling, you don't get good results."

---

drugs. After all, recovery is supposed to take place without the use of mind-altering substances. Neither naltrexone nor acamprosate has abuse potential, and, says Willenbring, "they don't change you as a person, they normalize some abnormal brain chemistry." Few treatment professionals advocate "white knuckle treatment" these days, but even with medications, recovery isn't easy. "When I was in medical school, psychoanalysis was still the predominant theory in psychiatry," Willenbring recalls. "The analysts used to argue about whether people should take antidepressants rather than work through their depression." Both counseling and medications are necessary, but the counselors have to accept medications first, he says.

Willenbring doesn't only study the effects of medications, but the effects of behavioral treatments as well. "We've learned how to do good studies on counseling," he says. "What we've learned is that the counseling school like cognitive behavioral therapy or motivational enhancement or 12-step facilitation isn't the most important thing. The outcomes are pretty similar—all good." What is important, he says, is (1) the decision by the patient to seek help, and (2) the skill of the counselor.

How is skill measured? "It's based on how empathic they are, which translates into skill," Willenbring says. "This is something for the field to really consider. Are we looking at counselor-level outcomes in our programs? It's like looking at a surgeon and their post-op infection rate.

Engagement, retention, initial outcomes, we ought to be looking at by counselor."

And for all counselors, says Willenbring, the medications will help improve their patients' outcomes. "Nothing can make recovery easy, but medications can make it possible for some people."

From *Alcoholism & Drug Abuse Weekly*, Volume 17, Issue 28, July 25, 2005, pp. 1–3. Copyright © 2005 by John Wiley & Sons. Reprinted by permission.

# A Teen Health Gap

**Adolescents have unique medical issues, and a growing specialty is aimed at addressing them.**

BARBARA KANTROWITZ AND KAREN SPRINGEN

Think about your pediatrician's office. Chances are that "Winnie-the-Pooh" or "Sesame Street" murals decorate the walls and restless toddlers pass the time before their appointments by playing on the floor with brightly colored toys. Now imagine you're a 16-year-old girl waiting for your checkup in this same room. How comfortable would you feel? How likely would you be to tell the doctor who has treated you since you were in diapers that you're thinking about sleeping with your boyfriend and you need birth control?

Help for such girls, and boys, may be on the way, thanks to a growing recognition in the medical community that teenagers have health-care needs that aren't always met by pediatricians (who officially treat patients from birth to 21) or doctors specializing in adult care. "Pediatricians spend most of their time with little babies and young children," says Robert T. Brown, president-elect of the Society for Adolescent Medicine (SAM) and chief of adolescent health at Children's Hospital in Columbus, Ohio. "Family practitioners spend most of their time with older people." Neither is generally trained to help teens, who are "the healthiest age cohort there is as far as organic disease," Brown says. "But it's sort of a paradox that at the same time, they have relatively high mortality and morbidity rates, and those come from behavior. That's what makes them different."

Since 1994, nearly 1,000 doctors have been certified in the subspecialty of adolescent medicine. Though most of them work in academic medical centers and are not available to help every teen in need, SAM hopes that, by highlighting the need and providing training and role models, the specialists will pass on their methods to many more doctors.

The most vital skill is how to talk to teens about sensitive issues: drinking, drugs, sex and violence. Dr. John Kulig, the current president of SAM and the director of adolescent medicine at Tufts-New England Medical Center, says pediatricians often just blurt out: "You're not having sex, are you? You're not drinking or smoking, are you?" And he adds, "They don't want to hear a yes—because they lack the time and skills to intervene." If Kulig were seeing a patient for the first time, he would take a different approach. "What's it like in your community, in your school?" he'd ask. "Do a lot of kids drink?" Then he would narrow the field: "Do your friends smoke or drink?" Finally he

would get personal. "What's your experience? How do you deal with someone who offers you a beer or passes you a joint?" The idea is to avoid being judgmental or threatening, Kulig says.

Finding the right approach is vital because this generation of adolescents faces unique pressures. They're more likely than their parents to be from divorced or unstable families, which contributes to emotional problems and a lack of support at home. Substance abuse and eating disorders appear to strike at younger ages. Emerging sexuality is more intertwined with the threat of disease than it was a generation ago, when avoiding pregnancy was the primary concern. This generation is also more likely to go far from home for college, which can be overwhelming for many young people.

According to a 2004 survey by the U.S. Substance Abuse and Mental Health Services Administration (SAMHSA), 18- to 20-year-olds have the highest rate of illicit drug use, with a remarkable 21.7 percent of that age group admitting to using illegal drugs in the previous month. Alcohol is also a major health threat. Another SAMHSA survey found that nearly one in five 12- to 20-year-olds was a binge drinker, which means five or more drinks on the same occasion on at least one day in the previous month. "They're abusing more of everything than any other age group," says Jim Steinhagen, executive director of the Hazelden Center for Youth and Families in Plymouth, Minn.

Teens in trouble often struggle for years before getting the help they need. Curtiss Schreiber started smoking pot and drinking when he was 13. By 14, he was in an outpatient rehab program with weekly counseling and drug tests. "That did not do much for me," he says. "I was depressed and angry, upset about a lot of things. The whole time, in the back of my mind, I was just waiting for the drug tests to stop." At 17 he was finally ready to get help. His parents signed him up for 60 days in a program for 13- to 18-year-olds in Oregon called Catherine Freer Wilderness Therapy, and he also went to a halfway house in Washington state called Gray Wolf Ranch. It worked. Now 19, Schreiber has been sober for two years. He's majoring in English and philosophy at Augsburg College in Minneapolis, where he's one of 36 recovering addicts who live together in a sober community called StepUP. Schreiber's grateful that he was able to turn his life around while he was still young. "I don't have the experience of failing out of college, of losing my family," he says. "A lot of people do. That's a terrible reality about this disease."

## Even for healthy young people, getting insurance can be a struggle.

Dealing with sexual issues is just as tricky as substance abuse. By the age of 20, about 75 percent of Americans have been sexually active, says David Landry, a researcher at the Alan Guttmacher Institute. "But many of them have just become sexually active, and they don't have a significant opportunity to discuss their health needs with medical personnel." Because the federal government is pushing abstinence instead of more comprehensive sex education in schools, many young people don't get accurate information about contraception and sexually transmitted diseases (STDs). That may be one reason that nationally, 15- to 24-year-olds account for half of new STD infections each year.

Even for young people who are healthy, getting adequate insurance can be a struggle. A Kaiser Family Foundation study found that a third of Americans 19 to 24 were uninsured, the highest rate of any age group. College students can rely on both their schools' health centers and their parents' plans. But young adults who don't go to college or have uninsured parents often are in lower-paying entry-level jobs that don't offer health benefits. If they get seriously ill or in an accident, they can find themselves with six-figure debt. "Getting out from under that debt is often impossible," says Catherine Hoffman, a registered nurse who is associate director of the Kaiser Commission on Medicaid and the Uninsured. Lack of insurance also means that young people don't get preventive care, such as regular checkups.

The old view of adolescence was that it ended at 18 or 19. Now, with many young adults in their early 20s still struggling to find their foothold in the world, doctors call the years from 18 to 28 the second decade of adolescence, which means there's an even greater need for doctors who understand their patients' distinctive concerns. "This age group is known for living hard and taking risks," says Dr. Frederick Blum, president of the American College of Emergency Physicians and an associate professor of emergency medicine and pediatrics at West Virginia University. With a little help, they'll learn how to channel those impulses and grow up safely.

# Teens Caught in the Middle: Juvenile Justice System and Treatment

Substance abuse treatment for adults in the criminal justice system is seriously inadequate, causing recidivism and other problems. But the situation is even worse in the juvenile system, according to a new report from Drug Strategies, a research institute based in Boston, Mass. The report, "Bridging the Gap: A Guide to Drug Treatment in the Juvenile Justice System," was released December 6, and focuses on the conflicts between treatment, on the one hand, and criminal justice, on the other. Nobody likes to use the word "punitive" to describe the criminal justice system, but compared to treatment, that's what it is, sources agree.

"The primary goal of drug treatment for adolescents is rehabilitation," Mathea Falco, president of Drug Strategies, told CABL. "But for the juvenile justice system, control is often the dominant concern."

However, the fact that juvenile justice is connected to substance abuse treatment also works in favor of these adolescents. If it were not for juvenile justice referrals, and treatment programs like those profiled in the Drug Strategies report, many of these teens would not be able to access treatment at all.

## Best Interests?

In most states, according to the report, the goals of the 51 different juvenile court systems are threefold: to protect public safety, reduce recidivism, and act in the "best interests" of the child. How a child's best interests are defined is up to interpretation, the report notes. But it adds that the juvenile justice goals and the goals of treatment are "not necessarily mutually exclusive" because teens who are not abusing substances are less likely to be rearrested.

In some areas, getting involved in the criminal justice system can be almost a guarantee of substance abuse treatment—for adults. In California, for example, Proposition 36 mandates treatment instead of incarceration for adults. "If we had that for adolescents, we'd have much better services," says Elizabeth Stanley-Salazar, director of public policy for Phoenix Houses of California, whose Phoenix Academy of Los Angeles is profiled in the Drug Strategies report.

"Kids who are at high risk—such as in foster care—simply don't have access to treatment," Stanley-Salazar told CABL. "We know we should be using evidence based practices, but there's only a veneer of funding for substance abuse services." Because of the

lack of funding, even teens in the juvenile justice system who need treatment have a hard time getting it in California, she says, but she adds that the courts provide one of the few "on-ramps" for treatment. "Most of the kids who come to us come through the court system—a kid almost has to get tied up in the criminal justice system before they can access treatment."

---

### Eleven Elements of Effective Drug Treatment in Juvenile Justice System

1. Systems integration
2. Assessment and treatment matching
3. Comprehensive, integrated treatment approach
4. Staff who are trained to recognize psychiatric problems
5. Developmentally appropriate program
6. Family involvement in treatment
7. A way to engage and retain teens in treatment
8. Qualified staff who have experience in diverse areas, such as delinquency, adolescent development, depression, or attention deficit disorder
9. Staff with gender and cultural competence
10. Process of continuing care that includes relapse prevention training
11. A way to measure treatment outcomes

Source: Drug Strategies

---

Are there differences between adolescents in treatment because of juvenile justice referrals, and other adolescents in treatment? "The ones in the juvenile justice system are more severe, because their drug use has reached a higher threshold," says Stanley-Salazar. "So at Phoenix House we're receiving kids who have very serious substance abuse problems." However, she says that "many of the kids who are not on probation look similar to kids who have been picked up by probation."

Some of the teens at Phoenix House are on "home probation" or "informal probation." According to Stanley-Salazar, what they have in common with those on formal probation are "very disordered lives." And for those on probation, those lives are more likely to have histories of violence and abuse and neglect.

# Multiple Agencies

The report builds on an earlier one from Drug Strategies called Treating Teens: A Guide to Adolescent Drug Programs, published in 2003. This report identified 9 key elements of treatment programs for adolescents (see box); this new report adds two elements that are specific to people coming through the juvenile justice system: (1) juvenile offenders are more likely to have co-occurring disorders, and (2) it's important to integrate functions of agencies.

Integrating agency functions is essential but often not done. One of the biggest challenges for a family in the juvenile justice system anywhere is navigating the bureaucracy. And this bureaucracy is particularly daunting in New York City. But this is the focus of Adolescent Portable Therapy (APT), a program of the Vera Institute, which acts as "a liaison" for people in the juvenile justice system, according to Evan Elkin, APT director. "You need to have a cultural understanding of the multiple agencies, of their fiscal, operational, and philosophical constraints, to make treatment work," Elkin told *CABL*. "You can't just ask for access, and come in and do treatment."

---

## Programs Profiled in Drug Strategies Report

Travis County Juvenile Justice Integrated Network (Austin, Tex.)
Tampa Juvenile Assessment Center (Tampa, Fla.)
King County Juvenile Treatment Court (Seattle, Wash.)
Adolescent Portable Therapy (New York, N.Y.)
Thunder Road Adolescent Treatment Center (Oakland, Calif.)
Chestnut Health Systems (Bloomington, Ill.)
Multidimensional Family Therapy (Miami, Fla.)
Multisystemic Therapy (Mount Pleasant, S.C.)
Phoenix Academy of Los Angeles
La Bodega de la Familia (New York, N.Y.)

---

The New York City Department of Juvenile Justice does assessment and pretrial detention but does not house adolescents when they are "placed" or sentenced, as it is called in the adult system—the state does, says Elkin. "Given how briefly a kid can be in the city's custody, it's impressive that the city agency has wanted to be involved in funding drug treatment for a kid who may quickly leave and enter the state system for placement." The city Department of Juvenile Justice, among others, funds APT.

# Clinic Without Walls

APT remains involved with an adolescent who is arrested, goes to court, and is sent to placement, as well as with the one who the judge allows to go home. The screening and assessment is integrated into the city's booking process, says Elkin. Then, during the first days of detention, APT assigns a therapist to him. "The kid may go to a residential placement facility for a year, but APT stays with the kid," says Elkin. "Then, they get four months of intensive home services when they get home." If the child is not placed, but returns home with services—which is happening more and more as New York State sends the message that it wants to rely less on institutional placement and more on home-based services—APT will treat that child as well. The key is portability. "We're a clinic without walls," says Elkin.

However, there's one down side to portability: payment. "The agencies who establish the standards of practice for alcohol and drug treatment do not yet recognize the reimbursability of portable home-based services," Elkin told CABL. "We would not get Medicaid reimbursement." APT is, however, licensed by the state Office of Alcoholism and Substance Abuse Services to provide this kind of treatment. "We are the only body that holds a license for this from OASAS," Elkin said proudly. "They created a special category for us 5 years ago."

Thanks to a grant from the Substance Abuse and Mental Health Administration (SAMHSA) for community-based adolescent drug treatment providers, APT was able to expand its services by over 50 percent for a four-year period. Under the SAMHSA grant, APT sees 90 additional teens a year returning home from state custody with the Office of Children and Family Services (OCFS). And under the Department of Juvenile Justice funding, they see 150 a year. That's about 250 families a year treated by APT. "We could triple in size and still not meet the need," says Elkin. The good news is that in recognition of the successful collaboration between APT and OCFS, the program is in the State's 2006 proposed budget for further expansion. "We hope also to remain in the City's budget in 2006."

# The Role of the Family

LaBodega de la Familia, a spinoff from the Vera Institute's pre-APT days, is another program profiled in the Drug Strategies report. This New York City-based program focuses on the family as a unit. "Some families come in and say, 'My kid is smoking pot, what should I do," says Carol Shapiro, founder and director of Family Justice, of which LaBodega is a direct service. "In other cases, the teen was arrested, but it's a family member with a drug problem." It's important to engage the whole family, Shapiro, who started LaBodega 10 years ago, told CABL.

By working with the government and families in tandem, LaBodega promotes the notion of family case management. This is an example of the juvenile justice system helping the treatment process, says Shapiro. "The escalation and the hammers of the justice system are an advantage," she says.

Unlike the "clinic without walls" concept of APT, LaBodega is "place-based," says Shapiro. "We have a storefront and a satellite in public housing in a neighborhood that is affected by drugs. We'll do home visits too." And LaBodega's services integrate into the community. "We engage in a lot of things that have nothing to do with drug treatment," says Shapiro. "We help with gardening, poetry, photography, we work with the housing police and the people who are the natural leaders, the social fabric of the neighborhood."

Getting judges to understand that the community, home, and home-based treatment might be in the child's "best interests" is an uphill battle. "We have a problem with getting the justice system to understand that if you match these kids to treatment, using the American Society of Addiction Medicine (ASAM) criteria, you'd be putting them in variable lengths of stay," says Stanley-Salazar, noting that the average stay at Phoenix House is 9 to 12 months. "But corrections doesn't always look through the lens of treatment. They place them because of their offense, but there's not enough capacity to provide the services."

Ideally, she adds, these patients should be treated earlier, before their problems get so severe. "But if they weren't in the justice system, who would pay for their treatment?"

# No Longer Theory: Correctional Practices That Work

Criminologists and politicians have debated the effectiveness of correctional rehabilitation programs since the mid-1970s when criminal justice scholars and policy makers throughout the United States embraced Robert Martinson's credo of 'nothing works.' Programs based around punishment and surveillance grew. They are being embraced even stronger today despite the fact that Martinson later admitted that he was wrong. An ample amount of research exists that suggest that there are successful programs available to reduce future criminality of not only offenders but also of potential offenders. This article presents correctional practices that effectively reduce recidivism rates and recommends two additional programs, Logotherapy and the Intensive Journal, proven to be cost-effective in the fields of prevention and rehabilitation.

HARVEY SHRUM

Life is difficult and seemingly unfair. When parents divorce, when one or both parents die, when we are bullied, or suffer a catastrophic illness or accident, when a friend is killed in an accident or war, we know that life is unfair and often very painful. But, Dr. Viktor Frankl (1997), survivor of the Holocaust, emphasized that the meaning of life is not what happens to us. It is what we do with that which happens to us.

When life appears to be unfair and painful many resort to self-medication. America comprises only five percent of the world's population, yet it consumes over 60 percent of the world's illicit drugs. Of those consuming illicit drugs, 77 percent are employed (Ferrell, 2003). Others attempt to divert pain and grief, usually onto those closest to them. Still others attempt to bury pain with their addiction to work, hobbies, or possessions. Often those who attempt to drug, divert, or bury their pain surround themselves with those of similar beliefs.

Sometimes laws are passed in the belief that they will make life fairer. Prisons are built at $100,000 per cell and $30–50,000 in annual costs per inmate are added to the tax burden. But, prisons and harsher laws tend to divert valuable funding away from public schools and other programs that tend to make our communities much safer. America has become so focused upon prisons as the answer to its social ills that today one in every 37 Americans is either in a state or federal prison or jail, or has been in the past (The Associated Press, August 18, 2003). The costs to American families are also enormous. The odds of a child of a recidivist father ending up in jail or prison at some point in his life are approximately 92 to one when compared to the general population. Increasing prison sentences do not reduce those odds.

Better ways do exist. Programs that lower recidivism rates result in less crime, lower costs for incarceration, fewer broken families, less welfare and social services, less prison overcrowding, less new prison construction, more funds for schools and alternatives to incarceration, and ultimately safer communities.

Recidivism and crime rates are readily reducible 16–62 percent and more by broader use of existing rehabilitation programs—substance abuse treatment, academic and vocational education, post-secondary education, intermediate sanctions, and alternatives to incarceration (Cypser, 1997). Some programs work so well that the rate of recidivism is as low as five to 15 percent (Manitonquat, 1996).

## Addictions and "Will to Meaning"

Over 80 percent of those incarcerated committed their offense under the influence of drugs, committed their offense to get money for drugs, or committed their offense under the influence of alcohol (Bureau of Justice Statistics, 1993). The majority of inmates with drug and alcohol problems still do not receive sufficient treatment while in prison. And the number of drug/alcohol-using arrestees who are probably in need of treatment exceeds two million (Lipton, 1995). Dr. Frankl (1997) noted that there tended to be a significant inverse relationship between drug involvement and meaning in one's life. Ninety percent of students in high school and college who were addicted to alcohol and one hundred percent who were addicted to drugs reported that "meaning" was lacking in their lives. They may have purpose, but they do not have meaning. When men and women in prison are offered a drug and alcohol rehabilitation program, it is generally limited to a 12-step program, the only program generally acceptable to many parole boards, and 12-step programs do not address the lack of meaning in their lives.

## Treatment for Addictions

The type of addiction treatment may not matter as much as whether sufficient treatment has been provided, usually a minimum of 12–24 months combined with education leading to a GED and/or vocational training. Addiction recovery begins with treatment inside prison. But, to be most effective, the addict must continue his treatment following his release to parole. The strongest predictors of outcome for substance abuse treatment, noted Condelli and Hubbard (1994), regardless of the type of treatment, are both time of duration and number of sessions in treatment. One program in Brooklyn (1996) placed second felony drug offenders into residential drug treatment usually for 18 to 24 months. After three years, the re-arrest rates for offenders who completed the program were 6.7–8.2 percent.

A study conducted for the state of California provided the most comprehensive cost-benefit examination on the effectiveness of substance abuse treatment. Looking at all treatment programs in the state, researchers concluded that every dollar spent on treatment resulted in seven dollars in savings on reduced crime and health care costs (Mauer & Huling, 1995). Caulkins et al (1997) demonstrated that treatment of heavy drug users is 15–17 times more effective in reducing crime than spending the same money on mandatory minimum sentences. In another study these same researchers noted that spending money on treatment reduces consumption of cocaine 3.7 times more than spending that same money on conventional enforcement, and 7.6 times more than spending it on mandatory minimum sentences for drug dealers.

Caulkins et al (1997) noted that spending money to treat heavy cocaine users was four times more effective in reducing total national consumption than spending it on conventional enforcement against drug dealers, and nearly eight times more effective than spending it on mandatory minimum sentences for the same dealers. Additionally, treatment reduces about ten times more serious crime than conventional enforcement and fifteen more than mandatory minimums.

In a joint study by the RAND Corporation, the U.S. Army, and the Office of National Drug Control Strategy, researchers Rydell and Everingham (1994) found that drug treatment programs are seven times more cost-effective in reducing cocaine consumption than other programs that aim at controlling the supply of drugs. Treatment is eleven times more effective than border interdiction and twenty-two times more effective than trying to control foreign production. This study further concluded that drug treatment could reduce cocaine consumption a third if extended to all heavy users.

## Cognitive Approaches to Addictions Treatment

Rational Emotive Behavior Therapy, developed by Dr. Albert Ellis, is a cognitive-behavior therapy approach to addictions (Dryden, 2002). The major reasons for its popularity are its effectiveness, short-term nature, and low cost. It works best for individuals desiring a scientific, present-focused, and active treatment for coping with life's difficulties. It is based on a few simple principles having profound implications: 1) You are responsible for your own emotions and actions. 2) Your harmful emotions and dysfunctional behaviors are the product of your irrational thinking. 3) You can learn more realistic views and,

with practice, make them a part of you. 4) You will experience a deeper acceptance of yourself and greater satisfactions in life by developing a reality-based perspective.

Another alternative to the 12-step program is Logotherapy, developed by Dr. Viktor Frankl (1997). In logotherapy, or "health through meaning" emphasis is given to the absence in the "will to meaning." When we lack a will to meaning, noted Frankl, we generally seek to fill the existential vacuum with a "will to pleasure" that often leads to addictions, or a "will to power" that often leads to violence. He also noted that "people are most likely to become aggressive when they are caught in this feeling of emptiness and meaninglessness" (Frankl, 1997). Robert Jay Lifton (1969) appeared to agree with Frankl when he stated that "men are most apt to kill when they feel overcome by meaninglessness."

Dr. Viktor Frankl (1984, 1997) noted that the predominant factor leading to incarceration is the lack of meaning in one's life and that a first-termer differs from those who have never been in prison with respect to purpose in life. Criminality and purpose in life, Frankl noted, are inversely related. The irony is that the more persistently one offends, the more likely he is to be sentenced to longer terms of imprisonment and the less likely he is to increase his sense of purpose in life, and so the more likely he is to continue offending when released. The spreading existential frustration lies at the root of this phenomenon.

Frankl (1997) repeatedly emphasized the importance of meaning, rather than pleasure and power, as essential for the health of the body, the mind, and the spirit. He believed that the key to a positive view of life is an awareness that life has meaning under all circumstances, and that we have the capacity to find meaning in our life "experientially, creatively, and attitudinally." We can rise above ill health and blows of fate if we see meaning in our existence. Logotherapy helps people say yes to life, whether the suffering they experience comes from difficult human relations, job dissatisfaction, life-altering illness, survivor's guilt, or death of a loved one, or from self-made problems such as hypochondria or an overwhelming hunger for pleasure and power.

Logotherapy was introduced to inmates at the California Rehabilitation Center in Norco about 40 years ago as a short-term project (Crumbaugh, 1972). The program aimed at giving inmates a purpose and direction in life, and at helping them acquire the knowledge needed to pursue a new direction during and after their prison experience. The inmates, who participated in the project learned to see that their very experiences as criminals gave them a unique opportunity to help other criminals, thus turning their liabilities into assets society could use. Only one group of inmates went through the program before it was terminated. The recidivism rate for those who completed the program prior to parole was only 5.5 percent. Furthermore, when utilized as an addictions treatment program, it was found to be four times as effective as any other program.

I re-introduced Logotherapy to inmates nearing parole at Folsom State Prison in 1990. In 1998 Drs. Viktor Frankl and Joseph Fabry were invited to conduct a workshop for men serving life sentences for violent crimes. Dr. Frankl was too ill and weak at the time, so Dr. Fabry agreed to conduct two workshops on the principles of Logotherapy. Nineteen men serving life sentences attended both workshops. I supplemented these with several followup workshops and correspondence study assignments. One of the men was assisted in putting together a fifteen-hour workshop that enabled him to present what he had learned to his fellow peers. Five of the original group of nineteen men paroled. Three of those discharged from parole. The rate of recidivism since 1998 is zero percent.

Drs. Viktor Frankl (1997) and his colleague and friend Joseph Fabry (1988, 1994, & 1995) attempted to introduce logotherapy to the inmates at San Quentin and Folsom State Prison. At San Quentin one group of inmates formed a support group based on the principles of logotherapy. The group maintained contact following each individual's release from prison. Only one inmate in the logo-group returned to prison. Dr. Louis S. Barber (Frankl, 1997) holds that logotherapy is particularly applicable to the treatment of juvenile delinquents, noting that "almost always the 'lack of meaning and purpose in their lives' appeared to be present, said Barber, 'We have one of the highest rehabilitation rates in the U.S. working with young people in a rehabilitation setting, a recidivism rate of less than 17 percent against an average of some 40 percent.'"

The value of writing in alcohol and drug recovery has long been noted in treatment and twelve-step circles. However, Dr. Ira Progoff (1992), creator of the Intensive Journal wrote that unguided journal writing results in decreasing effectiveness over time. He also noted that whereas unguided journal writing often declines into behavior analysis and circuitous thinking, the Intensive Journal process does not. Instead, through its non-judgmental, non-analytical nature, along with "Journal Feedback," it gives the writer a mirroring capability that increases the energy, power, and effectiveness of the process over time. This experience has an empowering effect upon the Intensive Journal writer.

First introduced in 1992 at Folsom State Prison, the Intensive Journal is a practical method of self-development that utilizes writing exercises through a unique journal writing system. It's based on depth psychology and helps people access and work with their life experiences, feelings about family relationships, job, health, and meaning in life. Through a two-day introductory workshop, inmates discover improvement in job retention (Sealy and Duffy, 1977), in dealing with the causes of substance abuse and relapse and in rehabilitation while incarcerated. The first workshop introduces inmates to the first half of the Intensive Journal process. A second two-day workshop introduces inmates to the second half of the Intensive Journal. In the ten years since its introduction at Folsom State Prison, not one inmate who had completed at least the introductory Intensive Journal workshop returned to prison. In 2003 the Federal Bureau of Prisons adopted the Intensive Journal into its comprehensive re-entry program for inmates nearing parole.

In a related study of the impact on inmates at Folsom State Prison, 308 men were asked to provide a list of eight to twelve significant emotional events—ups and downs—that appeared to help shape their lives. Specifically identified as "Steppingstones" this writing exercise is only one segment of the Intensive Journal process. The lists were provided anonymously over a six-month period. They included important events from childhood to the present education, relationships, family life, mental, physical and spiritual health, marriages and divorces, births and deaths, and significant conflicts. The men were asked not to make any judgment—criticism or praise—for the actions they took or for the circumstances that were forced upon them, only to list them in the order that they came to mind.

A pattern appeared to take place. Without positive intervention following significant emotional events, particularly when they were traumatic in nature, all resorted to self-medicating, diverting, and/or burying their childhood pain. Every individual had been, is, or will be a victim in some way or other to trauma that causes loss of meaning. One in every two men in this study experienced the death of a loved one as a significant emotional event. One in every three listed growing up in a single-parent home; in most cases the custodial parent was the mother. And one in every five listed experiencing some form of traumatic physical, emotional and/or sexual abuse in childhood. When questioned later, four in every five verbalized acceptance of childhood abuse as "normal" and therefore did not list it as significant in their list of Steppingstones. Many also accepted as normal parents self-medicating with illicit drugs in their presence. Without therapeutic intervention shortly after these events, they became at greater risk for antisocial behavior, low self-esteem, depression, low educational attainment, underemployment, substance abuse, mental illness, and suicidal ideation. The Intensive Journal enabled them to deal with their issues in a safe, supporting environment.

## Education and Recidivism

Nearly 80 percent of state prison inmates have not completed high school (Bureau of Justice Statistics, 1993). Eighty percent of these may have learning disabilities (Ross, 1987). A RAND study by the Office of Correctional Education (1994) noted that the cost effectiveness of graduation incentives, in serious crimes averted per million dollars spent, was calculated to be five times better than that of the 3-strikes program. Recidivism of young parolees is also related to the amount of prior education. Recidivism did not increase despite the fact that, as an incentive, graduates were released to parole about 10.6 months prior to their court determined minimum period of incarceration according to a 1996 legislative report by the New York Department of Correctional Services. Many states are granting early release to non-violent prisoners, cutting sentences, sending drug offenders to treatment centers, and revising tough-on-crime laws in reverse of a 20-year trend as cost-saving measures (McMahon, 2003).

One study found that the recidivism rate for those who received both the GED certificate and completed a vocational trade was over 20 percent lower than for those who did not reach either milestone. The overall recidivism rate for college degree holders was a low 12 percent, and inversely differentiated by type of degree: Associate, 13.7%; Baccalaureate, 5.6%; and Masters, 0% (U.S. Department of Education, 1988–1994). The more educational programs successfully completed for each six months confined the lower the recidivism rate (Harer,

1994). In 1983 a study of the Folsom State Prison college program revealed a zero percent recidivism rate for inmates earning a bachelors degree, while the average recidivism rate for the state's parolees was 23.9 percent for the first year, increasing to 55 percent within three years (Taylor, 1992). College education does reduce the likelihood of recidivism principally through post-release employment (Batiuk, Moke, and Rounree, 1997). Employed ex-felons become taxpayers and reduce the odds of their children eventually ending up in prison.

## Recommendations by Judges, Wardens and Police Chiefs

In 2003 Supreme Court Justice Anthony Kennedy suggested that "prison terms are too long and that he favors scrapping the practice of setting mandatory minimum sentences for some federal crimes" (Cearan, 2003). The American Society of Criminology recommended expanding drug courts, alternatives to incarceration for nonviolent offenders, and community-based sentencing and treatment for those arrested for drug crimes. Furthermore, in a survey of prison wardens across America over 90 percent supported greater use of alternatives to incarceration, drug treatment, vocational training, and literacy and other educational programs (Sullivan, 1995). In another nationwide survey nearly 60 percent of police chiefs said placing drug users in court-supervised treatment programs is more effective than sentencing them to jail or prison. Nearly half of them said that more resources are needed to improve education, prevention, and treatment (Law Enforcement News, 1996). Finally, the American Correctional Association President, Bobbie Huskey (Sullivan, 1995), emphasized promoting greater use of sentencing options for nonviolent crime.

Additional time served in prison has little impact on recidivism. How can sentencing a child to life in a federal prison for delivering a small package, containing a small quantity of crack cocaine, for her uncle make the public safer? This is a child who was doing well in school and had never been in trouble with the law. Policies such as "truth-in-sentencing" that lengthen prison terms may be ineffective in improving public safety. Longer prison terms may provide some additional incapacitation effects, but they do so at great cost to our social-economic system and at the expense of more effective alternatives that make our communities safer. It is time that correctional educators and the voters reverse the current trend, emphasizing rehabilitation rather than punishment. When we suspect that we are not being told the truth, we have a duty to do the research, educate policy makers and legislators, and take the positive steps that lead to programs that work, regardless of the prevailing trend.

## Summary and Recommendations

The background of this paper is a long-term interest in the psycho-spiritual nature of proven rehabilitation programs for offenders. I have focused on "What works?" Some clear conclusions and cause for recommendations have emerged.

- Rehabilitation does have an impact in reducing recidivism.

- Rehabilitation programs that have a significant impact on reducing recidivism rates are those which are intense, of 18–24 months minimum in duration and continue following release to the community.

- Program success depends on the selection of offenders who have the potential of assuming responsibility. It also depends on the patience and understanding of the program director in dealing with prison authorities, prospective employers, and clients, who are often suspicious, easily discouraged, and respond to negative peer pressure from fellow inmates.

- Logotherapy holds great promise in restoring the "will to meaning" to those who have lost it, not only to those in jail, prison, or drug/alcohol rehabilitation programs, but also to those in grades K–16. Dr. Fabry's Guideposts to Meaning (1988) is an excellent resource for program development.

- The Intensive Journal also hold great promise in rehabilitating inmates as well as preventing young people from taking the path that often leads to addictions and incarceration. It is not only conducive in fostering self-improvement, but also in fostering/developing vocational interests, in increasing awareness and healing of health, addictions, and relationships. It also improves writing and communication skills, enhances relationships with family, and achieves breakthroughs in issues and decision-making.

Methods of prevention and rehabilitation do work, but correctional, educational, spiritual and psychiatric staff on both sides of the prison walls must support these goals if reduction in recidivism rates is to be achieved. When we embrace rehabilitation as a goal, we embrace hope. Hopefully, prevention and alternatives to incarceration will be emphasized to a much greater degree in the future. In the words of Nietzsche: "When we treat a man as he is, he only becomes worse. But, when we treat a man as he can be, he will be that which he can be."

# References

Batiuk, Mary Ellen (June 1997). The State of Post-secondary Education in Ohio Journal of Correctional Education, 48 (2), 70–72.

Batiuk, M. E., P. Moke, and P. W. Rounree (March 1997). Crime and Rehabilitation: Correctional Education as an Agent of Change: A Research Note Justice Quarterly, 14, (1).

Caulkins, J. P., C. P. Rydell, W. Schwabe, and J. Chiesa (1997). Mandatory Minimum Drug Sentences: Throwing Away the Key or the Taxpayer's Money? RAND Corporation Study.

Condelli, W. S. & R. L Hubbard (1994). "Relationship between Time Spent in Treatment and Client Outcomes from Therapeutic Communities Journal of Substance Abuse Treatment, 77 (1), 25–33.

Crumbaugh, James C. (May 1972). "Changes in Frankl's Existential Vacuum as a Measure of Therapeutic Outcome" Newsletter for Research in Psychology, H (2).

Cypser, R. J. (October 1997). What Works in Reducing Recidivism and Thereby Reducing Crime and Cost. New York: CURE.

Dryden, Windy (2002). Handbook of Individual Therapy. Sage Publications, Fourth Edition.

Edelstein, M. R. and D. R. Steele (1997). Three-Minute Therapy: Change Your Thinking, Change Your Life. Clendbridge Publishing Company.

Fabry, Joseph B. (1988). Guideposts to Meaning: Discovering What Really Matters. Oakland, California: New Harbinger Publications, Inc.

Fabry, Joseph B. (1994). Pursuit of Meaning. Abilene, Texas: Institute of Logotherapy Press.

Fabry, Joseph B. (1995). Finding meaning in Life: Logotherapy. New York: Jason Aronson.

Ferrell, Vance (2003). Hard Drugs Can Ruin You. Altamont, Texas: Harvestime Books.

Frankl, Viktor (1984). Man's Search for Meaning. New York: Washington Square Press.

Frankl, Viktor (1997). Man's Search for Ultimate Meaning, New York & London: Plenum Press.

Gearan, Anne (April 9, 2003). Kennedy: Too Many People Are Behind Bars. The Associated Press.

Harer, Miles (1994). Recidivism Among Federal Prisoners Released in 1987. Federal Bureau of Prisons Office of Research & Evaluation.

Lifton, Robert Jay (1969). History and Human Survival. New York: Random House.

Lipton, Douglas S. (November 1995). The Effectiveness of Treatment for Drug Abusers Under Criminal Justice Supervision. National Institute of Justice Research Report.

Manitonquat (1996). Ending Violent Crime: A Vision of a Society Free of Violence. Publisher.

Mauer, Marc and Tracy Ruling (October 1995). Young Black Americans and the Criminal Justice System: Five Years Later. The Sentencing Project.

McMahon, Patrick (August 10, 2003). "States Revisit 'Get-Tough' Policies as Revenue Slows, Prisons Overflow." USA Today.

Progoff, Ira (1992). At a Journal Workshop. New York: Washington Square Press.

Ross, J. M. (1987). "Learning Disabled Adults: Who Are They and What Do We Do With Them?" Lifelong Learning 77, No. 3: 4–7, 11. (ERIC #EJ 361 993).

Rydell, Peter and Susan S. Everingham (1994). Controlling Cocaine: Supply vs. Demand Programs. A joint study by the RAND Corporation, the U. S. Army, and the Office of National Drug Control Strategy.

Sealy, S. A. and T. F. Duffy (1977). The New York State Department of Labor Job-Training Program: Applying the Progoff Intensive Journal Method. Abridged Report.

Sullivan, J. (1995). From Classrooms to Cellblocks: A National Perspective. Center on Juvenile and Criminal Justice.

Taylor, Jon M. (September 1992). "Post secondary Correctional Education: An Evaluation of Effectiveness and Efficiency" Journal of Correctional Education, 43 (3), 132–141.

Waldon Jr., Alton R. (April 1996). Unhealthy choice: Prisons Over Schools in New York State. State Senator, 10th District.

—— (March 1993). Survey of State Prison Inmates, 7997. Bureau of Justice Statistics, NCJ136949.

—— (1996). The Eighth Annual Shock Legislative Report 1996. New York Department of Correctional Services and the Division of Parole.

—— (1994). The Impact of Correctional Education on Recidivism, 1988–1994. Office of Correctional Education, U.S. Department of Education.

—— (1996). Brooklyn Treatment Alternatives to Street Crime (TASQ, 7997–7992.)

—— (April 30, 1996). Law Enforcement News.

—— (August 18, 2003). Study: 7 in 37 U.S. Adults Have "prison experience". The Associated Press.

—— (August 18, 2003). The Associated Press.

—— (September 30, 1996). U.S. News & World Report.

**Harvey Shrum**, Ed.D., is a Re-Entry teacher at Folsum State Prison. At the urging of the late Dr. Fabry, Institute of Logotherapy, Dr. Shrum is nearing completion of a self-help book entitled Seeking Meaning in a Cell.

# Parent Power

**The price young people pay for parental pessimism and nonchalance is high.**

JOSEPH A. CALIFANO JR.

The 10th Annual Survey of 12- to 17-year-olds by the National Center on Addiction and Substance Abuse at Columbia University (CASA) has a loud and clear message: Parents, if you want to raise drug-free kids, you cannot outsource your responsibility to their schools or law enforcement.

The odds are that drugs will be used, kept or sold—or all of the above—at the school your daughter or son attends and that laws prohibiting teen use of tobacco, alcohol, marijuana and other illegal drugs will have little or no impact on your child's decision to smoke, drink or use marijuana.

What will motivate your kids to stay drug free is their perception of how Mom and Dad will react to their smoking, drinking or drug use, their sense of the immorality of such use for someone their age, and whether they consider such use harmful to their health. It is not much of an overstatement to say that reducing the risk of teen substance use is all in the family. Engaged and nourishing parents have the best shot at giving their children the will and skills to say no.

For any who doubt the frontline importance of the family in combating teen drug use and for parents who think they can outsource their responsibility, this year's CASA survey sends a grim message that a teen's world outside the family is infested with drugs.

The most disturbing finding is the extent to which our nation's schools are awash in alcohol, tobacco, and illegal and prescription drugs. Since 2002, the proportion of middle schoolers who say that drugs are used, kept or sold in their schools is up by a stunning 47 percent, and the proportion of high schoolers attending schools with drugs is up by 41 percent. This year, 10.6 million high schoolers, almost two-thirds, and 2.4 million middle schoolers, more than a quarter, are attending schools where drugs are used, kept or sold.

Sadly, many parents accept drug-infected schools as an inevitable part of their children's lives. Half of all parents surveyed report that drugs are used, kept or sold on the grounds of their teen's school, and a despairing 56 percent of these parents believe that the goal of making their child's school drug free is unrealistic. When asbestos is found in a school, most parents refuse to send their children there until it is removed; yet these same parents send their kids to drug infected schools day after day. When parents feel as strongly about drugs in schools as they do about asbestos, they will give our teens a chance to be educated in a drug free environment.

The price young people pay for parental pessimism and nonchalance is high. Teens who attend schools where drugs are used, kept or sold are three times likelier to try marijuana and get drunk in a typical month, compared with teens who attend drug-free schools. Students at high schools with drugs estimate that 44 percent of their schoolmates regularly use illegal drugs, compared with a 27 percent estimate by students at drug free schools.

This year's survey provides overwhelming additional evidence of the increasingly drug drenched world of American teens. In just one year, from 2004 to 2005, the percentage of 12- to 17-year-olds who know a friend or classmate who has abused prescription drugs jumped 86 percent; who has used the drug Ecstasy is up 28 percent; who has used illegal drugs, such as acid, cocaine or heroin, is up 20 percent.

Given the availability of substances throughout their lives—in their schools, among their friends—it is no wonder that teens continue to name drugs as their number one concern, as they have since CASA began conducting the survey in 1996. This year 29 percent of teens cite drugs as their top concern. (Remarkably, many parents don't understand this. Only 13 percent of those surveyed see drugs as their teens' biggest concern; almost 60 percent of parents consider social pressures their teens' biggest concern, a view only 22 percent of teens share.)

And little progress, if any, has been made in curtailing teens' ability to buy marijuana. Forty-two percent of 12- to 17-year-olds (11 million) can buy marijuana within a day; 21 percent (5.5 million) can buy it within an hour. This situation has remained unchanged over the past three years.

The abysmal failures of our schools to achieve and maintain a drug free status and of our government to reduce the availability of marijuana should by themselves be enough to alert parents to the critical significance of their role. But the clincher comes out of the mouths of teens themselves, who make it clear that morality and parental attitude trump illegality as deterrents to their smoking, drinking and drug use:

- Teens who believe smoking cigarettes or drinking alcohol by someone their age is "not morally wrong" are seven times likelier to smoke or drink than those who believe teen smoking is "seriously morally wrong."

- Teens whose parents would be "a little upset or not upset" if they smoked or drank are much likelier to smoke or drink than those whose parents would be "extremely upset."
- Teens who believe using marijuana is "not morally wrong" are 19 times likelier to use marijuana than teens who believe it is "seriously morally wrong."
- Teens who say their parents would be "a little upset" or "not upset at all" if they used marijuana are six times likelier to try marijuana than those whose parents would be "extremely upset."

At the same time, most teens say legal restrictions have no impact on their decision to smoke cigarettes (58 percent) or drink alcohol (54 percent). Nearly half of teens say illegality plays no role in their decision to use marijuana, LSD, cocaine or heroin.

The point is not that criminal laws are irrelevant; they serve an important purpose to protect society and as a formal consensus of society's judgment about seriously harmful conduct. The point is that a child's sense of morality, which most 12- to 17-year-olds acquire from parents, and a clear appreciation of parental disapproval are far more powerful incentives to stay drug free.

Parents also have an important responsibility to monitor their children's conduct and know their children's friends. Forty-three percent of 12- to 17-year-olds see three or more R-rated movies in a typical month. These teens are seven times likelier to smoke cigarettes, six times likelier to try marijuana and five times likelier to drink alcohol than those who do not watch R-rated movies. Teens who report that half or more of their friends are sexually active are at nearly six times the risk for substance abuse as those teens with no sexually active friends. Similarly, teens who report that most of their friends drink or use marijuana are at much higher risk of substance abuse.

The good news is that strong, positive family relationships are a powerful deterrent to teen smoking, drinking and drug use. Teens who would go to either or both their parents with a serious problem are at half the risk of teens who would seek out another adult. The substance-abuse risk for teens living in households with frequent family dinners, low levels of tension and stress among family members, parents who are proud of their teen and a parent in whom the teen can confide is half that of the average teen.

Frequent family dinners are a simple yet powerful way to influence teen behavior. Compared to teens who have at least five family dinners a week, those who have family dinner less often than three times a week are much likelier to smoke, drink and use marijuana. Only 13 percent of teens who have frequent family dinners have tried marijuana, compared with 35 percent of teens who have dinner with their parents no more than twice a week.

Teens who attend weekly religious services—or who say that religion is an important part of their lives—are at half the risk of smoking, drinking or using drugs as those who do not attend such services. And it is unlikely in this nation that 12- to 17-year-olds go to church each week without their parents.

Parent power is the greatest weapon we have to curb substance abuse. When mothers and fathers realize how much power they have—and use it sensitively—we will turn back this scourge that has destroyed so many children and brought so much grief to so many families and friends.

This nation's drug problem is all about kids. CASA's research has consistently shown that a child who gets through age 21 without smoking, abusing alcohol or using drugs is virtually certain never to do so. The CASA survey and 12 years of my life devoted to understanding this problem have led me to this bottom line: America's drug problem is not going to be solved in courtrooms, legislative hearing rooms or schoolrooms—or by judges, politicians or teachers. It will be solved in living rooms and dining rooms and across kitchen tables—and by parents and families.

---

JOSEPH A. CALIFANO JR., chairman and president of the National Center on Addiction and Substance Abuse at Columbia University, was secretary of health, education and welfare from 1977 to 1979. His most recent book, *Inside: A Public and Private Life*, will be available in paperback.

# What to Say When Your Child Asks: Did You Ever Do Drugs?

If you have young children, you've probably been warned to prepare an answer to a key question: Where do babies come from? But another question that's just as important may hit even closer to home: Did you ever use alcohol or other drugs as a teenager?

Children who ask this question create a defining moment in their lives. In response, a parent might dodge the question or improvise an answer at the last minute. Another option is to prepare for this "teachable moment" with your child by thinking through your answers right now.

Of course, many parents can honestly say that they did not experiment with alcohol or other drugs as a teenager. Even so, they might worry about how to convince their children of the dangers of abuse and addiction.

It may help to remember that you're in a better position to respond to the question than parents of any previous generation. "Over the past decade we've learned a lot more about how drug use affects the brain," says Sue Thomas, an editor at Hazelden Publishing who specializes in developing materials about substance abuse prevention. "For example, we now know that the human brain continues developing past the age of adolescence and into a person's early twenties. Using alcohol or other drugs can have a specific and negative impact on this development—something we just didn't know earlier."

Another recent discovery is that early use of alcohol or other drugs can create long-term health risks. In one survey, adults who said that they first drank alcohol before age 15 were five times more likely to report alcohol dependence or abuse than people who first used alcohol at age 21 or older.

There's no perfect response to the "did-you-ever-use" question. Yet the following suggestions can help you give a more effective answer when the time comes.

**Remember that your child does not have to repeat your past.** "Just because a parent used when he or she was young doesn't mean it was a legal, safe or smart thing to do," Thomas says. "Remind your child that all it takes is one bad decision while using to cause a lot of trouble, such as getting drunk at a party and ending up in a violent or date rape situation, or getting into a car accident after driving home under the influence."

**Be honest, but stick to essentials.** If you don't tell the truth about your past use of alcohol or other drugs, you risk losing credibility when your child discovers the truth. At the same time, you don't have to share every detail. Find out why your child is asking about your drug use history. Then limit your response to exactly what's being requested.

**Understand how much the drug scene has changed.** Today teenagers are exposed to a greater variety of drugs than were available in their parents' generation. Even prescription drugs for anxiety, depression, and attention-deficit disorders can be abused.

"The drugs that are being used now are also much more potent and dangerous than earlier," says Thomas. "For example, ecstasy is often a mixture of many different kinds of drugs, so you never really know what the effect of using it may be."

**Take a cue from these examples.** You might get an idea or two from these sample answers, excerpted from "Growing Up Drug-Free: A Parent's Guide to Prevention," published by the U.S. Department of Education:

- "Everyone makes mistakes, and when I used drugs, I made a big one. I'm telling you about this, even though it's embarrassing, because I love you, and I want to save you from making the same stupid decision that I made when I was your age. You can learn from my mistakes without repeating them."

- "At your age, between homework, friends, sports, and other interests, there are a lot of fun things going on. If you get into taking drugs, you're pretty much giving up those other things, because you stop being able to concentrate, and you can't control your moods or keep to a schedule. You'll miss out on all these great experiences, and you'll never get those times back."

- "I did drugs because I was bored and wanted to take some risks, but I soon found that I couldn't control the risks—they were controlling me. There are much better ways of challenging yourself than doing drugs."

# Exercise and Drug Detoxification

SIMON ODDIE

## Introduction

Leeds prison is a local category B male prison serving the communities of North, West and East Yorkshire. Its operational capacity is 1,254 and is regularly fully used. Over a number of years the prison had noted an increase in prisoner use of substances, particularly class A drugs. Many prisoners suffer withdrawal symptoms and medication was viewed as the main means of managing their recovery. It has long been recognised, within the physical education community, that physical exercise has a major role in therapeutic detoxification and rehabilitation. As a result a research project was instigated at Leeds to move beyond anecdotal observations and towards the formation of a first stage detoxification programme. The programme itself is broken down into three stages:

- identification of the user type and history;
- a short induction period that places the emphasis on detoxification; and,
- a detoxification treatment programme with continuous individual reviews.

## Identification of Clients

When a prisoner arrives at Leeds prison they are processed through the reception centre. Important aspects of the reception process are individual interviews for medical assessment and CARAT assessment, these are the two methods used to identify substance misusers. The criteria for entry to the programme are that those referred should be identified as being:

- at risk of self-harm (F2052 SH);
- chaotic polydrug users;
- likely to be on a short sentence;
- having a history of mental health or suffers depression; a crack cocaine user; and,
- having not previously received drug treatment.

Spaces are limited to 12 per week. Programmes are voluntary and the initial contact is very important. The team have learnt the importance of the programme induction, particularly developing an environment of mutual respect and a genuine desire for the client to achieve success.

## The Induction Process

The induction process is important not only to set standards but also as a motivational tool. Induction sessions are held in groups to enable the development of trust and mutual support. Individuals are informed about the programme, making it clear that it is not rehabilitation, but is purely about detoxification and improving well-being. Clients are helped to recognise that they are at the start of the process and are aware of the next stages. Many report that they simply 'want to feel better' and this is a powerful motivation.

Many prisoners are sceptical about the process particularly those who are experiencing depression, finding it difficult to comprehend that exercise at an intense level will make them feel better. The vast majority have not engaged in any form of physical exercise and find it hard to believe that they can exercise at all. During a one-to-one appraisal they complete a medical questionnaire covering a variety of physical conditions that may affect exercise, which is also used as our compact and consent form. This is a valuable time where we can address their fears.

## Detoxification Programme and Individual Review

The programme is based on frequency and intensity. To promote improvement, the group exercises for one hour, starting at a low intensity, quickly rising as the sessions move on. The duration stays the same but the intensity increases, in most cases quite dramatically. From experience we aim to have a minimum heart rate of 130+ dependent on age and ability, it is at this level we have experienced greater feelings of euphoria when the individual has completed a session. This is due not only to the physical effects of exercise, but also the effects on the brain—the neurological effect. For the individual this gives them a feeling of well-being and in some cases a 'high' which we observe after each session. This feeling of well-being is most likely exaggerated due to the chemical suppression in the brain resulting from drug misuse.

It has been noted that, even on completion of the first session when the intensity is at the lowest level, individuals exhibit an improved sense of well-being. This is only short-lived but important as it can motivate the individual to continue. The sense of well-being develops during the detoxifying period and becomes self-perpetuating.

The exercise programme is as follows, changing every two days:

### Week one

- Day one and two—six sets of ten minutes
- Day three and four—four sets of 15 minutes

### Week two

- Day five and six—three sets of 20 minutes
- Day seven and eight—two sets of 30 minutes

This is not set in stone and often the group moves through the programme quicker than expeded, depending upon ability. There is just enough time between sets to have a drink and change machine. It is our experience that motivation is very important, as most of the clients have never used a structured exercise programme as a form of treatment.

The next step after the first two weeks detoxifying, is to encourage the individual to continue with a structured exercise regime on a regular basis. This can only have a positive effect towards drug abstinence.

## The Detox Gymnasium

Our aims at HMP Leeds detox gymnasium are:

> To have a positive effect on those who attend the programme, to help them detox efficiently and safely, helping to speed up the body's natural processes and its ability to heal itself.

The detox gymnasium consists of cardio-vascular equipment, bikes, rower, steppers and cross-trainers. These machines were chosen for safety and ease of use. All the machines can monitor heart rate and all are programmable. We also have an Infra-red Heat Therapy Sauna which has therapeutic benefits too numerous to list, but is primarily used for individuals who have joint conditions which could be made worse by exercise, and it is used as an incentive or reward. Fitech software is used to assess well-being. Many drug users are dangerously under weight, lacking vital fat and muscle, and it is important that this is discussed with the individual.

Keeping groups small (up to 12) allows us to monitor individual progress and set individual targets during the sessions. This intervention has been proved to achieve our aim.

## Building an Individual's Motivation to Achieve

Motivation is the key to success. Physical Education Officers are renowned for having good motivational skills. To deliver this kind of programme a basic understanding on addiction and how drugs affect the body is essential and understanding how exercise can be an effective treatment for withdrawal. This information plays a large part in the motivational aspect of delivering this programme. As already stated, the opportunity to get through the withdrawal quicker is a good start. Other techniques include setting individual goals, altering duration and intensity, using hill climbs, random and manual settings on a selected machine, creating a group atmosphere, and—would you believe it—singing! We have found that by putting the onus back to the individual (we are only there to guide them through the process, they are the ones who need to put the effort in), they gain control of their own therapy process. Peer motivation is also a very useful tool: for instance, when an individual is struggling, the group rally round and help. However, group competition is not encouraged, as we do not want to further reduce the self-esteem of the less capable. Individual goals are preferable.

Aches, pains, cramps and the general feelings of withdrawal should be expected, and being sick occasionally happens. These people are relatively ill and do not need to be encouraged to be ill, our aim is clear: positivity and understanding are more appropriate. This is why it is the combination of motivational techniques that get the best from a group or individual.

**Physical Education Officers are renowned for having good motivational skills.**

## Recovering from Addiction with Exercise

A drug is a chemical or mixture of chemicals which when taken alters the body's biological function (the way the brain/body works) and possibly its structure (body organs, liver brain, muscles etc) WHO 1980. One of the reasons that drug misuse can exert such powerful control over behaviour is that it has neurological effects: through the brain drugs take over the role of controlling behaviour. What happens in the brain is that drugs alter the way the pleasure centre and other parts of the brain function. This includes neuro-chemicals such as Dopamine (pleasure/reward), Serotonin (well-being, regulating mood, aggression, sexual activity, sleep and sensitivity to pain) and Endorphins (pain control). Drugs affect these parts of the brain, this is what provides the pleasurable and addictive qualities. However, recent evidence shows that long-term use is likely to impair the brain's ability to return to normal function, hence the withdrawal effects.

Pharmacological interventions are readily used to combat addictions. Today, the right amount of medication used in combination with a behaviour modification plan yields the best results during recovery from addiction. In order for the brain to re-establish a state of equilibrium, the user must use again or be treated with a different synthetic intervention that decreases cravings for illicit drugs. Unfortunately, using drugs to combat drug addiction is not always the most desirable approach because treatment medication may actually be affecting the brain in a similar way. Some illicit drugs such as crack cocaine do not have a synthetic intervention. The reality however, is that drugs provide the most immediate response to recovery from drug abuse. One of the keys to effective recovery and prevention is making the process both tolerable and attainable. This can be a difficult task when a drug user is comparing his/her feelings during recovery with the euphoric feeling of being on a 'high'.

So, can exercise serve as an effective treatment for the prevention and recovery of drug misuse? Recent research shows that as well as causing cardio-vascular affects, exercise changes behaviour, brain chemistry and brain growth. This is central to dealing with the affects of drugs described above. In particular, exercise stimulates the production of neuro-chemicals such as endorphins, which control pain. In light of this, exercise should certainly be considered as a treatment option. Its dual approach can be effective in correcting chemical imbalances in the brain resulting from drug misuse as well as repairing some of the damage.

Physical activity plays a significant role in providing the brain with nourishment and stimulation. This is especially true when complex skills are integrated as part of activity. Exercise is one of the vehicles that can facilitate an increase in brain activity, but more importantly it increases the amount of blood flowing to the brain. Certain levels of cardio-intense exercise will facilitate changes in brain chemistry. As the chemical needs of the brain are met, instinctive motivation becomes less of a priority. The need for the body to be active subsides and a state of equilibrium becomes more constant, this state helps the body to think and act more appropriately. Evidence supports the negative

role that depression, anxiety, stress and other debilitating moods play in recovery. If exercise can improve the subject's mood then its use in conjunction with other strategies is valuable. Helping individuals reduce the impact of depression alone may be significant enough to integrate exercise as a serious component of both recovery and prevention programmes.

# Evaluation

The evaluation of our programme is based on information collected on PE evaluation forms, which are completed confidentially by the prisoners following the two-week programme. Some of the results are shown in the graph on next page.

The prisoners also made further comments about the course. Their answers can be put into four sub headings: Physical, Mental Health, Service and Personal Comments.

## *Physical issues*

This evidence goes to show that after just two weeks we are getting a very positive response, individuals were 'feeling better and a lot fitter'. Comments like 'gets your detox done quicker' and 'it helps you get through your rattle (withdrawal) a lot easier' go to endorse our aim. We have found that individuals have gained a basic understanding about exercise and detoxification, 'it sweated a lot of shit out of my system', burns the rubbish out of your body' and 'because it does help sweat it out of you and improves your health'. Out of the 30 individuals questioned we did not receive any negative comments. 'I felt so good' is not the kind of comment you would usually expect from a withdrawing drug misuser, but was typical of the comments after the course.

## *Mental Health issues*

Again there was a very positive reaction, the main benefits in the short term seem to be directed at keeping the body and mind occupied: 'taken my mind off wanting to use by giving me something more to do than just lying on my bed and counting away the days'. Most found the course very motivating and made them feel better about themselves. One individual said he would recommend this course 'for someone who wants a positive outlook on life, to achieve his aims of staying off drugs, feeling good and gaining knowledge in all drugs areas'. The programme also encourages team effort ready for group work this is highlighted by comments like this, 'the lads open up and say what they really think, and feel relaxed enough with each other to say what problems they have had with drugs and achieve new goals in other ways', and 'the groups pull together'. Another stated 'thought I'd be the same when I went out

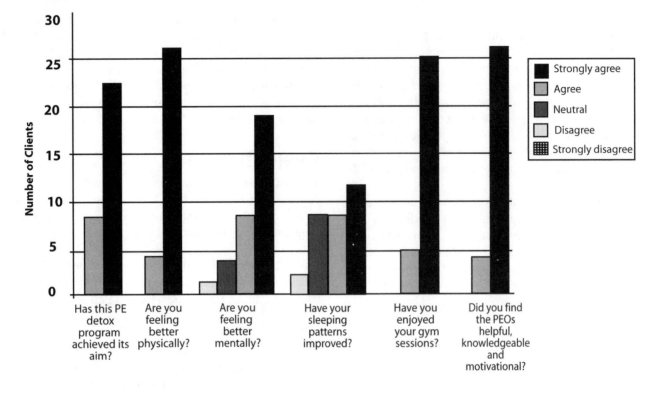

**Figure 1** Detox Gymnasium

but I'm more aware now, it's a lot better when you've got help'.

### Service issues

The course is generally thought of as 'an excellent course' where both PEOs and Officers are praised for making it 'a good experience'. One individual stated 'this is the first time I have been given any help in prison the staff were excellent caring and very patient'. Another said 'I've been to jail on several occasions and done many courses; this course is sensational and really serves its purpose well'. One of the main issues is the length of the course. Most of the groups wanted at least another week, as one individual said 'it's the best detox course I have done, needs to be twice as long you just get into it after two weeks'. All the above comments reflect the opinions of all the courses we have completed approximately 25 groups) not just the 30 individuals chosen.

### Personal Comments

Most of the personal comments are of thanks, but now and again you get a comment like 'I feel that being a member of such a group as this helps people that may be feeling isolated and find it hard to talk to people they don't know'. This course is not the easy option, individuals push themselves further than they may ever have done. However, they also get a lot of rewards from it, 'what you put in is what you get out, you learn stuff about yourself'.

**Exercise is proving to be a more beneficial therapeutic treatment to aid recovery than first thought.**

## Conclusion

Detox is a way of giving the individual an informed choice about the next step. Whether that next step is re-tox, maintenance or abstinence. Opiate based medical detox also suppresses the brains chemical activity in areas already covered and though assists in reducing the effects of withdrawal does not help to address the brains chemical balance. If this detox is not available then the individual's choice is influenced by the depressive nature of the addiction: no choice.

This paper has demonstrated the importance of intense exercise for drug addiction prevention and recovery. Physical education within prison and community based programmes has a major role in detoxification and rehabilitation. A simple structured programme based on the foundations of exercise, frequency and intensity as outlined above, will improve the physiological and psychological well-being of recovering drug misusers. It also has a dramatic effect on reducing the length of the withdrawal process. It is well documented that physical exercise/training has an increased effect on physical fitness, self-confidence, self-discipline, personal responsibility etc. Research and experience show that exercise is proving to be a more beneficial therapeutic treatment to aid recovery than first thought. Intense exercise should now be recognized as a fundamental part of any detoxification and rehabilitation programme for recovering drug misusers.

References are available from the author.

# Index

# Index

# Index

# Test Your Knowledge Form

We encourage you to photocopy and use this page as a tool to assess how the articles in *Annual Editions* expand on the information in your textbook. By reflecting on the articles you will gain enhanced text information. You can also access this useful form on a product's book support Web site at *http://www.mhcls.com/online/*.

NAME: DATE:

TITLE AND NUMBER OF ARTICLE:

BRIEFLY STATE THE MAIN IDEA OF THIS ARTICLE:

LIST THREE IMPORTANT FACTS THAT THE AUTHOR USES TO SUPPORT THE MAIN IDEA:

WHAT INFORMATION OR IDEAS DISCUSSED IN THIS ARTICLE ARE ALSO DISCUSSED IN YOUR TEXTBOOK OR OTHER READINGS THAT YOU HAVE DONE? LIST THE TEXTBOOK CHAPTERS AND PAGE NUMBERS:

LIST ANY EXAMPLES OF BIAS OR FAULTY REASONING THAT YOU FOUND IN THE ARTICLE:

LIST ANY NEW TERMS/CONCEPTS THAT WERE DISCUSSED IN THE ARTICLE, AND WRITE A SHORT DEFINITION:

# We Want Your Advice

ANNUAL EDITIONS revisions depend on two major opinion sources: one is our Advisory Board, listed in the front of this volume, which works with us in scanning the thousands of articles published in the public press each year; the other is you—the person actually using the book. Please help us and the users of the next edition by completing the prepaid article rating form on this page and returning it to us. Thank you for your help!

## ANNUAL EDITIONS: Drugs, Society and Behavior 07/08

### ARTICLE RATING FORM

Here is an opportunity for you to have direct input into the next revision of this volume.
We would like you to rate each of the articles listed below, using the following scale:

1. **Excellent: should definitely be retained**
2. **Above average: should probably be retained**
3. **Below average: should probably be deleted**
4. **Poor: should definitely be deleted**

Your ratings will play a vital part in the next revision.
Please mail this prepaid form to us as soon as possible.
Thanks for your help!

| RATING | ARTICLE | RATING | ARTICLE |
|---|---|---|---|
| | 1. Hey, You Don't Look So Good | | 32. The Best High They've Ever Had |
| | 2. Living the High Life: The Role of Drug Taking in Young People's Lives | | 33. Some Cold Medicines Moved Behind the Counter |
| | 3. Methamphetamine Across America: Misconceptions, Realities and Solutions | | 34. Facing an Uncertain Twilight |
| | | | 35. Meth Addicts' Other Habit: Online Theft |
| | 4. Balding, Wrinkled and Stoned | | 36. Mothers Addicted to Meth Face Losing Their Children |
| | 5. America's Most Dangerous Drug | | 37. The Role of Substance Abuse in U.S. Juvenile Justice Systems and Populations |
| | 6. With Scenes of Blood and Pain, Ads Battle Methamphetamine in Montana | | 38. My Spirit Lives |
| | 7. My Mother the Narc | | 39. When Drinking Kills |
| | 8. Pass the Weed, Dad | | 40. What Alcohol Does to a Child |
| | 9. Did Prohibition Really Work?: Alcohol Prohibition as a Public Health Innovation | | 41. The Problem with Drinking |
| | | | 42. ADHD Drugs and Cardiovascular Risk |
| | 10. Addiction Is a Brain Disease | | 43. High on the Job |
| | 11. Predicting Addiction | | 44. Administration Announces Anti-Methamphetamine Plan |
| | 12. Staying Sober | | |
| | 13. The Effects of Alcohol on Physiological Processes and Biological Development | | 45. Court Upholds Federal Authority to Reject 'Medical Marijuana' |
| | 14. The Toxicity of Recreational Drugs | | 46. Medical Marijuana, Compassionate Use, and Public Policy: Expert Opinion or Vox Populi? |
| | 15. Structural Differences Found in Brains of Heavy Marijuana Users | | 47. Is Drug Testing of Athletes Necessary? |
| | 16. Does Cannabis Cause Psychosis or Schizophrenia? | | 48. Meth Madness |
| | 17. A More Addictive Meth Emerges as States Curb Homemade Type | | 49. How to Stand Up to Big Tobacco |
| | | | 50. Cigarette Trafficking: Expanding Criminal Activity Attracts Law Enforcement Attention |
| | 18. Just Say No? No Need Here | | 51. Battles Won, A War Still Lost |
| | 19. A Harvest of Treachery | | 52. The War on Thugs |
| | 20. An End to 'Power Hour' | | 53. Arresting the Drug Laws |
| | 21. Helping Students Stay Clean and Sober | | 54. State's Evidence |
| | 22. The Power of Potent Steroids | | 55. How to Quit the Cure |
| | 23. Cannabis-Related Problems and Their Management | | 56. Drug Treatment and Reentry for Incarcerated Women |
| | 24. Pot Farms Ravaging Park Land | | 57. Combination Treatment of One Year Doubles Smokers' Quit Rate |
| | 25. Resurgence of Teen Inhalant Use | | |
| | 26. New Study Shows 1.8 Million Youth Use Inhalants | | 58. Medication & Counseling: The 'New Paradigm' in Alcoholism Treatment |
| | 27. The Changing Face of Teenage Drug Abuse—The Trend toward Prescription Drugs | | 59. A Teen Health Gap |
| | 28. OxyContin Acting as Pathway Drug for Adolescent Heroin Addiction | | 60. Teens Caught in the Middle: Juvenile Justice System and Treatment |
| | | | 61. No Longer Theory: Correctional Practices That Work |
| | 29. Club Drugs: Study Explores Reasons for Use by Young Adults | | 62. Parent Power |
| | 30. Rx for Trouble | | 63. What to Say When Your Child Asks: Did You Ever Do Drugs? |
| | 31. Studies Identify Factors Surrounding Rise in Abuse of Prescription Drugs by College Students | | 64. Exercise and Drug Detoxification |

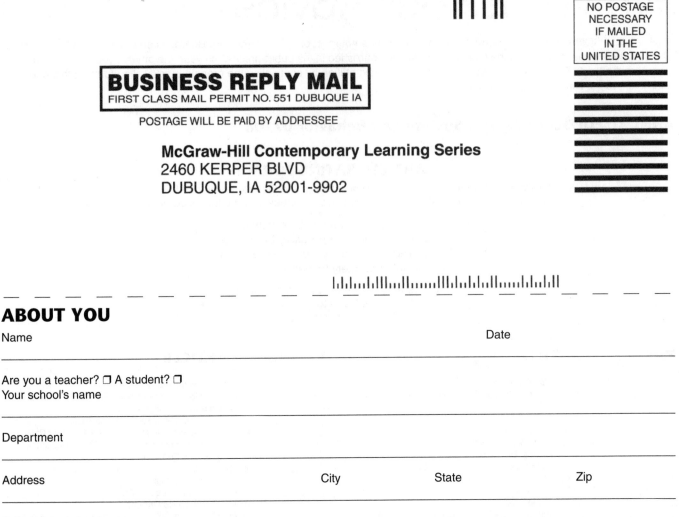

## BUSINESS REPLY MAIL
FIRST CLASS MAIL PERMIT NO. 551 DUBUQUE IA

POSTAGE WILL BE PAID BY ADDRESSEE

**McGraw-Hill Contemporary Learning Series**
2460 KERPER BLVD
DUBUQUE, IA 52001-9902

NO POSTAGE
NECESSARY
IF MAILED
IN THE
UNITED STATES

---

## ABOUT YOU

Name _____ Date _____

Are you a teacher? ☐ A student? ☐
Your school's name _____

Department _____

Address _____ City _____ State _____ Zip _____

School telephone # _____

## YOUR COMMENTS ARE IMPORTANT TO US!

Please fill in the following information:
For which course did you use this book?
_____

Did you use a text with this ANNUAL EDITION? ☐ yes ☐ no
What was the title of the text?
_____

What are your general reactions to the Annual Editions concept?
_____

Have you read any pertinent articles recently that you think should be included in the next edition? Explain.
_____

Are there any articles that you feel should be replaced in the next edition? Why?
_____

Are there any World Wide Web sites that you feel should be included in the next edition? Please annotate.
_____

May we contact you for editorial input? ☐ yes ☐ no
May we quote your comments? ☐ yes ☐ no